Governing in a Polarized Age

Many political observers have expressed doubts as to whether America's leaders are up to the task of addressing major policy challenges. Yet much of the critical commentary lacks grounding in the systematic analysis of the core institutions of the American political system including elections, representation, and the law-making process. *Governing in a Polarized Age* brings together more than a dozen leading scholars to provide an in-depth examination of representation and legislative performance.

Drawing upon the seminal work of David Mayhew as a point of departure, these essays explore the dynamics of incumbency advantage in today's polarized Congress, asking whether the focus on individual reelection that was the hallmark of Mayhew's groundbreaking book, *Congress: The Electoral Connection*, remains useful for understanding today's Congress. The essays link the study of elections with close analysis of changes in party organization, and with a series of systematic assessments of the quality of legislative performance.

ALAN S. GERBER is Divisional Director for the Social Sciences and Dilley Professor of Political Science at Yale University. Co-author of an award-winning textbook on experimental methods, his work has appeared in the leading journals in political science and has received various awards, including the Heinz Eulau Award for the best article in the *American Political Science Review*. He was elected to the American Academy of Arts and Sciences (2009) and the American Academy of Political and Social Sciences (2013).

ERIC SCHICKLER is Jeffrey & Ashley McDermott Professor of Political Science at the University of California, Berkeley. He is the author of *Disjointed Pluralism*, which won the Richard F. Fenno, Jr. Prize for the best book on legislative politics in 2002. He is the co-author of *Partisan Hearts and Minds*, which was published in 2002; *Filibuster*, which was published in 2006 and won the Fenno Prize; and *Racial Realignment*, published in 2016.

Governing in a Polarized Age

Elections, Parties, and Political Representation in America

ALAN S. GERBER
Yale University

ERIC SCHICKLER
University of California, Berkeley

CAMBRIDGE
UNIVERSITY PRESS

CAMBRIDGE
UNIVERSITY PRESS

One Liberty Plaza, 20th Floor, New York, NY 10006, USA

Cambridge University Press is part of the University of Cambridge.

It furthers the University's mission by disseminating knowledge in the pursuit of education, learning, and research at the highest international levels of excellence.

www.cambridge.org
Information on this title: www.cambridge.org/9781107479074

First published 2017

Printed in the United States of America by Sheridan Books, Inc.

A catalogue record for this publication is available from the British Library.

Library of Congress Cataloging-in-Publication Data
Names: Gerber, Alan S., editor. | Schickler, Eric, 1969- editor. | Mayhew, David R., honoree.
Title: Governing in a polarized age : essays on elections, parties and political representation in honor of David Mayhew / edited by Alan S. Gerber, Yale University ; Eric Schickler, University of California, Berkeley.
Description: New York, NY : Cambridge University Press, 2016. |
Includes bibliographical references and index.
Identifiers: LCCN 2016011189 | ISBN 9781107095090 (Hardback)
Subjects: LCSH: United States. Congress–Elections. | Incumbency
(Public officers)–United States. | Representative government and representation–United States. |
Polarization (Social sciences)–United States.
Classification: LCC JK1976 .G66 2016 | DDC 328.73–dc23 LC record available
at https://lccn.loc.gov/2016011189

ISBN 978-1-107-09509-0 Hardback
ISBN 978-1-107-47907-4 Paperback

Contents

Contributors

Christopher H. Achen, Department of Politics, Princeton University

Stephen Ansolabehere, Department of Government, Harvard University

R. Douglas Arnold, Department of Politics, Princeton University

Sarah Binder, Department of Political Science, George Washington University, The Brookings Institution

Joshua D. Clinton, Department of Political Science, Vanderbilt University

Katherine Levine Einstein, Department of Political Science, Boston University

Robert S. Erikson, Department of Political Science, Columbia University

Alan S. Gerber, Department of Political Science, Yale University

John Mark Hansen, Department of Political Science, The University of Chicago

Shigeo Hirano, Department of Political Science, Columbia University

Jennifer Hochschild, Department of Government, Harvard University

Gary C. Jacobson, Department of Political Science, University of California

Ira Katznelson, Department of Political Science, Columbia University

Keith Krehbiel, Graduate School of Business, Stanford University

John S. Lapinski, Political Science Department, University of Pennsylvania

Frances E. Lee, Department of Government and Politics, University of Maryland

David R. Mayhew, Department of Political Science, Yale University

Maxwell Palmer, Department of Political Science, Boston University

Eric M. Patashnik, Department of Politics, Watson Institute for International and Public Affairs, Brown University

Justin Peck, Department of Political Science, San Francisco State University

Representative David E. Pierce, U.S. House of Representatives

Eric Schickler, Department of Political Science, University of California, Berkeley

Benjamin Schneer, Department of Government, Harvard University

James M. Snyder Jr. Department of Government, Harvard University

I

Introduction

Alan S. Gerber and Eric Schickler

As President Barack Obama concludes his second term, the United States faces daunting economic and political challenges, from addressing persistent inequality and the looming fiscal burden of entitlement spending associated with an aging population to mitigating the environmental risks associated with climate change. Many political observers have expressed doubts as to whether our nation's leaders are up to these tasks. Yet much of the critical commentary on governmental performance lacks grounding in the systematic analysis of the core institutions of the American political system including elections, political representation, and the law-making process. *Governing in a Polarized Age* provides an in-depth examination of representation and legislative performance in American politics.

The three sections of this volume address a series of related questions about Congress and representation through the lens of David Mayhew's influential writings. The essays in Part I review the deep impact of Mayhew's early work on Congress and legislative studies more generally, and evaluate from a variety of perspectives whether the theory of congressional behavior outlined in Mayhew's seminal work, *Congress: The Electoral Connection* (1974a), remains useful for understanding contemporary congressional life. According to several of the authors, a model of today's members of Congress should add to the reelection motivation the desire to serve in the majority. The essays in Part II analyze the patterns of party organization at the state level and in Congress and detail how the partisan contest for control is reflected in the communications combat that pervades political life. Part III addresses the issue of legislative performance. Among other questions, the authors consider whether the absence of a significant relationship between divided government and legislative productivity found by Mayhew in the postwar period in *Divided We Govern* (1991) also applies to earlier eras in American politics and whether this finding continues to be valid today.

POLITICAL REPRESENTATION AND DEMOCRATIC ACCOUNTABILITY

The first part of the book explores how well the electoral connection between members of Congress and their constituents ensures both political responsiveness and democratic accountability in contemporary American politics. *Congress: The Electoral Connection* serves as an intellectual point of departure for these essays, which systematically consider whether and how shifts in the political system since the 1970s have changed fundamental processes of legislative representation.

Where *The Electoral Connection* treated members of Congress as independent operators able to build their own electoral coalitions separate from national party organization, today's members compete in a political environment characterized by the highest levels of partisan polarization and party-line voting since the early 1900s. The essays by R. Douglas Arnold and Gary Jacobson evaluate how well the analytic approach developed in *The Electoral Connection* holds up in this new electoral and institutional context.

Arnold's essay begins with a tour of the intellectual landscape at the time *The Electoral Connection* was published and demonstrates the profound effect of Mayhew's research on subsequent congressional scholarship. As Arnold's description makes clear, although the particular analytical categories Mayhew developed (credit claiming, advertising, position taking) have been used in subsequent scholarship, Mayhew's analytical strategy has arguably had a deeper effect. Prior to writing *The Electoral Connection*, Mayhew spent time as an American Political Science Association Congressional Fellow and had the opportunity to observe directly the complex constellation of motivations of our national legislators. However, when Mayhew turned to theorizing he employed a conscious simplification of legislators' motivations and argued that Members of Congress (MCs) can be usefully *modeled* as single minded seekers of reelection. This modeling decision, in both its parsimony and in its selection of reelection rather than other potential motivations (progressive ambition, good policy, power within the legislature, positioning for a career outside the legislature, pursuit of personal ideological ends, etc.) turned out to be an inspired choice, as demonstrated by its enormous and durable explanatory power. Further, the analytical choice to build a theory of Congress on the incentives and strategic choices of the *individual member*, with the implication that any additional analytical structures, such as parties, needed to be justified in terms of the strategies and preferences of this most basic unit, has shaped a generation of scholarship that seeks to construct theoretical accounts of the role of parties in Congress.

Beyond the broader theoretical significance of *The Electoral Connection* in the evolution of our understanding of legislatures and representation, Arnold argues for the enduring explanatory power of Mayhew's work as a theory of congressional behavior, observing that individual members continue to have strong incentives to engage in advertising, credit claiming, and position taking – the three activities highlighted by Mayhew – as they pursue reelection in the contemporary Congress. These individual incentives also continue to produce many of the collective results that prevailed in the 1970s: a focus on particularism and symbolism, servicing of the organized, and delay. In a world in which members of Congress continue to be rewarded for taking popular positions and delivering goods to local constituents, the core logic of the electoral connection remains in place.

This is not to say that nothing important has changed. Arnold observes that members of Congress vote much more on party lines than in the past, and party organizations play a much more active role in congressional deliberations. But Arnold argues that these shifts are rooted in individual members' electoral calculations: the southern realignment and the nationalization of elections have changed the optimal strategy for gaining reelection. Democratic and Republican members of Congress now come from quite distinct types of constituencies and they each face an environment where nationally oriented interest groups reward candidates for partisan and ideological loyalty. This new context dictates that pursuing reelection now involves a greater degree of partisan voting than in the past. It does not, however, logically imply the need for altering the parsimonious member-level reelection-oriented politician formulation to include the independent influence of "political party" to explain the greater partisan conformity we see in roll call voting.

Jacobson agrees with Arnold's contention that electoral incentives remain as potent as ever but proposes extending Mayhew's original formulation to add the member's desire to serve in the majority. This may easily be considered a friendly amendment, as it is natural that Mayhew did not focus on majority status in the 1970s, a time when the Democrats had held a firm majority of seats for decades and seemed to be the permanent majority party. Mayhew might even agree with Jacobson that MCs could believe that "it might even be worth trading a modest reduction in the probability of reelection for an increase in the probability of serving in the majority." However, this would have had no empirical relevance as Mayhew wrote in the 1970s, since in the prior era majority party status was not thought to be in question.

Jacobson also highlights a second significant change in the MC's electoral environment since the 1970s. In the modern era, the option of "build[ing] a power base that is substantially independent of party" (Mayhew 1974a) is no longer available. Jacobson demonstrates that the individual member's ability to build a personal vote that can withstand national partisan forces has greatly eroded. In earlier decades, many members of Congress were able to win reelection even if they were in a district that leaned toward the other party. Today, voting is more partisan and precious few districts elect members of Congress from the "wrong" party. Jacobson argues that this shift has had asymmetric effects on the parties because Republican voters tend to be distributed more efficiently than Democrats. Put simply, for Republicans to win a majority of House seats, they need only win the districts that lean toward the party in terms of their presidential vote and general partisanship. Democrats, by contrast, can only build a majority if they win GOP-leaning districts. This electoral arithmetic, a product of voting patterns, geography, and the details of drawing congressional districts, has important strategic implications; Republicans do best if the election is defined along sharply partisan lines, whereas Democrats benefit if party lines are blurred. Members' greater dependence on national partisan forces also means that they have a stronger reelection-based interest in shaping those forces. Republicans' "Strategy of 'No'" following Obama's 2008 victory makes sense in this new context: the way to win back Congress, in the view of GOP strategists, was to keep partisan divisions sharp and to deprive Obama of the kind of bipartisan policy victories that might burnish his and the Democrats' brand.

Robert Erikson's Chapter 4 provides an extended treatment of one critical issue highlighted in Jacobson's discussion of contemporary politics, the decline of the personal vote. Erikson describes the intellectual context and the aftermath of the seminal studies in this area, namely Erikson (1971, 1972) and Cover and Mayhew (1977), works that measured the size and growth of the incumbency advantage in congressional elections, and Mayhew (1974b), which demonstrated the decline in the number of competitive congressional elections. In his chapter, Erikson details how the incumbency advantage is measured and traces the changes in incumbency advantage over a sixty-year period. Erikson's analysis highlights a striking transformation: incumbency advantage – which has long been taken to be a central feature of congressional elections – has fallen substantially since about 1990. In the most recent election cycles, it appears that the edge reaped by the typical incumbent was roughly 2–3 points, comparable to the size of incumbency advantage in the 1950s, before the much-heralded increase in the value of incumbency in the 1960s through the 1980s.

This finding raises important questions for political scientists and the public. A rich literature has developed that aims to explain the origins of incumbency advantage; how well do these explanations hold up when it comes to accounting for the recent decline? Furthermore, is this shift in congressional election patterns mirrored by changes in other elections, such as those for governor, lower state-wide offices, and state legislature, which had also seen growing incumbency advantage in earlier decades? Finally, what implications does the erosion of incumbency advantage have for legislators' incentive to provide high-quality representation to their constituents?

There are two important differences in congressional politics in the 2010s versus the 1970s that are highlighted by Jacobson and Erikson: polarized voting in Congress and greater party line voting among the electorate. It is natural to consider how these developments are linked. Regarding the causes of the decline in the incumbency advantage, Jacobson suggests that greater congressional polarization and increased partisan voting "co-evolved." He explains, in Chapter 3:

any trends correlated with time will be correlated with each other, and correlations are silent about causation. Still, both logic and evidence point to an interactive process: voters have gradually sorted themselves into increasingly distinct political camps in response to the more sharply differentiated alternatives presented by the congressional parties and candidates, while the widening ideological gap between the congressional parties reflects their increasingly divergent electoral bases. The congressional parties were the first movers in this co-evolutionary process – as for example when the civil rights legislation of the 1960s initiated the southern realignment – but their drift toward the extremes was conditional on their members' avoiding punishment for it at the polls.

Erikson echoes this view and posits that there may be a link between congressional polarization and the decline of the personal vote, speculating that "the salience of the party brand limits the degree to which voters can detect nuances of congressional behavior that previously might have mattered. The result is a renewed fall-off in the personal vote in general and the incumbency advantage in particular." (Erikson, p. 24). An important research topic is to carefully model (and then test) how these central phenomena might be causally related. This research by its nature will link legislative politics (i.e., "institutions") and voting behavior.

Christopher Achen's Chapter 5 concludes this section with a cautionary note about how we conceptualize and measure incumbency advantage. The existence of an incumbency advantage has typically been attributed to the incumbents' successful efforts to insulate their positions from successful challenge though greater media exposure, constituency service, or other activities designed to produce a personal vote. These advantages are enhanced by the greater fundraising capacity of officeholders, who not only enjoy the ability to do favors that flows from current office holding, but are the likely winners of the next election as well. The advantages of office holding produce a "lock in" that has implications for social welfare if the effort to produce a personal vote or the insulation from electoral consequences that may result leads to waste or poor performance in office, or aggregate nonresponsiveness of the political system to voter sentiments.

Achen's analysis approaches the incumbency advantage from an entirely different perspective, by noting that the key thing to know about an incumbent is that the incumbent has (almost always) won an election. If we model elections as a contest between two individuals of observable quality selected at random from a population (quality is modeled as a random variable), it is mechanically true that the superior draw from the first two draws (which we will call "the incumbent") is likely to be of higher quality than a third random draw (which we will call "the challenger"). Thus, an "incumbency advantage" is produced without free congressional mailings and the other trappings of office. Achen works out a more detailed version of this model, which includes primary elections, and conducts empirical tests based on the model's predictions regarding the incumbency advantage for U.S. presidents. In the conclusion of his essay, Achen observes that his model of officeholder selection provides a baseline rather than a full theoretical or empirical account of incumbency. Attempts to explain the variation in reelection rates both across districts and over time would require additional work and will suggest further empirical tests. The empirical success of Achen's model in explaining U.S. presidential election outcomes suggests the direction Achen explores is a fruitful avenue for further investigation.

CONTINUITY AND CHANGE IN PARTY ORGANIZATIONS

A fundamental feature of legislative life is that members face a trade off between cooperating with one another to provide collective goods that benefit all members – such as policies that solve genuine problems or organizational arrangements that help keep all incumbents safe – versus focusing their energies on making the other side look bad. Mayhew's *The Electoral Connection* highlights the former set of incentives – in particular, the shared goal of providing incumbents with the kinds of perquisites and opportunities that help each member win reelection. But the terms of this trade off need not be constant over time. When members of Congress place little weight on the value of being in the majority party, it is far easier to form a cooperative incumbent cartel. By contrast, when majority status is seen to be at stake and valuable, the goal of making the other party look bad becomes more valuable to members. Party organizations can be used to achieve this very different type of collective goal.

This role for party organization is the motivating insight of Frances E. Lee's Chapter 6, which argues that legislative party organizations have seen dramatic growth and institutionalization over the past two decades, and have undertaken an array of political mobilization functions that they rarely performed in the 1960s and 1970s. Following several decades in which Democrats seemed to enjoy a permanent majority in Congress, the intense, prolonged competition for majority party control since the 1980s has prompted remarkable institutional innovation and expansion. Thirty or forty years ago, the national party organizations raised campaign funds but for the most part made no attempt to shape the messages, campaign activities, or electoral strategies of individual candidates. In sharp contrast, party organizations today seek to coordinate and orchestrate the political mobilization activities of their officeholders. Parties not only communicate their "brands" to the electorate, they also take positions on controversial issues, disseminate centrally approved "talking points" and speeches to individual candidates and office holders, claim credit for good economic and governmental performance when their standard bearer holds the presidency, and even seek to undercut the prestige and popularity of leaders of the opposing party.

Indeed, a central finding from Lee's work is that the job of opposing the president and undercutting his and his party's public support has become a focal point of activity for the out-party in Congress. The idea that the opposition party should hold the president's feet to the fire has deep roots. Along these lines, Mayhew's *America's Congress* (2002) demonstrates that one of the key roles played by Congress historically has been to mount oppositions to presidents. But can this opposition become pathological if it is entirely oriented toward short-term political gain? Is there a way to distinguish vigorous contestation from socially harmful obstruction? What role can the media and voters play in checking irresponsible obstruction – and encouraging the sorts of oppositions that Mayhew argues have played a key role in maintaining the constitutional balance of powers? The legislative dysfunction identified by many critics of today's Congress can be traced back to the very different incentives created by the race for majority party status.

The other two chapters in this section take a longer temporal perspective to assess the organization and cohesion of the major parties over the past three decades. Chapter 7 by John Mark Hansen, Shigeo Hirano, and James M. Snyder Jr., "Parties Within Parties: Parties, Factions, and Coordinated Politics, 1900–1980," builds upon classic works by V. O. Key and David Mayhew on party factionalism. Both Key and Mayhew noted the existence of "persistent factionalism" in dominant parties in many states and posed the provocative question of whether factions might function as "parties within parties" in states that lack effective two-party competition. This chapter takes a closer look at party factionalism, using a comprehensive database of primary election returns at the county level for nearly all of the states over the last century. Overall, Hansen, Hirano, and Snyder find little evidence of robust, deep, and durable factions within state parties.

A handful of states, however, did feature durable factions: Louisiana, North Dakota, Minnesota, and Wisconsin. Hansen, Hirano, and Snyder show that these four cases displayed a common pattern of an insurgency on the political left that met with a reaction from the center and right. Each faction constructed slates of candidates to contest offices; the factional identity of the candidates then served as a cue for voters that structured voting behavior. In each case, one-party dominance meant that ideological dissent was channeled through the primary process rather than interparty competition. Party factionalism gave way when the opposition party became a viable vehicle for opposition and two-party competition displaced one-party factionalism.

Chapter 8 by Joshua D. Clinton, Ira Katznelson, and John S. Lapinski focuses on the extent to which southern members of Congress constituted a durable faction within the national Democratic Party. The authors begin with the observation that scholars employing the standard NOMINATE methodology for estimating members' preferences have portrayed the Roosevelt and Truman years as a critical period during which the distance between the Democratic and Republican parties dramatically decreased compared with prior and recent moments. This characterization is at odds with historical accounts and empirical studies of party voting that suggest that southern Democrats largely stuck with their northern counterparts in the 1930s and that interparty conflict was actually quite high during the New Deal years.

Finding these differences to be puzzling, the authors explore diverse measures of preferences and behavior, raising questions about how problematic assumptions can sometimes drive historical assertions. They argue that DW-NOMINATE scores' assumption that member preferences change as a linear function of time leads to a misleading account of ideological shifts during the New Deal era. When one instead estimates ideal points using a more flexible approach, Clinton, Katznelson, and Lapinski find greater polarization during the early New Deal years. This, in turn, allows for a more nuanced understanding of the southern shifts that eventually gave rise to the cross-party conservative coalition that dominated American politics for much of the 1940s and 1950s.

Together, the chapters by Lee; Hansen, Hirano, and Snyder; and Clinton, Katznelson, and Lapinski illuminate how intraparty divisions and interparty competition shape law making and party dynamics both in particular regions and in the nation as a whole.

PARTISANSHIP AND GOVERNMENTAL PERFORMANCE

There is no simple set of metrics that can be used to judge the quality of political outcomes in the same way as is the case with economics. This raises difficult conceptual and measurement challenges for political scientists. What does it mean for Congress to be performing well? How can we know that it is doing a good job? How can we measure legislative performance? In his book, *Divided We Govern* (1991), Mayhew offers one approach to assessing legislative performance: he develops a coding system to evaluate the number of landmark laws passed by Congress and then applies that system to compile a list of significant legislation for the postwar period. He then uses this new data source to test the common claim that divided party control leads to poor legislative productivity. In contrast to that conventional wisdom, Mayhew showed that the volume of landmark laws enacted in the United States was not significantly higher when a single party controlled both Congress and the White House than under conditions of divided control.

In Chapter 9, Sarah Binder returns to Mayhew's (1991) finding about legislative productivity and divided party control, reconsidering his argument in light of two decades of rising partisan and ideological polarization on Capitol Hill. In doing so, Binder is adopting and extending a research paradigm that diagnoses the health of a political system based, in part, on legislative productivity. How does the rise in polarization affect the parties' incentives and capacity for securing compromise on major problems of the day? Binder finds that today's polarized conditions have led to unusually low productivity and high levels of stalemate. Her analysis concludes that these dynamics are unlikely to be self-correcting. The factors giving rise to high polarization – and, in turn, low productivity – do not appear likely to change anytime soon.

Chapter 10 by Stephen Ansolabehere, Maxwell Palmer, and Benjamin Schneer takes a broader sweep in applying the basic approach in *Divided We Govern* to more than 200 years of American political history. Ansolabehere and his collaborators enlisted the students in an undergraduate Congress course in a major effort to identify each landmark law passed from 1789 to the present. Each student was charged with becoming an expert on a particular decade – reading original materials and secondary sources – to develop a database of all significant legislation on which Congress took action in their decade. This approach allows the authors both to trace the aggregate level of legislative activity and to identify changes in the type of legislation adopted. Ansolabehere and his co-authors find that the nineteenth century Congress produced far fewer pieces of major legislation than the twentieth century Congress, with productivity peaking in the 1960s. Furthermore, they argue that while unified partisan control is associated with slightly greater production of landmark laws, it fails to explain the broad contours of legislative productivity.

Chapter 11 by Eric M. Patashnik and Justin Peck evaluates legislative performance through a different lens from that used by Binder and Ansolabehere and his co-authors. Rather than focusing on productivity, Patashnik and Peck assess how well Congress does policy analysis. Patashnik and Peck note that to perform effectively as a problem-solving institution, Congress must be able to identify failures in markets and government programs and craft effective, well-tailored solutions. That is to say, Congress must be a competent policy analyst. Patashnik and Peck draw upon an innovative survey of professional policy analysts to gain insight into the strengths and limitations of Congress as a policy analyst. A key move is to break down the policy analysis process into discrete tasks, which reveals the considerable variability in congressional performance. While the survey shows that policy experts believe that Congress does poorly in several areas – such as making policy decisions on the basis of empirical evidence and explaining issues to the public in plain language – it does better when it comes to crafting policies that reflect public opinion. Patashnik and Peck conclude that the "problem" when it comes to congressional policy analysis is not a lack of access to information and expertise, but rather legislative norms and practices that fail to promote a "culture of problem solving" (see Mayhew 2006, p. 230).

In Chapter 12, Katherine Levine Einstein and Jennifer Hochschild also consider a particular facet of legislative performance, asking how Congress responds to unexpected contingent events that create some perceived need or demand for a legislative response. Unexpected events (e.g., political scandals, the rise of social movements, crises such as 9/11 and Hurricane Sandy) are a frequent, if unpredictable, disruptive force that can compel politicians to react in novel, consequential ways. Under what conditions does Congress respond to such events with new policies or other substantive actions? The Einstein and Hochschild essay underscores the many obstacles to a sustained response to an exogenous shock. In thinking hard about the conditions in which a response is more likely, however, they take up a challenge posed by Mayhew (2005, 2009) in his recent work – that is, finding a way to incorporate contingency into the systematic study of American politics.

Finally, Chapter 13 by Keith Krehbiel explores a deep problem confronting legislative organization and performance. Krehbiel argues that there is an inherent tension facing legislators between maximizing the values of consensus, timeliness, and wisdom. Each of these values contributes to the likelihood of reaching a high-quality legislative outcome, yet one cannot maximize each of these values simultaneously. For example, provisions that encourage a timely decision (e.g., requiring only a simple majority to bring legislation to a vote) reduce legislators' incentive to build a broad consensus. At a deep level, Krehbiel argues that legislative majorities always retain the ultimate authority to set decision rules; but under what conditions will a majority choose to adopt procedures that limit its ability to bring matters to a speedy, if potentially rushed, conclusion?

Krehbiel traces how this "majoritarian tension" plays out in practice, with a particular focus on the House of Representatives' adoption of the Reed Rules in 1890. In contrast to accounts that treat the Reed rules as a "revolution," Krehbiel argues that these reforms continued a gradual process of adaptation in which the House moved toward majority rule at the agenda and decision stage. Crucially, this process was largely bipartisan: both Democrats and Republicans recognized that rampant obstructionism had gone too far in blocking legislative action, shifting the balance of considerations between consensus and timeliness. Krehbiel suggests that the Reed rules can be viewed as part of a much broader story in which legislative bodies balance considerations between consensus, timeliness, and wisdom, rather than as an example of a party-dominated transformation.

Taken together, the chapters in this part highlight the need for a multifaceted approach to evaluating congressional performance, rather than simply relying upon the volume of legislative productivity as a metric. A decade after writing *Divided We Govern*, Mayhew returned to the question of Congress's place in the American political system when he wrote *America's Congress* (2002). In the midst of popular demands for term limits on legislators, Mayhew began the book with the intuition that cutting off legislative careers after just six or eight years would undermine Congress's ability to perform its role in our political system. To test this intuition, Mayhew put together a unique dataset tracking what it is that members of Congress do that is "significant." His catalog of more than 2000 "significant actions" shows that much of what Congress does that is important does not involve legislation. Instead, members of Congress are, in large part, actors in a public sphere seeking to shape popular understandings of issues, controversies, parties, and public personalities (e.g., the president).

Crucially, a large number of these significant actions were undertaken by a relatively small number of long-serving members – among them Henry Clay,

Charles Sumner, John Sherman, George Norris, Robert Wagner, Lyndon Johnson, Wilbur Mills, Newt Gingrich, and Ted Kennedy. To Mayhew, Congress constitutes an unusual stage for performance: it provides individuals with the opportunity to change our understandings, not just to produce laws. In that sense, the "output" of the legislature is bound up with the process of legislating, investigating, and debating. But it can take years for a legislator to become known to the public and thus to acquire the resonance required to shape popular understandings. A career – such as Ted Kennedy's – has a narrative arc, and Congress as a national legislature provides a setting for that narrative to play out. To cut off careers at six years, Mayhew teaches us, would be to write a Shakespearean drama with only bit players who are on stage for minutes, rather than hours.

In today's Congress, the predominant role of parties – rather than term limits – poses the greatest threat to the vital role highlighted by Mayhew. In a legislative world in which each "character" is essentially seen as little more than a partisan warrior, fighting tooth and nail to make the other party look bad, there may be little room for the entrepreneurship and creative leadership of *America's Congress*. A Congress of "partisans" is in a fundamental sense contrary to our national DNA: from Madison's critique of factions in *Federalist 10* onward, our conception of what it means to be a good legislator has always included the idea of somehow rising above faction or party. Partisanship "pure and simple" has never been wholly legitimate, even as parties have played a vital role in structuring politics throughout our history. The question going forward is whether this tension – between the need for parties to organize politics and the value placed upon individual politicians engaging in arguments that reach beyond simple partisan appeals – has tilted all the way to one side. Mayhew's *America's Congress* teaches us that we should be worried about the partisan warfare in today's Congress less because it threatens to reduce the volume of laws passed and more because it may undermine each individual member's ability to play a constructive role in shaping a vibrant public sphere that citizens believe is worth their engagement.

CONCLUSIONS

The concluding section of the book includes reflections by Representative David Price (D-NC) and David Mayhew himself. Price, a Professor of Political Science for many years, assesses the contemporary Congress in light of both his academic expertise and his personal experience as a legislator. Striking themes consistent with the academic accounts that Jacobson, Erikson, and others present earlier in the volume, he argues that intense party competition for majority status combined with greater party polarization have undermined Congress's policy-making capacity, particularly by eroding the committee system and by privileging ideological position taking over the hard work of shaping good public policy.

In the final chapter, Mayhew provides a fascinating account of the intellectual origins of *Congress: The Electoral Connection*. Among other things, Mayhew details his methodical reading of the American politics literature, his immersion in the writings of V. O. Key, and the one hour each day (for many years) he spent working his way through the Congressional Record. He also provides some of the intellectual context for his work. Mayhew was a member of the Yale political science department in the early 1970s, a department he characterizes as committed to a vigorous pursuit of analytical rigor. Mayhew describes how the giants from an earlier era, including Dahl, Lindblom, Lane, and Kramer, as well as the extended analytical essay "An Economic Theory of Democracy" by Downs, shaped his thinking about political science, research design, and representation.

REFERENCES

Cover, Albert D. and David Mayhew. 1977. "Congressional Dynamics and the Decline of Competitive Congressional Elections." In *Congress Reconsidered*, eds. Lawrence C. Dodd and Bruce I. Oppenheimer. New York: Praeger.
Erikson, Robert S. 1971. "The Advantage of Incumbency in Congressional Elections." *Polity* 3: 395–405.
1972. "Malapportionment, Gerrymandering and Party Fortunes in Congressional Elections." *American Political Science Review* 65(December): 1234–1245.
Lee, Frances E. 2009. *Beyond Ideology: Politics, Principles, and Partisanship in the U.S. Senate*. Chicago: University of Chicago Press.
Mayhew, David R. 1974a. *Congress: The Electoral Connection*. New Haven: Yale University Press.
1974b. "Congressional Elections: The Case of the Vanishing Marginals." *Polity* 6: 295–317.
1991. *Divided We Govern: Party Control, Lawmaking, and Investigations, 1946–1990*. New Haven: Yale University Press.
2002. *America's Congress: Actions in the Public Sphere, James Madison Through Newt Gingrich*. New Haven: Yale University Press.
2005. "Wars and American Politics." *Perspectives on Politics* 3(September): 473–493.
2006. "Congress as Problem Solver." In *Promoting the General Welfare: New Perspectives on Government Performance*, eds. Alan Gerber and Eric M. Patashnik. Washington, DC: Brookings.
2009. "Is Congress 'the Broken Branch'?" *Boston University Law Review* 89:2 (April): 357–369.

PART I

POLITICAL REPRESENTATION AND DEMOCRATIC ACCOUNTABILITY

2

The Electoral Connection, Age 40

R. Douglas Arnold

Forty years ago David Mayhew changed the way scholars view the American Congress. His contributions were three. First, he demonstrated that rational choice theory is an effective way to generalize about how senators and representatives think, calculate, and act. Second, he showed how the quest for reelection shapes virtually everything that elected legislators do. Third, he demonstrated that most of what congressional scholars had discovered in the postwar period could be explained with his simple framework.

The postwar literature on Congress was large and illuminating. Using a variety of research methods, including case studies, historical analysis, participant observation, and quantitative analysis, scholars had explored wide swathes of the congressional landscape. We knew about careers, committees, parties, leaders, rules, seniority, voting, law making, appropriating, and taxing. We knew less about campaigns, campaign finance, elections, or interest groups. We knew very little about how these parts fit together. There were theories about the parts – about committees, budgeting, appropriating, roll call voting, and the like – but no theories about Congress as a whole.

Mayhew's *Congress: The Electoral Connection* (1974) changed all this. It was the first attempt to integrate what we knew about Congress into a single theory. Mayhew first assumed that legislators – both House members and senators – were "single-minded seekers of reelection." After defending his assumption, he showed how legislators engaged in three kinds of activities to advance their electoral interests – advertising, credit claiming, and position taking – and how engaging in those activities helped generate particularism, symbolism, delay, and servicing of the organized (all terms to be defined shortly). Particularistic goods aside, he argued that legislators had no electoral incentive to produce pleasing effects, only pleasing positions. He also showed how the basic organizational units on Capitol Hill – committees, parties, and offices – were well designed to advance legislators' electoral interests.

The book was influential because it took just about everything we knew about small segments of congressional behavior and explained it with a simple, parsimonious theory. Mayhew was not so much teaching us new things about Congress as he was teaching us how to understand what we already knew. His theory was the political science equivalent of plate tectonics theory, which had revolutionized geology a decade before.[1] Plate tectonics theorists assumed that the earth's outer shell was composed of a dozen or so large plates that were constantly moving and colliding. Those collisions explained everything from earthquakes, volcanoes, and mountain ranges to the continents' shapes and the worldwide distribution of species. Just as one assumption in geology explained a wide range of known phenomena, one assumption in politics explained a wide range of known behaviors in Congress.

This chapter explores how well *The Electoral Connection* has stood the test of time. Does it still provide a sound explanation for congressional behavior in the 1970s, when Mayhew was writing, or do more recent works offer superior explanations? How well does it explain congressional behavior today? Does a book that highlights the role of entrepreneurial legislators still have explanatory power in a dramatically changed world where parties are more important, interest groups more numerous, and campaigns more expensive?

RATIONAL CHOICE THEORY

The time was ripe for a rational choice explanation of congressional behavior. Although two economists had shown the way – Anthony Downs (1957) for political parties and Mancur Olson (1965) for interest groups – no one had attempted a comprehensive rational choice explanation for the major governmental institutions: legislatures, executives, courts, or bureaucracies. In retrospect, Mayhew chose the easier task. Downs and Olson attempted to explain the behavior of ordinary citizens who were deciding about issues that were peripheral to their lives – voting in elections and joining interest groups – whereas Mayhew was theorizing about the calculating behavior of full-time politicians managing their professional careers. Today we know that rational choice theory is more successful in explaining the behavior of elites, whose careers are on the line, than of citizens, who have little at stake as individuals. Mayhew also had an experiential advantage. He had spent a year on Capitol Hill, watching legislators practice their craft. He was not imagining how legislators might behave; he was theorizing about behaviors he had observed closely.

The influence of Mayhew's book was immediate. Although the 1970s were full of important books, including Manley (1970) and Fenno (1973) on

---

[1] I first made this argument in the foreword to the second edition of Mayhew's book (Arnold 2004).

committees, Kingdon (1973) and Matthews and Stimson (1975) on voting, and Fenno (1978) on representatives and their constituents, Mayhew's book changed the way scholars thought about and taught about Congress. His book was essential reading for every course on Congress. More importantly, it changed how scholars did their research.

In just a few years rational choice theory became the dominant way to theorize about Congress. Out went the norms, roles, and folkways of the more sociological theories; in came the rational, calculating, goal-oriented politicians of Mayhew's world. Of course, it helped that Richard Fenno, the discipline's most accomplished legislative scholar, had evolved in his own thinking. His magisterial *The Power of the Purse* (Fenno 1966), an intensive study of the House Appropriations Committee, demonstrated the power of sociological-type theories to explain congressional decision making. Seven years later Fenno found that framework less appealing for comparing six House and six Senate committees. In *Congressmen in Committees*, Fenno (1973) argued that legislators pursued three principal goals: reelection, influence within the House, and good public policy. Legislators who were strongly motivated by a single goal tended to join the same committee and structure each committee to achieve their common goal. His comparison of these twelve committees – and his demonstration that the new framework explained the politics of appropriations at least as well as his previous framework – underscored the power of rational choice theory.

The parsimonious Mayhew and the nuanced Fenno provided compelling theories about Congress. They also demonstrated the virtue of combining theoretical and empirical analyses. Their theories were rich because Mayhew and Fenno had spent so much time observing members of Congress. Their experiential advantage is most obvious if one compares their two books with the books of Downs (1967) and Niskanen (1971) – both economists – who created rational choice theories of bureaucratic behavior. Unfortunately, neither scholar had a deep knowledge of what made bureaucrats tick. Their works left only a faint imprint on bureaucratic scholarship.

Rational choice theories quickly became the new rage. Before the decade ended, Fiorina (1977) and Arnold (1979) explored the relationships between Congress and the bureaucracy; Shepsle investigated both committee assignments (1978) and committee power (1979).[2] The 1980s produced an explosion of research rooted in rational choice theory, mostly in articles, including Shepsle and Weingast (1981) and Weingast, Shepsle, and Johnsen (1981) on committees and distributive politics, and Weingast and Moran (1983);

---

[2] The reaction was so quick because all three scholars were steeped in rational choice theory before writing anything about Congress. Fiorina and Shepsle were part of the Rochester project to remake political science; Arnold studied formal theory with Kramer and game theory with Shubik before reading a single book about Congress. In short, when thinking about Congress, they had nothing to convert from.

McCubbins and Schwartz (1984); McCubbins, Noll, and Weingast (1987); and Moe (1987) on Congress and the bureaucracy. None of these works challenged Mayhew's basic premise or his central conclusions. A spate of books in the 1990s, all in the rational choice tradition, did challenge Mayhew, either in his assumption about single-minded seeking of reelection or in some of his conclusions. Rhode (1991), Kiewiet and McCubbins (1991), and Cox and McCubbins (1993) argued that political parties were central to understanding Congress. Krehbiel (1991, 1998) critiqued both the distributive view of committee power, arguing that committees served majoritarian interests, and the partisan view of congressional power, arguing that a nonpartisan majoritarian (or supermajoritarian) theory explained things nicely. Meanwhile, other scholars built on Mayhew's foundation. Arnold (1990) explored the conditions under which the quest for reelection could inspire legislators to produce not only group or geographic benefits but also general benefits; Hansen (1991) established the conditions under which interest groups serve legislators' electoral needs; and Hall (1996) investigated the conditions under which legislators participate in the difficult work of legislating, rather than just the simple act of voting.

The revolution that Mayhew sparked was quick and decisive. Before Mayhew, there was a rich congressional scholarship, firmly rooted in sociological-style theories. Soon after *The Electoral Connection* was published, all the influential theories were of the rational choice variety. Scholars might disagree about legislators' goals or about how they behaved in certain circumstances, but there was little disagreement that conceiving of legislators as rational, calculating individuals was a productive way to theorize about congressional decision making.

CONGRESS IN THE 1970S

How well did Mayhew's theory explain congressional behavior at the time he was writing? In my view, he got most things right. First, the book contained only one logical flaw. Mayhew worked valiantly to explain, as he called it, "How Congress stays afloat." He wrote, "If all members did nothing but pursue their electoral goals, Congress would decay or collapse" (p. 141). This is the classic collective action problem, where the solution is to provide selective incentives for some legislators to "man the helm" (p. 145). The selective incentives he introduced were power and prestige within Congress. The only problem with this solution is that power and prestige are additional goals for legislators – goals that impel leaders to do some things that are contrary to their own electoral interests (p. 146) – whereas Mayhew maintained that legislators were single-minded seekers of reelection. The better response would have been to admit that, although the electoral quest explains a great deal about Congress, it could not explain institutional maintenance. Put differently, if all legislators were singled-minded seekers of reelection, they would focus exclusively on near-term consequences, be unchecked in their eagerness to shower favors on both constituents and interest groups, and prefer funding governmental expenditures with deficits rather than taxes. This one limitation does not undermine the theory's power; it simply makes clear the theory's limits. No theory can explain everything.

Mayhew also seemed too pessimistic in his view that the electoral connection inspired legislators exclusively toward particularism – filling their districts with divisible benefits and serving organized interest groups – and never toward serving more general interests. To be sure, particularism was legislators' natural inclination. Individual legislators sought to claim credit for good deeds, and, as Mayhew argued, credit was available only for bite-sized policies for which individual legislators were plausibly responsible. But legislators also cared about general benefits, as their position-taking activities made clear. The challenge was to find ways for legislators to *produce* general benefits rather than merely acclaim them. Arnold (1990) showed that the key to whether legislators produced general benefits, rather than group or geographic benefits, was how coalition leaders defined policy options and framed voting choices. If citizens could trace general costs or benefits back to legislators' votes, they could hold legislators accountable for these effects. In order to forestall this electoral audit, rational legislators were forced to consider general costs and benefits. Thus, if legislators were asked to vote on a tax break for a narrow interest group, they would enthusiastically support this particularistic policy, whereas if they were asked to vote on a reform proposal that would eliminate many tax breaks, they would just as enthusiastically support a more efficient tax code.[3] In short, under the right conditions the electoral connection could produce either particularistic or general-benefit policies.

Both Mayhew and Arnold emphasized the importance of coalition leaders, but only Mayhew attempted to explain legislators' incentives to become leaders. He argued that legislators would build coalitions only when they could deliver particularized benefits or when "somebody of consequence" was watching, notably an attentive interest group (p. 115). The electoral incentive inspired legislators to deliver targeted group or geographic benefits, but not to build coalitions that would benefit the general interest. Later Hall (1996) developed a theory to explain why individual legislators would chose to invest their time and energy in advancing proposals. His explicit aim was to explain participation in committees: Why did some legislators show up at markup sessions, introduce amendments, participate in markup debates, round up support from fellow committee members, or defend a bill on the floor, while most committee members did nothing? Hall also assembled a

---

[3] Later Patashnik (2008) explained why some general-benefit reforms are fragile and soon dismantled (e.g., tax reform), while others are sturdy and lasting (emissions trading for acid rain).

rich data set on what individual legislators did in three House committees (from committee records) and what these legislators' interests were in each bill being considered (from interviews with legislators' staffers). Hall argued that activist legislators were largely self-starters; no one was required to participate in anything. He found that the electoral connection provided one motive for legislators to work on specific bills, especially if a bill affected an important segment of a legislator's constituency, but equally important were legislators' personal interests in specific policies. These personal interests reflected their previous employment or professional backgrounds, their identification with racial or ethnic groups, and their ideological commitments. In short, it is a mix of electoral and personal interests that explains individual activism.[4]

In the early years, then, the general reaction to Mayhew's book was acceptance, with some nibbling around the edges. Most works were building on his theory, not attempting to overturn it. Arnold did not dispute that legislators are inclined toward particularism; he merely argued that, under the right conditions, single-minded seekers of reelection could also produce general benefits. Hall did not dispute that the electoral connection impels some legislators to become entrepreneurs; he merely argued that other goals could also inspire legislative activism. Only the party-centric works (discussed later) directly challenged the centrality of the electoral connection to all that happens on Capitol Hill.

The principal advantage of Mayhew's theory is that it is a single-goal theory. Everything emanates from the quest for reelection; legislators never have to balance conflicting goals. Unfortunately, as it turns out, not everything flows from the electoral goal, especially leadership. Coalition leadership arises partly from legislators' quest for good public policy. Institutional leadership stems partly from legislators' quest for power. A more complete explanation, therefore, requires at least three goals – reelection, policy, and power – just as Fenno (1973) argued in his committee book. The downside is that three-goal theories get messy unless one knows the conditions under which one goal dominates.[5] Mayhew is on firm ground when he argues that reelection must be the *proximate* goal for everyone – the one that "must be achieved over and over if other ends are to be entertained" (p. 16). Beyond that, neither Mayhew nor his critics and followers have been able to specify exactly how legislators make trade offs among multiple goals.

---

[4] Later Wawro (2000) investigated whether legislators' overall entrepreneurial activities affected other people's behavior – citizens in elections, donors giving money, or leaders choosing other leaders.

[5] Those who have been most successful in developing multiple-goal theories include Schickler (2001) on institutional change, Lee (2009) on congressional partisanship, and Adler and Wilkerson (2012) on problem solving.

CONGRESS TODAY

How well does Mayhew's theory explain congressional behavior today?[6] It helps to begin with a discussion of the three activities that Mayhew identified as dominating legislators' lives, all of them designed to achieve their electoral goals. Do these three activities seem equally important today?

Advertising, which refers to activities that promote an individual legislator's brand name, but in messages without issue content, seems undiminished. Wherever the cameras are rolling, you find a gaggle of legislators jockeying for position; no microphones or scribes are required. Before the State of the Union Address, some House members wait patiently for up to ten hours to have an aisle seat and the chance to shake hands with the president as he walks down the aisle, all so the folks back home will see their representative sharing a brief word with the president. Moreover, aisle-seat squatting is a bipartisan affair; Republicans and Democrats are equally happy to wait all day for two seconds of prime-time exposure (Fahrenthold 2013). Yes, advertising is alive and well on Capitol Hill, as legislators seek publicity whenever and wherever they can find it.

Credit claiming, which involves generating the belief among constituents or other relevant actors that a legislator is personally responsible for delivering a valued good, also remains a central legislative activity. Although the delivery methods vary, fetching geographic benefits for constituent groups appears invariant over time. In Mayhew's time, bureaucrats allocated most geographic benefits in the form of grants, so legislators worked to ensure that their districts received adequate shares and that they earned lavish credit (Arnold 1979). Soon representatives removed the bureaucratic intermediaries by inventing earmarks – individual provisions, sometimes in omnibus bills, sometimes in committee reports – that deliver funds directly to district-based organizations (Evans 2004). Earmarks eventually became a growth stock, peaking in 2005 at more than 1 percent of the federal budget, before becoming a bridge-to-nowhere embarrassment. So Congress passed a general-benefit reform that sought to ban them. Of course, earmarks have not gone away; they are just hidden more carefully (Nixon 2012; Weisman 2012). Meanwhile legislators find many other ways to claim credit. For example, a senator who blocks nominees for the influential U.S. Court of Appeals for the District of Columbia Circuit – the court reviews regulations from most administrative agencies – can claim credit for eliminating any new judges who seem unfriendly to the various

---

[6] I do not address how well Mayhew's theory explains congressional behavior before the 1970s. The conventional wisdom suggests that his explanation works best for the post–World War II era. But Carson and Jenkins (2011) make a persuasive case that Mayhew's explanation works well beginning in the Progressive Era (1890–1920). Indeed, some elements of the theory can be seen in congressional practice in the early nineteenth century.

corporate interests that regularly appear before this court.[7] Such claims are completely credible in a world where the informed know which senator is blocking action and the inattentive do not notice or care. Legislators continue to insert special tax provisions in urgent fiscal bills. They force the Pentagon to acquire weapons that defense officials do not want. They hold up presidential appointments until the administration delivers little goodies. Yes, credit claiming is alive and well on Capitol Hill.

Position taking, which refers to making judgmental statements about matters that constituents or other relevant actors consider important, also seems unchanged. Legislators so enjoy taking public positions on some issues that House Republicans have voted fifty-six times (last count) to repeal, revamp, or delay Obamacare (Pear 2015). Presumably, after the first few votes Republicans realized that the Senate would not follow suit and that, even if it did, President Obama would veto the repeal. But was there a better way to demonstrate the depth of their opposition to the president's signature accomplishment? Was there a better way to make Democrats look bad than by repeatedly forcing them to support a program that pollsters declared unpopular? Meanwhile the Senate schedules what are called "vote-a-ramas" – occasions where some senators force other senators to take positions on hot-button issues that could be used against them in future campaigns. Recently the Senate pulled an all-nighter, voting on forty-two amendments to a necessary budget resolution, but a resolution that everyone knew would never have the force of law (Weisman 2013). In short, the amendments were of no policy consequence. It was pure position taking – pure symbolism. The actual production of laws is down considerably since Mayhew's time, but not the incidence of roll-call votes, especially in the House. In the productive 92nd Congress, when Mayhew was writing his book, the House voted 934 times on the way toward Congress enacting 607 public bills. Four decades later in the unproductive 112th Congress, the House voted 1,607 times on the way toward Congress enacting 283 public bills (Ornstein et al. 2014).[8]

Mayhew's insight was not merely that legislators care about using their positions to shape their images, but that they care more about the images they shape via position taking than the effects they actually produce. That much is obvious in the cases just discussed – repealing Obamacare and

---

[7] It was the refusal of Republican senators to allow any votes on President Obama's three nominees to fill vacant seats on this court – second in importance only to the Supreme Court – that prompted Democratic senators to modify the rules for overcoming Senate filibusters (Leonnig 2013).

[8] Roll call voting actually declined in the Senate during this period, with 955 votes in the 92nd Congress and 486 votes in the 112th (Ornstein et al. 2014). The Senate is now more the scene of obstruction than action and obstruction is more a consequence of credit claiming than position taking.

Senate vote-a-ramas – because no effects were on the table. These were purely symbolic occasions. But sometimes legislators must come together and produce effects. They must pass a budget or the government will shut down. They must raise the debt ceiling or the government will default. These are occasions when legislators struggle to keep their voting records pure while concealing their connection with unpleasant effects. House Republicans regularly face this dilemma. Although they are publicly opposed to increasing either taxes or debt, they can hardly be associated with default or the government shutting down. Their most recent solution, while struggling to avoid the fiscal cliff, was to delegate bill drafting to the Senate – once an unthinkable abrogation of House power – in order to distance Republican legislators from the distasteful policy of increasing taxes. On the New Year's Day 2013 vote to approve the Senate-designed tax package, most House Republicans voted "nay" (64 percent), but on the more crucial vote to allow the bill to reach the floor, Republican legislators voted overwhelmingly in favor (99 percent). The more visible final vote allowed them to remain firmly against all tax increases, while the less visible procedural vote kept the country from tumbling over the fiscal cliff. Yes, legislators' concern with symbolic position taking more than actual policy effects still captures the reality of congressional politics.

Mayhew also investigated the policy effects of a legislature filled with members engaged in advertising, credit claiming, and position taking. He argued that the inevitable results were particularism, symbolism, servicing of the organized, and delay. Once again, these patterns nicely describe more recent congresses. As discussed earlier, particularism and symbolism are alive and well. The proliferation of interest groups and the rise in campaign costs have made servicing the organized even more profitable for legislators. If anything, delay seems worse today than it was forty years ago. Presidential nominations to the courts languish for years, as do nominations for some agencies such as the National Labor Relations Board. The reauthorization of the No Child Left Behind Act is eight years overdue. It is down to the wire on budgets and raising the debt ceiling. Some of these delays have serious consequences. The 2011 fiscal follies produced a downgrade in the government's credit rating.

Mayhew's book does not introduce readers to some historic relic. Although the proper nouns have changed, the arguments are still fresh. Today's legislators sound remarkably like those of forty years ago. To be sure, Congress is more diverse, with many more female, black, Latino, Asian-American, gay, and lesbian legislators. The issues that animate legislators are also different. Terrorism has replaced communism as a pressing issue. Balancing the federal budget is more an issue than sharing abundant federal revenues with states and localities. Abortion and same-sex marriage have replaced school busing and hiring quotas. But the notion that legislators care more about reelection than anything else still rings true to my ear.

PARTY-CENTRIC THEORIES

Having advanced the notion that legislators are single-minded seekers of reelection, Mayhew argued, "No theoretical treatment of the United States Congress that posits parties as analytic units will go very far" (p. 27). Although this did not seem like a controversial statement in the mid-1970s, it has become increasingly contested over time. There is now a vast literature on the role of parties in Congress, ranging from Gary Cox and Mathew McCubbins (1993, 2005), who place parties at the center of their theorizing, to Keith Krehbiel (1993, 1998), who repeatedly asks, "Where's the Party?"[9]

One reason that parties seem more important today is that they are more homogeneous. In Mayhew's time, congressional Democrats came in three flavors – liberal, moderate, and conservative – and so did Republicans. Many policy coalitions in Congress were bipartisan, uniting like-minded legislators from both sides of the aisle. Today the congressional parties are better sorted, each with fewer flavors. In ideological terms, the most conservative Democratic legislator is less conservative than the most liberal Republican is. Although it took a generation for voters in the South to replace conservative Democrats with conservative Republicans, and for voters in New England to replace liberal Republicans with liberal Democrats, that transformation is now complete. Many policy coalitions in Congress are now composed of unified Democrats opposing unified Republicans.

The sorting of Democratic and Republican legislators into two homogeneous groups who often act in unison reveals little about whether parties are in any way responsible for legislators' cohesion. Are legislators voting together because they happen to share common policy preferences? Or do powerful party leaders force them to march in step? Isolating party effects is hard because there are few good measures of either legislators' policy preferences or party leaders' efforts. One study that did employ an independent measure of policy preferences (from campaign surveys) found modest party effects, especially for close votes, procedural votes, and votes on key party issues such as budgets and taxes (Ansolabehere, Snyder, and Stewart 2001). Other studies have shown that the occasional legislators who switch parties subsequently modify their voting decisions in the direction of their new parties (Hager and Talbert 2000; Nokken and Poole 2004). In short, although there is some evidence that party has an independent effect on roll call voting, it is still unknown how large is the effect or under what conditions it appears.

The existence of small party effects does not necessarily undermine Mayhew's theory. As with any monocausal venture, he made clear that he would be "satisfied to explain a significant part of the variance rather than all of it" (p. 9). It takes more than explaining a smattering of unexplained variance to undermine a theory. The real question is whether someone can construct a

---

[9] For a critical survey of the literature on party influence in Congress, see Smith (2007).

party-based theoretical edifice that can explain a significant part of the variance – say as much as Mayhew explained, or even half as much. There are two contenders.

Cox and McCubbins (1993, 2005) developed the most sophisticated party-based theory, known as *procedural cartel theory*, where legislators seek reelection, good public policy, and majority party status. According to cartel theory, legislators believe that reelection depends on their party's performance in office, which gives them a powerful interest in their party's brand name. Since party performance depends on collective action, majority-party legislators cede power to party leaders who then manage legislative affairs to their collective benefit. Party leaders promote issues that advantage their members and obstruct issues that would divide them. Among other things, party leaders use their procedural cartel to block bills from the floor that do not command majority support within the majority caucus.

There is much to admire in cartel theory. There is also much to question. First, the theory implies that legislators care as much about their party's brand name as they do about their own personal brands. I am happy to believe that legislators care about their party's brand name when it does not conflict with their personal brands. Perhaps now that parties are more homogeneous, the conflicts are fewer. When the two goals collide, however, I still observe legislators worrying more about their own personal brands than about their party's brand. When Republican leaders pulled the Hurricane Sandy relief bill off the House floor in early 2013, Representative Peter King (R-NY) responded indignantly on Fox News: "I'm saying anyone from New York and New Jersey who contributes one penny to congressional Republicans is out of their mind. Because what they did last night was put a knife in the back of New Yorkers and New Jerseyans. It was an absolute disgrace" (Dionne 2013). Notice how King distances himself from Republicans: What *they* did was a disgrace. Don't tar *me* with the Republican brand.

Second, the principal prediction of cartel theory is that House leaders will not allow a bill to reach the floor unless a majority of the majority party favors it. In Washington, this is called the Hastert Rule. Unfortunately, Republican leaders seem less enamored with cartel theory than are its scholarly proponents. Between January 2013 and February 2014, Republican leaders allowed six important bills on the House floor that Republican majorities opposed. Three of these bills were about tax and budget policy – the very core of Republican doctrine. The American Taxpayer Relief Act, passed in January 2013 with 64 percent of Republicans opposed, made the Bush tax cuts permanent, while raising taxes on the wealthy. The 2014 Continuing Appropriations Act, passed in October 2013 with 62 percent of Republicans opposed, reopened the federal government after a sixteen-day shutdown and raised the debt ceiling to avert the first-ever federal default. The Temporary Debt Limit Extension Act, passed in February 2014 with 86 percent of Republicans opposed, raised the debt ceiling for another thirteen months. The other three bills were important but less central to core Republican principles. The House passed the Hurricane Sandy Relief Bill in January 2013, with 77 percent of Republicans opposed, the Violence Against Women Reauthorization Act in February 2013, with 59 percent of Republicans opposed, and the American Battlefield Protection Act Amendments in April 2013, with 53 percent of Republicans opposed. Perhaps Republican leaders allowed these six exceptions because they were worried about the party's brand name. Tumbling over the fiscal cliff, defaulting on the national debt, raising income taxes across the board, denying aid to hurricane victims, favoring violence against women, and allowing the desecration of battlefield sites does not sound like clever brand management. Contrary to the predictions of cartel theory, however, two-thirds of Republican House members (averaged across the six bills) were *not* worried about their party's brand. The Hastert Rule is not much of a rule if the Republican majority violates it for some of the most important issues of the day.

Third, cartel theory requires more assumptions to make fewer predictions. Cox and McCubbins restrict their attention to agenda setting in a single chamber, the House of Representatives. They do not attempt to explain the full range of legislative behaviors in both chambers. Moreover, Cox and McCubbins require a three-goal theory to explain a narrow set of decisions. I still admire the range and parsimony of Mayhew, who offers a one-goal theory to explain a wide range of regularities in both House and Senate.

The other party-based theory – *conditional party government* – seeks to explain why party influence in Congress varies over time. This theory, originally developed by David Rhode (1991) and further developed with John Aldrich (Aldrich and Rohde 2001, 2010), is also a three-goal theory.[10] Here legislators seek reelection, good public policy, and power within Congress. The moving part in conditional party government is each party's preference homogeneity in Congress. When members of a party caucus disagree on important policy issues, as they did in Mayhew's time, legislators are reluctant to empower party leaders who might thwart their electoral or policy goals. When members of a party caucus agree on most policy issues, as they currently do, legislators are more comfortable empowering party leaders so that they can advance their common aims. Aldrich and Rohde largely accept Mayhew's explanation for the congressional behavior and organization of forty years ago. Given the heterogeneity of policy preferences within the parties, legislators had no reason to grant substantial powers to party leaders. The authors show that once policy preferences became more homogeneous, legislators willingly granted party leaders increased powers.

Three aspects of conditional party government are appealing. First, it is fundamentally an electoral story. Second, it is dynamic: It seeks to explain

---

[10] The foundation for the theory was Joseph Cooper and David Brady's (1981) argument that the degree of partisan polarization in Congress is a direct consequence of partisan polarization in the electorate.

change over time. Third, it incorporates most of Mayhew's theory for periods when party caucuses are heterogeneous, while showing how and why congressional behavior changes when parties become more homogeneous. Its principal contribution, then, is to transform Mayhew's static theory into a dynamic one. The legislators populating Aldrich and Rhode's theory closely resemble those populating Mayhew's theory. All that changes is the environment within which they think, calculate, and act.

ELECTORAL ROOTS OF PARTISANSHIP

Most of the causes of increased preference homogeneity in Congress have electoral roots. Voters in the South shifted from supporting conservative Democratic candidates to supporting conservative Republican candidates. Although these shifts were gradual, often coinciding with the retirement of senior Democratic legislators, the once solid Democratic South eventually became solid for Republicans. The Southern realignment involved many changes (Carmines and Stimson 1989). Southern voters first started to support Republican presidential candidates after these candidates distanced themselves from national policies on civil rights. After a while, new voters started to identify with the party that better reflected their conservative views and new legislative candidates started to run as Republicans. Over a generation, the old order disappeared, as voters, candidates, and legislators developed complementary ideological and partisan identifications. This made the Democratic caucuses in Congress more liberal and the Republican caucuses more conservative.

Voters across the nation also developed complementary ideological and partisan identifications (Levendusky 2009). Whether through conversion, replacement, or issue evolution, fewer Republican identifiers expressed liberal views and fewer Democratic identifiers expressed conservative views. Given that ideological extremists are more likely than moderates to vote in congressional primaries, Republican primary winners became increasingly conservative and Democratic primary winners became increasingly liberal. Even for districts filled with moderates, the choices in general elections were often between conservative Republican candidates and liberal Democratic candidates. Once again, this made the Democratic caucuses in Congress more liberal and homogeneous and the Republican caucuses more conservative and homogeneous.

All these explanations for increased partisanship emphasize the electoral connection. Republican candidates campaign as conservatives because their primary electorates are increasingly conservative. Once in office, they govern as conservatives because to do otherwise is to invite other candidates to challenge them in primaries. For the same reason, Democrats campaign and govern as liberals. Some observers believe that primary challenges today are more frequent than in Mayhew's time. That claim is not correct. Although primary challenges occurred more frequently in the most recent decade than in the 1980s and 1990s, they were even more common during the 1970s, when

Mayhew was writing, than they are today (Boatright 2013).[11] What *has* changed is the issue basis of the typical primary challenge. In yesteryear, challengers emphasized incumbents' age, incompetence, lack of accomplishments, involvement in scandals, or their positions on particular issues (abortion, busing, immigration, trade, Vietnam). Today's primary challengers more frequently emphasize incumbents' ideology: Republican incumbents are not conservative enough, and Democratic incumbents are not liberal enough (Boatright 2013).

The other big change is the nationalization of congressional elections. How general elections became nationalized is well known (Jacobson 2013). The more recent story is how congressional primaries became nationalized. Primaries were once localized events. Candidates challenged incumbents as old, out of touch, tainted by scandal, not doing their jobs, or wrong on some issue of local concern. Today national groups regularly threaten incumbents with primary challenges if they support the wrong side on national issues. They actively recruit challengers when incumbents fall short; they raise and disburse funds to promising challengers. Many of these groups care intensely about ideological purity (Boatright 2013). The Club for Growth recruits, endorses, and funds fiscally conservative candidates. MoveOn.org actively supports liberal candidates. Many other national groups are active in primaries, including organized labor, the National Rifle Association, and various Tea Party groups. All these organizations make congressional primaries more the scene of ideological conflict than they were in the 1970s.[12] Campaign finance is also more of a national affair than ever before (Heberlig and Larson 2013).

Notice that my discussion of the increased preference homogeneity and party loyalty in Congress is rooted in nothing more than legislators' quest for reelection. Legislators continue to adjust their behavior to avoid electoral problems. The only difference is that today's electoral problems are not the same ones legislators faced in the 1970s. Before citizens aligned their ideological and partisan preferences – associating Republicans with more conservative positions and Democrats with more liberal positions – legislators employed carefully crafted local strategies, matching their policy positions to the mix of ideological and partisan identifications in their districts. This was especially true in competitive districts, where the principal hurdle was the general election. Now that citizens have better aligned preferences, legislators play to their more partisan and ideological voters. This is especially true in districts where today's

---

[11] Primary challenges were even more frequent in the early twentieth century (Ansolabehere et al. 2006).

[12] Mayhew argued: "There is no reason to expect large primary electorates to honor party loyalty" (p. 25). My argument here is that the increased nationalization of campaign finance and the increased power of national groups in party primaries have changed this calculus. Senator McCain (R-AZ), once celebrated as a maverick presidential candidate, shed his independent stripes as his 2010 senatorial primary neared.

principal hurdle is now the party primary, a venue where ideological extremists dominate. Today's legislators are prevented from moving toward the center not by what party leaders might do to them but by what primary challengers and primary voters might do to them. In short, party discipline in today's Congress has deep electoral roots.

OVERALL ASSESSMENT

It is easy to identify aspects of congressional behavior and organization that require more than the electoral connection for a full explanation. Institutional maintenance (Fenno 1973) and coalition leadership (Hall 1996) are good examples. So are institutional development (Schickler 2001), partisanship (Aldrich and Rohde 2001), and problem solving (Adler and Wilkerson 2012). Each theory accomplishes this feat by employing more assumptions to explain a narrower range of regularities. Although these are important works that I admire greatly, they are not as ambitious as the one theory that explains more regularities with a single assumption.

What makes David Mayhew's book so enduring is that legislators on Capitol Hill are still the ultimate political entrepreneurs. They decide when and where to run. They build their own campaign organizations, hire their own legislative staffs, and choose what issues to emphasize. They survive in office as long as they can navigate the turbulent political waters, both at home and in Congress. Conceiving of them as single-minded seekers of reelection is just as useful today as it was forty years ago, when Mayhew first postulated that the quest for reelection dominated legislators' lives.

What has changed – and what will continue to change – is the turbulence of the political waters through which legislators navigate their careers. Most notably, party currents are stronger today than they were forty years ago. Voters are more likely to hold issue positions that are compatible with their party identifications and use a candidate's party as a quick measure of issue compatibility. Voters in primary elections are more likely to use party loyalty as an indicator of a legislator's fealty to past campaign promises. National groups that endorse and finance legislative candidates are more likely to monitor candidates' ideological and party loyalty. Given these changes, legislators have modified their strategies for staying in office, paying more attention both to those who vote in party primaries and to those who finance electoral campaigns. These strategic modifications are exactly what one would expect single-minded seekers of reelection to do. Legislators survive by adapting to a changing political environment.

Why is party voting in Congress more common today? The most persuasive answer is that legislators are less likely to see conflicts between what they prefer, what their fellow partisans believe, what their constituents want, and what party leaders request. Seeing no conflict, legislators vote with the herd (Kingdon 1973, p. 230). The trouble with herd voting is that one cannot disentangle what causes what. There is no variance to analyze. Are legislators following their personal policy preferences, their constituents' preferences, or party leaders' commands? Disentangling these causes requires that there be conflicts between what legislators, constituents, and leaders want. Fortunately, we still see many instances where these three factors pull in different directions.

Watching House Republicans wrestle with budget and debt-ceiling issues helps pinpoint legislators' electoral calculations. These are issues where Congress has little choice but to act. Annual appropriations are necessary to keep the government open; periodic increases in the debt limit are necessary to pay for expenses already incurred. The last four years were particularly difficult for House Republicans because managing fiscal bills is the responsibility of the majority party. To add to their plight, they could not enact fiscal bills on their own. Democrats controlled both the Senate and the White House, so House Republicans had to compromise. Finally, many House Republicans had promised Tea Party voters and conservative donors that they would never vote to raise the debt limit or increase taxes. In short, if House Republicans supported these must-pass fiscal bills, they would invite well-funded primary challengers who could highlight how legislators had broken their pledges to resist all debt and tax hikes. If House Republicans refused to act, however, a governmental shutdown or a federal default might produce serious economic consequences that could easily be traced to their inaction. Watching how Republican legislators negotiated these treacherous waters helps isolate the continuing importance of electoral calculations.

For four years, the script was the same. Speaker John Boehner (R-OH) or his lieutenants patiently negotiated with President Obama or with Democratic leaders in the Senate on must-pass fiscal bills. No matter how well Republican leaders did in these negotiations, the Republican caucus rejected each compromise. The cycle continued until time was about to run out – the government would shut down, the Treasury would default, the nation would pass over the fiscal cliff – and then Republican leaders suddenly negotiated a bill that minority Democrats and a few lonely Republicans could support. What is revealing about these theatrical experiences is that House Republicans sometimes had to vote twice, first on whether to allow a compromise bill to reach the floor, and then on whether to pass it. The first vote seemed procedural and technical – it was not *really* about raising taxes or the debt limit – so House Republicans grudgingly supported it. The second vote was the electorally dangerous one – the one that would violate their oath never to raise taxes or debt – so only the bravest and most electorally secure Republicans joined Democrats in doing what had to be done.

Electoral considerations were paramount in these fiscal votes. For example, late on New Year's Day 2013, just before the nation would have tumbled over the fiscal cliff with the expiration of all Bush-era tax cuts and the sequestration of more than $100 billion from agency budgets, House Republicans voted

232 to 2 to adopt a rule that would allow House floor consideration of a bill that would make the tax cuts permanent for all but the wealthy and delay sequestration for two months. An hour later, only 85 Republicans (joined by 172 Democrats) voted to approve the bill. Both votes made perfect electoral sense. The first vote guaranteed that the nation would not plunge over the fiscal cliff and, more importantly, that Republicans would not be blamed for the economic consequences. The second vote guaranteed that most Republican House members would not be punished for violating their pledge to oppose all tax increases. No matter how essential the first vote was to the whole scheme, it would be tough for any challenger to make a campaign issue out of a difficult-to-understand procedural maneuver.

It is easy to tell an electoral story for why 147 Republican House members switched sides in the space of an hour, voting first to move forward procedurally to avoid the fiscal cliff, and then voting against the actual bill. It is easy to tell a similar electoral story for why House Republicans used the same tactic two weeks later, voting 225 to 1 to allow floor consideration of a supplemental appropriations bill to provide recovery funds for Superstorm Sandy, and then voting 49 to 179 against the actual bill. It is very difficult to conjure up alternative explanations for these switches. Talking about the power of party leaders does not work, for Speaker Boehner was repeatedly embarrassed by his inability to corral Republican troops behind any feasible proposal. Talking about legislators' concern for their party's brand does not work, for the Republican brand suffered badly when Republicans shut down the government, allowed for an expensive downgrade of government debt, and politicized emergency relief. These sorts of stories demonstrate that legislators continue to allow electoral concerns – and specifically how their constituents, their donors, and their supporters in congressional primaries might react – to overwhelm other considerations.

The political world has changed over the past forty years. Parties are more important, polarization greater, interest groups more numerous, campaigns more expensive, and the media more decentralized. Despite these changes in the legislative environment, I know of no superior explanation for congressional behavior than this timeless book. Without the electoral connection, Congress becomes as muddled and confusing as it was before Mayhew introduced "single-minded seekers" into the congressional lexicon.

REFERENCES

Adler, E. Scott, and John D. Wilkerson. 2012. *Congress and the Politics of Problem Solving*. Cambridge: Cambridge University Press.
Aldrich, John H., and David W. Rohde. 2001. "The Logic of Conditional Party Government: Revisiting the Electoral Connection." In *Congress Reconsidered*, 7th edition, eds. Lawrence C. Dodd and Bruce I. Oppenheimer. Washington: CQ Press, 269–292.

2010. "Consequences of Electoral and Institutional Change: The Evolution of Conditional Party Government in the U.S. House of Representatives." In *New Directions in American Political Parties*, ed. Jeffrey M. Stonecash. New York: Routledge, 234–250.

Ansolabehere, Stephen, James M. Snyder, Jr., and Charles Stewart III. 2001. "The Effects of Party and Preferences on Congressional Roll-Call Voting." *Legislative Studies Quarterly* 26 (4): 533–572.

Ansolabehere, Stephen, John Mark Hansen, Shigeo Hirano, and James M. Snyder, Jr. 2006. The Decline of Competition in U.S. Primary Elections, 1908–2004." In *The Marketplace of Democracy: Electoral Competition and American Politics*, ed. Michael P. McDonald and John Samples. Washington: Brookings, 74–101.

Arnold, R. Douglas. 1979. *Congress and the Bureaucracy: A Theory of Influence*. New Haven: Yale University Press.

1990. *The Logic of Congressional Action*. New Haven: Yale University Press.

2004. "Foreword." In *Congress: The Electoral Connection*, 2nd edition, ed. David R. Mayhew. New Haven: Yale University Press.

Boatright, Robert G. 2013. *Getting Primaried: The Changing Politics of Congressional Primary Challenges*. Ann Arbor: University of Michigan Press.

Carmines, Edward G., and James A. Stimson. 1989. *Issue Evolution: Race and the Transformation of American Politics*. Princeton: Princeton University Press.

Carson, Jamie L., and Jeffery A. Jenkins. 2011. "Examining the Electoral Connection Across Time." *Annual Review of Political Science* 14: 25–46.

Cooper, Joseph, and David W. Brady. 1981. "Institutional Context and Leadership Style: The House from Cannon to Rayburn." *American Political Science Review* 75 (2): 411–425.

Cox, Gary W., and Mathew D. McCubbins. 1993. *Legislative Leviathan: Party Government in the House*. Berkeley: University of California Press.

2005. *Setting the Agenda: Responsible Party Government in the U.S. House of Representatives*. Cambridge: Cambridge University Press.

Dionne, E. J. 2013. "Peter King Accuses House Republicans of Putting a 'Knife' in the Back of New Yorkers and New Jerseyans." *Washington Post*. 2 January.

Downs, Anthony. 1957. *An Economic Theory of Democracy*. New York: Harper and Row.

1967. *Inside Bureaucracy*. Boston: Little, Brown.

Evans, Diana. 2004. *Greasing the Wheels: Using Pork Barrel Projects to Build Majority Coalitions in Congress*. Cambridge: Cambridge University Press.

Fahrenthold, David A. 2013. "State of the Union Squatters: Lawmakers Wait Hours on Aisle for Seconds with President." *Washington Post*. 11 February.

Fenno, Richard F., Jr. 1966. *The Power of the Purse: Appropriations Politics in Congress*. Boston: Little, Brown.

1973. *Congressmen in Committees*. Boston: Little, Brown.

1978. *Home Style: House Members in Their Districts*. Boston: Little, Brown.

Fiorina, Morris P. 1977. *Congress: Keystone of the Washington Establishment*. New Haven: Yale University Press.

Hager, Gregory L., and Jeffery C. Talbert. 2000. "Look for the Party Label: Party Influences on Voting in the U.S. House." *Legislative Studies Quarterly* 25 (1): 75–99.

Hall, Richard L. 1996. *Participation in Congress*. New Haven: Yale University Press.

Hansen, John Mark. 1991. *Gaining Access: Congress and the Farm Lobby, 1919–1981*. Chicago: University of Chicago Press.

Heberlig, Eric S., and Bruce A. Larson. 2013. *Congressional Parties, Institutional Ambition, and the Financing of Majority Control*. Ann Arbor: University of Michigan Press.

Jacobson, Gary C. 2013. *The Politics of Congressional Elections*, 8th edition. New York: Pearson.

Kiewiet, D. Roderick, and Mathew D. McCubbins. 1991. *The Logic of Delegation: Congressional Parties and the Appropriations Process*. Chicago: University of Chicago Press.

Kingdon, John W. 1973. *Congressmen's Voting Decisions*. New York: Harper and Row.

Krehbiel, Keith. 1991. *Information and Legislative Organization*. Ann Arbor: University of Michigan Press.

1993. "Where's the Party?" *British Journal of Political Science* 23 (2): 235–266.

1998. *Pivotal Politics: A Theory of U.S. Lawmaking*. Chicago: University of Chicago Press.

Lee, Frances E. 2009. *Beyond Ideology: Politics, Principles, and Partisanship in the U.S. Senate*. Chicago: University of Chicago Press.

Leonnig, Carol D. 2013. "Senate's Filibuster Decision Could Reshape Influential D.C. Federal Appeals Court." *Washington Post*. 21 November.

Levendusky, Mathew. 2009. *The Partisan Sort: How Liberals Became Democrats and Conservatives Became Republicans*. Chicago: University of Chicago Press.

Manley, John F. 1970. *The Politics of Finance: The House Committee on Ways and Means*. Boston: Little, Brown.

Matthews, Donald R., and James A. Stimson. 1975. *Yeas and Nays: Normal Decision-Making in the U.S. House of Representatives*. New York: Wiley.

Mayhew, David R. 1974. *Congress: The Electoral Connection*. New Haven: Yale University Press.

McCubbins, Mathew D., Roger G. Noll, and Barry R. Weingast. 1987. "Administrative Procedures as Instruments of Political Control." *Journal of Law, Economics, and Organization* 3 (2): 243–277.

McCubbins, Mathew D., and Thomas Schwartz. 1984. "Congressional Oversight Overlooked: Police Patrols versus Fire Alarms." *American Journal of Political Science* 28 (1): 165–179.

Moe, Terry M. 1987. "An Assessment of the Positive Theory of Congressional Dominance." *Legislative Studies Quarterly* 12 (4): 475–520.

Niskanen, William A., Jr. 1971. *Bureaucracy and Representative Government*. Chicago: Aldine.

Nixon, Ron. 2012. "Congress Appears to be Trying to Get Around Earmark Ban." *New York Times*. 6 February.

Nokken, Timothy P., and Keith T. Poole. 2004. "Congressional Party Defection in American History." *Legislative Studies Quarterly* 29 (4): 545–568.

Olson, Mancur. 1965. *The Logic of Collective Action*. Cambridge: Harvard University Press.

Ornstein, Norman J., Thomas E. Mann, Michael J. Malbin, and Andrew Rugg. 2014. *Vital Statistics on Congress*. Washington: Brookings. Online. Tables 6.1, 6.2, 6.4.

Patashnik, Eric M. 2008. *Reforms at Risk: What Happens After Major Policy Changes Are Enacted*. Princeton: Princeton University Press.

34   *R. Douglas Arnold*

Pear, Robert. 2015. "House G.O.P. Again Votes to Repeal Health Care Law." *New York Times*. 3 February.

Rohde, David W. 1991. *Parties and Leaders in the Postreform House*. Chicago: University of Chicago Press.

Schickler, Eric. 2001. *Disjointed Pluralism: Institutional Development of the U.S. Congress*. Princeton: Princeton University Press.

Shepsle, Kenneth A. 1978. *The Giant Jigsaw Puzzle: Democratic Committee Assignments in the Modern House*. Chicago: University of Chicago Press.

———. 1979. "Institutional Arrangements and Equilibrium in Multidimensional Voting Models." *American Journal of Political Science* 23 (1): 27–59.

Shepsle, Kenneth A., and Barry R. Weingast. 1981. "Structure Induced Equilibrium and Legislative Choice." *Public Choice* 37 (3): 503–529.

Smith, Steven S. 2007. *Party Influence in Congress*. Cambridge: Cambridge University Press.

Wawro, Gregory. 2000. *Legislative Entrepreneurship in the U.S. House of Representatives*. Ann Arbor: University of Michigan Press.

Weingast, Barry R., Kenneth A. Shepsle, and Christopher Johnsen. 1981. "The Political Economy of Benefits and Costs: A Neoclassical Approach to Distributive Politics." *Journal of Political Economy* 89 (4): 642–664.

Weingast, Barry R., and Mark J. Moran. 1983. "Bureaucratic Discretion or Congressional Control: Regulatory Policymaking by the Federal Trade Commission." *Journal of Political Economy* 91 (5): 765–800.

Weisman, Jonathan. 2012. "Fight Over Ferry on Lake Michigan Prompts Questions of Definition of Earmarks." *New York Times*. 30 November.

———. 2013. "Senate Democrats Offer a Budget, Then the Amendments Fly." *New York Times*. 23 March.

3

The Electoral Connection, Then and Now

Gary C. Jacobson

David Mayhew's lucid, concise, and tightly argued analysis in *Congress: The Electoral Connection* established the electoral incentive as the starting point for examining virtually every aspect of congressional behavior (Mayhew 1974a). Its influence on the subsequent congressional literature can scarcely be exaggerated.[1] Mayhew was careful to acknowledge that winning reelection was not members' only motivation – a caveat sometimes missed by careless readers – but made a compelling case that it took priority, if only because being in Congress is necessary to achieve anything else there.

As part of his argument, Mayhew had to demonstrate that, along with the motive, members had the means and the opportunity to pursue reelection successfully. His review of the evidence found both to be readily available, with members simultaneously creating and exploiting conditions that enabled them to carve out individual political franchises based on a substantial "personal vote" (Cain, Ferejohn, and Fiorina 1987). Official resources for reaching and serving constituents proliferated in the 1960s and early 1970s. Campaign money kept pace. Party loyalty among voters weakened during these years and the proportion of self-identified independents grew, opening a larger portion of the electorate to cross-party or nonpartisan appeals. Split-ticket voting became increasingly common, decoupling members' electoral fates from those of their presidential candidates and national parties (Jacobson 2013e, 39–46). The most conspicuous effect of these trends was the sharp rise in the value, in terms of vote share, of incumbency status (Erikson 1971; Kostroski 1973; Mayhew 1974b).

In the nearly forty years since *The Electoral Connection* appeared, life in Congress and the electoral landscape that its members must negotiate to win and retain their jobs has undergone gradual but cumulatively radical change,

[1] Google Scholar lists more than 4,500 citations to date.

responding to and reinforcing the widening partisan divisions among its members. In this chapter, I review some of the major developments since the 1970s that have reshaped the electoral motives, means, and, most crucially, opportunities of representatives and senators. I conclude that the electoral connection, although refashioned, remains as potent as ever, providing a firm basis for the polarized partisanship and intransigence observed in the contemporary Congress – particularly among Republican House members who, for structural reasons, thrive on nationalized, highly partisan elections.

MOTIVE: REELECTION PLUS MAJORITY STATUS

Mayhew began by asking, "First, is it true that the United States Congress is a place where members wish to stay once they get there?" (1974a, 13). The answer was unambiguously "yes." Despite changes that have made life in Congress considerably less pleasant (partisan acrimony, heightened media scrutiny, the incessant pleading for campaign money) and the rising opportunity costs of remaining there (ex-members can now earn multiples of their congressional salaries as lobbyists), the answer still seems to be "yes." The incidence of voluntary retirements has increased not a whit over the past forty years. The average number of terms served has fluctuated but the overall trend has been flat.[2] Members have invested ever more effort in amassing ever larger campaign kitties aimed at scaring off or, failing that, defeating potential rivals. The few members who have opted for short stays – such as Oklahoma's Steve Largent, a conservative firebrand from the Republican class of 1994 who said he wanted a career that was "brilliant but brief" (Koszczuk 1995, 3251) – have evidently selected themselves out, leaving no detectable trace in the averages.

The reelection incentive thus seems as compelling as ever, but it has now been joined by a heightened desire to win as part of a majority, especially in the House of Representatives. When Mayhew wrote, the Democrats were in the midst of four decades of uninterrupted control; their retention of majority status was simply not in serious question in the 1970s.[3] Moreover, at a time when the House's universalism could take on "the appearance of a cross party conspiracy among incumbents to keep their jobs" (1974a, 105), minority status was not nearly so demeaning and frustrating as it has since become. Today, control of the House is up for grabs almost every election year, and the stakes are much greater because the majority party now dominates a deeply divided legislature. Members have thus acquired a much stronger interest in their party's collective electoral performance and therefore have, for example,

[2] Regressing ether the frequency of retirements or mean years of service on time produces small, statistically insignificant coefficients and virtually no explained variance.
[3] Mayhew noted that "in both houses unbroken Democratic control in the years 1955–1974 has set durability records unmatched since the rise of the two-party system in the 1830s" (1974a, 104); the record for the House remained unbroken for another two decades.

become far more willing to share campaign resources (through leadership PACs, contributions to the Hill campaign committees, and direct transfers from their own campaign funds) with colleagues in tight races (Currinder 2003, 2008; Jacobson 2010). This has emphatically not come at the expense of their own reelection efforts, to be sure, for the growth in campaign money available to incumbents has far outpaced the growth in the funds they now share with their party and its other candidates. But it does suggest that members now have greater reason and are under more pressure to consider how their actions can contribute to their party's collective electoral performance as well as to their individual prospects. It may even be worth trading a modest reduction in the probability of reelection for an increase in the probability of serving in the majority. In short, the pursuit of reelection, while as diligent as ever, is no longer as single minded as it once was.

The same logic applies, albeit to a lesser extent, to the Senate. Majority control is now hotly contested (the Senate has changed party hands six times since 1980). The Senate's rules give minority members, individually and collectively, much more influence than House minorities enjoy, but partisan polarization and the battles it engenders nonetheless put a greater premium on majority status now than in the 1970s.

MEANS: ADVERTISING, POSITION TAKING, AND CREDIT CLAIMING

The electoral motive retains its potency. In some important respects, the means available to pursue reelection are, if anything, rather more abundant than they were in the 1970s. The resources that come with congressional office – staff, communication, and travel allowances – have stabilized at the high levels reached in the 1970s; the Republicans who took over the House after the 1994 elections advertised their frugality by reducing committee staff by one-third, but voted down any reduction in the personal staff that, among other things, delivers constituency services. Meanwhile, the money available for members' campaigns has increased steeply. Since 1974, campaign spending by House incumbents has grown by about 10 percent in real terms from one election cycle to the next, the average rising from less than $300,000 in 1974 to more than $1.7 million in 2012 (in current 2012 dollars). Senators' spending has risen by about 11 percent per election cycle, with the average growing from $2.1 million to $10.5 million over the same period.[4] By this measure, at least, members' resources for advertising themselves are far greater now than in the 1970s. Yet it is worth pointing out that their familiarity to voters, at least as measured by voters' ability to recall their representative's name, has fallen significantly since then (Jacobson 2013e, 131). Like other advertisers, members

---

[4] Based on my analysis of Federal Election Commission data.

of Congress evidently struggle to be heard over the noise generated by countless competitors for the fragmented attention of the citizenry.

Congress is still rife with opportunities for free-wheeling position taking as well, although the growth in party discipline and the introduction of party-generated "talking points" (Malecha and Reagan 2012) – position taking as a tag-team event – impose greater pressure for partisan conformity than existed in the 1970s (discussed in other contributions to this volume). One of Mayhew's key insights into position taking was that members often "had every reason to worry about whether they were voting on the right side but no reason to worry about what was passed or implemented" (1974a, 115). That this remains true is nicely illustrated by the vote to deal with the impending termination of the Bush tax cuts, scheduled to occur automatically in January 2013 if Congress did not act. President Obama had promised to veto any extension of the cuts that did not raise the taxes on the wealthiest families, but many Republicans had pledged never to vote for a tax increase. Out of options – taxes would go up one way or another, and more if nothing were done – they voted 232–2 in favor of the rule that brought the Senate-passed bill that included Obama's tax increase to the floor, then voted against the bill 85–151, which passed with a large majority of Democratic votes. "I thank all of you who will vote for it," said Representative Darrell Issa (R-CA). "I cannot bring myself to vote for it" (Steinhauer 2013). Like the other 150 Republicans, Issa maintained his position as an antitax purist in the happy knowledge that it would not prevail.

The Senate's rules have always allowed members to take highly public positions on whatever issue strikes their fancy, and the increase in partisanship has not imposed any serious constraints. Kentucky Republican Rand Paul's throwback filibuster in 2013 serves as an example. Paul held the Senate floor for thirteen hours to block a vote on Obama's nominee to head the CIA as a protest against the possible use of drone attacks against American terrorist suspects on American soil. He got the Obama administration to make it clear that the government would not use drone strikes at home against noncombatant American citizens suspected of terrorism. He also reaped a bonanza of publicity on a stance that was highly popular with the public, presumably boosting his presidential prospects for 2016 (Parker 2013). More generally, with the Senate's continuing tolerance of uninhibited individualism, cultivating a reputation for independence remains a feasible reelection strategy for senators, though one now considerably harder to execute.

Some opportunities for credit claiming have been curtailed, although mainly to further position taking. The Republican majority that took over the House in the 112th Congress (2011–12) put a moratorium on earmarks to demonstrate that they were serious about shrinking government and reducing "wasteful" spending. Although earmarks accounted for less than one-half of 1 percent of the federal budget (and eliminating them does not necessarily reduce spending, for money continues to be allocated to specific projects by executive branch agencies), they were an irresistible symbol of congressional profligacy.

The earmark ban has not stopped members from pushing local projects – as Tea Party star Michele Bachmann (R-MN) explained, "Advocating projects for one's district does not in my mind equate to an earmark" (Young 2010) – but surreptitious pursuit of pork at least complicates credit claiming. The moratorium has also been blamed for some of Congress's current dysfunction, making it more difficult, for example, for House Speaker John Boehner to round up Republican votes during various iterations of the fiscal face-off with Barack Obama (Greeley 2013; Ungar 2012). It is unlikely to end any time soon, for taking a position pleasing to their Tea Party faction evidently serves many Republicans' electoral objectives better than would delivering traditional particularized benefits. This reality points to the domain where the electoral connection has changed the most in the past forty years: the electoral arena.

OPPORTUNITY: THE CONTEMPORARY ELECTORAL ARENA

The electoral arena, described by Mayhew as one in which members "can – and must – build a power base that is substantially independent of party" (1974a, 26), has changed almost beyond recognition. As it turns out, Mayhew was writing at a point when party influences – on members, on voters individually and in the aggregate, and on campaign strategies and resources – were at a low point. Since then, all of the trends that weakened parties and enabled members to establish personal political franchises have shifted into reverse. The partisan, ideological, and policy views of voters have grown more internally consistent, more distinctive between partisan coalitions, and more predictive of voting in national elections. At the same time, the electoral units into which voters are sorted have become more homogeneously Republican or Democratic (Jacobson 2013c, 547–550). Members' capacity to withstand contrary national partisan tides and to win against the partisan grain has consequently diminished.

These developments are a direct consequence of a gradual but thorough ideological realignment of the Republican and Democratic parties. The realignment was driven by elite and popular reactions to political changes initiated in the 1960s and early 1970s. Chief among them was the civil rights revolution, crowned by the Voting Rights Act of 1965, which brought southern blacks into the electorate as Democrats, while moving conservative whites to abandon their historic allegiance to the Democratic Party in favor of the ideologically and racially more compatible Republicans. The rise of social issues – led by abortion after its legalization in *Roe v. Wade*, but also including other women's issues and gay rights – augmented this shift, as the Republican Party adopted the conservative positions favored by the evangelical Christians who populate southern electorates. This provoked a smaller countermovement among socially liberal and moderate Republicans elsewhere, particularly in the northeast, who no longer found themselves at home in the Republican Party and gradually adopted a Democratic identity.

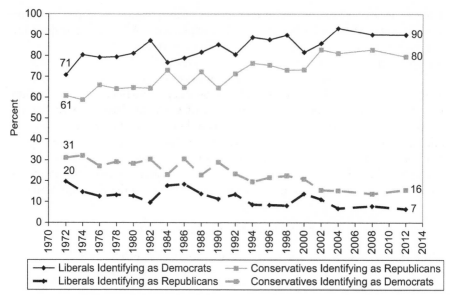

FIGURE 3.1 Ideology and party identification of Voters, 1972–2012. Source: American National Election Studies.

These changes were key components of a broader process of ideological sorting that has left partisans on opposite sides of a diverse and growing range of issues (Abramowitz 2010; Levendusky 2009). As a result, the mass bases of the two parties have grown increasingly distinct in their political values and ideological preferences. The data in Figure 3.1 summarize this trend (with end points labeled).[5] The Republican Party has always attracted the larger share of conservatives and the Democratic Party the larger share of liberals, but with far greater consistency now than earlier. In 1972, self-identified liberals and conservatives identified with the "appropriate" party 69 percent of the time; in 2012, they did so 87 percent of the time. The electorate's increasing partisan coherence is also evident in the growing correlation between partisanship and opinions on issues ranging from abortion to race to the proper role of government to global warming (Abramowitz 2010; Bafumi and Shapiro 2009; Jacobson 2011a). Most importantly for our purposes, these changes have sparked a revival of party loyalty in congressional elections.

[5] Ideology is respondents' self-location on a seven-point scale: extremely liberal, liberal, slightly liberal, moderate, slightly conservative, conservative, and extremely conservative. The proportion of voters calling themselves liberals or conservatives has grown over time; typically, about 80 percent of voters can place themselves on the scale, and about 70 percent of those voters place themselves either to the left or to the right of center.

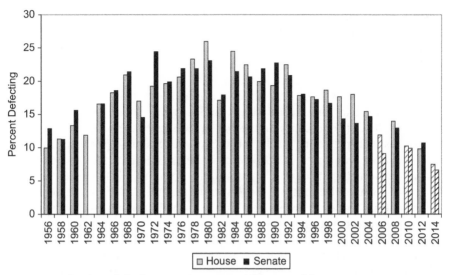

FIGURE 3.2 Partisan defection rates in contested House and Senate races, 1952–2014.
Source: 1956–2004, 2008, 2012: American National Election Studies; 2006, 2010, 2014:
Cooperative Congressional Election Study.

Voters

Party loyalty among voters in House and Senate elections reached its nadir in
the American National Election Studies (ANES) time series during the
1970s.[6] The defection rates for House elections peaked at 26 percent in
1980 and for Senate elections at 24 percent in 1972 (Figure 3.2). By 2012,
defections had dropped to 10 percent in House elections and 11 percent in
Senate elections. The proportion of the electorate composed of pure independents (leaning toward neither party) also dropped from about 9 percent in
the 1970s to 5 percent in 2012. Thus, the proportion of the electorate
consisting of loyal partisans was as high by the end of the 2000s as it had
been in the 1950s.

In 2012 and 2014, party-line voting also reached its highest levels ever for
House and Senate elections in the national exit polls[7] and the Cooperative

---

[6] The American National Election Studies (www.electionstudies.org) TIME SERIES CUMULA-
TIVE DATA FILE [dataset]. Stanford University and the University of Michigan [producers and
distributors], 2010 and the ANES 2012 Time Series Study [dataset]. Stanford University and the
University of Michigan [producers]. I use only the face-to-face component of the 2012 ANES
(N = 2056) to maintain comparability in the time series.
[7] The exit poll results are from www.foxnews.com/politics/elections/2012-exit-poll, November
18, 2012.

Congressional Election Study (CCES).[8] In the 2012 exit polls, about 93 percent
of partisans reported a vote for their party's House candidate, matching their
loyalty in the presidential election, which was also 93 percent. In the 2014
CCES, 92.5 percent of partisans voted for their party's House candidate, 93.4
percent for their party's Senate candidate.

These surveys also reported the lowest incidence of ticket splitting – voting
for a Democrat for president and a Republican for House or Senate, or vice
versa – in the last six decades. In the 1970s, a quarter of the House and Senate
electorates reported voting a split ticket; by the 2000s, the average incidence of
ticket splitting was down to 16 percent in House elections and 13 percent in
Senate elections (Figure 3.3). The rates in the 2012 ANES, 11 percent in both
House and Senate elections, are the lowest for the entire ANES series. Reported
ticket splitting was even lower in the 2012 exit poll, dropping to just 7 percent
for House voters. The previous low for an exit poll was 10 percent (in both
2004 and 2008); the 1976–2008 average was 15 percent. In the CCES, 9 percent voted a split House ticket in 2012, down from 11 percent in 2008; the rate
of ticket splitting among Senate voters was 8 percent, down from 9 percent in
2008.[9] Partisan defections and split-ticket voting have always strongly favored
incumbents, so the increase in party loyalty has come largely at their expense
(Jacobson 2013e, 128–130).

Districts and States

These changes in individual voting behavior have registered powerfully at the
district and state levels. The proportion of House districts delivering split
verdicts – pluralities for the president of one party and the House candidate
of the other – has fallen steeply since the 1970s (Figure 3.4), reaching a low of
only 6 percent in 2012, less than half the previous low of 14 percent (2004).
Landslide presidential elections such as 1972 and 1984 naturally produce a
larger number of split districts, but 2012 also stands out starkly in comparison
to other elections that were comparatively close (highlighted in black in the
figure). Senate elections have followed the same pattern, although split outcomes remain considerably more common in statewide elections because states
tend to have a more even partisan balance than congressional districts
(Figure 3.5). In 2012, only six states delivered split verdicts, and after the
election, only twenty-one senators represented states lost by their presidential
candidate, both sixty-year lows.

---

[8] The Common Content of the 2012 CCES includes 55,400 respondents, 36,097 of whom
reported voting for a major party House candidate, and 27,508 of whom reported voting for
a major-party Senate candidate. CCES results reported in this paper are based on these respondents (Ansolabehere 2013).

[9] These are national figures; the average rate of ticket splitting per state was 8.1 percent in the
2012 CCES.

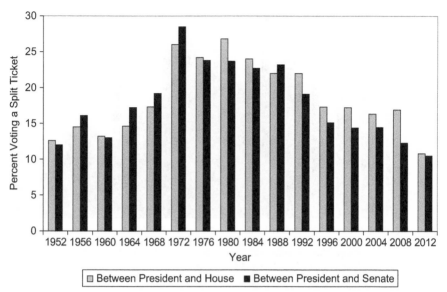

FIGURE 3.3 Ticket splitting in national elections, 1952–2012. Source: American National Election Studies.

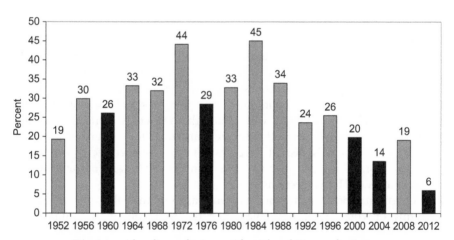

FIGURE 3.4 Districts with split results in presidential and House elections, 1952–2012. Source: Norman J. Ornstein, Thomas E. Mann, and Michael J. Malbin, *Vital Statistics on Congress 2008* (Washington, D.C.: Brookings Institution Press, 2008), Table 2–16; data for 2008 and 2012 data compiled by author.

The growing correspondence between presidential and congressional elections also shows up in the simple correlations between the percentage of votes won by the Democratic presidential and House candidates (in contested elections) at the district level (third column of Table 3.1; for midterm elections, the

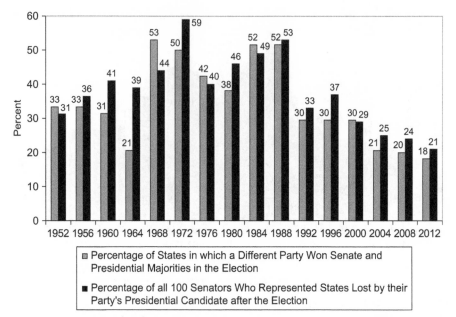

FIGURE 3.5 States with split outcomes, 1952–2012. Source: Compiled by author.

correlated presidential vote is from two years earlier[10]). The mean correlation between the district-level House and presidential vote fell from 0.81 in the 1950s to 0.60 in the 1970s.[11] By the 2000s it had returned to the levels of the 1950s and in the two most recent elections, it reached its highest points in the series for a presidential and midterm election year, 0.95 and 0.94, respectively. Not surprisingly, the accuracy with which the district-level presidential vote predicts the House winner followed the same trajectory (fourth column of Table 3.1).[12] Obama's district vote in 2012 by itself correctly predicts a remarkable 94.0 percent of the 2012 winners and 94.5 percent of the 2014 winners of House elections.

As partisan coherence in voting patterns has risen, the value of incumbency, in terms of vote share, has fallen. For the fifth column, I estimate the

---

[10] Data on the presidential vote for midterms after reapportionment have been recalculated for the new districts; these data are unavailable for more than half the districts in 2002 and 2006, so observations for these years are omitted.

[11] Decades are defined here by reapportionment cycles; the 1960s, for example, extend from 1962 to 1970.

[12] Estimated from logit equations in which dependent variable is 1 if the Democrat won the seat, 0 if a Republican won it, and the dependent variable is the share of the major-party presidential vote won by the Democratic candidate in the election (or previous elections for midterms). Uncontested districts are included in this analysis.

TABLE 3.1 *The District-Level Presidential Vote and House Results, 1952–2014*

House Election Year	Presidential Vote Year	House/ President Vote Correlation	% Winners Correctly Predicted	Value of Incumbency	
				Modified Gelman- King Index	Gelman- King Index
1952	1952	0.86	85.0	2.7	
1954	1952	0.85	84.8	1.3	2.4
1956	1956	0.83	85.1	0.2	2.5
1958	1956	0.74	80.1	4.3	3.2
1960	1960	0.76	77.1	4.9	5.0
1962					
1964	1964	0.63	68.2	3.8	3.6
1966					
1968	1968	0.68	77.2	7.6	5.0
1970	1968	0.63	75.6	8.8	7.4
1972	1972	0.54	60.7	7.7	
1974	1972	0.51	63.6	7.4	6.0
1976	1976	0.67	75.6	7.3	7.7
1978	1976	0.63	73.3	9.5	10.1
1980	1980	0.67	70.8	9.6	7.7
1982	1980	0.69	76.3	6.6	
1984	1984	0.71	76.8	9.8	9.3
1986	1984	0.63	74.7	12.2	12.3
1988	1988	0.65	74.3	8.9	11.3
1990	1988	0.62	73.8	6.1	8.2
1992	1992	0.70	69.8	7.3	
1994	1992	0.75	80.0	9.3	9.5
1996	1996	0.83	79.3	6.7	6.8
1998	1996	0.82	80.8	8.0	9.1
2000	2000	0.80	80.4	8.6	9.9
2002	2000	0.81	86.2	8.5	
2004	2004	0.84	86.4	6.8	7.1
2006	2004	0.84	83.5	6.5	7.4
2008	2008	0.85	80.7	7.1	6.7
2010	2008	0.92	91.3	4.8	6.3
2012	2012	0.95	94.0	2.4	
2014	2012	0.94	94.5	3.5	3.6

Note: data for 1962 and 1966 are too incomplete for analysis.

Source: 2012 presidential vote data are from David Nir and reported at www.dailykos.com/story/ 2012/11/19/1163009/-Daily-Kos-Elections-presidential-results-by-congressional-district-for-the- 2012-2008-elections?detail=hide (accessed April 5, 2013).

incumbency advantage with a variant of the Gelman-King index that has the advantage of applying to election years ending in 2. Gelman and King compute the incumbency advantage by regressing the Democrat's share of the vote on the Democrat's vote in the previous election, the party holding the seat, and incumbency, which takes the value of 1 if the Democrat is the incumbent, −1 if the Republican is the incumbent, and 0 if the seat is open. The coefficient on incumbency estimates the value (in vote percentage) of incumbency status for each election year (Gelman and King 1990). The Gelman-King model cannot be applied to elections following redistricting because it requires interelection comparisons between stable districts. I thus replace the lagged Democratic vote with the Democratic presidential candidate's share of the major party vote in the district in the current or, for midterms, previous election, avoiding this problem and allowing 2012 to be included in the analysis.[13] For comparison, the sixth column lists estimates of the Gelman-King measure of the incumbency advantage for the years it can be calculated. The two measures reveal the same trends, with the value of incumbency growing from the 1950s to the 1980s and subsequently falling back to its lowest levels.[14] In 2012, at 2.4 percentage points, incumbency was, according to the modified Gelman-King index, worth less than in any election since 1956. Both versions of the index indicate that incumbency's value remained at pre-1960s levels in 2014. The electoral effects of challenger quality have also shrunk significantly since the 1970s, another sign of a diminished "personal vote" (Jacobson 2013d, 137–138).

The growing dominance of state and district partisanship (as measured by the presidential vote) and the declining impact of incumbency have made it increasingly difficult for congressional candidates to win and hold constituencies against the partisan grain. Back in the 1970s, Democrats taking moderate or conservative positions on economic and social issues regularly won Republican-leaning districts. Not any more. As Figure 3.6 shows, the pivotal election was 1994, when almost half the districts that had been voting Republican at the presidential level 'while electing Democrats to the House finally stopped doing so, giving Republicans their first majority in forty years (Jacobson 1996). Backed by strongly favorable national tides, Democrats managed to augment their share of Republican-leaning seats to win majorities in 2006 and 2008, but they lost heavily in such districts in 2010, with additional losses in 2012 and 2014. Republicans have never been as successful as Democrats in winning uncongenial territory, but they, too, have found it increasingly

---

[13] I also replace their dichotomous measure of party currently holding the seat with a trichotomous measure, which takes the value of 1 if the seat was currently held by a Democrat, −1 if Republican, and 0 if it is a new seat created by redistricting and held by neither party.

[14] The two measures are correlated at .89; on average, the modified measure using the presidential vote as the independent variable delivers an estimate of the incumbency advantage 0.2 percentage points lower than the original Gelman-King index; the standard deviation of the difference is 1.3 points.

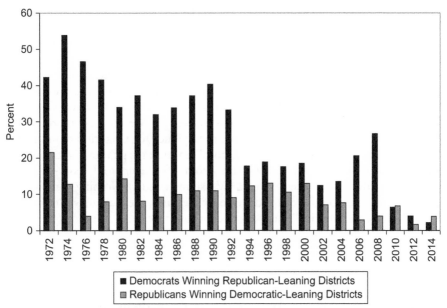

FIGURE 3.6 Winning against the partisan grain, 1972–2014. Note: "Leaning districts" are defined as those in which the district-level presidential vote was at least 2 percentage points higher than the national major party vote share for that party for that year's election, or, for midterms, the previous presidential election. Source: compiled by author.

difficult to win against the partisan grain. In 2012, both parties had remarkably little success on one another's turf; only twelve of the 406 districts with clear partisan leanings (those where Obama's district vote share was at least 2 points above or below his national vote share) went to the "wrong" party. That number did not change in 2014, when Democrats lost four of their nine Republican-leaning seats while Republicans were adding an equal number of new Democratic-leaning seats.

Obviously, the prospects for building a local power base on something other than a shared party label and the positions it implies are now greatly diminished. The fate of the moderate Democrats in 2010 illustrates the problem. The forty-six incumbent Democrats seeking reelection who represented Republican-leaning districts compiled moderate voting records (average DW-NOMINATE scores of –0.15, compared with –0.40 for other Democrats). On the most important legislation of the 111th Congress, the Patient Protection and Affordable Care Act (i.e., Obamacare), twenty-five voted with their party and president, and twenty-one voted against the bill. Twenty (80 percent) of the bill's supporters lost reelection bids, but so did thirteen (62 percent) of those who voted against it, an insignificant difference ($p = 0.175$).

More generally, moderation was no shield for Democrats in 2010. There was in fact a strong *negative* relationship between greater ideological moderation and electoral performance, although only because most of the moderate Democrats represented Republican-leaning districts (accounting for their moderation) that they could not hold against a strong Republican national tide (Jacobson 2011c). With district partisanship (measured by the 2008 presidential vote) controlled, DW-NOMINATE scores were unrelated to election results both for all Democrats and for the subset of Democrats representing Republican-leaning districts. The demise of the Blue Dog Coalition of moderate Democrats exemplifies present-day electoral realities: resignations, retirements, and defeats reduced their membership from fifty-seven to twenty-seven in 2010 and further to fourteen in 2012 (Wasserman 2012). Nothing comparable occurred on the Republican side if only because the category "moderate Republican representative" has been vacant for more than a decade (Jacobson 2013c).[15]

The Republican Advantage

The data in Figure 3.6 make it clear that the partisan effects of growing electoral coherence have been asymmetrical, hurting Democrats more than Republicans. This is because Republicans are finally reaping the full benefit of their long-standing structural advantage in House elections. The advantage lies in the fact that regular Republican voters are distributed more efficiently across House districts than are regular Democratic voters. Although Republican gerrymanders reinforced this advantage through redistricting after the 2000 and 2010 censuses (Jacobson 2013e, 15–16; 2013a, 148–149), it is nothing new, for it reflects coalition demographics. Democrats win a disproportionate share of minority, single, young, secular, and gay voters who are concentrated in urban districts that deliver lopsided Democratic majorities. Republican voters are spread more evenly across suburbs, smaller cities, and rural areas, so that fewer Republican votes are "wasted" in highly skewed districts. This was as true in the 1970s as it is today (Figure 3.7). Over the past four decades, a substantially larger proportion of House seats have leaned Republican than have leaned Democratic ("leaning" defined as having the district vote for their party's presidential candidate at least 2 percentage points above the national vote for that year or, for midterms, for the previous presidential election). Meanwhile, the proportion of closely balanced districts (delivering presidential results within 2 percentage points of the national vote) has declined and after 2012 was down to only 6.7 percent; very few representatives now serve districts without a clear partisan tilt.

---

[15] Walter B. Jones of North Carolina is the only House Republican serving in the past decade with a DW-NOMINATE score of less than 0.2.

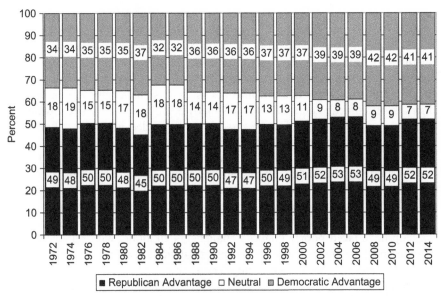

FIGURE 3.7 District partisan advantage, 1972–2014. Source: Compiled by author.

With the rise of party-line voting and decline in ticket splitting, the Republicans' structural advantage has become a formidable obstacle to the Democrats' pursuit of a House majority. Thus, for example, despite Barack Obama's decisive victory in 2012, Democrats picked up only six House seats, seventeen short of a majority. Obama won nearly five million more votes than Mitt Romney, but Romney nonetheless outpolled Obama in 226 districts, while Obama ran ahead in only 209. Democrats also won a majority of the major-party national vote cast for House candidates, their share rising from 46.6 percent in 2010 to 50.7 percent in 2012; but with party loyalty so high and split outcomes so rare, their seat share grew only from 44.4 percent to 46.2 percent. In sharp contrast to the 1970s, it is the Republicans who are now the "normal" majority party in the House.

Campaign Finances

The evolution of the congressional campaign finance system since the 1970s has also contributed importantly to the decline in members' ability to separate their fates from those of their parties and to win against the partisan grain. As noted earlier, the sums of money available to incumbents seeking reelection have risen steeply, far outstripping inflation. But so, too, has the money available to their challengers, especially in states and districts that are competitive or lean toward the challenger's party. Parties have become much better at distributing their resources efficiently and now adequately fund nearly every challenger with any plausible chance of winning (Jacobson 2010). Moreover, the Hill committees,[16] wealthy individuals, and nonparty interest groups, liberated by the Supreme Court to spend unlimited sums on independent campaigns, have become major sources of assistance to promising challengers. Independent campaigns help incumbents as well as challengers in competitive districts, and officeholders still typically enjoy a substantial resource advantage over their opponents even in the most lavishly funded campaigns. But campaign spending is more productive for challengers than for incumbents, and very few incumbents in potentially competitive states or districts can still hope to win simply by avoiding well-funded opponents (Jacobson 2013e, 51–59).

The growth in average campaign expenditures by challengers to House incumbents, broken down by district partisan leanings, is displayed in Figure 3.8.[17] Incumbents representing districts with a favorable partisan makeup have faced poorly financed challengers all along, with relatively little change since the 1970s. Those competing in balanced districts, in contrast, have faced increasingly well-funded opponents, but the greatest increase has occurred in districts where challengers enjoy a favorable partisan environment. The change over the past decade is particularly striking. This trend has not generally put incumbents at a financial disadvantage – in the last five elections for which complete data are now available (2004–2012), they have outspent the challenger in 89 percent of these districts by an average of more than $840,000 – but it has made it more difficult for them to prevail. Thirty percent of them lost during this period, compared to 17 percent in balanced districts and 2 percent in districts favoring the incumbent's party.

Independent spending has also strengthened competitive challengers. Party committees turned to independent spending in a big way after the Bipartisan Campaign Reform Act of 2002 turned off the soft-money spigot (Figure 3.9). Independent spending by nonparty groups has taken off even more spectacularly in recent elections (Figure 3.10). Outside spenders have targeted incumbents in House districts where the party balance favors the challenger (spending an average of $1.9 million for challengers in such districts in 2012) or has a close partisan balance (an average of $1.5 million for challengers in these districts). That is, outside spending increased the total expended on behalf of challengers in these competitive districts by about 50 percent above the averages shown in Figure 3.8. In 2012, candidates, parties, and independent groups

---

[16] They are the Democratic Congressional Campaign Committee (DCCC), the Republican National Congressional Committee (NRCC), the Democratic Senatorial Campaign Committee (DSCC), and the National Republican Senatorial Committee (NRSC).

[17] Again, districts where the Democratic presidential vote was at least two points above the national average are classified as leaning Democratic, those where the vote was at least two points below the national average are classified as leaning Republican, and those in between are classified as balanced.

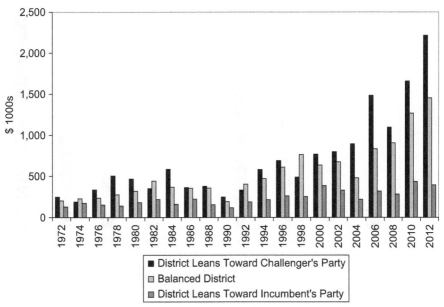

FIGURE 3.8 Challengers' campaign spending in House elections, 1972–2012 (adjusted for inflation, 2012 = 1.00). Source: Compiled by author from Federal Election Commission data.

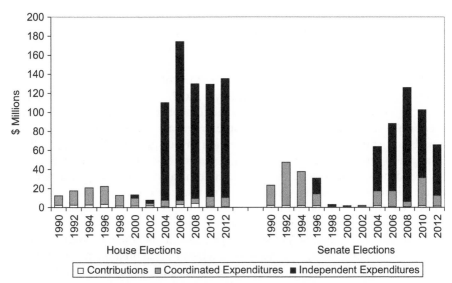

FIGURE 3.9 Party spending in congressional elections, 1990–2012 (adjusted for inflation, 2012 = 1.00). Source: Federal Election Commission data.

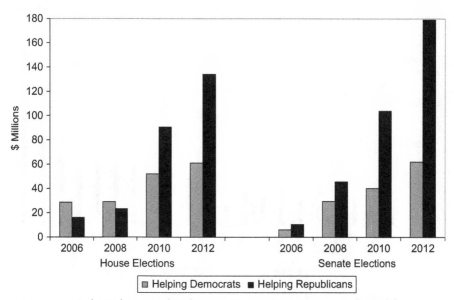

FIGURE 3.10 Independent spending by nonparty groups, 2006–12 (adjusted for inflation, 2012 = 1.00). Source: Campaign Finance Institute, "Reportable Spending by Party and Non-Party Groups in Congressional Elections, 2006–2010," at www.cfinst.org/pdf/federal/ PostElec2010_Table1_pdf. 2012: Center for Responsive Politics at www.opensecrets.org/ outsidepending/summ.php?cycle=2012&disp=C&type=S.

combined spent an average of more than $4 million opposing the eighteen incumbents defending districts whose partisan composition favored the challenger's party; eleven of them lost.

Outside spending was an even larger part of the resource mix in the 2012 Senate elections. Virginia led the way, with an astonishing $51 million spent by outsiders along with the $30 million spent by the candidates. However, on a per-voter basis, the most extravagant races were in the low-population states of Montana ($24 million in outside spending, $43 million total) and North Dakota ($16 million in outside spending, $26 million total). Independent spending was, as always, concentrated in the most competitive races. Eighty-two percent went to the eleven contests won with less than 55 percent of the vote; nearly half of the money spent on these races came from sources beyond the candidates' control.

Figure 3.11 displays the growth in independent spending from all sources, party and nonparty alike, from 1978 through 2012 (the preliminary totals from 2014 are higher yet). The consequences of the past decade's steep increase have yet to undergo sustained investigation by political scientists. Its clear tendency, however, is to nationalize campaigns (with the president or presidential candidates as focal objects), heighten partisanship, and undermine election strategies

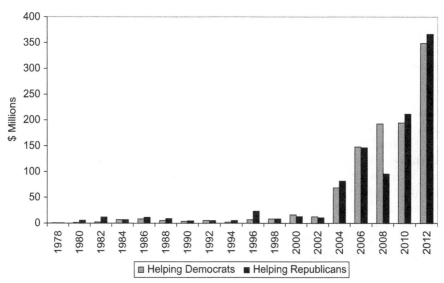

FIGURE 3.11 Independent spending in House and Senate races, 1978–2012 (all sources; adjusted for inflation, 2012 = 1.00). Source: 1978–2010: Campaign Finance Institute, "Political Party Contributors, Coordinated, and Independent Expenditures for Congressional Candidates, 1976–2010," at www.cfinst.org/pdf/vital/VitalStats_t12.pdf; "Non-Party Independent Expenditures in House and Senate Elections, 1978–2010," at www.cfinst.org/pdf/vital/VitalStats_t14.pdf. 2012: Center for Responsive Politics at www.opensecrets.org/outsidespending/summ.php?disp=C.

based on independence and soliciting a personal vote. Outside campaigns on behalf of the opposition make sure that any national issue, party leader, or roll-call vote potentially damaging to a vulnerable member is brought to the attention of voters. Even supportive independent campaigns may make it harder for members to shape and disseminate the campaign messages they think will best help them retain office (Jacobson 2013e, 85).

The possibility of a major assault by outside spenders also widens the set of actors whose reactions members need to ponder in figuring out how their actions in Congress might affect their reelection prospects. Mayhew noted that the "relevant political actors" incumbents had to consider while plotting reelection comprised "anyone who has a resource that might be used in the election," specifically including people outside the state or district who controlled campaign money (1974a, 39). But the relevance of this particular set of actors is obviously far greater than it was when he wrote. The era when members could reliably take comfort in the adage that "all politics is local" and, by assiduous personal attention to their constituencies, insulate themselves from national partisan issues and forces, is largely history.

It is not completely gone, however. A handful of members still manage to win against the partisan grain by emphasizing local ties and cultivating moderate records to distinguish themselves from their party and its national leaders. Doing so is evidently easier for senators (and senate candidates) than for representatives. Maine's two Republican senators, Olympia Snowe (now retired) and Susan Collins, for example, accumulated DW-NOMINATE scores two standard deviations more moderate than the Senate Republican average, enjoyed approval ratings above 70 percent among both Democrats and Republicans in their states, and were never seriously challenged.[18] Moderate Democrats have also managed to build cross-party coalitions in some red states in recent years, and even in 2012 it was possible to win a Senate seat despite representing the weaker party locally. Six Senate candidates, five Democrats and one Republican, won states lost by their party's presidential nominee. In three of these cases, the winner faced seriously flawed opponents, and had this not been the case, the 2012 entry in Figure 3.5 for split president–Senate outcomes would have been only 9 percent.[19] But the other three were moderate Democrats who defeated mainstream Republicans in states that went decisively to Mitt Romney.

Their victories suggest what it takes to win despite an adverse partisan environment. Incumbent Jon Tester (Montana) and open seat winner Heidi Heitkamp (North Dakota) were effective campaigners competing in states ideally suited to personal politicking: lightly populated and accustomed to face-to-face, friends-and-neighbors politics. Tester and Heitkamp had held prominent state-wide political offices (Heitkamp as North Dakota's attorney general, Tester as the president of the Montana Senate and then U.S. Senator) and were already thoroughly familiar to their electorates. They could credibly stake out positions separating themselves from Obama and the national Democratic Party because they were well-known quantities. Tester and Heitkamp won despite the huge investment of outside money aimed at tying them fatally to Obama, helped along by equally lavish spending by outside groups on their behalf. Joe Manchin, the other incumbent Democrat who won a state that went to Romney, was a popular former governor of West Virginia who had been careful to distance himself from the Obama administration, taking conservative positions on several salient issues and

---

[18] Based on averages of nine monthly polls taken between May 2005 and January 2006; see Jacobson (2006, 742–747).

[19] Democrat Joe Donnelly defeated Richard Mourdock, who had defeated veteran incumbent Richard Lugar in the primary, in Indiana; Democrat Claire McCaskill, considered the most vulnerable incumbent, defeated Todd Akin in Missouri; both Mourdock and Akin were extreme conservatives who offered bizarre reasons for forbidding women impregnated through rape to have abortions; appointed incumbent Republican Dean Heller defeated Shelley Berkeley, who was hurt by ethics charges sufficiently credible to be taken up by the House Ethics Committee and lost by 1.2 percentage points; see Jacobson (2103b, 13 and 31–32).

accumulating a DW-NOMINATE score of –0.128 through the 112th Congress.[20] He won easy reelection, running 25 points ahead of Obama.

As these instances suggest, Senate candidates are more successful in winning against the partisan grain in the less populous states. After 2012, more than a third (5 of 14) of the Senate seats in states with a single House seat were held by the "wrong" party.[21] For states with two to four House seats, the proportion was 25 percent (7 of 28); for the remaining states, it was 16 percent (9 of 58). Among House candidates, however, comparably low-population constituencies no longer routinely enable carefully adapted position taking and "home styles" to trump party affiliation (Fenno 1978). Incumbents are still more likely than nonincumbents to win districts favoring the other party – twenty-two of the twenty-six candidates who won districts lost by their party's presidential candidate in 2012 were current members – but the ranks of such candidates, incumbent or otherwise, have grown exceedingly thin (Figure 3.6).

CONSEQUENCES

Members of Congress are now much more likely to represent states and districts where their party is dominant than they were in the 1970s, and the electoral bases of the congressional parties have therefore become much more sharply divided along partisan and ideological lines. This has strengthened the electoral incentives for party loyalty, for "voting the constituency" increasingly means voting with one's party. Figures 3.12 and 3.13 document the widening gap between the congressional parties' respective electoral bases. The entries are differences in the mean share of the major party vote won by the Democratic presidential candidate between districts and states represented by congressional Democrats and Republicans (entries for midterms are based on the previous presidential election). Back in 1972, for example, House Democrats represented districts that were on average only about 7.6 percentage points more Democratic in their presidential vote than districts represented by Republicans. By 2014, the difference had grown to 26.5 points, with Obama winning an average of 67.4 percent of the vote in districts won by Democrats and only 40.9 percent in districts won by Republicans. States tend to be more diverse politically and less lopsided in their partisanship than House districts, but the comparable gap in the Senate has also widened from 1.3 to 16.7 points over the same period.

One important consequence of these trends is that the ideological leanings of the parties' respective electoral constituencies – defined as those voters who reported voting for the winning Republican and Democratic House and Senate candidates – have grown increasingly divergent (Figure 3.14). In the 1970s,

---

[20] For example, he was the only Senate Democrat to vote against repealing "don't ask, don't tell," and thus against allowing gay people to serve openly in the military.

[21] Defined as having gone to the other party's presidential candidate in 2012; all of them are Democrats (five of the seven single-district states are red states).

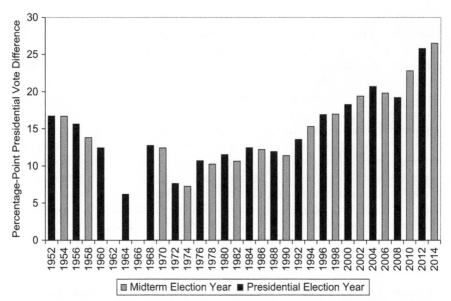

Midterm Election Year ■ Presidential Election Year

FIGURE 3.12 The polarization of U.S. House districts, 1952–2014. Note: Entries are the percentage-point differences in the average presidential vote between districts won by Democrats and districts won by Republicans; data for 1962 and 1966 are unavailable because of redistricting; entries for midterm elections are calculated from the previous presidential election. Source: Compiled by author.

average ideological differences between the parties' electoral constituencies were modest, about 0.5 points on the ANES's 7-point liberal–conservative scale.[22] By 2012, the ideological gap had more than tripled in both chambers.[23] Like the partisan divergence in House and Senate DW-NOMINATE scores over the same period, divergence in electoral constituency ideologies was more a product of Republicans moving right than of Democrats moving left.[24]

Another notable consequence is a decline in shared constituencies between presidents and members of Congress from the opposing party. In the 1970s and 1980s, senators and representatives from the rival party shared on average 37 percent of their voters with the president; the comparable figure for the

[22] See Footnote 5 for detailed coding..
[23] Realignment in the South explains only part of this change, since the gap between Republican and Democratic constituencies outside the South also grew (from 0.7 to 1.6 points in the House, from 0.6 to 1.4 in the Senate).
[24] The rightward movement of Republicans accounts for about 80 percent of the increase in mean partisan differences in DW-NOMINATE scores between the House and Senate parties since the 93rd Congress (1973–74); Republican voters account for about 60 percent of the increased partisan constituency differences on the liberal-conservative scale since then.

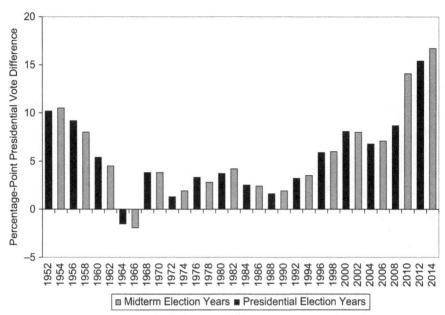

FIGURE 3.13 The polarization of state constituencies, 1952–2014. Note: Entries are the percentage-point differences in the average presidential vote between states won by Democrats and states won by Republicans in the Senate elections; entries for midterm election years are calculated from the presidential election two years earlier. Source: Compiled by author.

1990s and 2000s was 20 percent (Jacobson 2013e, 271–272). In 2012, according to the ANES, only 15 percent of House Republicans' electoral constituents and 10 percent of Senate Republicans' electoral constituents also reported voting for Obama, both lows for the entire 1952–2012 period. Meanwhile, the overlap between the electoral constituencies of the president and his own party's members has grown, reaching 90 percent in the House (an all-time high) and 88 percent in the Senate (matching the record set in 2008) for the 2012 election. Party differences in electoral bases are strongly related to party differences in presidential support and roll-call voting patterns (Jacobson 2003), so the observed increase in congressional party unity[25] and growing partisan differences in presidential support scores[26] have a solid electoral grounding.

[25] According to data from *CQ Weekly* archived at http://pooleandrosenthal.com/party_unity.htm, accessed April 17, 2013.
[26] According to data compiled by George C. Edwards III and posted at http://presdata.tamu.edu, accessed March 12, 2013.

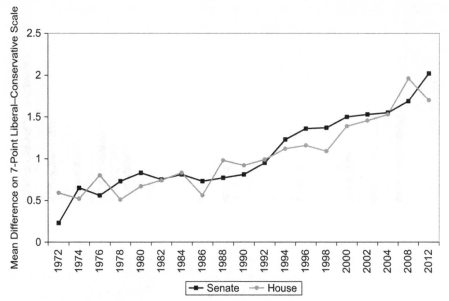

FIGURE 3.14 Ideological divergence of electoral constituencies of House and Senate parties, 1972–2012. Source: American National Election Studies.

The Electoral Connection Today

Member of Congress face a vastly different electoral landscape now than they did at the time Mayhew published his classic analysis. They retain the motive and means to pursue reelection, but the tightening of party lines and greater nationalization of electoral politics leaves them less opportunity to shape their own electoral fates. A handful may still be able to build a power base separate from their party, but for a large majority, the power base now *is* the party, and the most serious threat to reelection comes from within it. In particular, Republicans who stray from conservative orthodoxy risk well-funded challenges from the far right; the three Republican senators denied renomination in 2010 and 2012 show that the danger is real. Rhetorical declarations of independence and fealty to local interests are still common, but party loyalty serves most members' reelection needs – in relation to both voters and donors – quite well. When it does not, casting a locally unpopular vote for the party's sake is riskier than ever given the array of opposition forces primed to exploit it. Hence, for example, the votes cast by Democratic senators representing Alaska, Montana, North Dakota, and Arkansas against ending the filibuster that killed Obama's gun control legislation in April 2013.[27]

---

[27] Mike Begich (AK), Max Baucus (MT), and David Prior (AR) face reelection in 2014; Heidi Heitkamp (ND) had just been elected in 2012; Baucus announced his retirement a week later.

Although members may still regard national trends "as acts of God over which they can exercise no control" (Mayhew 1974a, 32), their diminished ability to defy national trends via their own efforts encourages them to at least try to shape them. The Republicans' lock-step strategy of "no" after Obama's election in 2008, rewarded by their historic victory in 2010, suggests that such collective efforts can pay off. Their subsequent project to make Obama a one-term president was, to be sure, less fruitful. Mayhew, in a footnote, raised and dismissed the possibility that "the party not in control of the presidency [might] try to sabotage the economy" to improve their electoral prospects (1974a, 31). But Republicans' resistance to Obama's proposals to stimulate the economy and advocacy of deep cuts in federal spending likely to dampen aggregate demand inspired some Democratic leaders to charge that this was exactly what they were doing (Cohen 2012).

More generally, opposition parties have more reason now than in the 1970s to deny presidents popular victories that might boost their approval ratings. The same logic gives the president's partisans a greater interest than before in his popular success. And all members now have a greater incentive to consider the effects of their behavior on their party's image, performance, and standing with the public. Indeed, it is probably no longer true that "the enactment of party programs is electorally not very important to members" insofar as success or failure affects the party's reputation and thus the value of its brand name, especially when the party's program is the president's program (Mayhew 1974a, 99). Of course, this is true only when the president's program is popular; Obama's landmark victories in the 111th Congress – on health care reform, the economic stimulus bill, and financial regulation – were legislative triumphs but political failures, at least in the short run (Jacobson 2011b). In this instance, it was a party's nearly unanimous opposition to the rival party's program that proved to be collectively beneficial. In any case, the huge impact of reactions to the Obama agenda in 2010, which was the most nationalized, president-centered midterm of the entire postwar period – until 2014, that is (Jacobson, 2015b) – underscores the large electoral stake members now have in popular evaluations of their respective national parties and leaders and therefore in doing whatever they can to promote their own side and discredit the other. With majority status now so valuable, this applies even to members safely lodged in deep red or blue states and districts.

Members' stakes in their national party's standing are not uniform across parties and chambers, however. House Republicans' structural advantage gives them a clear electoral motive for maintaining sharp differences between the parties even when moderation and compromise might better serve their party's presidential ambitions. Insofar as polarization in Congress inspires high levels of party loyalty among voters, it serves House Republicans' electoral interests quite nicely. It was Newt Gingrich's deliberate strategy of provocation and polarization that led to the Republicans' historic victory in 1994, and at present a party-line election guarantees Republican control of the House. Keeping the district party base satisfied and energized pays immediate electoral dividends even if the image conveyed hurts the party's long-term national prospects. It also suits the ideological inclinations of most of today's Republican members. Former Speaker John Boehner often struggled to unify his coalition, but only against departures toward the right, which are devoid of electoral risk.[28] Dallying with the Democrats *would* be risky, so Republican members have little incentive, electoral or ideological, to engage in bipartisan cooperation even when it would be generally popular. Democrats, in contrast, belong to a center-left coalition that can achieve majority status only by successfully reaching beyond the party's liberal base in a substantial number of districts. Thus, they have a collective interest in putting a moderate gloss on their party's image even if that means disappointing core Democratic supporters on the left.

Strategies of moderation that include cross-party cooperation continue to be pursued by some senators in both parties, mainly but not exclusively those who represent states where their party is in the minority.[29] The number of such senators has declined rather steadily (Figure 3.5), however, as the electoral process has culled their ranks in recent years.[30] Meanwhile, a growing number of senators are either veterans of party wars in the House (Theriault and Rohde 2011) or Tea Party enthusiasts who revel in ideological battle and find in the Senate's rules endless opportunities to harass their partisan rivals in the Senate and the White House. Bipartisan attempts by the more pragmatic senators to craft consensus legislation on major issues have thus rarely borne fruit.

Partisan Polarization

All of the trends considered here point to solid electoral underpinnings for the growing ideological divisions between the parties, the increase in party-line voting, and the widening partisan gap in presidential support observed in Congresses since the 1970s. Statistically, the linkages between the electoral and congressional polarizing trends are remarkably strong (Table 3.2). For example, the correlation across congresses elected since 1972 between the presidential vote gaps shown in Figures 3.12 and 3.13 and party differences in mean DW-NOMINATE scores is 0.97 for the House and 0.91 for the Senate; similarly, the ideological divergences of electoral constituencies shown in

---

[28] DW-NOMINATE scores were completely unrelated to vote share or probability of winning for Republican incumbents in 2012, with or without controlling for Obama's district-level vote.

[29] For example, the mean DW-NOMINATE score for Democratic senators from states won by Romney in 2012 was −0.23, compared with −0.40 for other Democrats; the mean for Republicans from Obama states was 0.41, compared with 0.52 for other Republicans.

[30] Of the fourteen Senate incumbents who lost general elections from 2004 through 2012, twelve were more moderate than their party's mean (according to their DW-NOMINATE scores), most of them substantially so; all four who lost primaries were also more moderate than average; two of the primary losers – Joe Lieberman and Lisa Murkowski – went on to win reelection, however, Lieberman as an independent, Murkowski as a write-in.

TABLE 3.2 *Correlations Between Electoral and Roll-Call Vote Gaps, 93rd–113th Congresses*

	Party Differences in Mean			
	DW-Nominate Scores		Presidential Support Scores	
	House	Senate	House	Senate
District/State Presidential Vote Gap (from Figures 3.12 and 3.13, N = 21)	0.97	0.91	0.92	0.77
Electoral Constituents Ideological Gap (from Figure 3.14, N = 19)	0.94	0.94	0.90	0.92

Figure 3.14 correlate at 0.94 with party differences in DW-NOMINATE scores in both chambers. Of course, any trends correlated with time will be correlated with each other, and correlations are silent about causation. Still, both logic and evidence point to an interactive process: voters have gradually sorted themselves into increasingly distinct political camps in response to the more sharply differentiated alternatives presented by the congressional parties and candidates, while the widening ideological gap between the congressional parties reflects their increasingly divergent electoral bases. The congressional parties were the first movers in this co-evolutionary process – as, for example, when the civil rights legislation of the 1960s initiated the southern realignment – but their drift toward the extremes was conditional on avoiding punishment for it at the polls (Jacobson 2000, 25–28; Levendusky 2009, 21–31). The electoral victims of polarization have mainly been moderates, whose departure automatically leaves the remaining party coalitions further from the center. In sum, party polarization in Congress, arguably the single most consequential development in national politics since the 1970s, is fully compatible with the persistence of a robust electoral connection.

CONCLUSION

The electoral connection remains as potent a force in shaping congressional life as it did when Mayhew published his seminal book four decades ago. Understanding the environment in which members win and hold office remains fundamental to explaining congressional behavior and institutional practices. That environment has grown ever more partisan, ideological, and national in focus since the 1970s, reducing the prospects for building personal coalitions independent of party and eroding the electoral value of incumbency.[31]

---

[31] Incumbents continue to win reelection at high rates, of course, but mainly because so many of them now represent districts with a favorable party balance (Jacobson 2015a).

Meanwhile, the individual and collective benefits of majority status have grown more valuable and thus worth fighting for. Changes in congressional organization, practices, procedures, and voting patterns reflect these realities, as other contributors to this volume attest. The 2012 elections extended all of the important trends, with party-line voting, straight-ticket voting, and the aggregate connection between presidential and congressional votes and victories reaching their highest levels in at least six decades. The sums invested in efforts to win House and Senate seats and thereby control of the chambers also broke all records. No surprise, then, that the 113th Congress was highly polarized and regularly paralyzed by partisan warfare over matters large and small. All of the crucial trends continued through 2014, producing the most partisan, nationalized, and president-centered midterm on record, offering no respite from partisan conflict in the 114th Congress (Jacobson 2015b).

Still, one clear lesson from the years since the publication of Mayhew's masterpiece is that Congress and its coordinate electoral environment are not immutable. Mayhew's analysis, as it turns out, captured an extreme point on the continuum between local, candidate-centered electoral politics and national, party-centered electoral politics. Electoral and congressional politics during the Obama administration may well represent the other extreme, the crest of another long wave catching our full attention just as it is poised to recede. The polarized ideological conflict and legislative gridlock of today are neither inevitable nor inalterable. However, respect for the power of the electoral connection leads me to believe that they won't diminish much until partisan warriors in Congress begin to pay a price at the polls.

REFERENCES

Abramowitz, Alan I. 2010. *The Disappearing Center: Engaged Citizens, Polarization, and American Democracy*. New Haven, CT: Yale University Press.
Ansolabehere, Stephen. 2013. *Cooperative Congressional Election Study, 2012: Common Content* [Computer File]. Release 1: March 13, 2013. Cambridge, MA: Harvard University [producer].
Bafumi, Joseph, and Robert Y. Shapiro. 2009. "A New Partisan Voter." *Journal of Politics* 71:1–24.
Cain, Bruce, John Ferejohn, and Morris P. Fiorina. 1987. *The Personal Vote: Constituency Service and Electoral Independence*. Boston: Harvard University Press.
Cohen, Michael. 2012. "Did Republicans Deliberately Crash the U.S. Economy?" *Guardian*, June 12, at www.theguardian.com/commentisfree/2012/jun/09/did-republicans-deliberately-crash-us-economy.
Currinder, Marian. 2003. "Leadership PAC Contribution Strategies and House Member Ambitions." *Legislative Studies Quarterly* 28:551–577.
　　2008. *Money in the House: Campaign Funds and Congressional Party Politics*. Boulder, CO: Westview Press.
Erikson, Robert S. 1971. "The Advantage of Incumbency in Congressional Elections." *Polity* 3:395–405.

Fenno, Richard F., Jr. 1978. *Home Style: House Members in Their Districts*. Boston: Little Brown.

Gelman, Andrew, and Gary King. 1990. "Measuring Incumbency without Bias." *American Journal of Political Science* 34:1142–1164.

Greeley, Brendan. 2013. "Earmarks: The Reluctant Case for Ending the Ban." *Business Week*, January 10, at www.businessweek.com/articles/2013-01-10/earmarks-the-reluctant-case-for-ending-the-ban.

Jacobson, Gary C. 1996. "The 1994 House Elections in Perspective." *Political Science Quarterly* 111:203–223.

2000. "Party Polarization in National Politics: The Electoral Connection." In *Polarized Politics: Congress and the President in a Partisan Era*, ed. Jon R. Bond and Richard Fleisher. Washington, DC: Congressional Quarterly Press, 9–30.

2003. "Partisan Polarization in Presidential Support: The Electoral Connection." *Congress and the Presidency* 30:1–36.

2006. "The Polls: Polarized Opinion in the States: Partisan Differences in the Approval Ratings of Governors, Senators, and George W. Bush." *Presidential Studies Quarterly* 36:732–757.

2010. "A Collective Dilemma Solved: The Distribution of Party Campaign Resources in the 2006 and 2008 Congressional Elections." *Election Law Journal* 9:381–397.

2011a. *A Divider, Not a Uniter: George W. Bush and the American People*, 2nd ed. New York: Longman.

2011b. "Legislative Success and Political Failure: The Public's Reaction to Barack Obama's Early Presidency." *Presidential Studies Quarterly* 41:219–242.

2011c. "The Republican Resurgence in 2010." *Political Science Quarterly* 126:27–52.

2013a. "Congress: Partisanship and Polarization." In *The Elections of 2012*, ed. Michael Nelson. Washington, DC: CQ Press.

2013b. "The Economy and Partisanship in the 2012 Presidential and Congressional Elections." *Political Science Quarterly* 128:1–38.

2013c. "No Compromise: The Electoral Origins of Legislative Gridlock." In *Principles and Practice in American Politics*, 5th ed., ed. Samuel Kernell and Steven Smith. Washington, DC: CQ Press.

2013d. "Partisanship, Money, and Competition: Elections and the Transformation of Congress since the 1970s." In *Congress Reconsidered*, 10th ed., ed. Lawrence C. Dodd and Bruce I. Oppenheimer. Washington, DC: CQ Press.

2013e. *The Politics of Congressional Elections*, 8th ed. New York: Pearson.

2015a. "It's Nothing Personal: The Decline of the Incumbency Advantage in U.S. House Elections," *Journal of Politics* 77:861–873.

2015b. "Obama and Nationalized Electoral Politics in the 2014 Midterm," *Political Science Quarterly* 130:1–26.

Kostroski, Warren Lee. 1973. "Party and Incumbency in Postwar Senate Elections: Trends, Patterns, and Models." *American Political Science Review* 67:1213–1234.

Koszczuk, Jackie. 1995. "Freshmen: New Powerful Voice." *Congressional Quarterly Weekly Report* 53 (October 28):3251.

Levendusky, Matthew. 2009. *The Partisan Sort: How Liberals Became Democrats and Conservatives Became Republicans*. Chicago, IL: University of Chicago Press.

Malecha, Gary Lee, and Daniel J. Reagan. 2012. *The Public Congress: Congressional Deliberation in a New Media Age*. New York: Routledge.

Mayhew, David R. 1974a. *Congress: The Electoral Connection.* New Haven, CT: Yale
   University Press.
   1974b. "Congressional Elections: The Case of the Vanishing Marginals." *Polity*
   6:295–317.
Parker, Ashley. 2013. "Republicans, Led by Rand Paul, Finally End Filibuster." *New
   York Times*, March 6, at http://thecaucus.blogs.nytimes.com/2013/03/06/rand-paul-
   does-not-go-quietly-into-the-night/.
Steinhauer, Jennifer. 2013. "Divided House Passes Tax Deal to End Latest Fiscal Stand-
   off." *New York Times*, January 1, at www.nytimes.com/2013/01/02/us/politics/
   house-takes-on-fiscal-cliff.html?pagewanted=all.
Theriault, Sean M., and David Rohde. 2011. "The Gingrich Senators and Party Polar-
   ization in the U.S. Senate." *Journal of Politics* 73:1011–1024.
Ungar, Rick. 2012. "Why Congress Cannot Operate Without the Bribing Power of
   Earmarks." *Forbes*, December 12, at www.forbes.com/sites/rickungar/2012/12/29/
   why-congress-cannot-operate-without-the-bribing-power-of-earmarks/.
Wasserman, David. 2012. "House Overview: How House Democrats Beat the Point
   Spread." *Cook Political Report*, November 8, at http://cookpolitical.com/house.
Young, Kerry. 2010. "An Earmark by Any Other Name." *CQ Weekly*, November 22,
   2698–2700.

4

The Congressional Incumbency Advantage over Sixty Years

Measurement, Trends, and Implications

Robert S. Erikson

In spring 1974, David Mayhew published his famous article in *Polity*, with the intriguing title of "Congress: The Case of the Vanishing Marginals" (Mayhew, 1974b). The reference, of course, was to the disappearing marginal or competitive congressional districts in the 1960s. The clue was the distinctive patterns in incumbent races and open seats. Open seats remained as close as they had before. But where incumbents were seeking reelection, the vote shifted considerably in the incumbents' favor, leaving few close contests. It turns out that there arose a mysterious growth in the size of the incumbency advantage.

Mayhew's findings raised the question of why this was so. His prize-winning book, *Congress: The Electoral Connection* (Mayhew, 1974a), offered an explanation: Congress had become increasingly organized as an institution designed to maximize the reelection chances of its members. By exploiting their franking privilege, appearing on local television, and other actions, members of Congress were increasing their exposure and tailoring it to their needs, such as by credit claiming for federal projects that touched their districts.

Conveniently, the time of this increased exposure coincided with a decline in party loyalty – what some have called a partisan dealignment. As voters became more reluctant to cast a party vote, beginning in the 1960s, they increasingly took into account the qualities of the actual candidates, which allowed incumbency to become an important voter cue (Cox and Katz, 1996).

If the marginal could vanish suddenly in the 1960s, one could imagine that the conditions could later become ripe for its return. For the remainder of the twentieth century and into the next, close House elections involving incumbents continued to be rare. Now, in the twenty-first century, signs indicate a turning

This paper benefits from my collaborations on congressional elections over the years with Gerald Wright, Thomas Palfrey, and Rocio Titiunik. I thank Eleanor Powell, Rocio Titiunik, and the editors of this volume for their helpful comments.

of the tide once again. By 2010, marginal incumbent races were returning to their mid-twentieth century frequency and some measures of the incumbency advantage began to shrink. As with the earlier spurt in the incumbency advantage, a shift in the nature of partisanship is a likely culprit, this time in the form of party polarization in Congress. As voters increasingly see partisanship as the defining cue for congressional behavior, House members are increasingly challenged when trying to enhance their constituency's support beyond its normal vote for their party.

The dynamics of the changing incumbency advantage and the concurrent vanishing and reappearing marginal are discussed in the pages that follow. The basic description of the changing marginals is presented graphically in three appendices. Appendix A to this chapter shows changes in the distribution of the vote over the years for incumbent-contested seats in the North. From the 1950s into the early 1960s, the distribution was unimodal, with a pro-Republican skew. Then, in the mid-1960s, the distribution became bimodal, with a hole where the marginal districts would be, just as Mayhew described. By 2012, the distribution had become decidedly unimodal and skewed Republican, much in the manner of the 1950s – portending a fresh diminution of the incumbency advantage and a new set of partisan consequences.

The distribution for *open* seats has remained unimodal, as shown in the decade-by-decade graphs (for northern districts) in Appendix B to this chapter. The marginals' vanishing act is restricted to incumbent-contested seats. Further, the distribution of the vote for president retains a Republican skew over the decades and has maintained its unimodal distribution, as shown in the graphs (for northern districts) in Appendix C to this chapter. Thus, a bipartisan incumbent gerrymander is not a likely cause of the underlying distribution of the House vote.[1]

INCUMBENCY: THE LITERATURE AND THE SIGNIFICANCE

Back in 1971, I published an article in *Polity,* dryly titled "The Incumbency Advantage in Congressional Elections." Erikson (1971) estimated the incumbency advantage in the 1950s to amount to only about 2 percentage points of the vote. A year later, Erikson (1972) reported that the incumbency advantage had grown in the 1960s from about 2 percentage points to about 5 points and possibly growing. This was consistent with Mayhew's "Vanishing Marginals."

Mayhew and I had the same general idea for estimating the incumbency advantage. These were the "sophomore surge" and the "retirement slump." Both terms were coined by Cover and Mayhew (1977). The sophomore surge is

[1] Another clue that proincumbent gerrymandering is not responsible for the bimodality is that the bimodality for incumbent-contested races is no more noticeable in the first years following redistricting (ending in 2) than in the final years of the decade, when any gerrymander effects would have faded.

the vote gain that accrues to freshman incumbents beyond their vote margin in their first election as nonincumbents (as open seat winners or successful challengers). The retirement slump is the vote loss to the incumbent's party once the incumbent retires. Each must be estimated while controlling for the partisan trend. Each has its potential biases, as discussed in the following.

The discovery in the 1970s of the growing incumbency advantage starting in the 1960s spurred a cottage industry of research on the topic. Much of the research in the 1970s centered on the "why." Was there an increase in congressional perks of office that members of Congress could exploit? Was it an increase in congressional casework (Fiorina, 1977)? Could redistricting (rampant in the 1960s post–*Baker v. Carr*) have contributed (Tufte, 1973; Ferejohn, 1977)? Was it due to the dealignment of voters so that a less partisan electorate would vote more on the basis of personal characteristics of the candidates, including incumbency (Ferejohn, 1977)? Was the growth of the advantage limited to relative congressional newcomers, or did old-timers get the benefit too? (Alford and Hibbing, 1981.)

Beyond the 1970s, scholars continued to debate the best way of measuring the incumbency advantage (Gelman and King, 1990; Alford and Brady, 1993; Levitt and Wolfram, 1997; Zaller, 1998; Lee, 2008), and even whether the marginals had really vanished at all (Jacobson, 1987; Ansolahebere et al., 1988). Did the incumbency advantage arise because it scared off worthy opponents (Cox and Katz, 1996, 2002)? Was it because incumbents could exploit their ideological representation of their constituencies (e.g., Erikson and Wright, 2000)? How much does the incumbency advantage have to do with the incumbents' known advantage in the size of their campaign war chest (Erikson and Palfrey, 1998; Ansolahebere et al., 2000)?

Why has the incumbency advantage attracted so much scholarly attention? The sizeable incumbency advantage has two effects on partisan outcomes of national elections, one more obvious than the other. The obvious impact is on the so-called "swing ratio," whereby a given change in the national vote margin has a specific effect on the seat margin. By some estimates, the swing ratio declined to about half its former value. The obvious implication is that the electoral consequences of vote swings get dampened in the process. A more subtle impact is on the partisan division of Congress. As is well known, the partisan division of congressional districts is skewed in a way that works against the Democrats, with Democrats clustered geographically in districts that are very safe for Democratic candidates, with no similar process for Republicans. Democratic votes go "wasted" while Republican voters are distributed efficiently. (This is over and above any skewness due to partisan Republican gerrymandering.)

If the vote is a very tight partisan vote with little variance due to the personal qualities of the candidates, then Republicans do quite well. President Obama, whose vote margins were tightly tied to local partisan strengths, carried only a minority of the congressional districts in 2012, despite his clear (but narrow) presidential victory with 52 percent of the two-party vote. A House of Representatives that reflected district partisanship and nothing else would almost always go Republican. But if the district House vote is jittered out of its partisan makeup, Democratic victories increase.

Consider that the timing of the surge in the incumbency advantage corresponded to the aftermath of the 1964 election, when the Democrats won many new seats in a landslide election. Gifted with a newly enlarged incumbency advantage, the Democrats freshly elected in 1964 were better able to survive the more Republican tide in 1966 and subsequent years.[2]

The mirror image, of course, applies to Republican landslides. The persistent GOP success in the aftermath of the 2010 Republican surge is an example. Today, incumbency gets tangled up with the dominant question of "polarization." With growing partisanship, we can imagine a "nationalized" vote, whereby notions that congressional voting is "local" become extinct. Further fueling such a national vote would be the perception that the national congressional verdict is "in play" and not an obvious conclusion, as it was during forty straight years of Democratic control of the House of Representatives. In the extreme, if voters were to vote for the House on the same partisan basis that they employ in their vote for President, the Republican advantage would increase.

In the pages that follow, I discuss the following matters: How should we measure the incumbency advantage? How big is it, really? Is the size of the advantage declining? What are the implications for current politics?

MEASURING THE INCUMBENCY ADVANTAGE: THE MODEL[3]

For fifty years, scholars have proposed different methods to obtain a valid measure of the incumbency advantage. One can identify three challenges. First, candidates who win elections tend to win because of their personal qualities (or "personal vote") apart from what they earn once becoming the incumbent. Incumbents would tend to win by larger margins than partisan expectations even if there were no incumbency advantage, simply because they tend to be the highest quality candidates. I will call this "electoral selection." Second, elections are usually contested by two major party candidates, and each can affect the vote margin. Candidates may become incumbents due in part to the poor quality of their opponents. Third, incumbents are strategic in deciding when to retire, and tend to quit whenever they are expected to do badly. All these complications present challenges to finding an unbiased measure of the incumbency advantage.[4]

[2] See Erikson, 1972; Gelman and King, 1991; and Cox and Katz, 2002 for discussions of the 1964 case.
[3] For a more elaborate discussion of the issues presented in this section, see Erikson and Titiunik, 2015.
[4] Strategic decisions by potential challengers could also be listed here. But this indirect scare-off effect is considered here as one aspect of the advantage candidates gain from incumbency.

Further, there are two different notions of an incumbency advantage – as a *personal* advantage that accrues to an incumbent by virtue of becoming the incumbent, and as a *party* advantage, defined with various nuances as the advantage to the current office-holder's party regardless of the identity of the current candidates. The party advantage is usually defined as the gain to a party from both the personal advantage from incumbency and any electoral advantage to a party stemming from holding the seat previously. Recent research by Fowler and Hall (2014) suggests that any electoral bonus from seat-holding is negligible: term-limited state legislators offer no carry-over electoral benefit to their parties' designated successors. In this paper, the focus is on the personal advantage, gained from earning incumbency, rather than the more inclusive (and elusive) party advantage.

The direct personal advantage includes all downstream advantages from becoming an incumbent – from constituency service, credit claiming, ideological representation, and the like – plus the amplification that stems from the incumbent's megaphone and presumption of future electoral success. One can also include, as I do here, the indirect advantage from the scare-off, which accrues from strong potential challengers being scared to contest a popular incumbent. All these sources of advantage represent the votes that an incumbent gains beyond those earned when the incumbent was a nonincumbent candidate.

The personal incumbency advantage has been measured in different ways. The "sophomore surge" estimates the within-individual electoral gain obtained by newly elected candidates in their reelection as freshmen. The "retirement slump" estimates the party's vote loss when its incumbent retires (Erikson, 1971, 1972; Cover and Mayhew, 1977). The "slurge" is the average of the surge and the slump (Alford and Brady, 1993). The Gelman and King (1990) method regresses the vote on the lagged vote and appropriate dummies for the incumbent's party and whether the incumbent runs.[5] Most recently, Lee (2008) estimated the party incumbency advantage using regression discontinuity (RD) analysis. Erikson and Titiunik (2015) discuss how the RD formulation can be employed to estimate the personal incumbency advantage.

The sophomore surge is the trend-adjusted vote gain once a candidate becomes an incumbent and runs as a freshman. The retirement slump is the party's trend-adjusted loss when its incumbent retires. Even with a perfect control for the partisan trend, each method suffers from a subtle bias. Fortunately, given very plausible assumptions, these biases operate in opposite directions. Thus, where the two estimates of the incumbency advantage diverge, we can at least expect the answer to be somewhere in between.

---

[5] Further variations include estimating the sophomore surge by restricting the analysis to races where the same candidates run in multiple elections (Levitt and Wolfram, 1997) and exploiting different kinds of natural experiments such as redistricting (Ansolabehere et al., 2000) or unexpected deaths (Cox and Katz, 2002).

In the following discussion I refer to the partisan baseline as "Par." Par represents district partisanship plus any electoral trend. In successive elections, Par will change in accord with the change in the electoral trend. Assume now that the vote is measured relative to Par, and is only a function of the vote-getting ability (quality) of the two major party candidates plus, possibly, random luck. Candidate quality is normed so that on average, conditional on Par and the seat being open, the quality of a party's candidate (apart from any scare-off in an incumbent race) is zero.

As the vote gain from election t (as a nonincumbent) to election $t+1$ (as an incumbent), the sophomore surge equals the incumbency gain plus the vote increment contributed by the replacement of the losing candidate at t with a draw of a new opponent at $t+1$. Sophomore surge is biased downward because it fails to adjust for the fact that initial victories are partially due to the draw of a poor opponent plus luck factors. This is clearest in the case of freshmen who win open seats rather than by defeating the previous incumbent.

For an open seat, both the winner and the loser contribute equally (on average) to the deviation of the vote from a simple partisan outcome (district partisanship plus electoral trend). Also, on average, the winning candidate is a stronger candidate than the loser. Thus, as an expectation, about half of the winner's vote that is unexplained by Par is due to the quality of the losing candidate. At the next election at $t+1$, running as a freshman incumbent, the time t winner draws an average candidate, apart from the contribution of the scare-off effect. (Recall that the scare-off is considered here as part of the incumbency advantage.) By this reasoning, the expected gain from t to $t+1$ represents the newly won incumbency advantage (including scare-off) minus half of the initial surplus (over Par) from $t+1$. This latter component biases the estimate downward.

When measuring the sophomore surge for successful challengers, the assumptions about the components of the vote surge are less clear. Technically, the surge should represent the winner's incumbency gain minus the loser's loss of an incumbency advantage. But the net incumbency bonus for successful challengers is not twice the bonus for open seat winners. In fact, on average, the sophomore surge for successful challengers is not much greater than it is for open seat winners. The combined gain from taking away the opponent's incumbency and gaining theirs minus the loss from losing the weak time t candidate (now a defeated incumbent) is not much greater than for open seat winners. This is an important clue that the rare incumbents who lose (losers to successful challengers) must on average be severely weak candidates.

The retirement slump is biased upward, because it represents both the retirees' loss of incumbency for their party and the loss of the net quality of the retiring incumbent. Incumbents generally tend to be of positive quality, so that their margin relative to Par exceeds their incumbency advantage. They tend to retire when their popularity is at low ebb, but still in positive territory. The result is a slight inflation of the incumbency advantage.

The Gelman-King method is best seen as an estimate of the party rather than the personal incumbency advantage. Gelman and King (1990) regress the vote on the lagged vote, year dummies, candidate incumbency, and the incumbent party. The lagged vote is intended to control for sources of the $t+1$ vote other than incumbency. However, this assumption leads to an unbiased estimate only if incumbent retirement decisions are unrelated to their expected vote share. This assumption is decidedly untrue, so that the lagged vote is a leaky control for the relevant nonincumbency causes of the time $t+1$ vote that it is intended to measure. The consequence is that nonincumbency factors masquerade as part of the incumbency advantage.

Lee's regression discontinuity method estimates the partisan incumbency advantage as the differential at $t+1$ from winning slightly less than 50 percent of the two-party vote at t to slightly more than 50 percent at t. As such it is an elegant estimate of the downstream prospects for a *party* from either winning or losing a very close election. Erikson and Titiunik show that under a set of assumptions, a regression discontinuity design can offer an unbiased estimate of the personal incumbency advantage. In particular, these assumptions are most likely to hold for open seats at time t. For close open seats, the differential from wining versus losing is twice the personal incumbency advantage. At the 50–50 juncture, winners and losers are of equal quality on average, so that twice both the $t+1$ vote and the t+1 vote gain are unbiased estimates of the incumbency advantage (including the scare-off).

The good news is that the different methods converge in their estimates of the size of the incumbency advantage. As an average over the period from the late 1960s to the early 2000s, the net incumbency advantage appears to be about 7 or 8 percentage points. While this is a convincing estimate of the incumbency advantage at *stasis*, we also want to be alert to any changes in magnitude.

MEASURING THE INCUMBENCY ADVANTAGE

In the following, I present estimates of the incumbency advantage over sixty years – from 1952 through 2012. Vote data come from standard sources, most notably the data assembled by Gary Jacobson. I exclude both the South and border states entirely.[6] I estimate Par, the sum of district partisanship plus year effects, from a regression equation predicting the two-party vote for open House seats (North only) from the current (or most recent) vote for president in the district, plus year dummies.

Several reasons guide the decision to exclude South and border states. Over the sixty years, the trajectory of southern politics has been decidedly distinct

---

[6] Excluded are all the former slave states, which were also the set enforcing compulsory racial segregation prior to *Brown v. Board of Education* (1954). Oklahoma is among the excluded states, as a formerly segregationist state that entered the union after slavery ended.

from that in the North, with the advance of Republicanism throughout the once-solid South. This Republican advance has occurred at different stages – and to different degrees, with subregional variation – for House and presidential elections in the South. As a result, for a long time, the relationship in the South between the district House vote and the district presidential vote was at variance with the same relationship in the North. For the North, throughout the period, the cross-district variation in the presidential vote could be understood as a proxy for the partisanship that also influenced House elections. This was not always the case in the South. As the South and border states turned Republican in various waves, the House voting wave generally lagged behind the presidential wave. Moreover, the Republican presidential wave was subject to interruptions, such as the candidacy of southerners Jimmy Carter and (to some extent) Bill Clinton. The general "problem" with the South extended to certain mid-South and border states where the Republican wave in House elections only recently arrived.

For northern districts, Par is measured as follows. The races with open seats are pooled across the years, with the Democratic share of the two-party vote predicted from the current (for presidential year) or most recent (for midterms) vote for president in the current district, plus dummy variables for the various years. The predicted values from this equation comprise the estimate of Par, or the net baseline from district partisanship plus year effects:[7]

$$\text{Dem.Vote(House)} = 0.90 \, \text{Dem.Vote(President)} + \psi$$

where ψ = year effects (not shown).

Figure 4.1 shows the relationship between the open seat vote and Par over six decades. One can see that the fit of the model varies, with the greatest deviations in the middle decades. The first panel suggests that in the 1950s, open seat elections were largely decided by partisanship (reflected in the presidential vote) plus year effects. The middle panels show a greater departure of the congressional vote from the presidential vote prediction, as if candidate quality began to matter more. The final panel suggests that the 2000s pattern began to revert to that of the 1950s. District-level congressional election outcomes are trending toward a simple party-line vote.

---

[7] The standard error for the presidential vote is 0.02. The adjusted R squared is 0.69. The standard error of the residuals is 7.07. As a measure of the candidate-generated variance, this approximates the variance of national presidential election vote outcomes. One can say campaigns and candidates matter about as much in open seat races as they do in presidential elections. The 0.90 coefficient for the presidential vote is quite insensitive to the years selected. For a similar use of Par, see Erikson and Palfrey (1998). There, Par was further refined as the open seat estimate from presidential voting, year effects, and equal Republican and Democratic expenditures. Expenditures are ignored here.

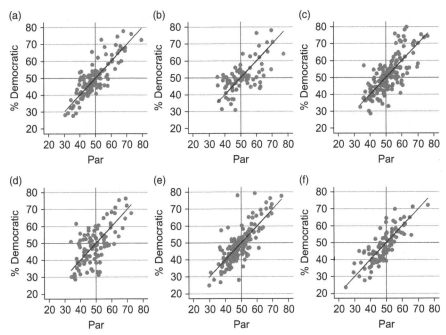

FIGURE 4.1 Major-party vote for the House of Representatives in open seats as a function of Par, by decade. (a) 1950s. (b) 1960s. (c) 1970s. (d) 1980s. (e) 1990s. (f) 2000s. North only. Par is a measure of voting support for the Democratic candidate based on presidential voting and year effects, estimated for open seats.

With Par measured, the differential between the congressional vote and the Par baseline becomes the subject of interest. Let us call this the "residual vote." The residual vote is the net vote due to candidate forces, including any incumbency advantage. The sophomore surge measure becomes the change in the residual vote from the time of the candidate's initial victory to the first election as a freshman incumbent. The retirement slump measure becomes the change in the residual vote from the incumbent's final race to the retiree's party's vote in the next election when it contests an open seat.

THE INCUMBENCY ADVANTAGE: HOW LARGE?

This section estimates the size of the incumbency advantage over the three decades of the 1970s, 1980s, and 1990s. This is a period when (we shall see) the size of the incumbency advantage appeared both large and stable. Both the sophomore surge and retirement slump are estimated. The sophomore surge is further divided into the surge for open seat winners and successful challengers. The surge for open seat winners is also measured as the adjusted surge,

74   *Robert S. Erikson*

TABLE 4.1 *Estimates of the Personal Incumbency Advantage, Based on Northern Districts, 1970s, 1980s, and 1990s[a]*

	N	Residual Vote, Election *t*	Residual Vote, Election *t*+1	Mean Change
Sophomore Surge (Freshmen elected at *t*)	462	+2.78	+8.70	+5.92 (0.38)
Successful Challengers	158	+1.02	+6.88	+5.86 (0.58)
Open Seat Winners	304	+3.69	+9.64	+5.95 (0.49)
Adjusted[b]	304	+1.85	+9.63	+7.80 (0.45)
Retirement Slump (Incumbent retires at *t*+1)	292	+9.55	+1.31	−8.24 (0.64)

Residual vote is the residual vote at *t* and at *t*+1 for the election *t* winner, as the deviation of the vote from Par. Standard errors (in parentheses) are based on the *t*-test for the mean change.
[a.] Election *t*: 1972–1978, 1982–1988, 1992–1998. Election *t*+1: 1974–1980, 1984–1990, 1994–2000.
[b.] The adjusted sophomore surge for open seat winners is the difference between the *t*+1 residual vote and half the *t* residual vote.

where the bias in the estimate is reduced by discounting the winner's lead over Par at election *t* by half. The results, discussed in the following, are summarized in Table 4.1.

Open Seat Winners. For the clearest visualization, let us begin with Figure 4.2, which depicts the sophomore surge for open seat winners from the 1970s through the 1990s. The figure displays the vote for open seat winners as a function of Par. The first panel shows the result when they win their open seats; the second panel shows the result for their reelection attempt as freshmen.[8]

In Figure 4.2a, the vote is truncated at the 50 percent line since we are observing the vote only for the winners of open seats. Many win in districts with adverse partisanship (as measured by Par) by doing better than Par. Others win, even comfortably, while running below Par. Winners in adverse districts owe their victory to a combination of their own strength as candidates plus the weakness of their opponent. In safe districts, how well they do versus Par is largely irrelevant.

---

[8] The open seat winners in Panel 1 and the freshman incumbents in Panel 2 are the same candidates, running in 1972–1998 for Panel 1 and 1974–2000 for Panel 2. While the observations in the two panels are identical, Par shifts between panels due to year effects and slight changes in presidential voting from one election to the next. Some extremely safe seats are cropped, as the two panels include only cases where Par for the open seat winner is less than 80 percent.

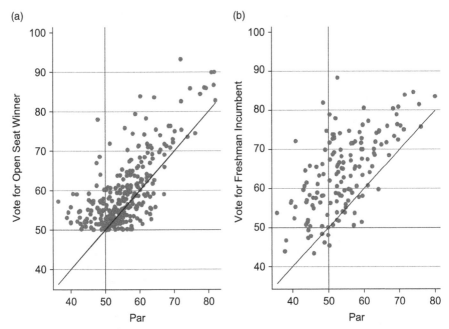

FIGURE 4.2 Vote for open-seat winners, as nonincumbents (a) and as freshman incumbents (b), 1972–1998 (a), 1974–2000 (b). Northern districts only. The candidates are identical in the two panels. No observations for paired elections that span Census redistricting. Par is a measure of partisan advantage for the open seat winner, adjusted for year effects.

Figure 4.2b shows the result in open seat winners' second elections, now as freshmen incumbents. Twenty-six (9 percent) of these 304 new incumbents fell (these are the data points below the 50 percent vote horizontal line). Virtually all those who were defeated had initially won by beating Par. Meanwhile, on average, the vote increased when moving from nonincumbent status (Figure 4.2a) to incumbency (Figure 4.2b). Further, this increase was most noticeable in the all-important competitive range where Par hovered around 50 percent. That is, incumbency advantage was greatest where it mattered the most.

We can see this in Figure 4.3, which graphs the lowess curves for the incumbency gain (sophomore surge) as a function of Par. Averaging the observed vote gains for freshman incumbents over the three decades, the sophomore surge is +5.95 percentage points. But it varies importantly by district competitiveness. For values of Par up to 60 percentage points for the incumbent party, the observed sophomore surge is in the range of seven points. Beyond 60 percentage points, the observed surge declines sharply and in fact slips slightly into negative territory around 80 percent. Those who do not need an incumbency advantage due to their safe seats (in terms of Par) rarely earn it. Presumably, this is because they see no need to try.

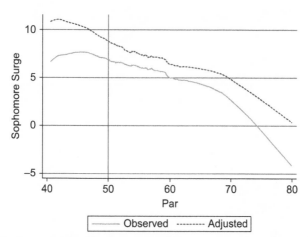

FIGURE 4.3 Sophomore surge for open-seat winners, 1974–2000, observed and adjusted, by Par. Northern districts only. The curves are lowess curves, with a 0.8 bandwidth. No observations for post-census elections, ending in 2. Par is a measure of partisan advantage for the successful challenger, adjusted for year effects.

Recall that the observed sophomore surge is biased for open seat winners. The candidate-generated variance in the first election is a dual function of the winner's and the loser's quality. If we assign all the variance of the residual vote (deviation from Par) in the open seat election equally to the two candidates, half of the residual is due to the loser. In the second election, a fresh draw produces an average candidate (except for the scare-off from the new incumbent's observed voting strength). Thus, one arrives at an adjustment to the sophomore surge: measure it as the residual vote in the second election minus one-half the residual vote in the first election.[9]

Adjusted, the mean sophomore surge for the three decades climbs to +7.80 percentage points. Its variation with Par is also shown in Figure 4.3. Adjusted, the sophomore surge climbs to over 10 percentage points for members who most need it – those who would expect to lose based on partisanship and year effects alone. To see its importance for the survival of new incumbents, consider the result if we simulate the incumbency advantage away to zero. Subtracting out the lowess-estimate of the sophomore surge specific to Par yields the

---

[9] Counting half of the residual vote in the first election as a nonincumbent is actually based on a conservative assumption. The assumption is that each candidate is responsible for half of the variance in the residual vote and ignores other idiosyncratic factors, which we can call short-term luck. Suppose that luck accounted for some proportion of the variance, λ. The losing candidate plus luck would then account for $(1-\lambda)0.5+\lambda$ or $0.5(1+\lambda)$. Adjusting for this unknown λ yields:

Adjusted sophomore surge = residual vote at $t+1$ minus $0.5(1+\lambda)$ multiplied by the residual vote at time t.

The utilized measure of the adjusted surge is conservative about the size of the incumbency-induced surge because it assumes $\lambda=0$.

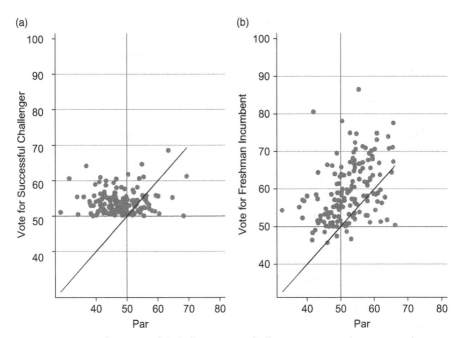

FIGURE 4.4 Vote for successful challengers, as challengers to incumbents (a) and as freshman incumbents (b); 1972–1998 (a), 1974–2000 (b). Northern districts only. The candidates are identical in the two panels. No observations for paired elections that span census redistricting. Par is a measure of partisan advantage for the successful challenger, adjusted for year effects.

inference that 28 percent of open seat winners would have lost their seats at their first reelection attempt were it not for incumbency advantage.

Successful Challengers. The other type of freshman incumbent is the successful challenger, who ascends to Congress by defeating a sitting incumbent. There were 158 successful challengers over the 1970s through the 1990s. Of these, only 9 lost their reelection bids. On average, successful challengers gained 5.86 points as a sophomore surge. Figure 4.4 shows the vote for successful challengers relative to Par first as winning upstarts in the first panel and then as freshmen seeking reelection in the second panel.

Successful challengers take away their opposition's incumbency advantage while gaining their own. It follows that the surge for successful challengers should be something like twice the size of the surge for open seat winners. Yet this expectation is decidedly unmet. On average, the surge for successful challengers is even slightly smaller than for open seat winners, only +5.86 percentage points. The likely explanation is twofold. First, defeated incumbents are less popular than average, so their personal vote is worse than that of the average candidate. This boosts the vote for successful challengers at election *t*. Second, successful challengers themselves are not as strong as open seat winners, perhaps because the strongest potential opponents to vulnerable incumbents are scared off. As poor candidates, successful challengers provoke less of a scare-off themselves at $t+1$, compared with successful challengers. We can see evidence of the relatively poor quality of successful challengers from Table 4.1 and from comparing the second panels of Figures 4.3 and 4.4. Successful challengers earn fewer votes than do open seat winners at the same level of Par.[10]

Despite being weaker candidates than the average open seat winner (conditional on Par), successful challengers lost only 6 percent of their reelection attempts in the data. It is the incumbency advantage that provided the protection. We can simulate the result that would have occurred if their incumbency advantage had been taken away from these successful challengers. For instance, dropping seven percentage points from their vote (i.e., requiring them to win with 57 percent, not 50 percent) yields a loss rate that rises to 42 percent.

Retirement Slump. Over the three decades of the 1970s through the 1990s, there were 292 useable retirements (including nonvoluntary ones from death or primary defeat), where one can compare the retiree's final vote margin with the vote for the retiree's party at the next election when the contest is an open seat. Measured relative to Par, the average slump was 8.24 percentage points. Although the expectation is that the retirement slump might inflate the incumbency advantage, its observed size is only slightly larger than the adjusted sophomore slump for open seat winners.

Figure 4.5 shows the two panels – before and after – for the retirement slump. In their immediate preretirement election, retirees display a residual vote 9.55 percentage points greater than Par. This is greater, for example, than the 8.70 average for the sophomore surge data (open seat winners plus successful challengers). The increment represents an upward creep in the incumbency advantage past the sophomore year, minus any selection effects whereby incumbents retire when their residual vote is poor. With the 9.55 starting point, the simple expectation is that the slump would go to zero, yielding, of course, a 9.55 point net slump. The observed 8.24 average slump varies from this expectation due to the fact that the retiree's party retains a slight advantage in open seat races (1.31 points on average). This could be a hidden effect of local party organization or it could reflect some leakiness in the Par variable.

Retirements obviously matter for party control of a seat. As it turned out, for our sample of retirees, the retiree's party failed to keep the seat a formidable 38 percent of the time. If we could assign these vulnerable replacement candidates an arbitrary 7 points incumbency advantage, only 10 percent would have been defeated.

---

[10] The average residual vote for successful challengers as freshmen is only +6.88, which represents the sum of their incumbency advantage (including scare-off) plus their quality and their opponent at $t+1$. The comparable residual vote for freshman open seat winners is +9.64.

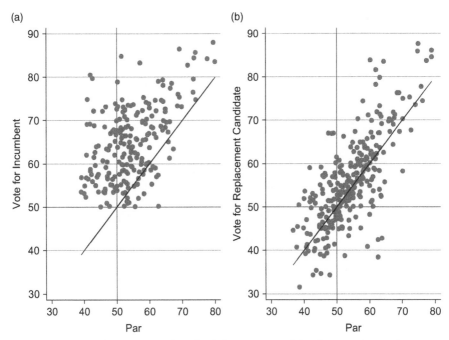

FIGURE 4.5 Vote for retirees in their final election (a) and for their parties' replacement candidates (b), 1972–1998 (a), 1974–2000 (b). Northern districts only. No observations for paired elections that span Census redistricting. Par is a measure of partisan advantage for the retiree's party, adjusted for year effects.

Summary. During the three decades of the 1970s, 1980s, and 1990s, the incumbency advantage was in the neighborhood of seven or eight percentage points. The size of the incumbency premium varied with the circumstances and was highest for those in competitive districts where working to please one's district had the greatest marginal value. Once in office, few incumbents lost. Seats were most likely to switch parties when the incumbent retired.

THE INCUMBENCY ADVANTAGE OVER TIME

The previous section treated the incumbency advantage as a stable entity that could be studied in detail by pooling data over three decades. We know, however, that the incumbency advantage increased in the 1960s. We see change again in the twenty-first century. This section explores the changing magnitude of the advantage over six decades, 1954–2010. It documents the growth in the 1960s. It also suggests that the incumbency advantage may be receding again.

Figures 4.6, 4.7, and 4.8 present various graphs of the advantage over time, as measured by various methods. Figure 4.6 shows the annual readings of the two standard measures, the sophomore surge (open seat winners and successful

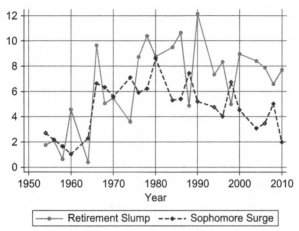

FIGURE 4.6 Retirement slump and sophomore surge, means by election year: 1954–2010. Northern districts only. No observations for post-census elections, ending in 2.

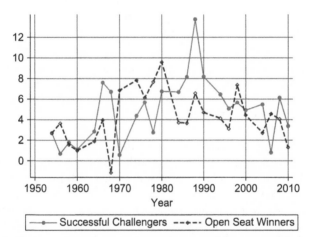

FIGURE 4.7 Sophomore surge for open seat winners and for successful challengers, means by election year: 1954–2010. Northern districts only. No observations for post-census elections, ending in 2.

challengers pooled) and the retirement slump. Figure 4.7 decomposes the surge into that for open seat winners and that for successful challengers. Figure 4.8 further compares the open seat winner surge that is observed with the adjusted version, which subtracts only half instead of all the time *t* (nonincumbent) residual vote. As elsewhere in this paper, all estimates are based on deviations from Par and only estimated for northern districts.

During the 1960s, the measures wobble some, due to low district continuity stemming from the continuous churning of court-ordered redistricting post–*Baker*

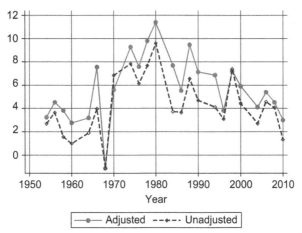

FIGURE 4.8 Sophomore surge for open-seat winners, 1954–2010, by election year mean. As observed and adjusted. Northern districts only. No observations for post-census elections, ending in 2.

v. Carr. Yet the pattern is unmistakable; we see the growth of the incumbency advantage that fuels the vanishing of the marginals. The average incumbency advantage rose from about two points to five points or higher. It rose higher still in the 1970s, when it more or less plateaued, at least through the 1990s.

What about today? In the 2000s (2004–2010), the graphs clearly hint at a reversal, with the incumbency advantage declining in strength. As measured by the traditional sophomore surge, the advantage in 2010 was only 2 percentage points, back where it was in the 1950s. The retirement slump did not recede in the same manner, suggesting a possible disconnection between the two measures. However, there is a ready explanation: retirees had built up electoral immunity, maintaining their incumbency advantage previously earned. The plunge in the vote following their exit revealed the degree to which the party success during their tenure had been incumbency-induced.

The clearest evidence for a new trend is the depiction in Figure 4.9. This graph shows the variance of the two-party district vote (percent Democratic, North only) by election year, subdivided into those races with and those without an incumbent candidate. Unlike for earlier graphic presentations, this method allows presentation for redistricted seats and ignores Par. Thus it can be extended continuously from 1952 through 2012.

Predictably, this graph shows that the variance of the vote is greatest with the incumbent in the race, as evidence of an incumbency advantage. Without incumbents, election results are a function of district partisanship and year effects plus candidate effects. With incumbents, they are a function of these forces plus an incumbency advantage that helps either the Democrats or the Republicans. But the gap between the two trend lines is clearest in the middle years, with recent elections reverting to the pattern of the 1950s.

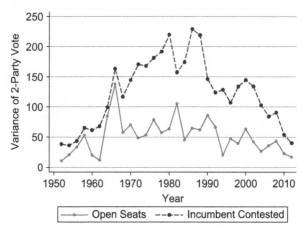

FIGURE 4.9 Variance of the two-party vote for open seats and for incumbent-contested seats, 1952–2012. North Only.

2012 AND BEYOND

Ideally, we would estimate the incumbency advantage for 2012. Estimation must, however, overcome a barrier. As for every election following a national census, the nearly universal redistricting pre-2012 prevents a simple measure of electoral change. Still, to estimate the sophomore surge, we can compare how well new winners in 2010 did relative to Par for that year with their 2012 freshman performance relative to 2012 Par as an incumbent in their new district. In this way, we can compare for each 2012 freshman the 2010 and 2012 residual vote even though their districts changed.[11] The limitation is that new incumbents in 2012 may have been less familiar to voters in the newly added segments of their districts. For the retirement slump, estimation is more problematic for 2012, as retirees would have represented only a fraction of the voters in the new district that they would be contesting if they had run for reelection.[12]

For 2012, I proceeded to estimate the sophomore surge by comparing the 2010 and 2012 residual vote of new incumbents, while ignoring the retirement slump. Table 4.2 shows the results. The table considers open seat winners and successful challengers separately.

For the nineteen northern open seat winners from 2010 (mainly Republicans), the average net gain (relative to Par) was only 2.02 points, similar to

[11] Recall that the Par measure is based on the prediction of open seat races from the current or most recent presidential election. Thus, Par for 2010 is the estimate of the 2010 vote in the district if it were an open seat, based on the Obama vote in 2008. Par for 2012 is the estimate of the 2012 open seat vote based on the Obama vote in 2012. Par takes into account both relative district partisanship and year effects.

[12] Also, the identities of the new districts of retiring incumbents are not always identifiable.

TABLE 4.2 *Estimates of the Sophomore Surge, Based on Northern Districts, for 2010–2012 Transition*

	N	Residual Vote, Election *t*	Residual Vote, Election *t*+1	Mean Change
Successful Challengers, 2010	32	−3.06	+3.38	+6.44 (0.97)
Open Seat Winners, 2010	19	+2.14	+4.16	+2.02 (1.04)
Adjusted[a]	19	+1.07	+4.16	+3.09 (0.87)

Residual vote is estimated for the election *t* winner, as the deviation of the vote from Par. Standard errors (in parentheses) are based on the *t*-test for the mean change.
[a] The adjusted sophomore surge for open seat winners is the difference between the *t*+1 residual vote and half the *t* residual vote.

2010 and to the 1950s. Thus, at least for this group, there was little incumbency advantage. The era of a massive incumbency advantage would appear to have ended.

Meanwhile, for the thirty-two successful challengers from 2010 (again, predominantly Republican), the net gain was 6.44 points, even larger than the average surge for successful challengers previously. It may seem puzzling that the gain for successful challengers in 2010 would be more than twice the gain from 2010 open seat winners, quite the opposite of the pattern for earlier years. Actually, successful challengers were no stronger relative to Par than were the comparable open seat winners with their modest gains. That is, in terms of their personal vote, successful challengers were less secure than the open seat winners in 2012. Their greater gain was due to revoking the incumbency advantage of their defeated 2010 incumbent opponents. In 2010, most successful challengers had a lesser vote share than Par (i.e., less than if it were an open seat). This is testimony to the size of the 2010 Republican wave, in that the 2010 incumbents who were vanquished still beat Par even as they lost. In 2012, the successful freshman challengers were given a bounce by the draw of a fresh (possibly scared-off) challenger rather than the strong incumbent.

Note again, from Appendix A, that the distribution of the 2012 district vote for incumbent candidates reverted to its shape from the 1950s. We have just seen evidence that the sophomore surge was weaker than usual in 2012. The world of congressional elections has changed once again.[13]

---

[13] Subsequent to the preparation of this chapter, Jacobson (2015) has shown that the diminution of the incumbency advantage was repeated in the 2014 midterm elections.

DISCUSSION

Before Mayhew, congressional elections were not seen as particularly interesting. As seen by the authoritative *American Voter* authors, for instance, congressional voters cast partisan ballots largely without knowing the candidates, yielding vote outcomes that were ratifications of the "normal vote" plus maybe some spillover from "short-term forces" (coattails).[14] This view was not necessarily wrong. By the time the marginals had been found to be missing, the nature of congressional elections had changed. Two developments were responsible. First, there began a decline in partisanship, or dealignment. As the public became less tied to partisanship, it became more attuned to individual congressional candidates. Second, now with a more attentive audience, members of Congress became more adept at exploiting their perks of incumbency. The result was the growth of the incumbency advantage. And, as the personal vote expanded in general as a factor in congressional elections, U.S. House elections became a more interesting venue for electoral scholarship.

Congressional elections now are undergoing a new shift. With today's polarization in Congress (if not the electorate), the dominant determinant of a candidate's behavior in the mind of the voter has become the party label. Candidates who previously would moderate their positions or perform extraordinary service now have less incentive to do so. One can speculate that the salience of the party brand limits the degree to which voters can detect nuances of congressional behavior that previously might have mattered. The result is a renewed fall-off in the personal vote in general and incumbency effects in particular.

If congressional elections are entering a new era of strictly partisan voting, who benefits? In the short term of 2012, the Democrats may have actually benefited in that the incumbency advantage for the Republicans' class of 2010 appeared weaker than for incumbents of previous years.[15] In the long term, more partisan district outcomes would mean more Republican victories. The Republican Party benefits from a well-known "natural" gerrymander in its favor in terms of underlying partisanship as reflected in presidential voting

---

[14] The classic *The American Voter* (Campbell et al., 1960) focused almost entirely on presidential elections. The authors turned to congressional elections in *Elections and the Political Order* (Campbell et al., 1966).

[15] A full analysis of partisan consequences is beyond the scope of this chapter. However, we can note the following. Of the 253 northern congressional districts with two-party competition in 2012, the average congressional vote was 55 percent Democratic. In these districts in 2012, Par (for the Democrats) exceeded 50 percent in 58 percent of the cases. However, the Democrats' 55 percent of the vote carried only 54 percent of these districts into the Democratic column, and they may have been lucky to earn that many. The Democrats' poor yield was helped by Republicans holding so many new seats by slim margins. If the Republicans' incumbency advantage had reached its historic norm, the Republicans would have won more.

(Erikson, 1972; Rodden, 2010). Just as the Electoral College "reform" of allotting wins by congressional district would help the Republicans win the presidency, the winner-take-all system of strict party voting benefits the Republicans when it comes to House elections.

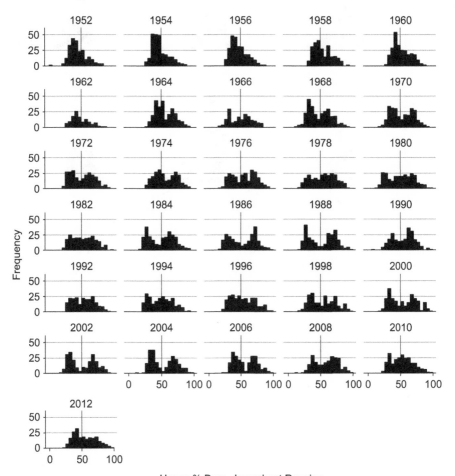

House % Dem., Incumbent Running

APPENDIX A Two-party vote in districts with incumbent candidates, by year, northern states only. Seats without major-party competition are not shown, for clarity. A bimodal distribution opens up in the late 1960s, and occasionally disappears. The distribution becomes less skewed over time. By 2012, however, the distribution begins to resemble the distribution of the 1950s.

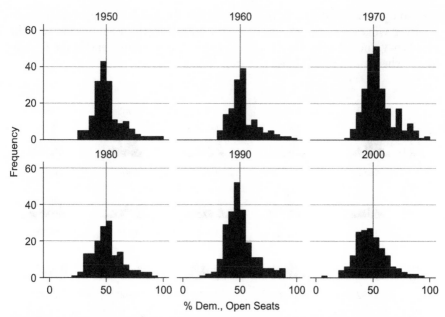

APPENDIX B Two-party vote in open seat districts by decade, northern states only. Seats without major-party competition are not shown, for clarity. For open seats there is no bimodality. The distribution is skewed somewhat in favor of Republicans.

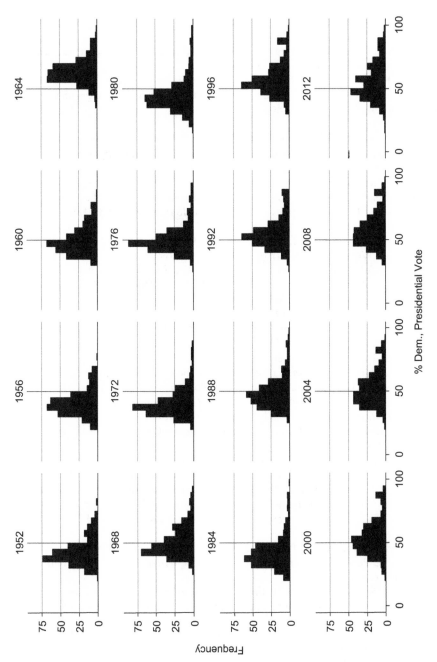

APPENDIX C Two-party vote for president in northern congressional districts, by year. The distribution is unimodal and skewed to favor Republicans, but decreasingly so over the years.

REFERENCES

Alford, John R. and John R. Hibbing. 1981. "Increased Incumbency Advantage in the House." *Journal of Politics* 43: 1052–1061.

Alford, John R. and David W. Brady. 1993. "Personal and Partisan Advantage in US Congressional Elections." In Lawrence C. Dodd and Bruce I. Oppenheimer, eds., *Congress Reconsidered*, 5th ed. Washington, D.C.: Congressional Quarterly Press.

Ansolahebere, Stephen and James M. Snyder, Jr. 2000. "Money and Office: The Source of the Incumbency Advantage in Campaign Finance." In David Brady, John Cogan, and Morris P. Fiorina, eds., *Continuity and Change in House Elections*. Palo Alto: Stanford University Press.

Ansolahebere, Stephen, David W. Brady, and Morris P. Fiorina. 1988. "The Vanishing Marginals and Electoral Responsiveness." *British Journal of Political Science* 22: 21–38.

Ansolahebere, Stephen, James M. Snyder, Jr., and Charles Stewart III. 2000. "Old Voters, New Voters, and the Personal Vote: Using Redistricting to Measure the Incumbency Advantage." *American Journal of Political Science* 44: 17–44.

Campbell, Angus, Phillip E. Converse, Warren E. Miller, and Donald E. Stokes. 1960. *The American Voter*. New York: Wiley.

   1966. *Elections and the Political Order*. New York: Wiley.

Cover, Albert D. and David Mayhew. 1977. "Congressional Dynamics and the Decline of Competitive Congressional Elections." In Lawrence C. Dodd and Bruce I. Oppenheimer, eds., *Congress Reconsidered*. New York: Praeger.

Cox, Gary W. and Jonathan N. Katz. 1996. "Why Did the Incumbency Advantage in US House Elections Grow?" *American Journal of Political Science* 40: 478–497.

   2002. *Elbridge Gerry's Salamander: The Electoral Consequences of the Reapportionment Revolution*. New York: Cambridge University Press.

Erikson, Robert. 1971. "The Incumbency Advantage in Congressional Elections." *Polity* 3: Spring, pp. 395–405.

   1972. "Malapportionment, Gerrymandering and Party Fortunes in Congressional Elections." *American Political Science Review* 65: December, pp. 1234–1245.

Erikson, Robert S. and Gerald C. Wright. 2000. "Representation of Constituency Ideology in Congress." In David Brady, John Cogan, and Morris Fiorina, eds., *Continuity and Change in Congressional Elections*. Stanford: Stanford University Press.

Erikson, Robert S. and Rocio Titiunik. 2015. "Using Regression Discontinuity to Uncover the Personal Incumbency Advantage." *Quarterly Journal of Political Science* 10: 101–119.

Erikson, Robert S. and Thomas R. Palfrey. 1998. "Campaign Spending Effects and Incumbency: An Alternative Simultaneous Equations Approach." *Journal of Politics* 60: May, pp. 355–373.

Ferejohn, John. 1977. "On the Decline in Competition in Congressional Elections. *American Political Science Review* 71: 166–176.

Fiorina, Morris. 1977. "The Case of the Vanishing Marginals: The Bureaucracy Did It." *American Political Science Review* 71: 177–181.

Fowler, Anthony and Andrew B. Hall. 2014. "Disentangling the Personal and Partisan Incumbency Advantages: Evidence from Close Elections and Term Limits." *Quarterly Journal of Political Science* 9: 501–531.

Gelman, Andrew and Gary King. 1990. "Estimating Incumbency Advantage without Bias." *American Journal of Political Science* 34(4): 1142–64.

  1991. "Systemic Consequences of Incumbency Advantage in US House Elections." *American Journal of Political Science* 35: 110–138.

Jacobson, Gary C. 1987. "The Marginals Never Vanished: Incumbency and Competition in Elections to the U.S. House of Representatives, 1952–1982. *American Journal of Poltiical Science* 31: 126–141.

  2015. " Its Nothing Personal: The Decline of the Incumbency Advantage in US House Elections ." *Journal of Politics*: 77: 861–873.

Lee, David S. 2008. "Randomized Experiments from Non-random Selection in U.S. House Elections." *Journal of Econometrics* 142(2): 675–697.

Levitt, Steven D. and Catherine D. Wolfram. 1997. "Decomposing the Sources of Incumbency Advantage in the U.S. House." *Legislative Studies Quarterly* 22 (1): 45–60.

Mayhew, David R. 1974a. *Congress: The Electoral Connection*. New Haven: Yale University Press.

  1974b. "Congressional Elections: The Case of the Vanishing Marginals." *Polity* 6: 3295–3317.

Rodden, Jonathan. 2010. "The Geographic Distribution of Political Preferences." *Annual Review of Political Science* 13: 297–340.

Tufte, Edward R. 1973. "The Relationship between Seats and Votes in Two-Party Systems." *American Political Science Review* 67: 549–553.

Zaller, John. 1998. "Politicians as Prize Fighters: Electoral Selection and Incumbency Advantage." In John Geer, ed., *Party Politics and Politicians*. Baltimore: Johns Hopkins University Press.

5

A Baseline for Incumbency Effects

Christopher H. Achen

THE PROBLEM

Incumbent presidents are often reelected. In the United States, approximately two-thirds of presidents who run for a second term are successful (Mayhew 2008). Just as American Members of Congress usually enjoy a "sophomore surge," winning their second election more easily than their first, so also incumbent presidents often coast to reelection. The standard interpretation of their second-round success is that they exploit office holding to bias the electorate in their favor. Media exposure and familiarity make them appear "presidential" in ways that challengers cannot match. In the Congressional case, the franking privilege (free mailing), constituency service, media exposure, and the resulting name recognition are all said to contribute to incumbent advantage. On this view, winning begets winning, in ways that may be worrisome for the health of democratic institutions.

One difficulty with this interpretation of incumbent advantage, as many have pointed out, is that it ignores the selection effect of prior victories. A champion prizefighter is likely to win his next match, not because of any incumbency benefit due to holding the title, but because a champion has already

In 2004, David Mayhew presented an early version of Mayhew (2008) to the Center for Political Studies, Princeton University. Stimulated by his work, this paper was given at a conference, Representation and Governance in Honor of David Mayhew, at the Center for the Study of American Politics, Yale University, New Haven, CT, May 30–31, 2013. Audience members made many insightful comments. Steve Ansolabehere, Doug Rivers, Henry Brady, Eric Schickler, and Alan Gerber provided subsequent advice and suggestions. David Mayhew gave me the benefit of a particularly close reading of a first draft, which saved me from errors of fact and interpretation. As my discussant at the New Haven conference, Larry Bartels produced a trenchant statistical critique of my argument, which I reply to in the text. I thank him for sharing his data, and I am grateful to all these colleagues for their assistance. The responsibility for remaining errors is my own.

proved that he is a great boxer. In the same way, political incumbents have almost always defeated other contenders at the polls to attain their current position.[1] Hence they are likely to be better-than-average candidates when they run again.

Two important articles have explored this aspect of incumbent electoral advantage. Zaller (1998) reviews the literature in detail, shows the empirical limitations of the conventional wisdom, initiates the boxing analogy, and skillfully lays out the substantive argument for electoral selection. Mayhew (2008) provides a sophisticated discussion of presidential incumbency advantages, including selection effects. He also compiles the full list of American presidential elections, with historical commentary, showing how often parties retain the office with and without incumbents running.

Because they have already proven themselves to be superior candidates at least once, incumbents will win reelection more than half the time even if there are no electoral advantages due to office holding itself. To demonstrate electoral bias due purely to incumbency, therefore, a researcher must show that reelection rates exceed the baseline rate due to selection effects. But what is that rate? How is it affected by the number of prior incumbent terms? And by the existence of primary elections?

This chapter demonstrates that these questions have a relatively simple mathematical answer under canonical assumptions about random selection of candidates. The analysis also gives insight into circumstances in which the simple answer will fail. The argument applies to electoral competition generally, for example to U.S. House and Senate races, where incumbents are usually returned to office (Erikson 1971; Mayhew 1974). However, coattail effects and House redistricting make the analysis of Congressional incumbency complex. The analysis here will therefore focus on the presidency.[2]

The only closely related prior investigation seems to be Rivers (1988), who was both the first to notice the selection effect of incumbency and the first to model it.[3] Alternate models of incumbency bias have also been proposed, for example, one-period reelection effects derived within the spatial modeling tradition, in which the voters have ideological preferences, the candidates have an "ability" dimension that may be due to a talent for constituency service, and challengers enter endogenously (e.g., Londregan and Romer 1993; Ashworth and Bueno de Mesquita 2008).

---

[1] The exceptions are incumbents appointed to office on the death or resignation of the previous officeholder.

[2] Boxing presents challenges for modeling, too: Champions can sometimes pick their opponent, while at other times they are required to face the highest-ranked challenger.

[3] Rivers (1988) is an unpublished paper not known to me at the time the present work was first drafted and which I have not yet seen. The author reports that it obtained some of the same results.

THE INTUITION

Suppose that candidates for a political office can be ordinally ranked in electoral appeal. That is, if candidate A would defeat candidate B under majority rule, and if candidate B would defeat candidate C, then A would defeat C. Downsian competition on a one-dimensional issue space ensures this kind of transitivity, for example. Now as Condorcet taught us, no such assumption holds in all conceivable elections. In practice, however, when voters are asked to compare prominent candidates in pairwise competitions, intransitivities among electoral outcomes seem to be rare. For example, Brady (1990, 1033–1034) finds no collective intransitivities among 1984 Iowa Democratic Party caucus-goers in pairwise comparisons among eight presidential candidates.[4] Thus, this chapter sets aside the special cases in which transitivity fails and proceeds on the same assumption that is common in sports: The number one-ranked player is likely to beat any of the other contestants, the second-ranked player is favored to defeat all lower-ranked contenders, and so on.

Now consider the case of a one-term incumbent in a competitive district. Suppose that this incumbent defeated a single opponent last time and faces another single opponent at the present general election. If all three candidates are independent random draws from a single pool of candidates (strong challengers are not "scared off" by incumbents), with no one-sided party advantage and no electoral benefits of incumbency itself, what is the chance that the incumbent will be reelected?

The easiest route to the answer is to consider the current challenger's chances of winning. Under the present assumptions, the challenger wins only if he or she is more electable than the incumbent. Now the incumbent is known to be more electable than the first-round opponent, since the incumbent won that election. Hence by transitivity, if the second challenger defeats the incumbent, that challenger must have been the most electable among the three candidates. But since all three candidates are independent random draws from the same distribution, the probability that the second challenger is the best of them is just one-third. Thus the incumbent's chance of reelection is two-thirds. (A formal derivation appears in the Appendix.) That is, first-term incumbents should win 67 percent of the time even if there are no pure incumbency advantages apart from selection effects. As of 2014, American presidential incumbents have won 22 of 32 contests, or 69 percent (Mayhew 2008), suggesting that pure incumbency advantages for presidents are probably quite small.

---

[4] The theoretical literature on how often collective intransitivities occur under various assumptions about the distribution of voter preferences includes DeMeyer and Plott (1970) and Weisberg and Niemi (1982). Speaking of legislative voting rather than mass electorates, the latter two authors conclude that "on balance our analysis confirms the less systematic hunches of most political scientists that the paradox of voting [i.e., collective intransitivity] is by far the exception and not the rule" (p. 230).

Reelection rates should rise with more terms of incumbency. A two-term incumbent has already defeated two prior challengers, so that a successful challenger has to be the best of *four* candidates. Under the model, this makes the challenger's chances one-quarter, so that the reelection probability for the incumbent is three-quarters. If electabilities are constant over a career, then the reelection rate for an n–term incumbent running for an $(n + 1)$st term is easily seen to be:

$$\text{Pr(incumbent re-elected}|n \text{ prior terms)} = \frac{n+1}{n+2}$$

Of course, this implies that as the number of prior terms grows, incumbents whose electabilities are not altered by a bad economy, a failed war, poor health, old age, or scandal will be reelected with ever-higher probabilities, asymptoting at 100 percent probability of reelection.

ADDING PRIMARIES

American general elections are usually preceded by primary contests settled by plurality rule. Any number of candidates may compete. To extend the analysis to this case, suppose that each candidate's electability meets an independence of irrelevant alternatives (IIA) assumption: The winner of a primary conducted under plurality rule is also the candidate who would have defeated all the other primary candidates in pairwise majority-rule competition (Arrow 1951).[5] For present purposes, the important implication is that the winner of a primary has the highest electability among the primary candidates.

IIA is not easily tested in most American elections. Ordinarily, there is no way to prove that a primary winner was more electable than any of the other primary candidates, since the primary winner faces an entirely new candidate in the general election. However, runoff primaries in the American South provide a partial test. Runoffs are usually won by the plurality leader of the initial primary, as required by IIA. For example, writing in the early 1950s, Ewing (1953, 87, 97) found that 84 percent of the winners of the first primary were nominated outright: They were unopposed, won a majority, or their opponents withdrew. In 73 percent of the remaining cases, they won the runoff. Thus altogether, 96 percent of first-round primary winners became the eventual nominee. Bullock and Johnson (1985, 941) find similar results for Georgia three decades later. In sum, IIA appears to be an excellent approximation for

---

[5] In analyzing presidential elections in the following, we will be including elections in which the party nominee was chosen by a convention system, by a primary system, or by a mixture of the two. We will make the implicit assumption that whatever the system, whatever the number and sequence of primaries, and whatever the convention voting rule, the winner obeys an IIA condition. That is, the nominee who beats three or four other contenders would also have beaten each of them in a pairwise competition under the same rules.

most American races. It is adopted in what follows as the best simple hypothesis about primary winners.[6]

Now consider the case of two parties, each with its own primary. Suppose that for open seats, each primary has k candidates. As before, each candidate is an independent random draw from the same distribution. Each primary then has a winner, and those two candidates face each other in the general election. The winner of the general election then becomes the incumbent. Then by the IIA assumption, the new incumbent had the highest electability among the $2k$ candidates who ran in the two primaries.

In subsequent elections, assume that the out-party again conducts a primary with k contestants, each of whom is an independent random draw from the distribution of candidates. The incumbent is assumed to face no primary opposition. This last postulate is another imperfect representation of reality, of course, but it seems closer to the truth than any other simple alternative. Incumbent first-term presidents and incumbent members of Congress who are scandal-free and in good health are almost always renominated.[7]

Now consider the chance that a one-term incumbent will win reelection. The easiest route to the answer is to consider the chance that any one challenger will win both the primary and the general election. To win the primary, the challenger must be the best of those k contestants. To win the general election also, the challenger must be better than the incumbent, who has already proven to be the best of the $2k$ candidates who ran at the first election (k from each party). To repeat, the incumbent is assumed to have no primary challenger. Then to win the office, the challenger must be the best of $3k$ candidates altogether, which has probability $1/3k$.

There are k such out-party candidates with this same probability $1/3k$ of winning it all. The events in which they each win are disjoint, and thus their probabilities add. It follows that the probability that *some* out-party candidate will win the general election is one-third, and thus the incumbent has a two-thirds chance of reelection. This is the same result as before: one-term incumbents have a two-thirds chance to be reelected. Adding primaries makes no difference. And so long as the number of candidates in both parties' primaries is the same, the number of primary opponents makes no difference.

The Appendix proves this result formally, demonstrating that with the primary structure assumed here, all the previous results for electoral systems

---

[6] Lamis (1984) reports that Utah used runoff primaries from 1937 to 1947. A study of those elections would expand our understanding beyond the Southern experience.

[7] Among incumbent presidents, only the disastrous Franklin Pierce actively sought his party's nomination and was denied it. The other immediate pre–Civil War president, James Buchanan, had pledged himself to a single term in his inaugural address. No other healthy American incumbent president who had won the office himself, and who had not already publicly precluded a second term, has been denied the nomination (Mayhew 2008, 223–224). Thus a potential selection bias, in which incumbents who would have done poorly choose not to run, is not of major concern.

without primaries continue to hold. Thus the probability that an n-term incumbent will be reelected is $(n + 1)/(n + 2)$, regardless of whether there are primaries. Again, it makes no difference how crowded the primaries become, so long as the crowd is of equal size in both parties.[8] And, of course, a little random variation in the number of primary candidates will essentially average out across elections to the same result, so long as neither party's primaries are systematically more crowded.

PREDICTING PRESIDENTIAL REELECTION RATES

Defining the Sample

This chapter was stimulated by David Mayhew's finding that almost exactly two-thirds of all incumbent presidents running for reelection have been successful. He also found that as of 2005, the twenty-two presidential elections with no incumbent running divided exactly evenly between those in which the incumbent party kept the office and those in which it lost it. (The 2008 election dropped incumbent party success rates in open seats to 11/23, or 48 percent.) This electoral even-handedness may come as a surprise, as Mayhew (2008, 201–202) notes. One might have guessed instead that long periods of party dominance would raise incumbent party success rates above 50 percent. But they do not: party competition for the presidency has been close throughout American history. Since the model of this chapter assumes that new candidates are all draws from the same distribution, a 50 percent success rate for in-parties not running an incumbent is precisely the proportion predicted. The two-thirds success rate for incumbents is also the proportion predicted. Thus the historical record broadly supports the key assumptions of this chapter, so that applying the model in more detail to American presidential elections is plausible.

Testing the model more seriously requires that the sample of presidential elections be confined to those conducted in a manner not too distant from the model's assumptions. Mayhew (2008) focused his empirical tests on incumbency itself, regardless of how it was achieved. For his purposes, that made perfect sense: His goal was to assess how often incumbents win, regardless of how they attained office.

The logic of this chapter is somewhat different: It deals with electoral selection as a potential *cause* of incumbent success. Thus the relevant data set comprises those presidential incumbents who won the previous election. Vice presidents who become president because of the death or resignation of the incumbent have not gone through electoral selection in the sense used here. Thus T. Roosevelt in 1904, Coolidge in 1924, Truman in 1948, Ford in 1976,

---

[8] If incumbents face primary competition, they are more likely to win the general election if nominated, but less likely to be reelected overall. See the Appendix.

and L. B. Johnson in 1964 were running as incumbents, but they had not led a presidential ticket to victory previously. Hence for the purposes of assessing pure selection effects, they are counted as new candidates.

Second, the model is designed to explain electoral popularity, not the elite-based politics of the early republic. As Mayhew (2008, 208) remarks, "popular vote totals for president are nonexistent or worthless before the 1830s." For testing purposes, then, this chapter follows the usual scholarly convention and begins with the Andrew Jackson presidency, when mass electorates (i.e., white male adults) entered in full force.[9] The 1864 election in the midst of the Civil War is also dropped, since the South was not voting and thus the 1864 mandate came from a population quite different from the 1860 electorate, a dramatic violation of democratic continuity (and of the model's assumptions).

Third, because the model is not directed toward explaining the vagaries of the Electoral College, winners will be declared on the basis of the popular vote.[10] Thus Hayes in 1876 becomes a loser, while Cleveland in 1888 becomes a winner, even though the Electoral College outcome was the opposite in each case. Cleveland in 1892 had actually won the popular vote in both the two prior contests, so that he is counted here as having had a three out of four chance to win his third presidential election.

Fourth, the methods outlined in the Appendix may be used to show that prior losers are less likely to win when they run again. Thus new candidate Truman in 1948 had a two-thirds chance to defeat prior loser Dewey, as did Taft in 1908 against Bryan.[11] Humphrey is also given a two-thirds chance of defeating Nixon in 1968, since Nixon is conventionally treated as having lost the 1960 popular vote (but see Gaines 2001). Thus Nixon's probabilities of winning in his three races are one-half, one-third, and one-half, respectively. Similarly, just one president in the post-1830 period ran as an incumbent in spite of losing the previous popular vote and without facing the previous popular vote winner, namely G. W. Bush in 2004. He is coded here as a previous popular vote loser, that is, a candidate running who had actually lost the prior presidential popular vote contest and thus had only a one-third chance to win the popular vote in his second election.[12]

---

[9] But compare Mayhew (2008, 206–207), who argues that the earlier elections involved "vigorous participatory politics" and thus deserve to be included in studies of incumbent success. As is shown in the following, adopting that approach makes no difference to the conclusions of this chapter.

[10] One might argue that "electability" *means* winning the Electoral College, however odd or adventitious its outcome might be. But then one is forced to say that Benjamin Harrison was more electable than Cleveland in 1884, but less so in 1888. It seems more sensible to say that Cleveland, who won the popular vote both times, was more electable in each year.

[11] Bryan had lost twice previously, but against the same candidate (McKinley) both times, so that under the model's assumptions, there is no new information in the second prior loss.

[12] I have chosen to ignore previous failures to get a nomination when a candidate succeeds in getting a subsequent party nomination. Thus, for example, Douglas in 1860 and Reagan in

Fifth, a few first-time winners beat incumbents who had won the popular vote at the previous election. These challengers had only a one-third chance to win their first race, as we have seen. Having won it, however, they are easily shown to have a three-quarters chance to win a second term. Post-1830 candidates who gained office by beating a previous popular vote winner are Wilson, F. D. Roosevelt, Reagan, and Clinton, all of whom proved to be formidable vote-getters in their reelection campaigns. (W. H. Harrison also beat an incumbent who had won the popular vote at the previous election, but Harrison did not live to run again.) Extending the same logic as in the Appendix demonstrates that F. D. Roosevelt's election probabilities in his four races are one-third, three-quarters, four-fifths, and five-sixths, respectively.

Last, first-term popular vote winners Jackson, Van Buren, McKinley, and Eisenhower, along with Cleveland in his third race, all faced the same candidate they had defeated in the popular vote in the prior race. Thus in the deterministic model of this paper, their probability of winning the popular vote again is 100 percent. All won except Van Buren, who was saddled with the brutal Panic of 1837.

First Historical Test

The initial test sample comprises nineteen elections in which the winner of the prior popular vote was running again, as set out in Table 5.1. Summing the probabilities in both columns of Table 5.1 shows that 14.8 of these elections should have resulted in another popular vote victory for the winner of the previous popular vote, with 4.2 losses. In fact, 14 previous popular vote winners won it again, with 5 losses. Thus the model's forecasts are quite good. By this measure, the advantages of presidential incumbency apart from electoral selection seem to be quite small.

Second Historical Test

A second sample consists of all the other post-1830 elections in which no winner of the previous electoral vote was running. (See Table 5.2.) With four exceptions, these elections all give the prior vote-winning party a 50 percent chance of victory. The four exceptions include Taft and Truman, who faced a prior loser in their first race and thus had a two-thirds chance to continue their party's previous success. They both won. The other exceptions are Nixon in 1968 and G. W. Bush in 2004, who had each lost a previous popular vote,

1980 are not counted as previous losers even though both unsuccessfully sought their party's nomination in the previous presidential election. Dealing with those complications would require many doubtful historical judgments, especially in the pre-primary era, while making only a very small difference in overall predicted reelection rates.

TABLE 5.1 *Presidential Popular Vote Winners Post-1830*

When the Previous Popular Vote Winner Runs Again[1] (with win probability for
previous vote winner in brackets)

Previous Vote Winner Wins Again (14)	Previous Vote Winner Loses (5)
1832 Jackson [1]	1840 W. Harrison (defeats Van Buren) [1]
1872 Grant [2/3]	1912 Wilson (defeats Taft) [2/3]
1888 Cleveland# [2/3]	1932 F. D. Roosevelt (defeats Hoover) [2/3]
1892 Cleveland* [1]	1980 Reagan (defeats Carter) [2/3]
1900 McKinley [1]	1992 Clinton (defeats G. H. W. Bush) [2/3]
1916 Wilson [3/4]	
1936 F. D. Roosevelt [3/4]	
1940 F. D. Roosevelt [4/5]	
1944 F. D. Roosevelt [5/6]	
1956 Eisenhower [1]	
1972 Nixon [1/2]	
1984 Reagan [3/4]	
1996 Clinton [3/4]	
2012 Obama [2/3]	

\# lost Electoral College.
* nonincumbent; lost Electoral College in previous race.
[1] Lincoln's 1864 victory omitted due to dramatic change in the electorate – 11 Confederate states
not voting.

giving the Democrats a two-thirds chance to win the popular vote again.
However, these two Republicans both won.

Altogether there are twenty-six elections in this sample. The expected
number of victories for the prior vote winning party under the model is 13.7
(the sum of the probabilities in Table 5.2) versus 12.3 losses. The actual
numbers are 11 wins and 15 losses.[13] Again the model's fit is quite
respectable, indicating that the key assumption of the model, that candidates'
electabilities are a random draw from the same distribution, is a reasonable
approximation.[14]

---

[13] There may be some evidence here that repeat winning parties have an elevated chance to lose
when they run fresh candidates (Bartels and Zaller 2001). However, even if that point is correct,
it does not bear on the central concern of this chapter, which is the respective power of selection
versus pure incumbency advantage when the same candidate runs again.

[14] As Mayhew (2008, 209) says, these historical comparisons are "marshy," and not too much
should be made of small deviations from forecasts. For example, Mayhew notes that Garfield
won in 1880 by no more than 10,000 votes, perhaps as few as 2,000 or even fewer: No one
knows. If he had lost the popular vote, then in Table 5.2, the 1880 and 1884 elections would
move into the party continuity column, producing thirteen wins by the prior vote winning party
compared to the model forecast of 13.7.

TABLE 5.2. *Presidential Popular Vote Winners Post-1830*

When the Previous Popular Vote Winner Does Not Run Again (with win probability for previous vote winner if not 1/2)

Same Party Wins Popular Vote Again (11)	Other Party Wins (15)
1836 Van Buren	1844 Polk
1856 Buchanan	1848 Taylor
1868 Grant	1852 Pierce
1904 T. Roosevelt+	1860 Lincoln
1908 Taft [2/3]	1876 Tilden#
1924 Coolidge+	1880 Garfield
1928 Hoover	1884 Cleveland
1948 Truman+ [2/3]	1896 McKinley
1964 L. B. Johnson+	1920 Harding
1988 G. H. W. Bush	1952 Eisenhower
2000 Gore#	1960 Kennedy
	1968 Nixon [2/3]
	1976 Carter [defeats Ford+)
	2004 G. W. Bush& [2/3]
	2008 Obama

lost Electoral College.
+ incumbent who had run as vice–president on winning ticket in prior race.
& incumbent who lost popular vote in prior race.

Additional Historical Tests

To further separate mere incumbency from the selection effect, it is helpful to examine post-1830 candidates who were incumbents but who had not won the popular vote the previous time. These are vice presidents who succeeded to the office on the death or resignation of the president (Tyler in 1844, Fillmore in 1852, A. Johnson in 1868, Arthur in 1880, T. Roosevelt in 1904, Coolidge in 1924, Truman in 1948, L. B. Johnson in 1964, and Ford in 1976), plus candidates who had lost the popular vote the previous time but became president anyway (B. Harrison in 1892 and G. W. Bush in 2004). To avoid biased sampling of only the stronger politicians, we have counted former vice presidents who became incumbents as reelection candidates even if they failed to get the nomination for a second term (the first four), as well as those who were renominated (the last five).[15]

---

[15] In terms of the model, the vice presidents who became president are new candidates and thus are assumed to face primary competition in their first electoral contest for the presidential office. In this group, longstanding powerful politicians such as T .R. Roosevelt in 1904 and L. B. Johnson in 1964 faced only an "invisible primary" in which no one else in their party was foolish enough to challenge them.

All these men enjoyed the benefits of incumbency but none of the selection effects. If incumbency itself matters, their reelection rate (in terms of the popular vote) should look something like that of other incumbent presidents (two-thirds). On the other hand, if only selection effects are at work, they should be reelected at a rate of 50 percent, since in electoral terms they are untried new candidates. In fact, the expected reelection rate of 50 percent is too high for the final two incumbents, since they are proven losers. We expect a one-third success rate for Bush and a 0 percent chance for Harrison, since Harrison was running again against the same candidate who had defeated him the time before. In addition, Truman faced a prior loser and thus had a two-thirds chance of reelection. Summing these probabilities, we expect five winners of the popular vote among these eleven incumbents. In fact, exactly five (T. Roosevelt, Coolidge, Truman, L. B. Johnson, and G. W. Bush) won the popular vote and served another term. The other six lost. Again, this suggests that selection is the more powerful force, and that incumbency *per se* plays a much smaller role.

Finally, we might look at the incumbent presidents who faced the same opponent twice – Van Buren, Harrison, McKinley, and Eisenhower.[16] If incumbency itself matters, their second two-party vote share should be consistently higher than their first. The actual vote share changes from the first to the second election for these four presidents are −11.2, −1.3, 0.5, and 2.4. Even if we drop the first observation (the Van Buren loss stemming from the Panic of 1837), the average vote gain for the incumbent is just half a percentage point. Again, it is difficult to see much evidence for incumbency advantage beyond selection effects.

Extending the Sample Makes No Difference

Historical judgment is required in all these tests, and other sample definitions are defensible. For example, if elections before 1832 are included, as Mayhew does, then incumbents are reelected at a two-thirds rate in that period as well.[17] Added to Table 5.1, they would not disturb its message. And if we add the appropriate pre-1830 contests to Table 5.2 (races without the previous winner), the split moves closer to 50–50 between in-party and out-party, making the model fit that table even better than before.[18] In short, the model tests are insensitive to the inclusion of pre-1830 elections.

---

[16] Since we are dealing with vote shares here, we exclude J. Q. Adams, whose initial Electoral College victory (and second-place vote share) in a splintered four-way race occurred before the era of widespread white male enfanchisement. More than three times as many votes were cast in his second race as in his first, so that the vote shares at the two elections are derived from noncomparable electorates.

[17] In pre-1830 races with an incumbent, Washington in 1792, Jefferson in 1804, Madison in 1812, and Monroe in 1820 win, while J. Adams in 1800 and J. Q. Adams in 1828 lose.

[18] Among pre-1830 races with no incumbent, in-parties win all three races before 1830 (J. Adams in 1796, Madison in 1808, and Monroe in 1816). Adding these three in-party victories to Table 5.2 results in a 14–15 split between in-party and out-party victories.

One might also question whether the one-party reelections of 1792 and 1820 count as incumbent successes against the competition, or whether the four-way races of 1824 and 1860 or Democrat Wilson's win in the three-way contest against two former Republican presidents in 1912 should be included in tests of a two-party model. Similarly, one may ask whether Chester Arthur in 1884 was too ill to be considered a competitor who lost the intraparty nomination battle, whether Kennedy was truly the popular vote winner in 1960, and several other questions. But these historical imponderables do not affect the probabilities in any consistent way. Resolving all these issues would have only small net effects, and they would not alter the conclusion that electoral selection predominates over the advantages of office in explaining presidential reelection rates.

What seems clear is that when one-term presidential winners run again (whether winning is defined as capturing the Electoral College or the popular vote), the chance that they will win again has historically been very near two-thirds. And when two candidates meet who have not run previously, the chance that the incumbent party will be victorious has been very near 50 percent. Both those fractions constitute the model forecast when there are no complications due to prior races by the same candidates. The sample sizes in all these tests are too small for overweening confidence, of course, as Mayhew (2008, 213) demonstrates. As he suggests (2008, 226), further work with larger samples of appropriate high visibility two-party races (perhaps American senatorial or gubernatorial elections in competitive states), done with appropriate contextual sensitivity, might improve our understanding of the advantages of incumbency.

TESTS USING VOTE SHARE

Thus far, the tests of the model have focused on wins and losses. A natural extension is to examine vote shares. Politicians who win big are conventionally thought to be stronger competitors than those who squeak into office. Hence if the model of this chapter is correct, presidential candidates who run twice should tend to have similar vote shares each time – not identical, because they typically face different opponents and different economic conditions each time, but nevertheless similar shares. On the other hand, two different candidates of the same party running for the same office in adjacent elections should have unrelated vote shares. Now in practice, this pattern will be modified slightly, since periods of party dominance will induce a small correlation between the shares of two different candidates of the same party. But that association should be dwarfed by the correlation when the same candidate runs twice.

In both cases, the statistical model to be estimated is

$$y_t = \alpha + \beta y_{t-1} + \varepsilon_t \qquad (5.1)$$

where y_t is a measure of vote strength at a presidential election, y_{t-1} is the corresponding value at the previous election, ε_t is an error term, and α and β are coefficients to be estimated. The model of this chapter predicts that β will be a substantial fraction when the same candidate runs at both times t and $t-1$, while β will be much smaller when there is no repeat contestant.

The first question is how to measure y_t. Electoral strength is most commonly computed as the share of the two-party vote, and this paper follows that tradition. Some scholars prefer the margin (the percentage point gap between the winner and the second-place finisher). When just two parties contest the election, these two measures are linear transformations of each other, and the choice between them makes no difference. The problem enters when third and fourth parties get substantial proportions of the vote. Either two-party shares or margins can be misleading in that case, depending on which major party is the principal source of the minor party votes. To avoid those situations, presidential elections in which the top two vote-getters received less than 85 percent of the vote have been set aside in all the subsequent analyses of this section.

The second issue that arises in defining y_t is less familiar. In statistical studies of presidential vote shares, y_t often refers to the incumbent's vote. That seems the natural way to proceed here; it has worked well in other contexts. However, in the presence of a lagged dependent variable, the conventional approach creates a subtle statistical problem. Incumbent vote shares have a special character: Presidents are much more likely to lose votes dramatically in their second election than to gain them dramatically. Four of the five largest changes in incumbent vote shares are negative, including the largest (Hoover's eighteen-point drop in 1932).[19] That negative skewness matters because incumbents' prior vote shares are nearly all above 50 percent. (That is how they won.) Hence large prior votes are associated with negative vote shifts. The result is that a substantial negative correlation is induced between prior vote shares and the disturbance term. By well-known results in econometric theory, the consequence is that the impact of prior vote shares on current vote shares is biased: it will be seriously underestimated. Hence prior electoral strength will seem not to carry over from one election to the next, which in turn would imply that the model of this chapter is overstated or mistaken.[20] But that critique of the model is incorrect due to the bias in the estimator.

To avoid the bias, the dependent variable here will be defined in a natural time series fashion as the Democratic candidate's share of the two-party vote.

---

[19] Van Buren lost 11.2 points in 1840 from his previous showing, F. D. Roosevelt lost 7.5 in 1940, Nixon gained 11.4 in 1972, and Carter lost 6.4 in 1980. Overall, in presidential elections with a previously elected incumbent running, the skewness in vote share changes is −0.8, with kurtosis = 3.8. That is, vote share changes are skewed left with somewhat long tails.

[20] This was the argument advanced by my discussant, Larry Bartels, at the Yale conference in honor of David Mayhew. Discussants must work quickly, and their task is to suggest counter-arguments and to point in new directions, not to work out the author's econometrics. I thank Larry very much for encouraging me to look closely at the vote returns and to think harder about their implications.

Since both Democratic and Republican incumbents sometimes suffer dramatic losses in vote share, those losses can either raise or lower the Democratic vote. Hence the correlation between prior Democratic vote and the disturbance term is minimized, leaving slope estimates and correlations (asymptotically) unbiased.

To further improve the estimates by removing large outliers in this small data set, some regressions reported in the following will control for or remove the three elections occurring in the worst depressions in U.S. history, the contests of 1840, 1876, and 1932, corresponding to the Panic of 1837, the Panic of 1873, and the Great Depression, respectively. The last two are the only post–Civil War contractions of more than 40 months (peak to trough) that overlap a presidential election (National Bureau of Economic Research 2010). The first panic predates good economic data but appears on the basis of contemporary reports to have been the worst until the Great Depression (Roberts 2013).[21] Thus "recession" is a dummy variable for the recession elections of 1840, 1876, and 1932, with its sign reversed when the incumbent is a Republican (because Democrats gain in those years). Thus recession = 1 in 1840, −1 in 1876 and 1932, and is zero otherwise. Coded in this manner, its coefficient is expected to be negative.

Table 5.3 sets out several regression estimates based on Equation (A.1) in the Appendix to this chapter when no repeat candidate is running, including both ordinary least squares (OLS) and, to cope with the long-tailed distribution of the error term, the more robust minimum absolute deviations (MAD) estimator. Again, the full sample consists of post-1830 elections in which both the current vote and the lagged vote can be meaningfully computed, that is, when the two main parties get 85 percent or more of the total vote. For ease of interpretation, vote shares are expressed as percentages, and they have been scaled as deviations from 50 percent, which is very close to the average Democratic party vote throughout the sample. Thus the intercept picks up systematic Democratic advantage expressed in percentage points; it should be near zero throughout. The lag coefficient estimates the proportion of a party's above- or below-average performance at one election that is carried forward to a different candidate of the same party at the second election. We expect the lag slope to be quite small in Table 5.3.

Table 5.3 shows, as the model predicts, that the previous party vote share does not predict the current election outcome when new candidates run. Controlling for major recessions makes no difference. (There is only one major recession year in the sample of Table 5.3, so that controlling for it is equivalent

---

[21] The Panic of 1884 was milder, occurring during a contraction of 38 months duration beginning in 1882. No other recession overlapping a presidential election since 1857 has come close to forty months in duration, including the Great Recession, which began officially in December 2007 (National Bureau of Economic Research 2010).

TABLE 5.3 *Predictors of Democrats' Two-Party Vote Share*

Years 1832–2012. No repeat candidate running.

	OLS		MAD	
Lag	0.136	0.158	−0.022	−0.022
Stnd. Error	0.225	0.234	0.258	0.252
Recession		−3.08		−1.44
Stnd. Eerror		6.22		6.69
Intercept	−0.513	−0.650	−0.067	−0.067
Stnd. Error	1.36	1.42	1.56	1.52
R2/Pseudo-R2	0.02	0.04	0.002	0.02
Adjusted R2	−0.04	−0.08	–	–
σ	5.82	5.95	–	–
N	19	19	19	19

to dropping it.) Throughout the table, the estimated lag coefficients are tiny and far from statistically significant, and the R^2 values are vanishingly small – about what one would expect from a random number generator. The intercept estimates are all less than a percentage point in absolute value and statistically insignificant, as expected. The more robust MAD estimator finds even less evidence of predictive power. In sum, once again, the evidence here firmly supports the model's assumption that new candidates are a random draw from the pool of all candidates.

Tables 5.4a and 5.4b repeat the analysis using the election years in which at least one candidate had run at the previous election. In this part of the sample, there are two major recession years, so that controlling for recessions and deleting them from the sample are different; the table presents both results. Also included is a variable representing incumbency (+1 for Democrats, –1 for Republicans) to estimate the pure impact of incumbency net of selection effects.

The pattern in Tables 5.4a and 5.4b is quite different from that of Table 5.3. When the same candidate runs again, the vote share from the previous election is a powerful, statistically significant predictor of the current vote share, with a coefficient typically near unity. Controlling for major recessions or deleting them makes no difference, nor does using a robust estimator. By contrast, incumbency itself has a tiny estimated effect of one percentage point or less, not close to statistical significance. As noted earlier, pure incumbency effects of this magnitude are similar to what one sees in election pairs with the same two candidates facing each other both times. The office itself adds very little.

TABLE 5.4A *OLS Predictors of Democrats' Two-Party Vote Share*

Years 1832–2012. At least one repeat candidate running.

			Recessions Out	
Lag	0.548*	1.04***	1.10***	0.836**
Stnd. Error	0.278	0.228	0.211	0.355
Recession		-15.0***		-14.6***
Stnd. Error		3.65		3.74
Incumbent				1.36
Stnd. Error				1.76
Intercept	-0.902	-1.65	-2.43**	-1.42
Stnd. Error	1.58	1.12	1.10	1.17
R2	0.21	0.64	0.68	0.66
Adjusted R2	0.15	0.59	0.65	0.58
$\hat{\sigma}$	6.28	4.38	4.01	4.44
N	17	17	15	17

* significant at 0.10;
** significant at 0.05;
*** significant at 0.01.

Presidents tend to get the same vote share at their second election that they received the first time.[22]

Thus in presidential elections, candidate strength matters a great deal; incumbency at most only a little. Selection effects are most of the value of incumbency. That is precisely what the model of this chapter predicts.

CONCLUSION

Under the assumptions that all candidates are independent random draws from a common distribution, and that electability in two-party majority rule competition is constant over a career and forms a transitive scale (if A beats B, and B beats C, then A beats C), this chapter has shown that n–term incumbents will be reelected with probability $(n + 1)/(n + 2)$. Adding primaries makes no difference: If nonincumbent candidates must first win a k-candidate primary to become the general election challenger against the incumbent, while

---

[22] A pure version of the model in the appendix would predict a lag coefficient of 0.5 rather than the 1.0 that is observed. Whether the voters reward those incumbents who avoid recessions or whether strong incumbents draw weaker challengers at their second election is a subject for further investigation.

TABLE 5.4B *MAD Predictors of Democrats' Two-Party Vote Share*

Years 1832–2012. At least one repeat candidate running.

	Recessions Out			
Lag	1.00**	1.12***	1.12***	1.16*
Stnd. Error	0.448	0.339	0.256	0.633
Recession		−10.4*		−10.5
Stnd. Error		5.41		6.67
Incumbent				−0.228
Stnd. Error				3.14
Intercept	−1.50	−1.78	−1.78	−1.78
Stnd. Error	2.55	1.66	1.33	2.09
Pseudo-R2	0.25	0.47	0.52	0.47
N	17	17	15	17

* significant at 0.10;
** significant at 0.05;
*** significant at 0.01.

incumbents face primary competition only when they run the first time (when they themselves are not yet incumbents), and if primary winners are the strongest electorally among the primary contestants, then the same reelection probabilities hold. With the customary caveats imposed by small samples, the model seems to predict historical presidential reelection rates quite well. In turn, this suggests that the relentless publicity generated by presidential campaigns minimizes the electoral advantages of office holding.

A variety of statistical tests confirmed the underlying logic of the model, demonstrating that its predictive success is no accident. In particular, "electability" does seem to be a property of candidates, not parties. Thus presidents who win big the first time are more likely to win big the second time, while the vote share of each successful new candidate is unrelated to the vote share obtained by his or her party at the previous election.

This model of electoral selection is a simple baseline. It is obviously not a full theoretical or empirical account of incumbency, nor is it meant to be. Even as a baseline, this very simple structure will fail to predict accurately when its assumptions do not hold. For example, and most importantly, uncompetitive districts should have higher reelection rates than those predicted here (Zaller 1998, 164–165), as should entrenched incumbents in low-visibility races. In such districts, challengers draw their electabilities from a different distribution with a lower mean than the distribution that generates incumbents. Hence incumbents will tend to stay in office longer than the model of this chapter predicts.[23] Many contemporary American congressional districts fit this pattern, with incumbents replaced only when their electability is changed by retirement, ill health, scandal, or substantial electoral tides. House reelection rates between 1982 and 1990 were 95 percent for one-term incumbents, for example, and fully 84 percent for one-term incumbents even in competitive districts (Zaller 1998, 164).[24] Modeling reelection rates in such circumstances would require extensions of the model, as would applications to multiparty systems, especially those with proportional representation.

The empirical evidence in this chapter derives entirely from presidential elections. That small evidentiary base encourages modesty about causal claims. Nonetheless, on the basis of Zaller's (1998) arguments and those of other scholars, along with the findings reported in this chapter, it seems quite likely that electoral selection is a powerful force for presidential reelection, dwarfing the effect of pure office holding. As a profession, we owe thanks to David Mayhew for pointing out, in a series of publications, the questions and the evidence that have led to this quite different way of thinking about incumbency.

Appendix

The result used throughout this chapter answers this question: Suppose that candidates can be ranked by their electability. Then if candidate A is the best (most electable) of k_1 independently drawn candidates from a common distribution, and if B is the best of another such sample of k_2 additional candidates drawn from the same distribution independently of the first group, then what is the probability that A is better than B? The following proposition shows that this probability does not depend on the form of the distribution function (df).

Proposition. Let x^* be a scalar random variable with twice-differentiable distribution function $F = F(x)$ and density $f = f(x)$.[25] Let $\{x_{11}, x_{12}, ..., x_{1k_1}\}$ and $\{x_{21}, x_{22}, ..., x_{2k_2}\}$ be two finite independent random samples of size k_1 and k_2 respectively, drawn from F, and mutually independent of each other. Set $x_1^m = \max\{x_{11}, x_{12}, ..., x_{1k_1}\}$ and $x_2^m = \max\{x_{21}, x_{22}, ..., x_{2k_2}\}$. Then

---

[23] However, as Zaller notes, factional competition in primaries sometimes replaces general election competition in one-party districts, preventing incumbents from being responsible only to the Grim Reaper.

[24] At the other extreme, in a country with a decades-long stagnant economy, most incumbent leaders might lose. Incumbency would then become a disadvantage.

[25] For precise mathematical definitions of a random variable, a distribution function, and a density, see any text on probability or statistical theory. A classic, thoughtful exposition is Cramer (1946, 56–58, 151–154).

$$\Pr\left(x_1^m > x_2^m\right) = \frac{k_1}{k_1 + k_2}. \tag{A.1}$$

Note that twice-differentiability for F means that f is differentiable and hence continuous. Thus ties in candidate electability occur only on a set of measure zero, and the possibility of ties may be set aside.

An initial lemma is helpful. It is a special case of a standard result in basic statistical theory, the distribution of the quantiles of a sample (e.g., Cramer 1946, 370):

Lemma. Under the conditions of the proposition, the random variable defined as the largest of k independent random draws from F, namely $x^m = \max\{x_1, x_2, ..., x_k\}$, has density kfF^{k-1}.

Proof. The probability that any given observation, say x_1, is the largest of k independent observations from F is just the probability that the other $k - 1$ observations are smaller, that is, $F^{k-1}(x_1)$. Second, the density of a given observation x_1 is $f(x_1)$. Hence by Bayes' Theorem, the density for the largest of k_1 draws from F is proportional to the product of these two quantities, fF^{k-1}.[26] To find the normalizing constant for this density, use integration by parts ($\int g'h = gh - \int gh'$), and then the defining properties of distribution functions:

$$\int_{-\infty}^{\infty} f(x)F^{k-1}(x)\,dx = F^k(x)\Big|_{-\infty}^{\infty} - (k-1)\int_{-\infty}^{\infty} f(x)F^{k-1}(x) \tag{A.2}$$

$$= 1 - (k-1)\int_{-\infty}^{\infty} f(x)F^{k-1}(x)\,dx \tag{A.3}$$

Solving gives $\displaystyle\int_{-\infty}^{\infty} f(x)F^{k-1}(x)\,dx = 1/k$, so that the normalizing constant is just k, and the proof is complete.

Turn now to the proof of the proposition:

Proof. The probability that a given observation is larger than k_2 other independent random observations from the df F is F^{k_2}. By the lemma, the density of observations that are the largest of k_1 independent random observations is $k_1fF^{k_1-1}$. Hence the probability that an observation that is the largest of k_1 observations exceeds the largest of an independent random sample of k_2 observations is given by the integral of the product of these two quantities. But the integral is of the same form as that in the Lemma, and so:

---

[26] That is, if L denotes the event that x_1 is the largest of the k draws, then $f(x_1|L) = f(L|x_1)f(x_1)/ \Pr(L)$. But $\Pr(L)$ is a constant, so that $f(x_1|L) \propto f(L|x_1)f(x_1)$.

$$\Pr\left(x_1^m > x_2^m\right) = k_1 \int_{-\infty}^{\infty} f(x) F^{k_1+k_2-1}(x)\, dx \tag{A.4}$$

$$= \frac{k_1}{k_1 + k_2} \tag{A.5}$$

Recall that we have assumed that incumbents running for the first time face k challengers in their own party primary. After n terms, they have also defeated n challengers from the other party, each of whom by assumption was the best of k primary challengers. Hence incumbents are the best of $(n + 1)k$ candidates, while the current challenger is the best of k. The following corollary is then a routine consequence of the Proposition.

Corollary. Let "n-term incumbent electability" denote the largest of $(n + 1)k$ independent random draws from the df F, and let "challenger electability" denote the largest of another k independent random draws from the same df. Then the probability that the n-term incumbent electability exceeds the challenger electability is $(n + 1)/(n + 2)$.

REMARKS

1. The Corollary can be used to establish the distribution of the length of incumbent careers, as in Zaller's (1998, 156–164) simulations. Thus one-third of incumbents should lose their first reelection attempt and thereby serve only one term; another group should win their first reelection campaign and lose the second, thus serving two terms, which has probability $(2/3)(1/4) = 1/6$; and in general, it is easily shown that the probability of serving exactly n terms is $2/[(n + 1)(n + 2)]$. Empirically, however, these baseline calculations need to be limited in two respects. First, they will not apply to uncompetitive districts or to nearly invisible campaigns against familiar incumbents. Second, electabilities may not be constant as incumbents enter old age and choose to retire, or are defeated by more vigorous opponents. In that case, the forecasts will be inaccurate for older incumbents. Hence empirical tests should focus on competitive districts with visible challengers and should use a right-censored version of the implied distribution, with elderly incumbents omitted. Some allowance for electoral tides would also be needed.

2. The Proposition can also be used to find reelection rates under assumptions different from those of the current chapter. For example, suppose, somewhat implausibly, that incumbents face k new primary competitors every election (rather than just being one of k new competitors at their first primary contest and then being unchallenged in primaries afterward). Then an n-term incumbent will be the best of $(2n + 1)k$ candidates after winning the current primary. Challengers will continue to be the best of k candidates. Hence by the Proposition, the reelection

rate for incumbents, conditional on winning the primary, will be $(2n + 1)/(2n + 2)$, which is higher than under the Corollary. For example, one-term incumbents who are renominated will win 75 percent of their general election contests. Note, however, that incumbents with continuing primary competition also have only probability $(2n)/(2n + 1)$ of winning the primary $(n \geq 1)$. Hence the chance to win both the primary and the general election is $[2n(2n + 1)]/[(2n + 1)(2n + 2)] = n/(n + 1)$, and this is obviously smaller than $(n + 1)/(n + 2)$. Under the model, then, more primary competition for incumbents reduces their reelection rates, as it should.

3. When electability is measured on an interval or ratio scale, for example by the vote shares or logistic transformations of vote shares, the approach used thus far has the advantage that it makes testable predictions about the shape of the vote share distribution for incumbents of varying length of service. However, when electability is unmeasured except by wins and losses, a simpler method of derivation is to observe that "electability" is an unmeasured, purely ordinal concept in that case, so that its scale may be modified in any smooth (i.e., differentiable) manner without altering any of its properties used in the proofs. In particular, if F is the original df for x^*, we may transform x^* to $x^{\#} = F(x^*)$. The resulting random variable has support only on the unit interval, and it is uniformly distributed. Hence there is no loss in assuming from the beginning that the distribution of electabilities is uniform. In that case, $F(x) = x$, $f(x) = 1$, and the proofs here may be done with beginner's calculus – a possible class assignment for those otherwise dull calculus reviews in political science graduate school "math camp."

To see the simpler mathematics of the uniformly distributed case, begin with the probability that an initial-term incumbent is reelected. Now first, the probability that a candidate with electability x defeats a randomly chosen opponent is the probability of drawing a new electability value less than x, which in the uniformly distributed case is just x. Thus by Bayes' Theorem, the electability of a first-time winner has density f proportional to x, a triangular distribution with domain and range (height and width) both equal to one. Hence from elementary geometry, the normalizing constant must be 2, making the density of electabilities among first-term incumbents $2x$. Next, the probability that an incumbent with electability x defeats a new randomly drawn challenger is again x. Then by the usual rule for computing a mean, the probability that the incumbent will be reelected is the product of these two quantities integrated over the range of the density. This yields:

$$\int_0^1 2x^2 dx = (2/3)x^3 \Big|_0^1 = 2/3. \tag{A.6}$$

REFERENCES

Arrow, Kenneth. 1951. *Social Choice and Individual Values*. New York: Wiley.

Ashworth, Scott, and Ethan Bueno de Mesquita. 2008. Electoral Selection, Strategic Challenger Entry, and the Incumbency Advantage. *Journal of Politics* 70, 4 (Oct.): 1006–1025.

Bartels, Larry M., and John Zaller. 2001. Presidential Vote Models: A Recount. *PS: Political Science and Politics* 34, 1 (Mar.): 8–20.

Brady, Henry E. 1990. Dimensional Analysis of Ranking Data. *American Journal of Political Science* 34: 1017–1048.

Bullock, Charles S., III, and Loch K. Johnson. 1985. Runoff Elections in Georgia. *The Journal of Politics* 47: 937–946.

Cramer, Harald. 1946. *Mathematical Methods of Statistics*. Princeton: Princeton University Press.

DeMeyer, Frank, and Charles R. Plott. 1970. The Probability of a Cyclical Majority. *Econometrica* 38: 345–354.

Erikson, Robert. 1971. The Advantage of Incumbency in Congressional Elections. *Polity* 3: 395–405.

Ewing, Cortez A. M. 1953. *Primary Elections in the South*. Norman: University of Oklahoma Press.

Gaines, Brian J. 2001. Popular Myths about Popular Vote-Electoral College Splits. *PS: Political Science and Politics* 34, 1 (Mar.): 70–75.

Lamis, Alexander P. 1984. The Runoff Primary Controversy: Implications for Southern Politics. *PS: Political Science and Politics* 17: 782–787.

Londregan, John, and Thomas Romer. 1993. Polarization, Incumbency, and the Personal Vote. In W. A. Barnett et al., eds., *Political Economy: Institutions, Competition, and Representation*, Cambridge: Cambridge University Press, pp. 355–377.

Mayhew, David R. 1974. Congressional Elections: The Case of the Vanishing Marginals. *Polity* 6: 295–317.

2008. Incumbency Advantage in U.S. Presidential Elections: The Historical Record. *Political Science Quarterly* 123, 2: 201–228.

National Bureau of Economic Research. 2010. US Business Cycle Expansions and Contractions, www.nber.org/cycles/cyclesmain.html, accessed March 23, 2014.

Rivers, Douglas. 1988. Partisan Representation in Congress. Paper presented at the Seminar on Congressional Elections, University of California, Los Angeles.

Roberts, Alasdair. 2013. *America's First Great Depression*. Ithaca, New York: Cornell University Press.

Weisberg, Herbert F., and Richard G. Niemi. 1982. Probability Calculations for Cyclical Majorities in Congressional Voting. In Richard G. Niemi and Herbert F. Weisberg, eds., *Probability Models of Collective Decision Making*, Columbus, Ohio: Charles E. Merrill Publishing, pp. 204–231.

Zaller, John. 1998. Politicians as Prize Fighters: Electoral Selection and Incumbency Advantage. In John G. Geer, ed., *Politicians and Party Politics*, Baltimore: Johns Hopkins University Press, pp. 125–185.

PART II

CONTINUITY AND CHANGE IN PARTY ORGANIZATIONS

6

Legislative Parties in an Era of Alternating Majorities

Frances E. Lee

> Alternation in party control has at least temporarily ceased, with the Democrats becoming something of a "party of state" at the congressional level; in both houses unbroken Democratic control in the years 1955–74 has set durability records unmatched since the rise of the two-party system in the 1830s.
>
> David R. Mayhew (1974), 103–104

The reemergence of party competition for control of Congress is undoubtedly one of the most significant changes in the American political landscape since *Congress: The Electoral Connection* was published in 1974. For decades before 1980 the Democrats were, to all appearances, simply Congress's natural majority party. Even after President Richard Nixon won one of the largest popular vote shares ever recorded in a presidential election, Democrats in 1973 still held 57 Senate seats and 291 House seats; those margins grew substantially larger after the 1974 midterms. With the exception of two Congresses, the 80th (1947–48) and the 83rd (1953–54), Democrats maintained both House and Senate majorities from 1933 until 1981.

Democrats were not merely the congressional majority party during this half-century; they were an overwhelmingly dominant party most of the time, holding on average 60 percent of House and Senate seats and, with some regularity, majorities of 2:1. Given such persistent and predictable Democratic majorities, caucus organization and effort did not appear necessary for Democrats to continue in power, and stronger organization seemed unlikely to significantly improve Republican chances of winning a majority. It is not surprising, in such an environment, that key elements of the party system in Congress atrophied.

I thank Kelsey Hinchliffe for excellent research assistance on this project. For comments on earlier drafts, I am grateful to the editors of this volume, as well as to Morris Fiorina, Emery Lee, David Karol, Kris Miler, Irwin Morris, Konrad Mugglestone, Walter Oleszek, and Ric Uslaner.

Competition is a powerful spur to party organization (Schlesinger 1985; 1991). In this sense, 1980 represents a turning point. In the elections of that year, Republicans "shocked even themselves by winning a Senate majority for the first time since 1954" ("The Senator from Tennessee" 1981). Republicans gained twelve Senate seats, thirty-five House seats, and won the presidency in an Electoral College landslide. In the wake of those elections, the first since the New Deal in which Republicans captured the presidency with a candidate from the conservative wing of the party, Republicans began to see themselves as a fully viable national alternative to the Democratic Party, a party that should not have to settle for minority status any longer.

Congressional Republicans of early 1981 even "talked optimistically about winning control of the House next year and increasing their margin in the Senate" (Roberts 1981). It would, of course, be fourteen more years before Republicans won a House majority. But, in the interim, a band of insurgents under the leadership of Rep. Newt Gingrich (R-GA) steadily gained sway within the House Republican conference (Arieff 1979; Remini 2006, 457–485). In 1983, Gingrich founded the Conservative Opportunity Society, relentlessly arguing to his colleagues that a Republican majority was within reach. As a means of winning the majority, he urged fellow Republicans to organize themselves to forcefully confront the Democrats (Roberts 1983). Gingrich would go on to claim vindication of his strategy when he assumed the House speakership after the 1994 elections.

After the losses of their chamber majorities in 1980 and 1994, Democrats never came to see themselves as a permanent minority. Instead, Democrats constantly stayed within striking distance of a return to power. They never held fewer than 44 Senate seats or 188 House seats between 1980 and 2017.

In short, competition for party control of Congress has been a more-or-less continuous reality since 1980. Control of the Senate shifted seven times during this period, with Democrats and Republicans each in the majority for nine Congresses. Control of the House of Representatives shifted three times, also with Democrats and Republicans each in the majority for nine Congresses. In both House and Senate during the post-1980 period, the majority party's average margin of control was roughly one-half the size of the majority's average margin between 1932 and 1980. "Alternation in party control" thus returned to a central place in congressional politics.

This paper argues that the continuous prospects for change in party control have altered congressional incentives. In a world where the overall institutional division of party power is largely taken for granted, members would understandably focus solely on their own individual reelection prospects. But in a world where party control of Congress is an open question, members have strong reasons to create and empower party organizations in hopes of affecting their party's overall fate. Members of Congress unquestionably have multiple goals, including personal power, reelection, and good public policy (Fenno 1973). Despite this complexity, Mayhew (1974) demonstrates the utility of a thought experiment giving primacy to the reelection goal. What can we understand about Congress better, he asks, if we assume that members are "single minded seekers of reelection" (Mayhew 1974, 5–6)? In this paper, I analyze congressional politics and institutional development giving primacy to the goal of winning and holding party majorities. What can we learn about congressional organization and behavior if we assume that members are seekers of partisan majorities?

To advance this analysis, this paper first details the strategies legislative parties employ to make the case for majority status, including their use of both programmatic legislation and partisan communications. Second, it takes stock of the volume and content of partisan communication in the contemporary Congress. Concepts identified in *Congress: The Electoral Connection* to understand individual members' reelection efforts – namely, advertising, credit claiming, and position taking – prove no less valuable for understanding partisan communications. Third, the paper traces the institutional development of legislative parties since 1960. In particular, the period since 1980 has been one of enormous growth and change for party organizations in Congress, especially in terms of their capabilities for developing and disseminating party "message" communications. If the parties' decisions about allocation of staff are indicative, the growth in legislative party organizations over the past three decades has been aimed more at improving partisan public relations than toward winning programmatic policy victories.

THE QUEST FOR MAJORITY CONTROL

> What is the job of Republican leader in the minority? It's to hold the job for as short a time as possible.
>
> Rep. John A. Boehner (R-OH), in a 2006 letter to Republican House colleagues[1]

The central question of *Congress: The Electoral Connection* is whether "congressmen in search of reelection are in a position to do anything about it" (Mayhew 1974, 28). In answer, Mayhew argues (1) that members believe that they can affect their own prospects for reelection and (2) that members' activities do indeed have electoral impact. The goal of these reelection-seeking activities is to increase the "expected incumbent differential," which is defined as "any difference perceived by a relevant political actor between what an incumbent congressmen is likely to do if returned to office and what any possible challenger ... would be likely to do" (Mayhew 1974, 39).

---

[1] Quoted in Hulse 2006.

One might press the parallel question of whether congressional partisans in search of legislative majorities are in a position to do anything about it. How might members enhance the chances of their party holding a congressional majority? Unlike the pursuits discussed in Mayhew (1974), winning and holding partisan majorities are not goals that members of Congress believe they can pursue effectively on their own as individual lawmakers. Majority seeking requires collective effort. As such, it is foremost a job for congressional leaders. In the quest for legislative majorities, members expect party leaders to coordinate their party in enterprises that will widen the "expected party differential."[2] To reappropriate Mayhew's definition, the goal of these activities is to amplify the differences that voters and other relevant political actors perceive between what an incumbent party is likely to do if returned to power and what the opposition party will do.

Whether or not there is solid empirical evidence for such a view, there seems little doubt that members of Congress *believe* that collective efforts can affect their party's chances for winning and holding legislative majorities. The fate of party leaders following disappointing electoral or public relations efforts bears this out. Congressional leaders regularly face blowback from rank-and-file party members after electoral reversals. This blowback may or may not involve leaders' removal and replacement, but leaders inevitably come in for some level of criticism and blame from rank-and-file members in the wake of public disapproval or poor election results.

House leaders, especially Republicans, have been subject to accountability for adverse electoral outcomes. After only four years as speaker, Gingrich – the "Moses" who led the Republicans out of forty years in the wilderness of minority status – was summarily dispatched when Republicans "turned on him after the unexpected losses" in the 1998 elections (Gugliotta and Eilperin 1998). Former Speaker Dennis Hastert (R-IL) also stepped down from the leadership after Republicans lost their majority in the 2006 elections, tacitly accepting blame for failing to contain the public relations fallout from the late-breaking sex scandal involving Rep. Mark Foley (R-FL). Although Speaker Nancy Pelosi did not bow out after the Democrats' loss of the majority in 2010, she endured reproach from within her caucus and a contested vote on her bid for the minority leadership.

Senate leaders do not experience the same level of pressure to resign as House leaders following contrary election outcomes. They do, however, typically come in for criticism after electoral disappointments and, in the post-1980 era, have often reorganized their leadership offices in response. Following their losses in the 2010 elections, for example, Senate Democrats met at their annual retreat, where "there was a lot of frustration and venting about communication

---

[2] The term "expected party differential" originates with Downs (1957, 38–9), who defines it as the difference in the utility that voters believe they would receive were each party in office.

failures"; the upshot was a major redesign of Democratic Leader Harry Reid's public relations operation (Pierce 2010). Similarly, in the immediate wake of the Democratic takeover of Congress in January 2007, "senior aides to Senate Minority Leader Mitch McConnell (R-Ky.) and Senate Republican Conference Chairman Jon Kyl (R-Ariz.) met with Republican press secretaries to address last year's communications shortcomings" (Bolton 2007).

Even between elections, leaders come under continuous pressure from rank-and-file members when the party seems to be failing to get its "message" out or otherwise appears to have wound up on the wrong side of public opinion. A typical news story begins: "Sen. Bill Frist (R-Tenn.), seeking to rebound from several high-profile setbacks in his message battle with Minority Leader Harry Reid (D-Nev.), is beginning his last year as majority leader with a newly assembled rapid response and message development team" (Stanton 2006). The story goes on to report that Frist initially resisted the reorganization, but pressure for change mounted as "conference members were frustrated . . . by the seeming lack of coordination" (Stanton 2006). Clearly, rank-and-file members see their leaders as responsible, at least to some extent, for the aggregate outcomes of congressional elections, as well as for the state of their party's public image at any given point.

What activities are useful for increasing the expected party differential? Given that party differentials exist in the world of perceptions and beliefs about future party performance, efforts to enlarge these differences involve both legislation and communication. Indeed, modern congressional leadership offices are organized around these two functions, with division of labor between policy advisors and communications specialists. Public relations efforts to heighten party differences can be pursued at all times. Legislative victories, however, are only sometimes valuable for this purpose.

Party leaders who want to use legislation to widen the expected party differential need to be able to pass bills or amendments via party-line votes. Of course, there are cases when it is politically advantageous for a party to dodge a partisan fight. On issues where a party is perceived as being on the wrong side of public opinion, party leaders may try to narrow a party differential. In these cases, they would want to arrive at bipartisan deals and to avoid party-line votes. Avoiding party conflict, however, is never a good way to increase the expected party differential. Members and leaders who want to amplify the differences that voters perceive between the parties need to provoke some partisan fights.

Actual legislating is not generally useful for a minority party's effort to enhance party differences. In most cases, minority parties cannot expect to enact party programmatic legislation in the face of majority party opposition. Although there are occasional examples in which a minority party succeeds in fracturing the majority party and enacting legislation, this is not usually a realistic option. Charles O. Jones (1970) details the minority party's central dilemma: when the minority works "constructively" with the majority party in order to successfully modify legislation toward its preferences, it hinders its ability to make an effective political case for retaking the majority. "In the long run, [a strategy of] constructive opposition ensures that [the minority] will not achieve the goal of majority party status . . . . The minority party may be creative and responsible and *not only remain the minority party but even ensure the continued success of the majority party*" (Jones 1970, 24; see also Green 2015).

A more achievable legislative strategy for a minority party seeking to dramatize party differences is to craft appealing legislative alternatives that will go down to defeat at the hands of the majority party – thus creating an issue to take to the voters in the quest to regain control (Egar 2016). To serve their political purpose, these legislative alternatives need not be workable, realistic, or carefully designed in policy terms. All that is necessary is that they sound good to constituencies outside the Congress. Another effective minority party strategy is to vote en masse against the majority's legislative initiatives, provided that the majority's proposals are not so popular that such behavior creates undesirable contrasts. Most of the time, legislative defeats, rather than legislative successes or compromises, best serve the minority party's interest in emphasizing party differences.

But legislative victories are by no means always necessary for a congressional majority party to make the case for its continuation in power. After all, even if it holds its own ranks together, a majority party probably still will not be able to deliver programmatic legislation, given many other institutional veto points. Bicameralism, separation of powers, and other aspects of national institutions usually force congressional leaders to legislate by assembling large, bipartisan coalitions (Krehbiel 1998; Mayhew 1991), rather than in a way that would permit the majority party alone to claim credit. Under these constraints, a majority party's supportive constituencies will often be disappointed by the sort of legislation that can actually be enacted. These kinds of bipartisan legislative victories can blur the majority party's distinctive image, undermining the expected party differential.

To be sure, majority parties bear a greater burden of expectations to deliver on legislation, both from their base voters and (probably) from the public at large. A majority party that successfully legislates will likely be seen as more competent in terms of government management, assuming that the legislation it passes is not unpopular. Such considerations give majority parties greater incentive to succeed at legislating.

Nevertheless, the majority party, like the minority party, will also find unsuccessful legislative efforts politically useful. For example, a House majority party may prefer to pass legislation on a party-line vote, even if doing so will harm the bill's prospects for further action in the Senate or with the president, because party votes work better for clarifying its image relative to the opposition. Unsuccessful party-line cloture votes in the Senate also effectively communicate what a majority party stands for, even when they achieve nothing in terms of public policy. In short, a majority party has a stronger partisan incentive than a minority party to achieve legislative victories, but it also can derive political value from legislative defeats. A majority party may well prefer to keep an issue alive for electoral purposes rather than accept an compromise (Gilmour 1995; Groseclose and McCarty 2001). In short, both majority and minority parties often find it in their electoral interests to fail legislatively. Legislative success is not necessary for increasing expected party differentials; indeed, legislative enactments may even cut against the purpose.

PARTISAN COMMUNICATIONS: ADVERTISING, CREDIT CLAIMING, AND POSITION TAKING

Congress: The Electoral Connection famously identified three activities that reelection-seeking members constantly undertake: advertising, credit claiming, and position taking. What do these activities have in common? They are all forms of communication. Among them, only credit claiming depends to even a limited extent upon achieving any kind of legislative success. Despite being developed for another purpose, these three concepts are remarkably helpful tools for analyzing party leaders' communications efforts. Leaders continually engage in all of these activities as they craft and manage message operations to widen the expected party differential and thus make the case for their own party's majority status.

Advertising. Any review of the communications from congressional party leaders and leadership offices will quickly encounter examples of advertising – as in efforts to "create a favorable image but in messages having little or no issue content" (Mayhew 1974, 49). For example, leadership offices work to enhance their party's image by holding "listening sessions" with various constituencies. The Democratic Steering and Outreach Committee regularly sponsors such open-ended discussions, such as a March 13, 2013, meeting with fourteen "leaders in workforce development from across the country." Holding a meeting of this kind has advertising value for a party, as does a press release describing it.[3] Similarly, leadership offices across the Congress wanted the public to know that they were "praying for Boston" following the bombings at the Boston Marathon in April 2013. They were quick to express their condolences for those affected by the 2012 massacre at Sandy Hook Elementary School in Newtown, Connecticut. Parties offer many generic statements of their general goodwill toward the American people. In 2013, for example, House Republicans held a press conference in front of a large sign that read "Working for All Americans" in order to assure everyone that "the House is

---

[3] United States Senate Democratic Steering and Outreach Committee, "Senate Democrats Host Meeting With Workforce Development Leaders," Press release, March 13, 2013, www.dsoc .senate.gov/2013/03/13/senate-democrats-host-meeting-with-workforce-development-leaders-3/.

focused on growing our economy, creating more jobs, and helping hardworking Americans all across the country."[4]

Advertising is useful for improving a party's image. It is also useful for damaging the opposing party's image. Often, the goal is to embarrass the opposition in some way. Minority Leader Boehner, for example, stressed what he called "entrepreneurial insurgency" tactics to all the Republican committee press secretaries, enlisting them to capture Democratic witnesses or members in gaffes on video and then to disseminate the content via YouTube (Kucinich 2009). The House Republican conference produced a video ridiculing President Barack Obama for completing his NCAA basketball brackets on time while failing to meet the deadline for submitting a budget to Congress.[5] Partisan communicators compile long lists of reasons why their party opponents are "out of touch with reality" or are misleading the American people. Taken together, congressional parties produce a fair amount of largely issue-free public relations content designed to either promote their party image or undercut that of the opposition.

Credit Claiming and Blaming. Partisan communications frequently aim to foster the belief that one party is responsible for good policies and the opposing party is responsible for undesirable policies. Credit claiming and blaming are distinct from advertising in that these communications have issue content and involve attributions of responsibility for outcomes or actions.

Credit is much easier to claim for parties than for individual members. The challenge for individual members is to establish personal responsibility for any policy outcome at all in a Congress of 534 other members (Mayhew 1974, 53–61). Parties, by contrast, do not find it difficult to assert credit for the passage of laws or good policy outcomes, including for far-downstream effects such as lower unemployment or a growing economy, matters for which no individual member of Congress could credibly claim responsibility. The Senate Democratic Steering and Outreach Committee regularly crowed about good economic news during the Obama presidency.[6] For his part, Speaker John Boehner trumpeted that "GOP control ... saved taxpayers more than $400 million and counting" in the House operating budget.[7]

Parties also make use of a negative variation on credit claiming: blaming. Incumbent members of Congress can rarely blame their challengers for bad

---

[4] Video from the press conference was uploaded to the House Republican Conference's blog on April 24, 2013, at www.gop.gov/blog/13/04/24/4-24-13-republican-leadership.

[5] House Republican Conference, "Budgets or Brackets?," Video, GOP.gov, March 19, 2013, www.gop.gov/blog/13/03/19/budgets-or-brackets.

[6] United States Senate Democratic Steering and Outreach Committee, "Good Economic News: April 23, 2013," Press Release, www.dsoc.senate.gov/2013/04/23/good-economic-news-april-23-2013/.

[7] John A. Boehner, "Under GOP Control, House Operations Have Saved Taxpayers More than $400 Million & Counting," Press Release, April 25, 2013, www.speaker.gov/press-release/under-gop-control-house-operations-have-saved-taxpayers-more-400-million-counting.

policy outcomes. Partisan communications, however, pervasively engage in finger pointing, lambasting the other party for any and all policy problems for which it is purportedly responsible. The Senate Republican Policy Committee apprised the public that the "Obama economy continues to struggle," especially as compared with the economic recovery under President Reagan.[8] House Minority Leader Nancy Pelosi declared that "the GOP earns an 'F' on the first 100 days of Congress" for their "failed leadership."[9] Speaker John Boehner wanted it known exactly who was responsible for blocking the construction of the Keystone Pipeline: President Obama.[10]

Position Taking. Like individual members, parties enunciate "judgmental statements" on matters of political interest (Mayhew 1974, 61). Leaders regularly stage roll call votes for the purpose of partisan position taking, a phenomenon members refer to as "message votes," which they explicitly distinguish from votes that are actually intended to affect policy outcomes (Lee 2011). Party leaders devise many different ways to communicate positions. They put together party agenda documents. They hold press conferences. They and their offices stage media stunts or partisan events. Leadership aides prepare talking points on virtually all major political issues, along with graphs, videos, and other supporting materials. They organize teams of members to deliver these talking points in floor speeches and across all forms of media (Evans 2001; Evans and Oleszek 2002; Harris 2005; Sinclair 2006, 263–307; Sellers 2010). The Senate Republican Conference sometimes keeps track of precisely how much time senators of each party consume on the floor, and metrics are provided to members during the party's weekly lunches when necessary. "We're a competitive lot," noted Sen. John Cornyn (R-TX), "so when you tell Republican senators that we're being out-spoken by Democrats, it gets 'em going. It provides the additional nudge to get them on the floor" (Parnes 2008). As with partisan credit claiming and advertising, partisan position taking often takes a negative form – as in communications attempting to refute the other party's policy positions.

THE VOLUME AND CONTENT OF PARTISAN COMMUNICATIONS

The contemporary legislative branch includes a workforce of hundreds of professional communicators who work full-time on partisan public relations.

---

[8] Senate Republican Policy Committee, "The Obama Economy Continues to Struggle," April 25, 2013, www.rpc.senate.gov/policy-papers/the-obama-economy-continues-to-struggle.

[9] Democratic Leader Nancy Pelosi, "Pelosi: The GOP Earns an 'F' on the First 100 Days of Congress," Press Release, April 12, 2013, www.democraticleader.gov/Pelosi_Statement_on_First_100_Days_of_113_Congress.

[10] Katie Boyd, "Pressure Mounts on President Obama to Approve Keystone Pipeline," Speaker's Blog, March 27, 2013, www.speaker.gov/general/pressure-mounts-president-obama-approve-keystone-pipeline.

They generate an enormous amount of output. Table 6.1 offers a tally of the number of public relations items released by each House and Senate leadership office in the first four months of 2013, excluding tweets. Items vary in length, but most are short, a paragraph or two in length. They take the form of blog posts, press releases, policy notes, and reports. In some cases, blog posts are just video clips uploaded with a title and brief description. The list sums to 1,211 items, which averages about ten items a day, including Saturdays and Sundays. For the offices that put out a large number of items, the flow of output is relatively consistent on a day-to-day basis. The Senate Republican Policy Committee, for example, puts out a daily "policy note" when the Senate is in session. Boehner's blog on the Speaker.gov site posted two to three items on average each day of the work week. The Hoyer Press Staff Blog on the DemocraticWhip.gov site was only slightly less prolific. The steady production stream from many of these offices reflects the large number of staff aides employed specifically for this purpose.

Note that this tally was taken at the very start of a Congress, meaning that all of these items were published at least nineteen months before the next scheduled congressional elections. The Republican Party outpaced the Democratic Party in volume during this period, with House Republicans producing 499 items to the House Democrats' 399 and Senate Republicans producing 251 items to the Senate Democrats' 112. This discrepancy may reflect a greater industriousness among the party not controlling the presidency or perhaps a tendency of the party controlling the presidency to look to the executive branch for leadership on party communications strategies. Additional research would be necessary to determine if control of the presidency has an effect on congressional party messaging efforts. It is also worth noting that both parties' House leadership offices generated more output than their parties' respective Senate leadership offices. Despite these differences in the overall amount of activity, it is clear that both parties in both chambers have institutionalized a high capacity for continuous partisan public relations.

In order to gain insight into the types of messages these offices disseminated, I took a stratified random sample constituting 10 percent of all the items published by each leadership office during the first quarter of 2013. Each item was classified into one of six categories: positive advertising, negative advertising, credit claiming, blaming, position taking, and position refuting. Fully 96 percent of all the items could be designated in one of these categories. In most cases, items that could not be classified were announcements regarding changes in leadership or staff personnel. The results are displayed in Figure 6.1.

Among the output of leadership offices, "partisan blaming" was the single most common type of communication. Fully 35 percent of all the items were efforts to tar the opposing party with responsibility for undesirable actions or policy outcomes. If one examines all the items aimed at assigning responsibility for policy actions or outcomes, only 28 percent reflected a party's effort to take credit for positive outcomes, while 72 percent were efforts to blame the

TABLE 6.1 *Tally of Written Public Relations Output, House and Senate Leadership Offices, Excluding Tweets, January–April 2013*

	Office	Web Address	Output
House Republicans	Speaker	www.speaker.gov	239 blog posts and press releases
	Majority Leader	www.majorityleader.gov	75 press releases
	Majority Whip	www.majoritywhip.gov	45 blog posts and press releases
	GOP Conference	www.gop.gov	72 blog posts
	GOP Policy Committee	policy.house.gov	18 press releases
Total			*449 items*
House Democrats	Minority Leader	www.democraticleader.gov	167 blog posts and press releases
	Minority Whip	www.democraticwhip.gov	204 blog posts and press releases
	Democratic Caucus	www.dems.gov	28 press releases
Total			*399 items*
Senate Democrats	Majority Leader	democrats.senate.gov	70 press releases and blog posts
	Democratic Policy and Communications Center	www.dpcc.senate.gov	18 press releases, reports and blog posts
	Democratic Steering and Outreach	www.dsoc.senate.gov	24 press releases
Total			*112 items*
Senate Republicans	Minority Leader	www.mcconnell.senate.gov	108 press releases
	GOP Policy Committee	www.rpc.senate.gov	119 policy notes and statements
	Republican Conference	www.republican.senate.gov	24 blog posts
Total			*251 items*
Grand Total			*1211 items*

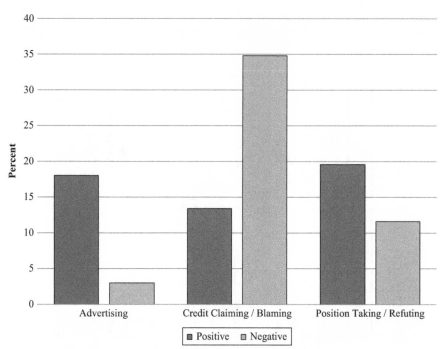

FIGURE 6.1 Content of public relations output, House and Senate leadership offices, January–April 2013. Source: Random sample drawn from items in Table 6.1 (n = 112).

opposition for negative outcomes. A strong preference for "blaming" over "credit claiming" is also true of each party's output analyzed separately. The tilt toward blame probably reflects the fact that there was not a lot for Congress to take credit for in early 2013, given the sluggish economy and the public's dissatisfaction with government performance. Still, it is fair to say that partisan finger pointing seems to be the primary job description of the communications professionals working in Congress's leadership offices.

Items classified as "advertising" (20% of the total) and "position taking" (31%) were less common than "credit claiming/blaming" items (48%). In contrast to credit claiming/blaming, advertising and position-taking was more positive than negative. The advertising items for both parties were usually efforts to improve the image of one's own party (87%), rather than to tear down the opposition (12%). Similarly, more of the position-taking items were efforts to affirm one's own party's positions (63%) than to refute the opposing party's positions (37%). Unlike with advertising, where there was no difference between the parties in the percentage of positive and negative items, there was some partisan difference in position taking, in that 80 percent of the Democrats' position-taking items were positive, as compared with only 50 percent of the

Republicans' items.[11] A presidency controlled by the opposing party provided a target-rich environment for Republican efforts to refute Democratic policy positions. Meanwhile, a presidency controlled by one's own party seems to impose a requirement to defend the administration's positions, at least to some extent.

Across the board, a key difference between communications designed for partisan purposes and those designed for individual members' reelection is that partisan communications are far more pervasively focused on the opponent. Aggregating across all the output of congressional leadership offices, about half of the total items were positive (51%) efforts to shore up perceptions of one's own party and half (49%) were negative attacks on the opposition party's image, policy positions, or policy actions.[12] The difference makes a lot of sense, when one considers the competitive environment for parties as opposed to that of individual members. Individual members of Congress engage in reelection-seeking activities under circumstances where they frequently do not know the identity of their opponent, or even when that opponent will emerge – whether in a primary, in the general election, or at all. Parties seeking majority control of Congress, by contrast, always know the identity of their opponent. Even when individual members of Congress know who their opponent is, incumbents will typically prefer to avoid acknowledging challengers by name as long as possible. Given the competitiveness of the two parties in the battle for control of Congress, parties do not have the luxury of refusing to "go negative." Like incumbents facing a competitive challenger, parties are forced to draw explicit contrasts.

THE INSTITUTIONALIZATION OF PARTISAN COMMUNICATIONS

Since the publication of *Congress: The Electoral Connection*, the role and scale of congressional party leadership operations has grown dramatically. In both chambers of Congress and among both Republicans and Democrats, members have built an elaborate infrastructure for the creation and dissemination of partisan communications. A snapshot comparing the House and Senate of 1975 and 2012 offers a sense for the extent of the change.[13]

---

[11] This difference of means is not statistically significant at conventional levels ($p = 0.07$), given the small n of the sample.

[12] The overall balance was more negative among Republican communications than for Democratic communications: 56 percent of Republican items were attacks on the opposition party, while 40 percent of Democratic items were negative. This difference is not statistically significant ($p = 0.08$). This difference in emphasis seems to derive from the Republican tendency to attack the Obama administration and Democrats' efforts to defend it.

[13] Data here and in the following compiled from *Congressional Staff Directories*.

In 1975, none of the Senate's top party leadership offices employed a press secretary or any public relations aides. In the House of 1975, there was a grand total of six press aides working for congressional leaders: one each for the Speaker of the House, the Minority Leader, and the Majority Whip, along with two editors and a publisher working for the Republican Conference. Among the 584 staffers employed by all the standing committees of the House, there were two press assistants, one working for the Agriculture Committee and the other for the Ways and Means Committee. Among the 489 staff employed by the standing committees of the Senate, there were no press aides.

In 2012, there were fifty-seven public relations professionals working for House leaders, summing to more than a quarter (27%) of all staff employed in their offices. A list of job titles offers a sense of the extensive specialization and division of labor involved. For example, the Speaker of the House employed a director for communications, a digital communications director, an assistant communications director, two press secretaries, a deputy press secretary, an assistant press secretary, a director of public liaison, a director of advance, a digital production manager, a director of speechwriting, a director of outreach, and a special events coordinator, among others. The office of the House Majority Leader employed a comparable (albeit smaller) array, augmented with a new media director and a strategic communications director. The Republican Conference employed a director of digital media, a director of coalitions, a director of rapid response, a posters and visuals director, a video and TV director, and a website director. The House minority party was no less staffed by communicators. Looking to the standing committees of the House, every committee aside from Ethics had at least one media-relations officer. There was a total of ninety-seven committee staffers employed in communications, comprising 12 percent of all House committee staff.

In the Senate of 2012, there were seventy-three public relations aides working for party leadership offices, constituting fully 45 percent of all staff working for leadership. All the top party leaders of the Senate had communications directors, press secretaries, and speechwriters.[14] The Senate Democratic Media Center encompassed a new media director, a deputy director of new media, a director of broadcast media, a press assistant, a senior developer, a multimedia specialist, six video specialists, and a graphic designer. The Senate Democratic Policy and Communications Center employed a communications director, a director of Hispanic media, a regional media director, a deputy press secretary for Hispanic media, a media events director, and a morning press assistant, among others. Communications staffs for the Senate minority party were organized along similar lines, with no less specialization in roles. There

---

[14] These counts are of employees working for the leadership offices and do not include communicators working for the member's personal office staff.

was a total of fifty-four communications staffers working for the standing committees of the Senate, constituting 7 percent of all committee staff.

For a more complete picture of the changes over time, Figure 6.2 displays the total number of aides working for congressional leadership offices, as well as the share of that total with job titles in communications between 1961 and 2012.[15] The figure is on two axes, with the bars indicating the number of leadership staffers and the trend line showing the percentage working in communications.

As shown in Figure 6.2a, there were no Senate leadership staffers working in communications before 1977. Between 1977 and 1986, the number of leadership staff more than doubled (from 46 to 104) and the share in communications quintupled (from 5% to 25%). The period between 1986 and 1996 was one of relative stability in the overall share working in communications, though the total number of leadership staff continued to grow. The share in communications moved up to 30 percent in 1997, holding steady at that level until a jump to 40 percent in 2007. By the end of the series, leadership staff levels were at their highest point to date, and communicators approached half of all Senate leadership staff aides (45%).

Shown in Figure 6.2b, the trends in the House are more gradual. The share of leadership staff in communications held steady around or below 10 percent through the early 1990s. Because the total number of staff working for House leadership offices was on the rise throughout this period, however, the absolute number of communicators was increasing, albeit not their overall share. Between 1989 and 1999, the number of leadership staff doubled (from 83 to 166), and the share working in communications nearly tripled (from 7% to 20%). After 2002, the number of leadership aides jumped from 170 to around 200. After 2008, the share working in House party communications advanced to more than a quarter (27%) of leadership aides, while the total number continued to hover around 200.

DRIVERS OF INSTITUTIONAL CHANGE

One simply cannot attribute all the growth in the public relations capacities of congressional leaders to the increased competition for control of Congress. The growth of public relations activity on the part of congressional leaders has not occurred in a vacuum. Beyond the leadership offices, the contemporary

---

[15] Senate leadership offices include the offices of the majority leader, minority leader, majority whip, minority whip, Republican conference, Democratic Policy Committee, Democratic Steering and Coordination Committee, Democratic Technology and Communications Center, and the Republican Policy Committee. House leadership offices include the offices of the Speaker of the House, majority leader, majority whip, minority whip, Democratic Caucus, Republican Conference, Democratic Steering Committee, Republican Policy Committee, the Democratic Study Group (when it existed), the Republican Committee on Committees, and the Democratic Policy Committee.

(a)

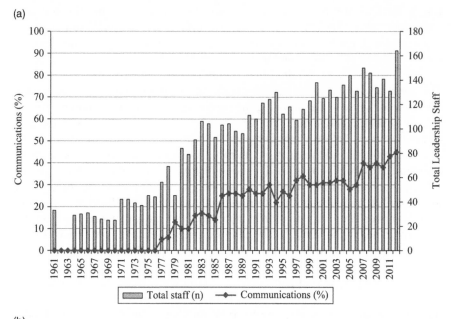

(b)

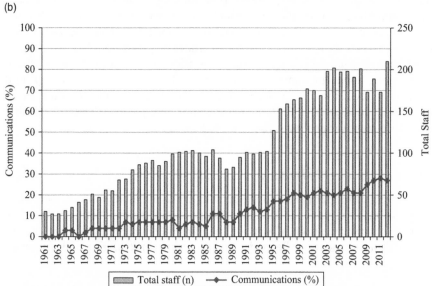

FIGURE 6.2 Total number of leadership staffers and share in communications, 1961–2012. (a) Senate. (b) House.

Congress as a whole is far more oriented toward external audiences than the Congress of the 1950s and 1960s (Harris 1998; Malecha and Reagan 2012; Sinclair 1989; 2006). The job of press secretary has also proliferated in individual member offices, reflecting a heavier emphasis on professional communications work throughout the legislative branch (Cook 1989; Hess 1991). The twenty-four-hour news cycle undoubtedly places huge demands on Congress to supply material, cope with journalists' needs, and answer charges in a more confrontational media environment. The rise of the congressional flack, in turn, echoes broader institutional changes both inside and outside of government. After all, the public relations professional has become a fixture of all large organizations, public and private sector alike. A Government Accountability Office study estimated the cost of public relations and advertising among seven cabinet-level agencies at $1.6 billion over 30 months between 2003 and the middle of fiscal year 2005.[16] Congressional parties are hardly alone in spending enormous sums on flackery.

Even so, the management of their party's public image has become a far more salient aspect of congressional leaders' jobs than it was in the 1960s and 1970s. If political science research offers any guide, the responsibility to win and hold party majorities did not even figure prominently among the tasks of congressional leaders during the long years of the so-called "permanent" Democratic majority. Scholarship on Congress from the 1960s and 1970s had hardly anything to say about members' or leaders' efforts to affect their party's majority status. For example, a 1981 round-up of scholarship on congressional leaders (Mackaman 1981) – a 300-page volume that included entries by many of the leading academics in the field – contains a mere five paragraphs on the responsibility of party leaders to seek or maintain partisan majorities. None of the chapters on leading the House of Representatives mentions this aspect of the party leader's job. Only Robert Peabody's chapter on the Senate briefly discusses the Republican leader's efforts to seek the "conversion of the Republican Party into a majority" (89–90). Similarly, Barbara Sinclair's 1983 and 1995 analyses of what House members expect from their party leaders contain no sustained discussion of winning or holding party majorities, although the penultimate chapter of the 1995 book examines leaders' efforts to promote the party's public image.

In the last two decades, however, scholars have made members' motivations to win and hold majorities a central feature of theories of congressional leadership. A fundamental assumption of Cox and McCubbins' (1993; 2005) influential cartel theory is that members view majority status as vital to their personal power and therefore organize Congress to that end. Along the same lines, Smith (2007) grounds his theory of congressional parties as seeking two goals: majority party status and policy. Green (2010) also posits maintaining the party's majority status as one of the House Speaker's principal objectives. Recent work

---

[16] Government Accountability Office, Report to Congressional Requesters, "Media Contracts: Activities and Financial Obligations for Seven Federal Departments," January 2006, GAO-06–305.

now details the mechanisms by which congressional leaders seek to enhance their party's public image (Sellers 2010; Sinclair 2006, 263–307).

This shift in the congressional literature is probably not the result of scholarly misperception in either earlier eras or the present. It is more likely that majority status and partisan image-making were simply much less salient concerns for members and leaders during a period when there was so little prospect for alternation in party control. The quest for majority status only became a central focus when the return of competition threw control of Congress into continuous doubt.

Furthermore, the pace and timing of staff changes relates in notable ways to the rise of two-party competition for control of Congress. Public relations professionals arrived relatively late to congressional leaders. Looking to individual member offices, the growth of press secretaries in Congress occurred in the 1960s and 1970s, well before the explosion of public relations capabilities documented here among congressional leaders. By the time party leaders began growing their communications staffs, nearly every senator and the vast majority of House members already had press secretaries (Cook 1989; Hess 1991). Competitive circumstances also seem to affect the incidence and rate of growth in communications staffers during recent decades. Figure 6.3 displays the percentage of staff with communications job titles for Senate Republicans and Democrats for each year between 1961 and 2012, with vertical lines indicating switches in party control.

One of the most notable patterns is that Senate Republicans began devoting staff resources to communications before Senate Democrats. Republicans hired their first communications specialists in 1977. Reporters at the time observed that Senate Republicans were reorganizing their staffs in order to do open battle with the Carter administration (Rich 1977), with the goal being to develop policy alternatives to "take to the public in the next election" (Malbin 1977). With an unpopular president and an economy plagued by stagflation, the late 1970s presented Republicans with their best opportunity in many years for a shot at winning control of the Senate, a fact noted by Peabody (1981, 89). Senate Democrats, by contrast, only began to escalate their spending on public relations after losing the majority in 1980. Newly in the minority, Democratic Leader Robert C. Byrd (D-WV) hired a small communications staff for the Senate Democratic Policy Committee for the first time. He appointed the high profile Greg Schneiders, a former aide to President Jimmy Carter, as communications director. Byrd made these staff changes at the same time as he undertook a variety of other initiatives to raise the public visibility of the Democratic Party, including appointing senators to partisan study groups, instituting regular party strategy meetings, and holding a Saturday morning news conference (Gailey 1982). Prior to 1980 Democrats did not hold weekly luncheon meetings to discuss partisan and other issues.

After 1980, both parties drastically escalated expenditures on public relations. Starting at a lower level in the 1970s, Democrats first caught up to

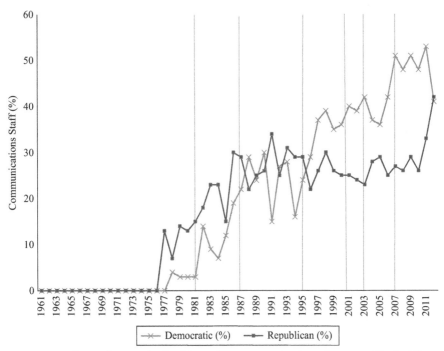

<small>FIGURE 6.3</small> Share of Senate leadership staff in communications, by party. Vertical lines indicate party switches.

Republicans in their overall share of staff devoted to communications in 1988, shortly after they resumed control of the Senate in 1987. Between 1988 and 1996, the two Senate parties allocated roughly proportionate shares of their leadership staff to public relations (around 25% of leadership staff). After the Republican take-over in 1994, however, Democrats dramatically intensified their communications efforts until they began to substantially outspend Republicans in 1996 (at 37% of their leadership staff). Democrats continued to outspend Republicans between 1996 and 2012, despite (very) narrowly retaking the majority briefly in 2001 and again in 2007. After the disappointing outcome of the 2004 elections, Senate Democrats under Minority Leader Harry Reid (D-NV) established a "war room," organized to churn out rapid response to Republican claims, place Democratic-friendly content in media outlets, and coordinate the Democratic Party message (Grove 2005). After the 2010 elections, when Republicans failed to win control of the Senate despite a highly favorable political environment, Senate Republicans stepped up expenditures on communications (from 26% of leadership staff in 2010 to 42% in 2012). In 2012, Senate Republicans and Democrats stood at rough parity in their allocations on public relations.

FIGURE 6.4 Share of House leadership staff in communications, by party.

Patterns in the growth of partisan communications in the House bear key similarities to the Senate. Figure 6.4 displays the percentage of staff with communications job titles for the House parties over time, with vertical lines denoting switches in party control. As in the Senate, House Republicans began to allocate staff resources to communications first, well before the majority-party Democrats. The discrepancy between the two parties was rather wide during the 1970s, when Republicans had already begun using the Republican Conference to publicly promote the party while the Democrats had no comparable leadership office. House Democrats only began to prioritize public relations after the 1980 elections. In 1979, none of the leadership offices of the Democratic Party even employed a press secretary; by 1983 all the top leaders of the Democratic Party had press secretaries. Speaker Tip O'Neill (D-MA) maintained a higher level of visibility on television news than any previous House speaker (Harris 1998). In part, the Democrats' new emphasis on publicity was a response to the Reagan Administration's attacks on the Democratic Party (Harris 1998; Sinclair 1995, 260–295). At some level, House Democrats may have recognized the greater precariousness of their House majority in the wake of the party's loss of the Senate.

Resembling an arms race, House Democratic and House Republican expenditures on public relations closely tracked one another as both parties steadily increased the share of leadership staff allocated for the purpose from 6 percent in 1985 to around 12 percent in the early 1990s. After they lost their House majority in 1994, Democrats revamped and strengthened their public relations capabilities throughout their years in the minority, going from 14 percent of leadership staff devoted to communications in 1994 to 25 percent in 2006. After their loss of the majority, Republicans redoubled their efforts with another expansion of communications staff, swelling their staff share working in communications to 32 percent in 2010 just before they took control of the House. In 2012, like the Senate parties, the two House parties allocated the same share of staff (41–42%) to communications.

In short, the history of how House and Senate parties built their public relations capabilities over time relates to the parties' competitive circumstances. It is likely that increased capacity for professional communications would have developed among congressional leaders, as it has in all large institutions. Nevertheless, party leaders only began employing large numbers of communicators when competition for control of Congress intensified – at a point well after most individual member offices had already developed professional press relations capabilities. Generally speaking, parties in the minority tended to innovate, increasing their share of staff allocated to public relations, in tandem with other efforts to raise their visibility. Parties in the majority showed more complacency, though divided government also puts extra pressure to "go public" on a congressional majority party. Although there was variability, and it often took time for a party to "catch up" after it fell behind, the minority party also usually outmatched the majority party in the share of its staff devoted to communications.[17] Even if the growth of congressional communications capabilities mirrors the growth of public relations in other public and private institutions, it is also influenced in key ways by the competitive challenges the parties faced.

Finally, it is important to note what the decisions about staffing suggest about members' priorities in an era of intense party competition for control of Congress. Congressional leadership has increased in importance and capabilities across many dimensions since the 1960s and 1970s. Leadership staff levels have also been on the rise throughout the entire period (Glassman 2012). Before 1980, however, the focus was largely on enhancing party capabilities to develop party policy and coordinate members internally. House leadership offices grew by 230 percent between 1961 and 1981, but only 11 percent of that growth was focused on public relations. Similarly, Senate leadership offices grew by 154 percent between 1961 and 1980, but only 16 percent of that increase occurred in the area of communications.

---

[17] In the House, the minority party devoted more staff to communications for twenty-five of the thirty-six years of the study. In the Senate, the minority party designated a larger share of staff to communications for twenty-one years.

By contrast, if we examine the growth of leadership staff since 1980, the emphasis tilts far more strongly toward communications. In both House and Senate, the number of people employed by leadership offices has more than doubled since 1980. Half or more of that total increase (51% of the growth in the House, 57% in the Senate) is attributable to expansion of the parties' communications staffs. Developments in committee staffing also deserve mention in this context. Between 1980 and 2010, the overall level of committee staff in House and Senate declined, with House committee staff cut by 32 percent and Senate committee staff reduced by 5 percent (Peterson, Reynolds, and Wilhelm 2010). At the same time, the share of committee staff devoted to public relations grew to 12 percent in the House and 7 percent in the Senate. Since alternation in party control of Congress resumed in 1980, members of Congress have been at least as interested in enhancing their institutional capabilities for partisan communications as in improving either their party or their committee staffs as repositories of policy expertise.

THE ZERO-SUM POLITICS OF PARTY CONTROL

The second half of *Congress: The Electoral Connection* begins with an inscription, a quotation from former Rep. Clem Miller (R-CA) describing the experience of serving in the House of Representatives: "We live in a cocoon of good feeling – no doubt the compensation for the cruel buffeting that is received in the world outside" (Mayhew 1974, 79). It is difficult to imagine a member of either the House or Senate at any time in recent decades describing congressional service as a "cocoon of good feeling." A more representative description of the atmosphere in Congress today employs words such as "toxic" and "hyper-partisan."[18] In the contemporary Congress, members and leaders of each party continually launch attacks at the other, with hundreds of communications aides throughout the legislative branch laboring full time to devise new broadsides in an ongoing permanent campaign. As shown in the analysis here, the single most common public relations gambit emanating from a congressional leader or leadership office during the first months of 2013 was an attack blaming the other party for some bad outcome or action.

In accounting for this change, scholars usually emphasize the role of ideological polarization. Long-term realignments have sorted voters ideologically, resulting in a more homogeneously liberal Democratic Party and a more homogeneously conservative Republican Party. These better-sorted parties are undoubtedly mirrored in a more uniformly and intensely partisan Congress. These important political shifts have been widely and comprehensively documented (Abramowitz 2010; Fiorina et al. 2005; Jacobson 2012; Rohde 1991).

---

[18] See, for example, the remarks of Rep. Louise Slaughter, *Congressional Record*, January 1, 2013, H7532.

Accounts stressing ideological polarization, however, often fail to consider how the battle for control of Congress factors into the story. The return of two-party competition for majority status brings back to congressional politics a "zero-sum edge" that had been "eroded away" (Mayhew 1974, 105) by the long years when Democratic Party control of Congress could seemingly be taken for granted. Setting aside the question of which party will hold the majority, members of Congress can all pursue their own individual reelection without running afoul of one another. Without harming the interests of any other member, all members of Congress can advertise, take positions, and claim credit to enhance the "expected incumbent differential" vis-à-vis any potential challenger. This is the world described in Mayhew (1974), published at a time when no close observers of Congress envisioned a change of congressional majority at any point in the foreseeable future. Competition for control of Congress, by contrast, is inescapably zero sum in nature. In the battle for congressional majorities, any public perception that advantages Republicans necessarily disadvantages Democrats and vice versa. With considerations of party control in mind, the political interests of Republicans and Democrats are diametrically at odds.

The contemporary era of party competition for control of Congress has persisted for more than three decades. It is not clear how long these highly competitive conditions will endure. It currently appears that Republicans hold a solid edge in retaining control of the House of Representatives, such that an exceptionally large partisan wave would be necessary to return Democrats to a House majority (Jacobson 2012). A pro-Democratic wave of this scale seems unlikely until there is a landslide election of a Democratic president or a large midterm backlash during a Republican presidential administration. According to the thesis advanced here, a widely perceived advantage for one party in maintaining majority control would undercut the partisan incentives identified here. Nevertheless, one would be hard pressed to claim that the post-1980 era of intense two-party competition has come to a close. The balance of party identification in the national electorate remains close, with an edge to Democrats (Pew Research Center 2015). Control of both the presidency and the Senate remain highly competitive, with speculation about the possibility of yet another change in party control of the Senate in 2016.

Since 1980, both parties have built elaborate infrastructures to wage continual partisan public relations warfare against one another. Every day, these institutions generate material to assist party leaders and members in advertising, credit-claiming, and position-taking to improve their party's political position relative to its opposition. These strengthened leadership institutions coordinate the activities of rank-and-file members, prodding them to take to the floor and to all forms of media with the prepared talking points endorsing the party's "message" and, no less pervasively, denouncing the party opposition. Whether these actions actually help parties win additional seats in congressional elections is very much an open question. What cannot be doubted, however, is that members believe that these public relations efforts are important. Congressional leaders can expect to be held accountable by rank-and-file members for "communication failures" whenever election or polling results are disappointing for the party.

Furthermore, the timing of these institutional innovations corresponds with the parties' competitive circumstances. The minority party tends to be more innovative in growing and reorganizing its communications functions, though divided government (and party competition for control of the presidency) also seem to be motivating factors for the majority party. Examining the share of leadership staff employed in communications in recent decades, the two parties have been locked in an arms race, steadily escalating their capacities for party message development and dissemination. If decisions about staff allocation are a valid indicator, since 1980, party communications has been a higher priority than enhanced policy expertise. If one examines the institutional growth of congressional parties prior to 1980, by contrast, communications was clearly a much lower priority.

If, in the spirit of Mayhew (1974), we posit members of Congress as seekers of party majorities, what can we learn about congressional behavior and organization? Party institutional development in both chambers makes more sense if viewed in light of members' efforts to enhance the "expected party differential." Congressional parties have strengthened in numerous ways since 1980, but those enhanced capabilities are hardly confined to advancing members' policy aims. Parties need to be understood as organizations aimed at assisting members to win party majorities, not just organizations designed to help the majority party pass desired policies (Rohde 1991) or block the passage of undesired policies (Cox and McCubbins 2005). Contemporary legislative parties pervasively and continuously attempt to affect their public reputations through communications. Theories of conditional party government or cartel theory tend to center on the majority party, but a focus on parties as PR operations sheds light on the role and function of the minority party as well. After all, both parties have many tools to use in message politics. It is not even clear that the majority party is advantaged over the minority in the messaging arena. In short, parties are important to members not just if they can be shown to help them achieve nonmedian outcomes or to block legislation disfavored by a majority of the majority party. Parties are also important to members because they are vital to the sort of collective message politics that members believe are necessary for success in the quest for party majorities.

Just as Mayhew (1974) emphasizes members' incentives to take positions and advertise themselves rather than to do the hard work of building legislative coalitions, a focus on members' desire to win and hold majority status draws attention to parties' incentives to engage in similar varieties of "cheap talk." A Mayhew-inspired analysis of congressional parties highlights the extent to which these are organizations designed to wage the permanent campaign. The concepts of "advertising," "credit claiming," and "position taking" are as relevant for understanding congressional party politics as they continue to be for understanding individual member behavior. It was just as easy to apply this conceptual scheme to partisan communications as to individual members' communications (see, e.g., Grimmer et al. 2012). The ease with which these concepts "travel" from one setting to the other reveals something important about congressional parties as institutions.

Political scientists have historically viewed parties as mechanisms of collective accountability for policy. This line of thinking dates back to the American Political Science Association's 1950 Report on Political Parties and before. It endures today in theories of legislatures that stress the incentive of congressional majority parties to deliver on programmatic legislation as a way of advancing members' policy goals (Rohde 1991) or preserving their party's "brand name" (Cox and McCubbins 1993; 2005). Applying Mayhew (1974) to congressional party organizations and activities makes an important contrary point about the role and function of legislative parties: enacting legislation is simply not essential to partisan public relations.

The role of legislative success in the quest for majority party status is actually rather ambiguous. After all, success in passing programmatic legislation is by no means necessary for a party to engage in advertising, position taking, and partisan blaming. All of these forms of communication are available even if a party has not achieved anything whatsoever in terms of legislation. There are many circumstances when legislative failure is more advantageous to a party's majority-seeking aims. In fact, legislative failure is usually a better strategy for a minority party seeking to increase the "expected party differential." Under some circumstances, a majority party can also benefit politically from failed legislative efforts. In the end, the only partisan message that legislative failure impairs is credit claiming. But considering the difficulty of actually enacting partisan legislation in the U.S. system (as opposed to merely passing a partisan bill through the House of Representatives), credit claiming for programmatic legislation is beyond a party's grasp most of the time, in any case. Given the way the U.S. system stymies parties in their policy aims, stronger congressional parties may be little more effective for purposes of policy accountability than the weaker parties of earlier eras. Perhaps today's stronger congressional parties are mainly just better organized for partisan image making.

REFERENCES

Abramowitz, Alan I. 2010. *The Disappearing Center: Engaged Citizens, Polarization, and American Democracy.* New Haven: Yale University Press.

American Political Science Association, 1950. "Toward a More Responsible Two-Party System: A Report of the Committee on Political Parties." *American Political Science Review* 44 (September): 1–14.

Arieff, Irwin B. 1979. "House Freshmen Republicans Seek Role as Power Brokers." *Congressional Quarterly Weekly Report*, July 7, 1339–45.

Bolton, Alexander. 2007. "Senate GOP Begins Repair of Messaging," *The Hill*, January 17.

Cook, Timothy E. 1989. *Making Laws and Making News: Media Strategies in the U.S. House of Representatives*. Washington, DC: The Brookings Institution.

Cox, Gary W., and Mathew D. McCubbins. 1993. *Legislative Leviathan: Party Government in the House*. Berkeley: University of California Press.

2005. *Setting the Agenda: Responsible Party Government in the U.S. House of Representatives*. New York: Cambridge University Press.

Downs, Anthony. 1957. *An Economic Theory of Democracy*. New York: Harper and Row.

Egar, William T. 2016. "Tarnishing Opponents, Polarizing Congress: The House Minority Party and the Construction of the Roll-Call Record." *Legislative Studies Quarterly*. doi: 10.1111/lsq.12135

Evans, C. Lawrence. 2001. "Committees, Leaders, and Message Politics." In *Congress Reconsidered*, 7th ed., Lawrence C. Dodd and Bruce I. Oppenheimer, eds. Washington, DC: CQ Press, 217–43.

Evans, C. Lawrence, and Walter J. Oleszek. 2002. "Message Politics and Senate Procedure." In *The Contentious Senate: Partisanship, Ideology, and the Myth of Cool Judgment*, Colton C. Campbell and Nicol C. Rae, eds. New York: Rowman and Littlefield, 107–30.

Fenno, Richard F. 1973. *Congressmen in Committees*. Boston: Little, Brown & Co.

Fiorina, Morris P., Samuel J. Abrams, and Jeremy C. Pope. 2005. *Culture War? The Myth of a Polarized America*. New York: Pearson Longman.

Jones, Charles O. 1970. *The Minority Party in Congress*. Boston: Little, Brown.

Gailey, Phil. 1982. "From Majority Leader to Minority Leader." *New York Times*, March 9, A20.

Gilmour, John B. 1995. *Strategic Disagreement: Stalemate in American Politics*. Pittsburgh: University of Pittsburgh Press.

Glassman, Matthew. 2012. "Congressional Leadership: A Resource Perspective." In *Party and Procedure in the United States Congress*, Jacob R. Straus, ed., Lanham, MD: Rowman & Littlefield, 15–34.

Green, Matthew N. 2010. *The Speaker of the House: A Study of Leadership*. New Haven: Yale University Press.

2015. *Underdog Politics: The Minority Party in the U.S. House of Representatives*. New Haven: Yale University Press.

Grimmer, Justin, Solomon Messing, and Sean J. Westwood. 2012. "How Words and Money Cultivate a Personal Vote: The Effect of Legislator Credit Claiming on Constituent Credit Allocation." *American Political Science Review* 106 (4): 703–19.

Groseclose, Tim, and Nolan McCarty. 2001. "The Politics of Blame: Bargaining before an Audience." *American Journal of Political Science* 45: 100–19.

Grove, Benjamin. 2005. "In Reid's War Room, the Battle Rages On." *Las Vegas Sun*, November 6.

Gugliotta, Guy and Juliet Eilperin. 1998. "Gingrich Steps Down in Face of Rebellion." *Washington Post*, November 7.

Harris, Douglas B. 1998. "The Rise of the Public Speakership." *Political Science Quarterly* 113 (2): 193–212.

2005. "Orchestrating Party Talk: A Party-Based View of One-Minute Speeches in the House of Representatives." *Legislative Studies Quarterly* 30 (1): 127–41.

Hess, Stephen. 1991. *Live from Capitol Hill: Studies of Congress and the Media.* Washington, DC: The Brookings Institution.

Hulse, Carl. 2006. "G.O.P. in House Gears Up for New Leadership Fight." *New York Times*, November 15.

Jacobson, Gary C. 2012. *The Politics of Congressional Elections*, 8th edition. New York: Pearson.

Krehbiel, Keith. 1998. *Pivotal Politics: A Theory of U.S. Lawmaking.* Chicago: University of Chicago Press.

Kucinich, Jackie. 2009. "Boehner Expands GOP Communications Plans." *Roll Call*, April 13, www.rollcall.com/issues/54_115/-33933-1.html.

Lee, Frances E. 2011. "Making Laws and Making Points: Senate Governance in an Era of Uncertain Majorities." *The Forum* 9 (4): Article 3.

Mackaman, Frank H., ed. 1981. *Understanding Congressional Leadership.* Washington, DC: Congressional Quarterly Press.

Malbin, Michael J. 1977. "The Senate Republican Leaders: Life Without a President." *National Journal*, May 21, 776.

Malecha, Gary Lee, and Daniel J. Reagan. 2012. *The Public Congress: Congressional Deliberation in a New Media Age.* New York: Routledge.

Mayhew, David R. 1974. *Congress: The Electoral Connection.* New Haven: Yale University Press.

  1991. *Divided We Govern: Party Control, Lawmaking, and Investigations.* New Haven: Yale University Press.

Parnes, Amie. 2008. "GOP Senators Using Online System." *Politico*, May 22.

Peabody, Robert L. 1981. "Senate Party Leadership: From the 1950s to the 1980s." In *Understanding Congressional Leadership*, Frank H. Mackaman, ed. Washington, DC: Congressional Quarterly Press.

Peterson, R. Eric, Parker H. Reynolds, and Amber Hope Wilhelm. 2010. "House of Representatives and Senate Staff Levels in Member, Committee, Leadership, and Other Offices, 1977–2010." Congressional Research Service Report, R41366, August 10.

Pew Research Center. 2015. "A Deep Dive Into Party Affiliation: Sharp Differences by Race, Gender, Generation, Education," April 7, www.people-press.org/2015/04/07/a-deep-dive-into-party-affiliation/.

Pierce, Emily. 2010. "Reid Turns Messaging Over to Schumer, Stabenow." *Roll Call*, November 15.

Remini, Robert V. 2006. *The House: The History of the House of Representatives.* New York: HarperCollins.

Rich, Spencer. 1977. "New Staff, Mission Planned for Senate GOP Policy Unit." *Washington Post*, January 1, A4.

Roberts, Steven V. 1981. "In Era of Permanent Campaign, Parties Look to 1982." *New York Times*, January 26.

  1983. "One Conservative Faults Two Parties." *New York Times*, August 11.

Rohde, David W. 1991. *Parties and Leaders in the Postreform House.* Chicago: University of Chicago Press.

Schlesinger, Joseph A. 1985. "The New American Political Party." *American Political Science Review* 79 (4): 1152–69.

  1991. *Political Parties and the Winning of Office.* Ann Arbor: University of Michigan Press.

Sellers, Patrick. 2010. *Cycles of Spin: Strategic Communication in the U.S. Congress.* New York: Cambridge University Press.

"The Senator from Tennessee May Hold the Key to Reagan's Economic Plans." 1981. *National Journal*, April 11.

Sinclair, Barbara. 1983. *Majority Leadership in the U.S. House.* Baltimore: Johns Hopkins University Press.

    1989. *The Transformation of the U. S. Senate.* Baltimore: Johns Hopkins University Press.

    1995. *Legislators, Leaders, and Lawmaking.* Baltimore: Johns Hopkins University Press.

    2006. *Party Wars: Polarization and the Politics of National Policy Making.* Norman: University of Oklahoma Press.

Smith, Steven S. 2007. *Party Influence in Congress.* New York: Cambridge University Press.

Stanton, John. 2006. "Frist Launches Message Shop." *Roll Call*, January 19.

7

Parties within Parties

Parties, Factions, and Coordinated Politics, 1900–1980

John Mark Hansen, Shigeo Hirano, and James
M. Snyder Jr.

INTRODUCTION

Elections are at the heart of democratic accountability. They are the link
between the hopes and desires of the citizens and the policies and pronouncements of the government. In elections, those who aspire to leadership submit
themselves to the judgments of voters, and to the candidates preferred by the
majority accrues the mandate to exercise the powers of the state.

Elections alone, however, do not ensure responsibility to the voters. By itself,
voting does not a democratic election make. Rather, there are institutions that
inhabit the space between citizens and candidates for leadership and make
choices comprehensible, for the choices that citizens are offered and the choices
that citizens make carry little meaning in and of themselves, in isolation in time
and space. Meaning arises only as the choices are organized.

Nowhere is such organization more important than in the United States,
a polity that holds elections at multiple levels of government for multiple
legislative and multiple executive offices independently. In the United
States, accordingly, political parties have played an important role in the
interstice of candidates and citizens, in coordinating electoral politics, both
as organizations and as objects of popular attachments. Their activities as
organizers of choice have been the subject of numerous important studies,
none more thorough and none more perceptive than that of David
R. Mayhew.[1]

This paper is part of ongoing projects supported by National Science Foundation grants
SES-0617556 and SES-0959200. The opinions, findings, and conclusions or recommendations
expressed in this manuscript do not necessarily reflect the views of the National Science
Foundation.
[1] David R. Mayhew, *Placing parties in American politics* (Princeton: Princeton University
Press, 1986).

This paper explores an alternative institutional formation for coordinating choice in elections: the faction. Factions operate within (and occasionally across) political parties, and they lack the formal legal powers and privileges of parties, most importantly the right to place candidates on the ballot and the right to identify institutional affiliations on the ballot. Factions are also unlimited in the potential of their appeal to voters, unlike political parties, whose prospects are circumscribed by the attachments we call partisan identification. For this reason, the possibility of factional competition exists even when party competition does not. For long periods of time in broad swaths of the country, to the extent that politics was organized at all, it was organized by factions.

An inquiry into factional politics necessarily proceeds in the long shadow cast by V. O. Key and his masterly work on politics in the southern states. In the South in the first half of the twentieth century, he explored (in depth) the several varieties of factional politics that flourished within Democratic Party monopolies. His statement on the "nature and consequences of one-party factionalism" is one of the all-time most influential interpretations of a form of politics in all of political science.[2]

The larger project of which this essay is a part will survey factional politics geographically and historically, doing for party factions what Mayhew did for traditional party organizations. Our aims in this paper are necessarily more modest. We focus our attention on four of the states that our data show to have had a high degree of cohesion in voting in primary elections: Louisiana, Minnesota, North Dakota, and Wisconsin. We examine in depth the processes in state politics that had such an influence on the primary electorates. The analysis confirms that all four states had robust and durable organizations that put up competing slates of candidates for nominations to multiple public offices. Our analysis, that is, verifies the relationship between factions in the electorate and factional organizations, to adapt Frank Sorauf's venerable distinction.[3]

That established, our main purpose is an exploration of the phenomenon of parties within parties. What exactly did the factions do that produced such high levels of cohesion in voting across offices? What brought them into being and what caused them to compete rather than collude? What caused their influence on the electorate to wax and to wane? What, finally, caused them to fail?

We will show that the factions in Louisiana, Minnesota, North Dakota, and Wisconsin undertook a common set of activities: they endorsed candidates in the party primaries and they electioneered on their slates' behalf. They followed a common sequence in their development: an insurgency on the political left and a reaction on the political center and right. They displayed a common pattern in the ebb and flow of their effectiveness: it varied with their

[2] V. O. Key Jr., *Southern politics in state and nation* (New York: Alfred A. Knopf, 1950).
[3] Frank J. Sorauf, *Party politics in America* (Boston: Little, Brown, 1968).

organizational resources, the degree of discord within the ranks of their own elites, and the power of incumbency. Finally, they met a common end: in every case, factional competition in single-party states gave way to party competition in two-party states.

In the next section, we discuss our electoral data and the information they contain about the strength of factions in the electorate. We then examine each of the four states, recounting the activities of the factions that operated within their dominant parties and presenting alongside the responses of the voters, moving west to east to south. Finally, we discuss the cases in comparison with each other and in relation to Mayhew's portrayal of party organizations. Our conclusion presents a summary of the patterns of factional politics across the country and the contribution that an analysis of "parties within parties" might make in understanding factions *and* parties.

FACTIONS AND SLATING

Of the features characteristic of traditional party organizations, the most central is their ability to control nominations by slating.[4] Successful slating implies the power to signal or to direct voters to support preferred candidates. If factions are strong, all the candidates they endorse will receive support from the same voters.

Building on this insight, we use the correlations in the votes in primaries for candidates for different offices across counties to identify states with factional competition. If a faction presents a slate of candidates in a primary and it is successful in drawing voters to support it, then the candidates on its ticket will receive similar levels of electoral support in any given area.[5] In other words, when factions are well organized, primary candidates' vote shares will be correlated across offices.

We are not the first to identify factions in this manner. In *Southern Politics*, Key displayed scatterplots of the vote shares of pairs of candidates for different offices by county in runoff (second) primaries.[6] They helped him to identify cohesive factions in Louisiana and more occasional instances of correspondence in Florida, Georgia, and Tennessee.

Our analysis is in the same spirit but even more comprehensive. We exploit a new data set of county-level primary election returns for seven state-wide offices: governor, lieutenant governor, secretary of state, attorney general, treasurer, auditor (or controller), and U.S. senator. The data encompass the forty-eight contiguous states for most primary elections from

---

[4] Mayhew, *Placing parties*: 18–20.
[5] To the extent that factions are concentrated geographically, as the secondary literature generally finds.
[6] Key, *Southern politics*: 66, 104, 109, 170–72.

1908 to 2008.[7] Because of the nature of our measure, we exclude states with fewer than twenty counties and primary elections with fewer than three contested nominations.[8]

We derive the "slates" themselves from the data, by connecting one candidate to another according to the highest correlations. The first slate is the set of candidates, one per office, with the highest average correlation across the set, and the second slate is the set of candidates with the second highest average correlation. (The details are in the Appendix to this chapter.) The figures present the average correlation for the first slate. Thus, our measure represents the cohesion in voting across the best-organized slate.

Factional Slating in the United States

Figure 7.1 presents the slate correlations for both major parties in all states in all the years in our dataset. Three features in the data stand out. First, most of the "slate" correlations are low: 93 percent are below 0.6, 75 percent are below 0.38, the overall average is 0.31, and the median is 0.26. Second, only five states have slate correlations above 0.6 in the same party for three or more elections – Louisiana Democrats, Minnesota Republicans, New Mexico Democrats, North Dakota Republicans, and Wisconsin Republicans. Four of these states will be our main interest in this paper. Finally, the slate correlations are even lower after about 1960. Before then, 90 percent of the correlations are below 0.6 with an average correlation of 0.32; after, 99 percent are below 0.6 with an average correlation of 0.28. The typical circumstance in party primaries is quite low levels of association in the votes across offices.

Our focus in this paper is the exceptions, four states – North Dakota, Minnesota, Wisconsin, and Louisiana – that had extended periods of factional conflict that played out in primary voting. (We will discuss the exclusion of New Mexico in the concluding section.) These four states, we will also show, had well-elaborated factional organizations that endorsed, advertised, and electioneered for their slates, that is, they had factions that operated in primary elections as parties operate in general elections.[9] The most developed and disciplined of all the party factions was a pair of organizations that competed for nominations in North Dakota's Republican Party primaries. In recognition of its archetypal status, we will give a fairly detailed account of the historical development of factional competition in North Dakota and then discuss the

---

[7] The sources include ICPSR Studies Nos. 71 and 72; official election returns from each state's election office (usually the secretary of state or the state board of elections); state government manuals ("Blue Books") and statistical registers; and reports in newspapers.

[8] The exclusions affect Maine, New Hampshire, and New Jersey and any primary election with no contestation for down-ballot nominations.

[9] Key notes Louisiana, North Dakota, and Wisconsin as states with factional slating. V. O. Key Jr., *American state politics: an introduction* (New York: Alfred A. Knopf, 1963): 128n.

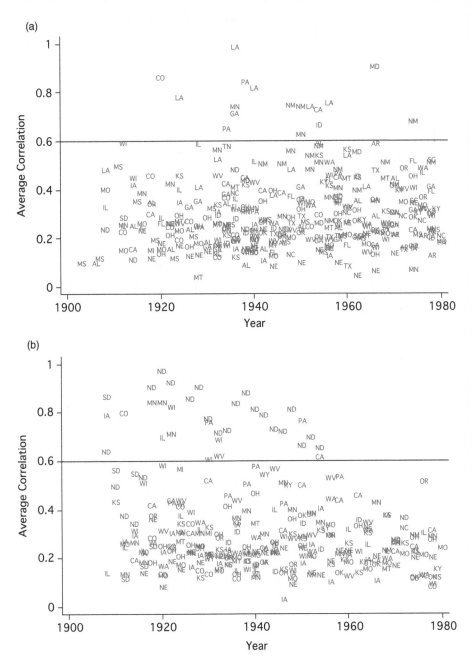

FIGURE 7.1 Average correlations in top slates. (a) All states, Democratic primaries. (b) All states, Republican primaries.

other three states in a more compact fashion. We will develop some comparisons and contrasts, and some final thoughts about factions and parties, in the Discussion section.

FOUR CASES OF PARTIES WITHIN PARTIES

North Dakota

The most impressive record of competitive two-party politics within a political party belongs to the Republican Party in North Dakota. For forty years, from the middle 1910s through the middle 1950s, North Dakota Republicans voted for factional slates with a consistency rivaling voters in partisan general elections. Figure 7.2 shows the patterns.

The impetus for the creation of two parties within the North Dakota Republican Party was the formation of the Farmers' Nonpartisan Political League in February 1915. The brainchild of Arthur C. Townley, a veteran Socialist Party organizer, the Nonpartisan League (NPL) was the result of a decade of agitation for the interests of farmers. Capitalizing on the failure of the North Dakota legislature to authorize the expenditure of state funds to build and operate a terminal grain elevator – in the heat of the moment, a state representative reportedly told the assembled masses of farmers in the gallery to "go home and slop the hogs and leave the lawmaking to us" – Townley recruited a cadre of organizers and sent them out into the countryside. North Dakota was the most agrarian state in the country, with more than 70 percent of its population resident on farms. By the end of the year, the Nonpartisan League had a political program, a monthly newspaper, and 40,000 dues-paying members.[10]

The League held county conferences in February 1916, leading up to its first nominating convention in Fargo in March 1916. A "league" and not a "party," and "nonpartisan" in its approach to the two major political parties, the NPL endorsed a slate of candidates for each of the state-wide offices, all but one of them for nomination in the Republican primary. One was an incumbent, Secretary of State Thomas Hall. Three others had already announced their candidacies, including William Langer, the Morton County state's attorney, for attorney general, and Carl R. Kositzky, the secretary of the Tax Commission, for auditor. The rest of the slate reflected the determination of the League to present a "farmers ticket." For treasurer, the League endorsed a Democrat, Patrick M. Casey, a county leader in the Society of Equity, a farm organization with a large following in the state. For governor, it chose a Pembina County

---

[10] On the history of the Nonpartisan League, see Robert L. Morlan, *Political prairie fire: the Nonpartisan League, 1915–1922* (Minneapolis: University of Minnesota Press, 1955) and Larry Remele, "Power to the people: the Nonpartisan League," pp. 66–92 in Thomas W. Howard, ed., *The North Dakota political tradition* (Ames: Iowa State University Press, 1981).

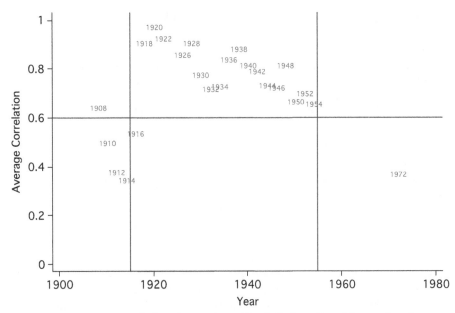

FIGURE 7.2 Average correlations in top slates, North Dakota Republican primaries.
Missing primary election data for 1924.

farmer and political novice, Lynn J. Frazier. The NPL's newspaper, the *Non-partisan Leader*, proclaimed him "the new Cincinnatus."[11]

With the energy of the new organization behind it, the NPL slate swept the Republican primary in June. Frazier received a majority of the vote and carried forty-six of fifty-three counties, defeating a progressive candidate, former lieutenant governor Usher L. Burdick, and a conservative candidate, sitting lieutenant governor John H. Fraine. The rest of the NPL slate won Republican nominations as well, and in the fall election, they all won offices, bringing along a majority in the lower house of the legislature as well.

The League's slating made a tremendous impact on the 1916 primary. The NPL endorsed Republican candidates for five of the six top state-wide offices,

[11] In addition to Morlan, *Political prairie fire*, good sources of information about North Dakota party politics include Edward C. Blackorby, *Prairie rebel: the public life of William Lemke* (Lincoln: University of Nebraska Press, 1963); Edward C. Blackorby, *Prairie populist: the life and times of Usher L. Burdick* (Bismarck: State Historical Society of North Dakota, 2001); Elwyn B. Robinson, *History of North Dakota* (Lincoln: University of Nebraska Press, 1995): chaps. 15–20; and the articles in Howard, *The North Dakota political tradition*. Another valuable source of information about North Dakota politics is www.ndstudies.org, which presents excerpts from the local newspaper dispatches of the era. For an analysis of the League's electoral strategies in North Dakota and other states, see Samuel P. Huntington, "The election tactics of the Nonpartisan League," *Mississippi Valley Historical Review* 36 (March 1950): 613–32.

with only a single incumbent among them.[12] Table 7.1 shows the correlations of their primary votes across the fifty-three North Dakota counties. Frazier's share of the vote was very highly correlated with the votes for the League's candidates for lieutenant governor, Anton T. Kraabel, and attorney general, William Langer. His vote was strongly related to the vote for Carl Kositzky, the NPL candidate for auditor, but only modestly related to the vote for Thomas Hall, the NPL candidate for secretary of state and the only incumbent.[13]

Table 7.1 also reveals the extent to which the NPL, running on an agrarian socialist platform, remade the political landscape in North Dakota. Before 1916, the primary cleavage in the Republican Party in North Dakota, as elsewhere, was between conservatives and progressives, the inheritance of populism and a later campaign against the Republican "machine" of Alexander McKenzie.[14] The Leaguers occupied an ideological space closer to that of progressives than regulars, hence the vote for Frazier overlapped the vote for Burdick, the progressive, more than the vote for Fraine, the conservative. The League was not, however, just a new name for North Dakota progressivism. The progressive program addressed the needs of educated citizens and commercial interests in North Dakota's "urban" counties – such as they were, in a state with only three municipalities over 10,000 in population – rather than the needs of farmers. Accordingly, the Nonpartisan League did not make an endorsement in the race for the GOP nomination for the U.S. Senate, which offered a clear ideological choice between a progressive, Ward County state's attorney Ragnvald A. Nestos; a conservative, Governor L. B. Hanna;

[12] North Dakota elected a large number of state officers, including an insurance commissioner, a commissioner of agriculture and labor, a superintendent of schools, and tax and railroad commissioners. We focus on the six top offices with general responsibilities.

[13] Our aggregated county-level data do not allow us to observe the actual content of individual ballots, of course, but we do not believe that ecological inference is so hazardous in this case. Ecological correlations are seriously misleading when the probability that individuals of a particular social kind take a particular action depends inversely on the aggregate proportions of individuals of their kind in their environs. The classic illustration is the aggregate correlation between the African American population and the Democratic Party vote across southern counties, which arose because white voters in heavily black counties were more likely to support Democratic candidates than white voters in counties with few black residents. Our variables, however, are not social characteristics but candidate vote shares. In order for a negative individual-level correlation to be observed as a positive aggregate correlation, conservatives in areas with high support for Frazier for governor would have to be much more likely to support Langer for attorney general than conservative voters in areas with low Frazier support, which seems unlikely and, in fact, contrary to the response we would expect the social forces to produce.

[14] See Robert P. Wilkins, "Alexander McKenzie and the politics of bossism," pp. 3–39, and Charles N. Glaab, "John Burke and the progressive revolt," pp. 40–65, in Howard, *The North Dakota political tradition.*

TABLE 7.1 *1916 Republican Primary*

	Gov	Lt Gov	Atty Gen	Sec State	Auditor
NPL nominee	Frazier	Kraabel	Langer	Hall	Kositzky
Kraabel	0.94				
Langer	0.92	0.89			
Hall	0.34	0.31	0.35		
Kositzky	0.56	0.61	0.51	0.40	
Not NPL endorsed					
Gov: Burdick	−0.31	−0.17	−0.21	−0.49	−0.50
Gov: Fraine	−0.75	−0.82	−0.75	−0.04	−0.32
Sen: Hanna	−0.63	−0.61	−0.61	0.12	−0.42
Sen: McCumber	−0.05	−0.09	−0.08	0.06	0.19
Sen: Nestos	0.50	0.51	0.51	−0.19	0.13

and the standpat incumbent, Porter J. McCumber, an associate of Alexander McKenzie, despite the progressive's clear appeal to NPL voters.[15]

In office, Governor Frazier pursued the NPL program aggressively, assisted in the legislature by Townley and NPL counsel William Lemke, who took it upon themselves to whip the faction's supporters. Although much of the program was standard progressive fare that passed easily into law – a nine-hour work day for women, a state grain-grading system, a land-title registration system, regulation of railroad rates and practices – other parts were proudly radical. The most controversial was a plan to amend the state constitution to broaden the initiative and referendum, to establish the recall, to raise the state debt limit, and to create the constitutional support for state-owned enterprises. The legislation passed the state house but died in the state senate, which was controlled by conservative and progressive Republican holdovers.

The constitutional legislation, and the strong-arm tactics that Townley and Lemke used to advance it, united the opposition. In April 1917, fifty-eight lawmakers opposed to the League, a combination of conservatives and progressives, convened an "anti-socialist conference" to map a strategy for resistance. They created a new organization, the Lincoln Republican League, and then met the next month in Minot to endorse candidates in the Republican primary. For the gubernatorial race against Governor Frazier, they nominated state treasurer John Steen, the only state officer not endorsed by the NPL in 1916. They also recruited candidates for all of the other constitutional offices. One was an incumbent, Anton T. Kraabel, the lieutenant governor and a

---

[15] Burdick was well regarded in agrarian circles and the NPL leadership attempted to persuade Nestos to withdraw from the Senate race so that Burdick might run for the senatorial nomination instead, with the NPL's endorsement. Burdick explained some of the circumstances in Usher L. Burdick, *History of the farmers' political action in North Dakota* (Baltimore: Wirth Brothers, 1944), chap. 9.

progressive.[16] To broaden their appeal, particularly to crossover Democrats, the conferees adopted a new name, the Independent Voters Association (IVA). They attacked the League for its "socialism" and its lack of vigor in the war effort.[17]

With a limited budget and only a month to campaign, the Independents were overwhelmed. The NPL candidates scored a big victory in the 1918 Republican primary. Frazier won renomination, and reelection in the fall, as did every other NPL nominee for state-wide office except one. The League defended its majority in the state house and captured a majority in the state senate. The scatterplot of Frazier's vote with his ticket mates' shows a very close correspondence, with their highest support in the central and northwestern parts of the state and their lowest in the east, along the Red River.[18] In 1916, the vote for Frazier for governor correlated with the vote for Kraabel for lieutenant governor at 0.94. In 1918, with Kraabel's defection to the Independent ticket, the Frazier vote and the Kraabel vote correlated at −0.91. *That* is slating.

With the support of fresh majorities in both chambers of the state legislature, the League passed the most radical economic program ever enacted by an American state, including a state-owned bank, a state-owned mill and elevator, a state home mortgage finance association, and a state hail insurance plan.

The contest between the Nonpartisans and the Independents set the course of North Dakota Republican politics for the next two generations. As factions, the two sides were very competitive and unusually disciplined. Their effectiveness was not accidental. It was the product of thorough organization.

From the very start, the NPL had a highly elaborate political structure. It had a central organization, a triumvirate of A. C. Townley, William Lemke, and Fred B. Wood. It endorsed candidates at state conventions and selected the delegates in meetings at the county and precinct level. It publicized its slates through its house organ, the *Nonpartisan Leader*, and a chain of newspapers that it began to assemble in 1916. Finally, it had a membership of dues-payers. The opportunities for involvement, the steady communications, even the demands for dues were part of a considered strategy to win commitment from campaign activists and instill loyalty – a kind of factional partisan identification – in voters. As Townley explained it in a (presumably affectionate) testimonial to the psychological impact of paying dues, "Make

---

[16] Burdick, who witnessed the events, reports that Kraabel broke with the League in 1917, having "lost confidence" in its leaders. Morlan, who made a careful study of the period, says that the NPL left Kraabel off its 1918 ticket and instead endorsed Howard R. Wood, the state house speaker and the son of an NPL organizer. Burdick, *History of the farmers' political action*: 85; Morlan, *Political prairie fire*: 95, 186.

[17] On the origins and activities of the IVA, see D. Jerome Tweton, "The anti-League movement: the IVA," pp. 93–122 in Howard, *The North Dakota political tradition*.

[18] The only exceptions to the pattern of correlation were a few counties in south central North Dakota with the state's largest populations of Russian-Germans, the voters most committed to an isolationist foreign policy. Almost all of the politicians in North Dakota opposed the war, so Frazier was not unique, though perhaps better known than most.

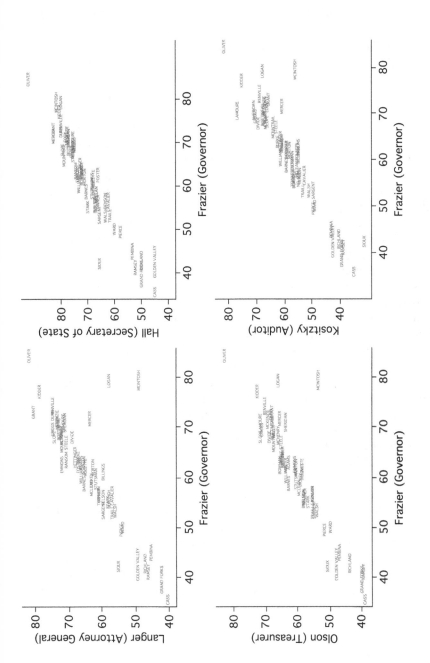

FIGURE 7.3 North Dakota NPL candidates in 1918.

the rubes pay their God-damn money to join and they'll stick – stick till hell freezes over."[19] The NPL was, truly, a party organization, and a robust one by any standard.

The IVA copied the NPL model almost exactly. In December 1918, one of the conveners of the 1918 Independent conference, state representative Edwin W. Everson, invited eight associates to a meeting in Cooperstown. They incorporated the IVA, wrote its bylaws, designated themselves as its first executive committee, and elected a president, Edwin Everson, and a full-time secretary, Theodore G. "Two-Bit" Nelson, formerly an organizer for the Society of Equity.[20] They laid plans for local organizations, state-wide conventions, and ten-dollar memberships. (At that point, NPL memberships, originally $6, cost $16 for two years.) The IVA held its first state convention in January 1919 in Bismarck, mostly to plan strategy for the upcoming legislative session. In March it published the first issue of the *Independent*.

The effects of organization were soon felt. On the heels of electoral victory and legislative triumph, Governor Frazier's administration broke apart. Treasurer Olbert A. Olson and Secretary of State Thomas Hall resisted Townley's direction and criticized Frazier's legislative program. Carl Kositzky's audits found featherbedding, padded expenses, and frivolous spending in League-administered state agencies. Most seriously, Attorney General William Langer upheld the election of an Independent as state superintendent of education, exposed financial improprieties in the NPL's acquisition of a bank, and engaged in a war of denunciations with A. C. Townley. Townley, Langer said, "might as well realize that the state's officers respect the people of North Dakota, and are not the petty hirelings of a dictator."[21]

The result of the strife was a mass defection to the Independent ticket in 1920. Langer led the "Anti-Townley" ticket, challenging Governor Frazier for the gubernatorial nomination. He was joined there by Thomas Hall and Carl Kositzky, seeking renomination to their offices on the IVA line. The incumbents – Governor Frazier, Lieutenant Governor Wood, Secretary of State Hall, and Auditor Kositzky – all won.[22] Through it all, though, the factional lines held. Table 7.2 shows the correlations across counties between the vote shares of the gubernatorial candidates and their down-ballot running mates. The vote for Frazier for governor was very highly correlated with Wood's vote for lieutenant governor (0.97), Lemke's vote for attorney general (.98), and Walker's vote for treasurer (0.97) (and, likewise, Langer's vote with Streeter's,

---

[19] Morlan, *Political prairie fire*: 27.
[20] Both Everson and Nelson were former Leaguers. Everson was reelected to the state house with NPL endorsement in 1916 but quickly fell out with Townley and Lemke.
[21] Tweton, "The anti-League movement": 103.
[22] Senator Asle J. Gronna, however, lost the nomination to the NPL's candidate, Edwin F. Ladd, a chemist at North Dakota Agricultural College and the administrator of the state's pure-food laws. A progressive, Gronna had no enthusiasm for the NPL and declined its endorsement.

TABLE 7.2 *1920 Republican Primary*

	Governor	Lt Gov	Atty Gen	Sec State	Treasurer	Auditor	Senator
NPL	Frazier	Wood	Lemke	Cahill	Walker	Poindexter	Ladd
IVA	Langer	Streeter	Gallagher	Hall	Steen	Kositzky	Gronna
r		0.97	0.98	0.96	0.97	0.97	0.93/0.91

Gallagher's, and Steen's).[23] Even more impressively, Frazier's vote was as highly correlated with Hall's and Kositzky's in the negative direction in 1920 as it was in the positive direction in 1918.

Indeed, the factional lines between the NPL and the IVA held throughout the following decade. Their influence on voters survived the campaign to recall Governor Frazier in 1921, the first – and until 2003 the only – successful effort to replace a chief executive, and the inauguration of an Independent, Ragnvald Nestos, as his successor. It survived the failure of both factional newspapers, the *Nonpartisan Leader* in 1923 and the *Independent* (by then the *Rural Independent*) in 1924, and the retirements of A. C. Townley and Two-Bit Nelson. It survived the rise of popular incumbents, such as Attorney General George F. Shafer (IVA), Auditor John Steen (IVA), and Secretaries of State Thomas Hall (IVA) and Robert Byrne (NPL), all of whom enjoyed extended periods of service.[24] With a strong hold on Republican voters, the NPL and the IVA remained robust as slate makers. Every two years, in the months before the June primary, they convened to choose candidates for the Republican nominations, and every two years they presented voters with two choices – and usually *only* two choices – for the main state offices. From 1924 to 1932, through the gubernatorial terms of Ragnvald A. Nestos (IVA), Arthur G. Sorlie (NPL), and George F. Shafer (IVA), the two factions produced a high level of cohesion in primary voting.

The early 1930s, a time of party realignment in national politics, was also a time of factional realignment in North Dakota Republican politics. The realignment began, inauspiciously enough, in 1928, when William Langer received an endorsement for the Republican nomination for attorney general – from the NPL. He lost, but the race reintroduced him to the NPL and the North Dakota electorate. Invigorated, and still burning with ambition, Langer turned his energies to the rejuvenation of the League. He was a capable organizer with

---

[23] The two correlations reported for the Senate vote indicate the presence of a third candidate in the primary; the first indicates that the vote for Frazier correlated with the vote for Ladd at 0.93 and the vote for Langer correlated with the vote for Gronna at 0.91.

[24] As we will show, incumbency had a weakening effect on factions in other states.

the personal wealth to build up a new NPL infrastructure, including a new NPL newspaper, the *Leader* (in 1933). Four years and $20,000 later, he had a dominant influence in it. The NPL gave him its endorsement in the race for governor, and with the IVA saddled with Herbert Hoover, he won the Republican nomination. The NPL candidates for four of the five major state-wide offices won the GOP nominations alongside him. In November 1932, Langer was elected to be the seventeenth governor of North Dakota.

Throughout his career, Bill Langer showed a magnificent ability to inspire voters and a prodigious tendency to alienate colleagues. Bohemian German and Catholic by descent, the son of a well-to-do farmer and investor, he had a strong following among farmers and Russian Germans. After his defection to the IVA in 1920, he gradually restored ties with the NPL's group of "radicals," although many of them, including Senator Lynn Frazier, were still chary about him. (He was never on good terms with Senator Gerald P. Nye, an NPL "moderate.") His success in rebuilding the League's organizational capabilities made the NPL comeback in 1932 possible and, not coincidentally, gave Langer firm control of the machinery.[25]

Langer's term as governor was marked by radical populist policies and by legal actions that resulted in his removal from office and the inauguration of three new governors in the span of seven months.[26] For the next ten years, the two factions in the North Dakota Republican Party were defined by Bill Langer, by his personal supporters and opponents. Langer controlled the NPL, so his allies ran on the Nonpartisan slate. The anti-Langer faction, a combination of the NPL "moderates," the scattered remnants of the Independents, and fresh enemies alarmed by his ruthlessness and ambition, typically claimed the "Progressive" label. They were also generally known, however, as "rumpers."

The divisions over Langer first expressed themselves at the League's convention in 1932. By a narrow majority, the delegates voted to endorse Langer for governor rather than NPL moderate T. H. H. Thoresen, its gubernatorial candidate in 1928. Langer's opponents balked. They withdrew from the

---

[25] See Glenn H. Smith, "William Langer and the art of personal politics," pp. 123–50 in Howard, *The North Dakota political tradition*; and Glenn H. Smith, *Langer of North Dakota: a study in isolationism, 1940–1959* (New York: Garland Publishing, 1979): chap. 1. Although not Russian in origin himself, Langer spoke fluent German and shared the dialect and the culture of the German diaspora. See Timothy J. Kloberdanz, "Volksdeutsche: the eastern European Germans," pp. 117–82 in William C. Sherman, ed., *Plains folk: North Dakota's ethnic history* (Fargo: North Dakota Institute for Regional Studies, 1988): 147–48.

[26] Federal authorities accused Langer of requiring federal employees to donate to the NPL. A federal jury found him guilty, but the conviction was reversed on appeal. Of the three succeeding governors, the first and the third were Leaguers nominated on Langer's slates in 1932 and 1934. Both became opponents. The second, Thomas H. Moodie, was a Democrat who defeated Langer's wife, Lydia, his replacement on the Republican ticket in 1934. The state supreme court later ruled that Moodie did not meet the state's residency requirement. For the details, see Roy L. Miller, "The gubernatorial controversy in North Dakota," *American Political Science Review* 29 (June 1935): 418–32.

convention and chose an alternative slate of candidates for several of the state offices, awarding the gubernatorial endorsement to I. J. Moe, a lawyer and sometime minor office holder. The rump convention in 1932 gave the anti-Langer faction a nickname. Running as the Progressive Republican ticket, they also gave it a name.

By 1934, the new alignment in North Dakota factional politics was fully developed. Governor Langer was under indictment. Lieutenant Governor Ole H. Olson and Secretary of State Robert Byrne publicly opposed him. The NPL's convention built a new slate around Langer, endorsing Walter Welford for lieutenant governor and James D. Gronna for secretary of state. Attorney General Peter O. Sathre, a loyalist for the moment, received the endorsement for renomination for his office.[27] For the second time, the Progressives held a second NPL convention and endorsed a second NPL slate for most offices: Olson for lieutenant governor, Byrne for secretary of state, and Thoresen for governor. The Independents met one last time, but they could not even fill out a full slate for state senator James P. Cain, the IVA's last nominee for governor. Langer won going away, with Thoresen second and Cain third.

Thus, the conflict between the NPL and the IVA gave way to the conflict between the NPL and the NPL Progressives, between the NPL factions for and against Bill Langer. But the face of North Dakota Republican politics changed hardly at all. Tables 7.3, 7.4, and 7.5 show the realignment in process. From 1932 to 1936, four NPL officials, all of them nominated with Langer, moved off the NPL slate and on to the Progressive ticket: Lieutenant Governor Olson and Secretary of State Byrne in 1934 and Attorney General Sathre and Lieutenant Governor Welford (running as the incumbent governor) in 1936. Voters did an about-face on each and every one of them. Running on the same ticket, Langer's vote correlated with Olson's at 0.88, with Byrne's at 0.78, and with Sathre's at 0.81; running on opposing tickets, Langer's vote correlated with Olson's at –0.77, with Byrne's at –0.89, and with Sathre's at –0.96. Each lost his nomination and his job. Welford, who faced off against Langer for the 1936 gubernatorial nomination, won the Republican nomination. He lost his office, however, when Langer entered the general election as an independent and won, with NPL support. As a slate-maker, A. C. Townley had nothing on Bill Langer. With a strong basis in grassroots organization, the slating power of the North Dakota factions was still impressive almost twenty years later. The transition from one bifactional alignment to another was remarkably smooth.

The new alignment in North Dakota Republican politics – one faction of a faction facing another – proved unstable. The problem, as in party politics, was the minority faction's inability to compete. After Welford's victory over Langer in the 1936 GOP primary, nullified by Langer's victory in the general election,

---

[27] Arthur J. Gronna, the NPL's 1932 candidate for attorney general, and James D. Gronna, the NPL's nominee for secretary of state in 1934 and 1936, were the sons of progressive senator Asle J. Gronna, whom Edwin Ladd and the NPL ousted in 1920.

TABLE 7.3 *1932 Republican Primary*

	Governor	Lt Gov	Atty Gen	Sec State	Treasurer	Auditor	Senator
NPL	Langer	O H Olson	A Gronna	Byrne	Dale	B E Baker	Nye
Progressive	Moe	Cuthbert		Byrne			
IVA	Hyland	R Johnson	Morris	Garnes	Wardrope	Steen	Shafer
r		0.88/0.33/ 0.77	0.66/–/ 0.73	0.78/ −0.10/0.86	0.78/–/ 0.88	0.65/–/ 0.68	0.54/–/0.48

TABLE 7.4 *1934 Republican Primary*

	Governor	Lt Gov	Atty Gen	Sec State	Treasurer	Auditor	Senator
NPL	Langer	Welford	Sathre	J Gronna	Gray	B E Baker	Frazier
Progressive	Thoresen	O H Olson	Crum	Byrne			Frazier
IVA	Cain	Fredrickson	T Johnson		Wright	McFadgen	Buck
r		0.94/0.88/ 0.79	0.81/0.76/ 0.85	0.89/ 0.81/–	0.89/–/ 0.81	0.58/–/ 0.75	0.62/ – 0.15/0.89

TABLE 7.5 *1936 Republican Primary*

	Governor	Lt Gov	Atty Gen	Sec State	Treasurer	Auditor
NPL	Langer	Crockett	Owen	J Gronna	Gray	B E Baker
Progressive	Welford	Thoresen	Sathre	Pippin	Aljets	
r		0.98	0.96	0.77	0.81	unopp

the Progressives won just a single major state office for the remainder of their existence. The anti-Langer faction managed to influence state-wide elections only by lining up behind the Democrats' nominee for governor, John Moses, who won each of his three terms by defeating an NPL Republican.[28]

---

[28] The rumpers' only win was Thomas Hall's return to statewide office as secretary of state, which he achieved running on a cross-party ticket as a Democrat in 1942. (He subsequently ran as a Republican.) The Progressives had better success in congressional elections, where they often split the House seats with the NPL. They also endorsed Senator Gerald Nye's successful bid for

In the years following the IVA's death and the NPL's split, independent Republicans made several attempts to organize a more effective opposition, without much success. In 1943, however, three veteran state senators mapped out a plan for a new independent political organization, with an executive committee, an executive secretary, and a statement of principles. The prime mover in the effort was Milton R. Young, the senate majority leader, who took responsibility for building up county organizations state wide. They called their creation the Republican Organizing Committee (ROC).[29]

The advent of the Republican Organizing Committee realigned the factions in the North Dakota Republican Party for the third time. In 1944, the ROC held its first convention in Bismarck. Its supporters, one observer reckoned, were about one third carryovers from the IVA, about one third disaffected Leaguers, and about one third young people with no set allegiances. For governor, the convention endorsed its keynote speaker, Fred G. Aandahl, a farmer and former state senator. The remainder of the ROC ticket featured names familiar from earlier iterations of the Progressive slates. The advertisements for the Aandahl slate promised "the American Way – less and better government" and urged the citizens of the state to "vote for trustworthy men in the best interests of North Dakota." Their allies in the press preached against the evils of Bill Langer, "still the ringmaster and guiding genius of the political machine which he built up while governor," dismissing Attorney General Alvin G. Strutz, the NPL's gubernatorial candidate, as "merely a glorified office boy for Mr. Langer."[30] The ROC ticket swept to victory in the June primary, carrying every nomination for the major state offices except auditor, held by a five-term incumbent, Berta E. Baker. Even though Strutz ran as an independent in the fall, the ROC Republicans also won big in November.[31] The "independents" gained control of the top state executive offices for the first time in twelve years.

The third factional "party system" in the North Dakota Republican Party was still robust in its influence on voters. As shown in Table 7.6, the

renomination in his 1938 race against Langer. On the period, see Adam J. Schweitzer, "The political campaign of John Moses," *North Dakota History* 32 (January 1965): 18–39.

[29] On the creation of the Republican Organizing Committee, see Dan Rylance, "Fred G. Aandahl and the ROC movement," pp. 151–82 in Howard, *The North Dakota political tradition*.

[30] Rylance, "Fred G. Aandahl": 172–73.

[31] The Nonpartisans gained a measure of satisfaction in the race for the U.S. Senate. Senator Nye received a reluctant endorsement from the ROC but won a three-way race for the nomination nonetheless, defeating the NPL candidate, Representative Usher L. Burdick, and an independent, Lynn U. Stahlbaum. Stahlbaum then ran as a third candidate in the general election, tipping the seat to Governor John Moses, a Democrat. Some saw the sinister hand of Senator Langer in Nye's defeat. When Burdick lost the primary, Langer openly encouraged Stahlbaum to take a second shot at Nye in the general. A former national commander of the American Legion, Stahlbaum siphoned Republican votes away from Nye, an outspoken isolationist. Moses died shortly after taking office, and Governor Aandahl appointed Milton Young to the seat. Young later won a special election for the remainder of the term, defeating Nye for the Republican nomination.

TABLE 7.6 *1944 Republican Primary*

	Governor	Lt Gov	Atty Gen	Sec State	Treasurer	Auditor	Senator
NPL	Strutz	Hagen	Garberg	C Anderson	Gilbreath	B E Baker	Burdick
ROC	Aandahl	Dahl	N Johnson	Hall		Krueger	Bryant	Nye
r		0.95	0.68	0.82	0.64	0.61	0.83/0.07

correlations between the vote at the top of the ticket and the votes down the ballot were still quite high.

But forces were building that would bring the factional competition within the Republican Party to an end. The Farmers Union, at 33,000 members the largest lobbying group in the state, was influential within the NPL and closely aligned at the national level with labor and liberals in the Democratic Party.[32] One by one, slowly at first, League politicians declared themselves Democrats rather than Republicans, and, increasingly, young NPL "insurgents" pressed the NPL "old guard" for a change in affiliation. One of the leaders in the insurgent effort was Quentin N. Burdick, the son of an NPL mainstay, U.S. Representative Usher L. Burdick. In 1942, the younger Burdick was the NPL's choice for the Republican nomination for lieutenant governor. In 1946, he was the Democratic gubernatorial nominee.

In 1956, the insurgents gained the upper hand. Although the NPL continued to elect its candidates to Congress and the down-ballot offices, it had not won a single gubernatorial nomination in the last six attempts. Democrats were hopeful, moreover, that the unpopularity of U.S. Agriculture Secretary Ezra Taft Benson and his Republican farm policy would allow them to make gains in November. The old guard absented itself and the League convention voted 173-3 to file its candidates in the Democratic primary. The delegates endorsed Quentin Burdick for the senatorial nomination and Wallace E. Warner for the gubernatorial nomination. Like Burdick, Warner was previously an NPL candidate (for the Republican gubernatorial nomination in 1954) and formerly the state's attorney general (elected on the NPL Republican line in 1948). The North Dakota Democratic Party accepted the nominees and a merger, becoming the Democratic–Nonpartisan League Party, still the official name of Democratic Party in North Dakota.[33]

[32] Ross B. Talbot, "The politics of farm organizations in North Dakota," doctoral dissertation, University of Chicago, 1953: 167–99.
[33] Talbot, "The politics of farm organizations": 183–95; Ross B. Talbot, "North Dakota – a two-party state?" *North Dakota Quarterly* 25 (Fall 1957): 93–104; Robinson, *History of North Dakota*: 470–72.

The NPL's old guard stood fast with the Republicans. In 1956, the Republicans convened a unity conference to make peace between the NPL tories and the ROC. The participants included almost all the League's incumbents, among them Attorney General Leslie R. Burgum, Secretary of State Ben Meier, and Congressman Usher Burdick. (Senator Langer stayed in the GOP fold as well and ran for reelection on the Republican ticket in 1958.) An old-guard Leaguer and former lieutenant governor, Ray Schnell, mounted a primary challenge to the endorsed unity candidate, state senator John E. Davis. (Davis won.) Every other unity candidate for the top state-wide offices ran in the primary unopposed.[34]

Thus, two-faction Republican politics in North Dakota gave way to two-party national politics in North Dakota.

Minnesota

The NPL took the same principles and the same tactics next door to Minnesota, but without equivalent success. For a short time, the competition between the NPL and GOP regulars ordered Republican voters. Factional contestation quickly gave way, though, to two-party competition. Figure 7.4 shows the slate correlations.

The NPL crossed the Red River into western Minnesota in 1916. It made Minnesota a main focus of its missionary work the following year. In January 1917, the League's leaders announced the creation of the National Nonpartisan League and the appointment of A. C. Townley as its president. Seeking a more central staging point for its efforts, it moved the national headquarters from Fargo to St. Paul. Its organizers helped to found the Minnesota Nonpartisan League in March 1917.[35]

At the time of the League's entry into Minnesota politics, the state's Republican Party was dominated by the typical midwestern mix of progressives and conservatives, typified by Senator Knute Nelson and Governor Joseph A. A. Burnquist. As in North Dakota, the League reoriented and sharpened the factional divisions. In 1918, it endorsed a slate of candidates for the Republican

---

[34] Congressman Burdick served his last term in Congress from 1957 to 1959. His son Quentin won the seat in 1958 as a Democrat, the first North Dakota had ever elected to the U.S. House. Shortly after, Senator Langer died, and Quentin Burdick won the special election for his seat in 1960, narrowly defeating Governor Davis. Later in 1960, Democratic state representative William L. Guy defeated Lieutenant Governor Clarence P. Dahl to earn the first of his four terms as governor. On the shift of the NPL from the Democrats' perspective, see William L. Guy, *When seldom was heard a discouraging word: Bill Guy remembers* (Fargo: North Dakota Institute for Regional Studies, 1992).

[35] The League's activities eventually encompassed thirteen states as distant as Oklahoma and Washington, as well as two Canadian provinces, Saskatchewan and Alberta. Seventy percent of the NPL's membership, though, was in the two Dakotas, Minnesota, and Montana. After North Dakota, its greatest influence was in Minnesota.

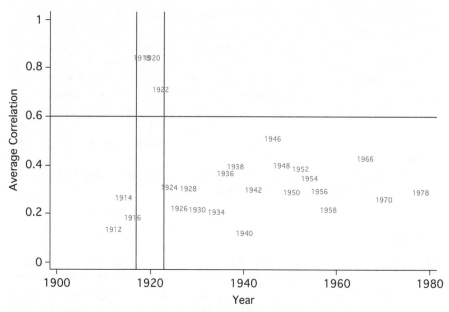

FIGURE 7.4 Average correlations in top slates, Minnesota Republican primaries.

nomination for most of the state-wide offices, led by Charles A. Lindbergh, a former five-term congressman and a well-known author and lecturer. They challenged Governor Burnquist and a ticket of incumbents and lost every race. Bidding for a better outcome in 1920, the Leaguers combined with a labor group behind a new slate headed by Henrik Shipstead, a dentist by profession and the NPL's most successful unsuccessful candidate in 1918. They squared off against a slate of regulars led by a protégé of Senator Nelson, the state auditor, Jacob A. O. Preus. The coalition ticket lost again, but Shipstead's slate, like Lindbergh's, induced a high degree of cohesion in the Republican primary voting (see Table 7.7).[36]

As in North Dakota, one factor in the polarization of the Minnesota electorate was the fierce reaction of the state's Republican leadership to the radical

[36] The sources on this period in Minnesota politics include Morlan, *Political prairie fire*; Carl H. Chrislock, *The progressive era in Minnesota, 1899–1918* (St. Paul: Minnesota Historical Society, 1971): chaps. 11, 13–15; and Millard L. Gieske, *Minnesota Farmer-Laborism: the third-party alternative* (Minneapolis: University of Minnesota Press, 1979): chaps. 3–4. On Lindbergh and the 1918 campaign, see Robert L. Morlan, "The Nonpartisan League and the Minnesota campaign of 1918," *Minnesota History* 34 (Summer 1955): 221–32; Bruce L. Larson, *Lindbergh of Minnesota: a political biography* (New York: Harcourt Brace Jovanovich, 1973): chaps. 9–10; and Barbara Stuhler, *Ten men of Minnesota and American foreign policy, 1898–1968* (St. Paul: Minnesota Historical Society, 1973): chap. 2. The famed aviator was Lindbergh's son. On Shipstead and the 1920 campaign, see Martin Ross, *Shipstead of Minnesota* (Chicago: Packard and Co., 1940): chap. 3; Stuhler, *Ten men of Minnesota*: chap. 4.

program of the Nonpartisan League. Coming at the time of the Bolshevik Revolution in Russia and the engagement of the American Expeditionary Force in France, 1918 was an inauspicious moment for the League's debut, and Lindbergh, a strident isolationist, was a controversial messenger. The pressure on the League was intense. The regulars attacked the NPL as "self-seeking demagogues" and agents of the Kaiser, the Wobblies, and the "Red Socialists." A state agency, the Commission of Public Safety, orchestrated a campaign of harassment against the NPL and its candidates. Nineteen counties forbade NPL meetings and rallies. The League's candidates and supporters suffered arrests, intimidation, beatings, tarring and feathering, and hangings in effigy. The 1920 campaign was not much more elevated, even though the Public Safety Commission was well on its way to extinction by then. The regulars painted the Leaguers as "professional Socialist agitators." A few weeks into the campaign, Shipstead discovered that his running mate, an army boxing champion, was keeping an automatic pistol close at hand during all their campaign stops.[37]

The other important factor in the coordination of the Minnesota Republican electorate was the League's political apparatus, imported directly from North Dakota. The Minnesota League solicited memberships, chartered county organizations, convened state nominating conferences, and published an official newspaper, the *Minnesota Leader*. The regulars never achieved such thorough organization. In 1918, as incumbent officeholders, they drew on the resources of the state, as we have seen, in an extraordinary way. In 1920, lest rivalries for the gubernatorial nomination create an opening for the farmer–labor league ticket, they held an unprecedented "eliminating convention" in St. Paul, with only partial success.

As it turned out, the regulars did not need organization. At its best, the League and its labor partners in coalition managed only to win the moral victories of near misses. In 1920, Henrik Shipstead carried 52 of 87 counties and 39 percent of the vote, but Jake Preus got 41. The League's only winner, other than two incumbent congressmen running with its endorsement, was O. J. Kvale, a Lutheran minister, who upset Congressman Andrew J. Volstead, the chair of the House Judiciary Committee and the author of the national prohibition act. The victory, though, was short-lived: in an odd and ironic twist, the state supreme court ruled that Kvale had committed a campaign infraction by calling Volstead an atheist, and it restored the nomination to the incumbent.

Minnesota, of course, was more different from North Dakota than similar to it. Minneapolis, St. Paul, and Duluth together exceeded the entirety of North Dakota in population. Farmers were a large fraction of the electorate but not a

---

[37] Gieske, *Minnesota Farmer-Laborism*: chap. 3; Morlan, "Minnesota campaign of 1918"; Carol Jenson, "Loyalty as a political weapon: the 1918 campaign in Minnesota," *Minnesota History* 43 (Summer 1972): 43–57; Stuhler, *Ten men of Minnesota*: chaps. 2, 4; Martin Ross, *Shipstead of Minnesota* (Chicago: Packard and Co., 1940): chap. 3. The words are Burnquist's and Preus's.

TABLE 7.7 *1920 Republican Primary*

	Governor	Lt Gov	Atty Gen	Sec State	Treasurer	Auditor
League	Shipstead	Mallon	Sullivan	Vollom	Lund	
Regular	Preus	Collins	Hilton	Holm	Rines	Chase
r		0.80/0.71	0.90/0.76	0.92/0.73	0.82/0.62	unopp

wholly dominant part. Labor unions represented thousands of workers in the manufacturing and transportation centers but also in the lumbering and mining areas of the state. The business community that wielded such influence in Republican politics was much larger and much wealthier.

The NPL was alive to the possibility of cooperation with labor in their shared battle with business for control of the Republican Party. Many of the NPL leaders, after all, had histories as socialist organizers. In 1918, it invited union leaders to attend the League's convention as observers, and it offered its endorsement for the nomination for attorney general to the mayor of Hibbing, an ally of the mineworkers union, who declined it. The League's interest in making common cause with labor increased again as elections passed without results. The NPL sent a representative to the 1918 convention of the Minnesota Federation of Labor (MFL) and applauded in 1919 when the Federation created a political auxiliary on the NPL model, the Working People's Nonpartisan Political League. In 1920, the farmers' league and the workers' league met separately in the same St. Paul hotel but negotiated a common slate for the 1920 Republican primary, balancing a farmers' candidate for governor, Henrik Shipstead, with a workers' candidate for lieutenant governor, George H. Mallon, a union pipefitter, Army veteran, and winner of the Medal of Honor for valorous service in France (and, as such, an answer to attacks on the ticket's loyalty as well).

Of even greater importance, the League and the unions made common cause behind independent candidates in the general election. After Charles Lindbergh lost the GOP nomination to Joseph Burnquist in 1918, the NPL and the Federation of Labor agreed to back an abbreviated slate in the fall campaign: David H. Evans, a progressive Democrat and political novice, for governor, and Tom Davis, a lawyer and state representative, for attorney general. Forced to adopt a party label by a ruling of the state's attorney general, they ran the general election race as the candidates of the Farmer-Labor Party. After Henrik Shipstead lost the GOP nomination to Jake Preus in 1920, moreover, the farmers' and the workers' leagues commenced negotiations toward a unified fall slate. When they could not agree, they each offered partial tickets in mirror image. Shipstead, Mallon, and the NPL's candidate for attorney general filed as Independents. Three fresh candidates chosen by the workers' league ran for the other state-wide offices on the Farmer-Labor Party line. In both years, the farmer-labor ticket lost to the Republican nominees but outpolled the Democratic nominees.

The farmer-labor coalition ended the two-party competition within the Minnesota Republican Party. Governor Preus, Senator Frank B. Kellogg, and most of the other state-wide officeholders faced primary challengers in 1922. While the challengers tapped into the residuum of support for the League in the primary, they were not Nonpartisan candidates. The NPL and the Working People's Nonpartisan League no longer contested nominations in the Republican Party.

In March 1922, the farmers' and the workers' leagues once again met separately but in close proximity, this time in Minneapolis. Despite the League's inability to win Republican nominations in Minnesota, Townley counseled patience in the pursuit of the "balance of power" within the political parties, but his authority was undermined by the internal strife and conservative backlash in North Dakota. Activists in both leagues, on the one hand socialists seeking a more radical alternative, on the other hand progressives seeking a more independent option, argued instead for a third party.[38] After the NPL had a last and brief dalliance as partner in a merger with the Democrats, the farmers' league joined with the workers' league to create the Farmer-Labor Party of Minnesota. Within two years, Henrik Shipstead and Magnus Johnson were Farmer-Labor Party senators from Minnesota and O. J. Kvale and Knud Wefald were Farmer-Labor Party congressmen from Minnesota.

"Paradoxically," one historian observed, "the Nonpartisan League helped restore partisanship to Minnesota." The NPL helped to give birth to the Farmer-Labor Party but it lost its own identity in the process. By 1922, the NPL, Minnesota's most successful party within a party, "had in effect been superseded."[39]

Wisconsin

The main cleavage in the Wisconsin Republican Party was already well established by the time of the adoption of the direct primary in 1903 (when it passed the legislature) and 1904 (when it won approval in a referendum). Indeed, the primary was itself an outcome of the factional struggle that pitted "insurgents" against "stalwarts," or, to take the names they gave to themselves, "progressives" against "regulars." Figure 7.5 shows the patterns of factional cohesion in Wisconsin Republican primaries.

---

[38] William Mahoney, the president of the Working People's Nonpartisan League, and Henry G. Teigan, the executive secretary of the NPL, both socialists, were particularly strong proponents of a new political party.

[39] Chrislock, *The progressive era*: 182; Morlan, *Political prairie fire*: 343.

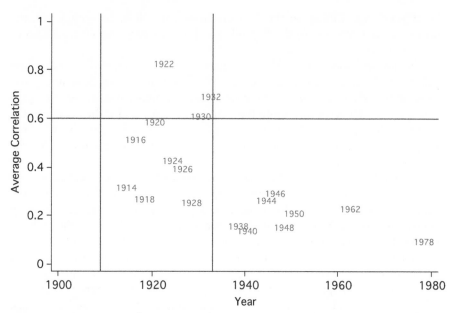

FIGURE 7.5 Average correlations in top slates, Wisconsin Republican Primaries. Missing primary elections for 1908 and 1954.

The cleavage opened with the mobilization of the progressive movement in the 1890s. Two Republicans, Robert M. La Follette and Nils P. Haugen, former colleagues in Wisconsin's U.S. House delegation, began a crusade against the conservatives and business interests that dominated the Republican Party in the state of its birth. They each made unsuccessful bids for GOP nominations for governor in 1894 (Haugen), 1896 (La Follette), and 1898 (La Follette). In 1900, though, La Follette gained the support of the regulars, the nomination, and the first of his three terms as chief executive. The rapprochement did not last, however. Once in office, La Follette advanced a progressive program of business regulation, tax reform, and political reengineering. Thus began the division between progressives and stalwarts that defined Wisconsin politics for half a century.[40]

[40] For an overview of the period, see Robert Booth Fowler, *Wisconsin votes: an electoral history* (Madison: University of Wisconsin Press, 2008): chaps. 4–6. On progressivism in Wisconsin and neighboring states, see Russel B. Nye, *Midwestern progressive politics: a historical study of its origins and development, 1870–1958* (East Lansing: Michigan State University Press, 1959). Good sources on Wisconsin Republican politics during this period include John D. Buenker, *The history of Wisconsin: the progressive era, 1893–1914* (Madison: State Historical Society of Wisconsin, 1998); Paul W. Glad, *The history of Wisconsin: war, a new era, and depression, 1914–1940* (Madison: State Historical Society of Wisconsin, 1990); Jonathan Kasparek, *Fighting son: a biography of Philip F. La Follette* (Madison: Wisconsin Historical Society Press, 2006); Patrick J. Maney, *"Young Bob" La Follette: a biography of Robert M. La Follette Jr.,*

The regulars were a minority presence in the early primary elections from 1906 to 1912, able to influence outcomes only by exploiting divisions among the progressives. The stalwart faction invigorated itself in 1914, led by a Milwaukee refrigerator-car company executive, Emanuel L. Philipp. One of La Follette's conservative supporters in 1900, Philipp took the governor's program of railroad taxation and regulation as a personal betrayal. Over the next decade, he authored tracts critical of progressive government and mobilized opposition to the progressive regime in Madison. Meeting in Madison in June 1914, a convention of Republican regulars endorsed Philipp for governor and slated candidates for each of the state-wide offices. Meanwhile, a rift between Senator La Follette and Governor Francis E. McGovern brought two formidable progressive candidates into the race for the Republican gubernatorial nomination. They split the progressive vote, and Philipp won the GOP primary in September by a plurality. Although La Follette tried to head off Philipp's election by running a progressive as an independent, he was elected in November as the first stalwart Wisconsin governor in fourteen years. The progressives, three incumbents and a new lieutenant governor, won every other state office.

The 1914 GOP primary exemplified one pattern of factional competition in Wisconsin: multicandidate races between regulars and two (or even more) varieties of progressives and weak factional cohesion. The 1916 GOP primary exemplified another: head-to-head contests between a stalwart slate and an insurgent slate and substantial factional cohesion. Meeting in July, the regulars endorsed Governor Philipp for renomination as the Republican Party candidate for governor, along with candidates for the other offices (including the incumbent treasurer, a convert to Philipp's side). The progressives settled on a ticket behind William H. Hatton and Fighting Bob La Follette himself, seeking renomination and reelection to the U.S. Senate seat he first assumed in 1906. The voters' loyalties were tested by the option of former governor Francis McGovern, running alone as an "independent progressive." Republican primary voters awarded the nominations to every incumbent, including Governor Philipp and Senator La Follette. Even so, the voters' choices cohered around the two competing tickets, as shown in Table 7.8.[41]

1895–1953 (Columbia: University of Missouri Press, 1978); Herbert F. Margulies, *The decline of the progressive movement in Wisconsin, 1890–1920* (Madison: State Historical Society of Wisconsin, 1968); Herbert F. Margulies, *Senator Lenroot of Wisconsin: a political biography, 1900–1929* (Columbia: University of Missouri Press, 1977); Robert S. Maxwell, *La Follette and the rise of the progressives in Wisconsin* (Madison: State Historical Society of Wisconsin, 1956); Robert S. Maxwell, *Emanuel L. Philipp: Wisconsin stalwart* (Madison: State Historical Society of Wisconsin, 1959); Thomas C. Reeves, *Distinguished service: the life of Wisconsin governor Walter J. Kohler Jr.* (Milwaukee: Marquette University Press, 2006): chap. 3.

[41] The coefficients are the correlations between the vote for the gubernatorial candidate and the corresponding down-ballot candidates. They differ because of the presence of multiple candidates, in this case a third candidate for governor.

TABLE 7.8: *1916 Republican Primary*

	Governor	Lt Gov	Atty Gen	Sec State	Treasurer	Senator
Progressive	Hatton	Dithmar	Owen	Hull	Peterson	La Follette
Regular	Philipp	Cousins	Hicks	Harrington	Johnson	Jeffris
r		0.38/0.30	0.42/0.49	0.58/0.58	0.36/0.32	0.42/0.62

If the correlations across slates were weaker and more variable in Wisconsin than in North Dakota and Minnesota, and they generally were, there was a good reason: the progressive and the regular factions were not the disciplined organizations of the NPL, IVA, and ROC type. The regular Republicans had a network of county leaders, and they typically issued their endorsements in state conventions. In some elections, the two sides campaigned and publicized as teams. In newspaper advertisements in 1916, for example, the stalwarts offered "reasons why Emanuel L. Philipp should be renominated on Sept. 5," comparing the taxes paid in Dane County during his administration and the preceding progressive McGovern administration, and urging Republican primary voters to support the entire ticket of regulars. On the opposite side, Senator La Follette headlined a "ticket ... endorsed by five hundred progressive leaders representing every county in Wisconsin," led by the progressive candidate for governor, William H. Hatton of New London. (See Figure 7.6) In other elections, one side or the other or both seem not to have put the energy into a unified campaign. The progressives were always the looser of the two organizations. Sources tell of county organizations and canvass lists originally compiled for use in the competitions for control of the Republican nominating conventions in the years before primaries. Slating, however, was tightly controlled by Senator La Follette and his closest associates, giving frequent rise to stalwart attacks on the "bossism" of the "Madison Ring."

The variability in factional cohesion had several sources. One was the state's lax ballot-access laws. Nothing other than prudence seems to have deterred entry into primaries, and the gubernatorial contests in particular were often crowded affairs, with several rival factional candidates – usually progressives – in line for the nomination. Six candidates (three progressives) ran in the 1914 primary, six candidates (three progressives) ran in the 1920 primary, and four candidates (two progressives) ran in the 1926 primary for governor.

The second reason for the variability in factional cohesion was division within the factions themselves, particularly within the progressive ranks. Senator La Follette was the movement's most inspiring and most polarizing figure, with an extreme need for personal loyalty, and his personal likes and dislikes

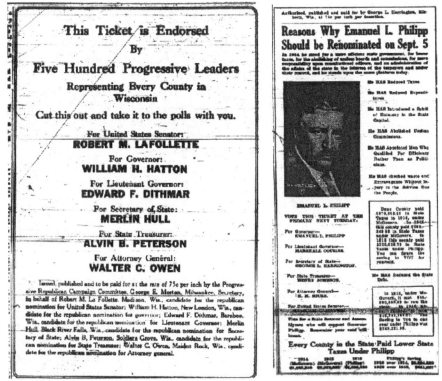

FIGURE 7.6 Wisconsin slate advertisements, 1916 election. Source: *Wisconsin State Journal*, September 1, 1916.

figured in many of the slating decisions. In 1906, for example, he recruited a protégé, state assembly speaker Irvine L. Lenroot, as a candidate in the primary against his own successor, Governor James O. "Yim" Davidson, whom he viewed as a lightweight.[42] He saw other progressive politicians as threats to his leadership. Governor McGovern, for instance, emerged to state-wide leadership out of the municipal reform movement in Milwaukee, giving him a strong following in southeastern Wisconsin and the urbanized areas of the state. La Follette, whose power base was rural, recruited Lieutenant Governor Tom Morris to run against him in the 1914 senatorial primary, and when that failed,

---

[42] The attempt to substitute the Swedish Lenroot for the Norwegian Davidson did not succeed, but it strained the senator's relationship with the state's large and loyally progressive Norwegian community, flushed with national pride after Norway's independence from Sweden in 1905. See Jørn Brøndal, *Ethnic leadership and midwestern politics* (Northfield, Minn.: Norwegian-American Historical Association, 2004): 185–203; Padraic M. Kennedy, "Lenroot, La Follette, and the campaign of 1906," *Wisconsin Magazine of History* 42 (Spring 1959): 163–74.

he sat out the general election and allowed McGovern to lose to a progressive Democrat, Paul O. Husting.[43]

Issues divided the progressives and (to a lesser extent) the regulars as well. The policy of national Prohibition under the 18th Amendment, for example, received strong support from puritan Yankees and pietist Scandinavians. On the other side, the state's large German community regarded Prohibition as a cultural affront, and heavily German Milwaukee, the center of the brewing industry, considered it a mortal threat. The state branch of the Anti-Saloon League regularly endorsed the "dry" candidates in the Republican primaries and the Order of Camels, an antiprohibition fraternal organization, the "wet" candidates.[44] In 1918 and 1920, and again later in the decade, independent wets and drys were frequent fringe candidates in the GOP primaries, particularly for senator, governor, and attorney general. They never won, but they played havoc with factional coalitions.

The final contributor to weak factional cohesion was incumbency. The progressives dominated the down-ballot state offices and, once nominated and elected, which in heavily Republican Wisconsin was about the same thing, progressive lieutenant governors, attorneys general, secretaries of state, and treasurers tended to stay until they left voluntarily, particularly in the 1920s, regardless of the outcomes at the top of the ticket. Henry A. Huber served four terms as lieutenant governor and John W. Reynolds served four terms as attorney general, both starting in 1925. Treasurer Solomon Levitan served five terms and Secretary of State Theodore Dammann six. All four persisted through the election of Fred Zimmerman as a renegade progressive in 1926, through the state's turn to stalwart Walter J. Kohler in 1928, and through the state's turn back to a La Follette, the second son Philip, in 1930.[45] As in two-party politics, the personal vote for incumbents eroded the party vote for factions.

When the stakes were high enough, however, the progressives could rise to the occasion and achieve the discipline to run as a team. The progressives faced their greatest challenge during the Great War. Senator La Follette was a leader in the "little band of willful men" who opposed President Wilson's policy of "armed neutrality" and the declaration of war against Germany in April 1917. The issue split the progressives and inflamed the Republican Party. The votes on the war finalized La Follette's break with U.S. Representative Irvine Lenroot,

---

[43] Herbert F. Margulies, "The background of the La Follette–McGovern schism," *Wisconsin Magazine of History* 40 (Autumn 1956): 21–29.

[44] Founded in Milwaukee the day Prohibition began, the Order paid wry tribute to the camel for its "ability to withstand a long drought." "Notes on secret societies," *Fortnightly Review* 27 (1920): 313.

[45] In 1932, Dammann alone among the progressives survived the renomination of Walter Kohler and, in the fall, the Roosevelt landslide and the election of a Democratic governor, Albert G. Schmedeman. He served as Secretary of State until 1939, finally as a Progressive Party office holder under Progressive Governor Philip F. La Follette.

once a rising star in the progressive firmament, and alienated La Follette from longtime supporters. Nationalist leaders organized over 300 chapters of the Wisconsin Loyalty Legion, pledging not only to support the war but also to expose "traitors" and "slackers." In the Wisconsin legislature, state senator Roy P. Wilcox of Eau Claire, an "ultra-loyalist," introduced a resolution censuring Senator La Follette for his "failure to see the righteousness of our nation's cause" and "to support our government in matters vital to the winning of the war." The measure passed 22–7 in the state senate and 53–32 in the state assembly.[46]

In 1920, the blood enemies of the La Follette progressives were both candidates for the Republican nominations for office, Lenroot for the U.S. Senate, Wilcox for governor, both for the second time. In the senatorial primary, the progressives endorsed a La Crosse lawyer, James Thompson, in a rematch against Senator Lenroot, the candidate of the stalwarts. In the gubernatorial primary, the two sides ganged up again to defeat Roy Wilcox.[47] Three progressive officeholders sought the nomination for governor, but the La Follette organization fell in behind Attorney General John Blaine and a slate of candidates for the down-ballot offices, three of them from the NPL. Declining the regulars' reendorsement himself, Governor Philipp engineered the selection of Gilbert E. Seaman, a colonel in the U.S. Medical Corps just returned to Milwaukee from service in France.[48] The six-way race for the gubernatorial nomination was complicated, but the Blaine team ran a campaign that produced a significant degree of voter unity across the slate. (Given the welter of alternatives, Table 7.9 shows only the correlations for the progressive-NPL coalition slate.)

In 1922, La Follette and the progressives sought "vindication" for the attacks they suffered during the war. He and Governor Blaine led the

---

[46] Margulies, *Decline of the progressive movement*: 211–13. La Follette and the antiwar progressives were not the only targets of the loyalists. The Social-Democratic Party of Wisconsin had a strong base in Milwaukee, which elected two SDP mayors in the 1910s. Its leader, Victor L. Berger, an immigrant from Austria-Hungary, was an outspoken opponent of the war. The first Socialist elected to Congress (in 1910), Berger was tried and convicted for violating the 1917 Espionage Act and refused the Fifth District seat in the U.S. House that he won in 1918 and again in the special election to fill the vacancy in 1919.

[47] In 1918, the progressives cared more about defeating Senator Wilcox than winning the governorship for themselves, and so they tacitly coordinated with Governor Philipp to that end. They endorsed J. N. Tittemore, a perennial progressive candidate but not an insider, but they gave him no real support. Philipp defeated Wilcox for the nomination by the narrowest of margins: 440 votes.

[48] In a retort to Wilcox's attacks on his patriotism, Philipp labeled him "the drum major of the stay-at-home division of the state," an unflattering contrast with Seaman, who was fifty-one and had also served in the Philippines and Cuba during the Spanish-American War. Margulies, *The decline of progressivism*: 270. See also Herbert F. Margulies, "The election of 1920 in Wisconsin: the return to 'normalcy' reappraised," *Wisconsin Magazine of History* 41 (Autumn 1957): 15–22.

TABLE 7.9 *1920 Republican Primary*

	Governor	Lt Gov	Atty Gen	Sec State	Treasurer	Senator
Progressive	Blaine	Comings	Kenneberg	Hall	Levitan	Thompson
r		0.56	0.67	0.51	0.63	0.64

progressive slate. Weighted down by a depressed farm economy, a railroad strike, President Harding's veto of a veterans' bonus bill, and a developing scandal in the U.S. Interior Department,[49] the dispirited regulars met in Milwaukee. They endorsed a lackluster ticket behind Attorney General William J. Morgan, a partner in Wilcox's campaign against "radicals" of all types, running for governor, and William A. Ganfield, president of tiny Carroll College and a resident of Wisconsin for less than two years, running for senator. In desperation, the stalwarts tried to paint themselves in progressive hues. "Don't be fooled next Tuesday," the advertisements for the Blaine ticket countered, vouching for its progressive authenticity with a photograph of Senator La Follette. Going head-to-head, the progressives and the regulars induced a high level of unity in primary voting, and the progressives won big (see Table 7.10).

After a period of declining factional coherence in the 1920s – the effect of conservative collapse, progressive rivalries, and incumbency – the two factions remodeled themselves. In 1925, in a bid to regain control of the Wisconsin Republican Party, conservative regulars created the Republican Voluntary Committee (RVC), designed to slate and fund stalwart candidates for office.[50] Two years later, in an attempt to reunite, the progressives held a state-wide meeting to decide the slate for the 1928 Republican primary. The regulars and the progressives both presented complete tickets for the first time since 1922.

Finally, the onset of the Great Depression reignited the passions that divided progressives from regulars at the very start. Heading the progressive ticket in

---

[49] In 1922, Senator La Follette led the initial congressional investigation into charges that Interior Secretary Albert B. Fall had received bribes from petroleum companies in exchange for low rates on leases on Navy oil reserves in California and in Wyoming at Teapot Dome.

[50] The founder of the Republican Voluntary Committee was William J. Campbell, a lumber broker and conservative activist, who called the group together in his hometown of Oshkosh. The regulars were infuriated that the state Republican Party snubbed President Coolidge and endorsed Senator La Follette and his Progressive Party ticket in 1924 instead. The extraparty structure enabled the RVC to bypass state requirements for the selection of party leaders and state limits on party fundraising. RVC leaders later incorporated under the name "Republican Party of Wisconsin," and after 1934 it functioned, de facto, as the party apparatus. The Democrats created a parallel organization in 1948. See Frank J. Sorauf, "Extra-legal political parties in Wisconsin," *American Political Science Review* 48 (September 1954): 692–704.

TABLE 7.10 *1922 Republican Primary*

	Governor	Lt Gov	Atty Gen	Sec State	Treasurer	Senator
Progressive	Blaine	Comings	Ekern	Zimmerman	Levitan	La Follette
Regular	Morgan	Young	Baker	Paulson	Johnson	Ganfield
r		0.82/0.80	0.86/0.82	0.87/0.86	0.83/0.79	0.95/0.97

the 1930 primary, Philip F. La Follette challenged Governor Walter J. Kohler, a stalwart and the president of the well-known plumbing fixtures company. La Follette's victory gave the progressives control of all state-wide elected offices for the only time in Wisconsin history. Kohler and the regulars mounted a furious comeback in 1932, attacking La Follette's administration for an "orgy of spending" and its inability to remedy the plight of the state's unemployed. Kohler defeated La Follette for the Republican gubernatorial nomination; the regulars also defeated Senator Blaine and every progressive candidate for a down-ballot office except one. They all lost in turn (one excepted) in November to Albert G. Schmedeman, the mayor of Madison, and the rest of the Democratic ticket. Tables 7.11 and 7.12 show the two slates in the Kohler–La Follette match and rematch, a pair of head-to-head races that again gave sharp order to the voting in the Republican primary.

At that, though, the progressives pulled out of the Republican Party. In May 1934, the faction's leaders met in Fond du Lac and turned themselves into the Progressive Party of Wisconsin. Their motives were pragmatic and principled. As progressives discovered in 1932, with the rise of the Wisconsin Democratic Party, the "fair-minded Democrats" whom the progressives counted on to cross over to vote in the Republican primary participated in the Democratic primary instead, leaving the Republican Party in the grip of conservatives. Rather than cast their lot with big-city machine bosses and southern reactionaries, however, the Wisconsin progressives decided to set their own course as an independent party. At first, the strategy was a success. In November 1934, running as Progressives rather than Republicans, Robert M. La Follette Jr. renewed his lease on his Senate seat, Phil La Follette regained his office in the Statehouse, and seven veteran progressives, many formerly Republican candidates and officeholders, won seats in the U.S. Congress. Two years later, in 1936, the Progressives took back all the constitutional offices from the Democrats with a slate of familiar names: Phil La Follette, Ted Dammann, Sol Levitan, and Orland Steen "Spike" Loomis.[51]

---

[51] The Wisconsin Progressive Party eventually failed. It lost its hold on state government in the Republican landslide of 1938 and won only two statewide offices thereafter. In 1946, no longer

TABLE 7.11 *1930 Republican Primary*

	Governor	Lt Gov	Atty Gen	Sec State	Treasurer
Progressive	La Follette	Huber	Reynolds	Dammann	Levitan
Regular	Kohler	Dahl	Eberlein	Peplow	Samp
r		0.85	0.45/0.58	0.77	0.42

TABLE 7.12 *1932 Republican Primary*

	Governor	Lt Gov	Atty Gen	Sec State	Treasurer	Senator
Progressive	La Follette	Huber	Fons	Dammann	Levitan	Blaine
Regular	Kohler	Dahl	Bancroft	Gettelman	Samp	Chapple
r		0.74	0.61	0.95	0.71	0.96

Thus, in Wisconsin, as in Minnesota, two-party competition superseded factional competition.

Louisiana

At the other extreme of the country (in more ways than one), the Democratic Party was the host of a bifactional politics that was often as robust as North Dakota's and Wisconsin's. In Louisiana, as in Wisconsin, its core was a family dynasty, in this case the brothers, cousins, and son of Huey P. Long Jr. and the Kingfish himself. Figure 7.7 shows the patterns.

With its rich social gumbo, Louisiana had a long history of factional strife: populist against conservative, rural against urban, Catholic against Protestant, Anglo against Cajun and Creole. Courthouse cliques directed the rural parishes while the New Orleans Regular Democratic Organization, known as the "Choctaws," dominated the Crescent City. The Old Regulars, as they were also called, generally aligned with the state's conservative sugar, plantation, and petroleum industry interests.[52]

hopeful for a resurgence, Progressive leaders voted to rejoin the Republican Party. The welcome was not a warm one: in the Republican primary, Senator La Follette lost to Joseph R. McCarthy, a Marine Corps captain who went on to an infamous career in Washington.

[52] Sources for Louisiana include Doris Dorcas Carter, *Robert Floyd Kennon: reform governor* (Lafayette: Center for Louisiana Studies, 1998); Edward F. Haas, *DeLesseps S. Morrison and the image of reform: New Orleans politics, 1946–1961* (Baton Rouge: Louisiana State University Press, 1974); Perry H. Howard, *Political tendencies in Louisiana*, rev. ed. (Baton Rouge:

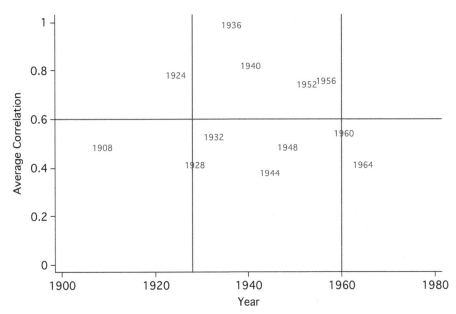

FIGURE 7.7 Average correlations in top slates, Louisiana Democratic primaries. Missing primary elections for 1904, 1912, 1918, and 1980.

Long hailed from Winn Parish in northern Louisiana, populist territory, and started his career in politics by winning a seat on the Railroad Commission in 1918. He fought successfully for regulatory authority over pipelines and other utilities, and used the agency – reorganized as the Public Service Commission in 1921 – to antagonize the Standard Oil Company, the utilities, Governor John M. Parker, and the Old Regulars, in approximately that order. In 1924, at age thirty, he ran a surprisingly strong race for the Democratic nomination for governor, finishing a close third in a contest that was polarized by region and religion.[53]

Long did not stop running, and four years later he squared off against Governor Oramel H. Simpson and Congressman Riley J. Wilson in the

Louisiana State University Press, 1971); Michael L. Kurtz and Morgan D. Peoples, *Earl K. Long: the saga of Uncle Earl and Louisiana politics* (Baton Rouge: Louisiana State University Press, 1990); Jerry Purvis Sanson, *Louisiana during World War II: politics and society, 1939–1945* (Baton Rouge: Louisiana State University Press, 1999); Allan P. Sindler, *Huey Long's Louisiana: state politics, 1920–1952* (Baltimore: Johns Hopkins University Press, 1956); T. Harry Williams, *Huey Long* (New York: Alfred A. Knopf, 1969); and, of course, Key, *Southern politics*: chap. 8.

[53] Lieutenant Governor Hewitt Bouanchaud was a Catholic from southern Louisiana. He led in the first primary but lost the runoff to Henry L. Fuqua, also from southern Louisiana, but like Long a Protestant. The Ku Klux Klan, stridently anti-Catholic in its second incarnation, was at the peak of its activity in Louisiana in 1924 (as it was elsewhere in the country). The correlations between Bouanchaud's vote and the votes for other offices in the first primary range from 0.77 to 0.90.

TABLE 7.13 *1928 First Democratic Primary*

	Governor	Lt Gov	Atty Gen	Treasurer
	Long	Cyr	Reid	Conner
Cyr	0.85			
Reid	0.44	0.50		
Connor	0.25	0.12	0.16	

Democratic gubernatorial primary.[54] Aspirants to the top two executive offices in Louisiana traditionally paired as running mates on "tickets," leaving the "lesser offices to [whomever] wanted to scramble for them."[55] Long recruited a larger but still partial slate – in the Louisiana political patois, a "bobtailed ticket" – including candidates for lieutenant governor, attorney general, treasurer, and superintendent of education.[56] He balanced it carefully, choosing a Cajun dentist from Iberia Parish in the south; a school superintendent from Claiborne Parish in the north; a lawyer from one of the Florida parishes, Tangipahoa; and a past Masonic grand master from one of the upriver parishes, Concordia. He campaigned throughout the state on a populist platform of highway construction (popular in rural areas), free school textbooks (popular in Catholic areas), and an increase in the severance tax on oil. Long led the first primary by a considerable margin and won election as governor when Congressman Wilson, in second place, conceded the runoff.

The slating effort had very little to do with the victory, however. Long carried along with him only his candidates for lieutenant governor and treasurer and a minority of affiliated state legislative candidates. The correlations of his parish vote and his running mates', moreover, were sizable only in the case of his lieutenant governor, Paul N. "Doc" Cyr (see Table 7.13). That more might be possible was suggested only by the switch in the alignment of the vote for Cyr: when Cyr ran for lieutenant governor in 1924 on the Bouanchaud ticket against Long, the correlation of his vote and Long's was –0.61! If nothing else, 1928 demonstrated Long's ability to attract support in francophone Louisiana.[57]

---

[54] Governor Fuqua died in office in 1926 and was succeeded by the lieutenant governor, O. H. Simpson.

[55] Williams, *Huey Long*: 263.

[56] The incumbent secretary of state ran unopposed for renomination.

[57] During a stop in St. Martinville in Cajun country, under the Evangeline Oak made famous by Longfellow's poem, Long delivered one of the most brilliant of all American campaign speeches. Recounting the long history of failings of the government of the state, Long closed his address

Long's governorship was one of the most turbulent ever, in any time in any state, marked by threats, clashes, fallings out, allegations of corruption, thuggery, occasional violence, and an impeachment drive. Long ejected Senator Joseph E. Ransdell from his seat in the 1930 primary but postponed his oath of office in Washington to tend to his more important business in Baton Rouge.[58] As the end of his term approached, he searched for a compliant candidate for his successor and found one in O. K. Allen, a neighbor from Winn Parish and his floor leader in the state senate. The 1932 "Complete the Work" ticket that Long assembled listed candidates for all nine state offices. Personal loyalty counted above all else, even blood relation: for lieutenant governor, Long slated John B. Fournet, the speaker of the Louisiana house, who had protected him during impeachment proceedings, over his own brother, Earl, who was not nearly as dependable. (Earl, in a pique, joined George S. Guion's slate, one of the two bobtailed tickets on the anti-Long side.) All nine of Long's candidates won their primaries in 1932. (Later on in the congressional primaries, Long's favored Senate candidate also prevailed, ousting the incumbent.) The ticket captured fifty-four out of sixty-four parishes – including Orleans, owing to a momentary accommodation with the Choctaws – "a feat of organization unexampled in Louisiana politics."[59] (See Table 7.14.)

Once again, however, the Long faction was better at picking winners than it was at making winners. Higher up on the ticket the correlations of votes across offices were respectably high; further down the ticket, they were negligible.[60] Slate-building was still more a job of assembling personal followings than mobilizing support for a platform.

By the 1940s, however, Louisiana factional politics was in a completely different position. First, the factional slates were expanded. Extending the practice it pioneered in 1932, the leading Long factions fielded full slates, and so did the anti-Long factions – and even some of the schismatic candidates within both factions. The number of serious candidates for the down-ballot nominations typically matched the number of serious pairings for governor and lieutenant governor. "Since 1932," Sindler observed in 1956, "all major candidates for state office have run on state tickets."[61] Second, the competing slates increasingly comprised factional "regulars" who cycled from ticket to ticket within factions. In a few cases, they were entrenched incumbents in lower

---

with an appeal that registered deep in the Acadian psyche: "Evangeline wept bitter tears in her disappointment. But they lasted through only one lifetime. Your tears in this country, around this oak, have lasted for generations. Give me the chance to dry the tears of those who still weep here."

[58] By then, Lieutenant Governor Cyr was one of his bitterest enemies, so he could not leave the state.

[59] Williams, *Huey Long*: 539.

[60] Reported are the correlations across the slates. Despite Earl Long's position on an anti-Long ticket, the Long name was still a draw to Longite voters: the parish votes for Allen and Long correlated at 0.24.

[61] Sindler, *Huey Long's Louisiana*: 275.

TABLE 7.14 *1932 First Democratic Primary*

	Governor	Lt Gov	Atty Gen	Sec State	Treasurer	Auditor
Long	Allen	Fournet	Porterie	Conway	Cave	Baynard
Anti-Long	Guion	E Long	Hamlin			
Anti-Long	D LeBlanc	Hendrick	Saint			
r		0.55/0.40/0.74	0.65/0.58/0.46	0.53/–/–	0.52/–/–	0.48/–/–

offices, who sometimes ran unopposed for renomination and who often received multiple endorsements.[62] In most cases, though, they were politicians who were identified as either Longites or anti-Longites.[63]

Finally, the factions became more readily identifiable ideologically. Even though there were divisions within the Long faction, which often expressed themselves in rival slates in first primaries, the Longites were generally more favorable to government action, more supportive of the national Democratic Party, and more sympathetic – or at least less hostile – to African Americans and the poor. In reaction to the populist program and the strong-arm tactics of the Kingfish, Huey Long, plus the spectacular venality of his successors, the anti-Longites generally rallied around the cause of "reform," even though they disagreed about its substance. A dominant conservative group including governors Sam H. Jones, Jimmie Davis, and Robert F. Kennon allied itself warily with a more liberal group led by New Orleans Mayor deLesseps S. "Chep" Morrison and Second District congressman T. Hale Boggs.[64] Personal rivalries

[62] The leading examples were state treasurer A. P. "Pat" Tugwell and secretary of state Wade O. Martin Jr., who both served in their posts for thirty-two years. Both were originally the nominees of the Long faction, Tugwell on the Leche ticket in 1936 and Martin on the Morgan ticket in 1944, but both were frequently at odds with Earl Long. In 1940, Tugwell charged Long with various financial improprieties, after which he generally ran only on tickets that did not include him (1948 was an exception). Martin's differences with Long started in 1940, when he encouraged Lewis Morgan to stay in the runoff and thereby denied Long the nomination for lieutenant governor. He and Long had a spectacular falling out in 1956, when Long dismantled the secretary of state's office. By then, though, Tugwell and Martin had no trouble getting nominations on other slates.

[63] Sindler examined several Longite politicians who failed to make the runoff and endorsed anti-Longite candidates in the second primary (in 1940 and after) and concluded that none was able to deliver their votes to the other side. Sindler, *Huey Long's Louisiana*: 265–73. In one of the same instances, James A. Noe's endorsement of Sam Jones in the 1940 runoff, Key reached exactly the opposite conclusion. See Key, *Southern politics*: 174–75.

[64] Jones supported the Dixiecrat ticket in the 1948 presidential election, Kennon endorsed Dwight D. Eisenhower in 1952, and both endorsed Barry Goldwater in 1964. Earl Long and Huey's son, Russell, elected U.S. Senator in 1948, quietly supported Truman and worked actively for Stevenson.

FIGURE 7.8 Posters advertising the Long slate. Source: State Library of Louisiana and Louisiana State Archives (used by permission).

and ideological divisions also ensured that the anti-Long forces fielded multiple candidates in first primaries as a matter of course.

The effect of competitive slating, though, was to identify politicians publicly as members of the Long faction or the anti-Long faction. The factions themselves advertised as teams. The Longite circulars in 1936 and 1940, for example, identified the faction's candidates, reviewed the faction's platform – "free school books," "debt moratoriums," "free poll tax," "good roads," and so forth – and summoned the memory of the martyred Huey (cut down by an assassin's bullet in 1935) and the tragic O. K. (felled by a stroke in 1936, days after winning the nomination for Huey's Senate seat) as reason to "carry on." (See Figure 7.8.) The press also drew the connections. In 1952, under the headline "Lincoln Parish gives entire Kennon ticket victory in runoff poll," for instance, a northern Louisiana newspaper reviewed the performance of the entire anti-Long slate, noting as well that two of its members started out on the Boggs slate but moved onto the Kennon ticket when his candidates missed the runoff.

The advent of two-party competition in the Louisiana Democratic Party gave strong signals to the electorate. In 1936, the sympathy vote for Huey's ticket delivered control of state government in Baton Rouge to the Long faction for the third consecutive term (Table 7.15). (Later in the year, the Longites also held on to Huey's Senate seat, nominating state house speaker Allen Ellender, from Terrebonne Parish in the southern "Sugar Bowl.") By 1940, however, the flagrant corruption of the Richard W. Leche administration – a succession of

TABLE 7.15 *1936 First Democratic Primary*

	Governor	Lt Gov	Atty Gen	Sec State	Treasurer	Auditor
Long	Leche	E Long	Porterie	Conway	Tugwell	Baynard
Anti-Long	Dear	Moss	P Coco	Williams	Mayo	Begnaud
r		0.99	0.99	0.99	0.99	0.98

outrages known collectively as "the Scandals" – led Leche to resignation in 1939 and prison in 1940. Anti-Long candidates won the next two state-wide elections, in 1940 and 1944 (Tables 7.16 and 7.17). In 1940, Sam H. Jones, an attorney from Lake Charles in southwestern Louisiana, a past state commander of the American Legion, and a political neophyte untainted by actual experience in elected office, ran for governor as a "reformer," defeating Earl Long. In 1944, Jimmie Davis, a singer, songwriter, and movie actor known for his signature hit, "You Are My Sunshine," gave "reform" a second term, upending the Lewis Morgan and Earl Long ticket. Whatever the rise and the fall of each faction's fortunes, however, the factional divisions in the electorate were sharply drawn.

Bifactional politics reached its apogee in Louisiana in 1948. The marquee event was the grudge match between Earl Long and the man who beat him out for a full gubernatorial term in 1940, Sam H. Jones. Jones enjoyed the tacit support of Governor Davis – his Sunshine Band played at Jones's campaign stops – and he rounded out his slate with Davis's lieutenant governor and attorney general. Long, on the other hand, mixed veteran Longites in the down-ballot offices and up-and-comers at the top. Two other candidates fielded full slates: Judge Robert F. Kennon led an "all-G.I." anti-Longite ticket and Congressman James H. Morrison headed a rump Longite group. Except for the votes for treasurer and auditor, held by long-term incumbents, the four factions in 1948 were exceptionally well-defined. Long won the rematch (Table 7.18).[65]

The Long and anti-Long factions appeared robust throughout the 1950s. Allan Sindler's analysis of Louisiana's "bifactional politics" – he coined the term – extended through 1952, the year Bob Kennon reclaimed the governorship for the anti-Longites, defeating Carlos Spaht, and saw its publication in 1956, the year Earl Long won his second gubernatorial election, defeating Chep Morrison. In both elections, the factions were still very strongly delineated.

Within a few years, however, two-party politics in the Louisiana Democratic Party ended abruptly. In 1959, for the first time in a generation, the Long faction failed even to make the runoff. The two Longites, former governor

---

[65] Huey's son Russell narrowly defeated Kennon in the senatorial primary later in the year.

TABLE 7.16 *1940 First Democratic Primary*

	Governor	Lt Gov	Atty Gen	Sec State	Treasurer	Auditor
Long	E Long	Peltier	Burns	Conway	Christenberry	Baynard
Anti-Long	Jones	Mouton	Stanley	Gremillion	Tugwell	Goyne
r		0.89/0.86	0.94/0.74	0.78/0.91	0.78/0.39	0.87/0.82

TABLE 7.17 *1944 First Democratic Primary*

	Governor	Lt Gov	Atty Gen	Sec State	Treasurer	Auditor
Long	Morgan	E Long	Cawthorn	Martin	Daigle	Bourg
Anti-Long	Davis	Verret	F LeBlanc	Gremillion	Tugwell	Gallion
r		0.50 /0.25	0.68/0.29	0.81/0.38	0.42/0.49	0.36/0.43

James A. Noe and Auditor Bill Dodd, finished behind Willie Rainach, a leader in the segregationist Citizens' Council movement, leaving Jimmie Davis and Chep Morrison to compete in the finals. (Davis won.) John J. McKeithen's successful nomination bid in 1963 was the Long faction's last hurrah. He had a sterling Longite pedigree: state house floor manager for Earl Long from 1948 to 1952; Carlos Spaht's running mate in 1952; Huey Long's legatee on the Public Service Commission, noted for his attacks on Southern Bell Telephone; so close to Blanche Long, Earl's widow, that she managed his 1963 campaign. In 1963, McKeithen positioned himself rightward, first to edge out Congressman Gillis W. Long, Huey's and Earl's cousin, and then to defeat Chep Morrison in the runoff. In the electorate, though, the Long and anti-Long factions were in utter disarray.[66] They never recovered.

One factor in the collapse of factional politics in Louisiana was the fading magic of the Long name. Huey Long had been dead for twenty-five years. Earl Long, always erratic, died in 1960 after years of increasingly bizarre behavior.[67] Once elected, Russell Long maintained a distance from his Uncle Earl and

[66] William C. Havard, Rudolf Heberle, and Perry H. Howard, *The Louisiana elections of 1960*, Louisiana State University Studies, Number 9 (Baton Rouge: Louisiana State University Press, 1963).

[67] His denouement included an affair with a striptease dancer, an unhinged rant before a joint session of the legislature, and an epic battle against his wife's motion to commit him to a state psychiatric hospital.

John Mark Hansen, Shigeo Hirano, and James M. Snyder Jr.

TABLE 7.18 *1948 First Democratic Primary*

	Governor	Lt Gov	Atty Gen	Sec State	Treasurer	Auditor
Long	E. Long	Dodd	Kemp	Martin	Tugwell	Baynard
Anti-Long	Jones	Verrett	F LeBlanc	Durham	Tugwell	Bannister
Anti-Long	Kennon	Deshotels	McNeill	R Fontenot	Champagn	Kolb
Long	J Morrison	J Fontenot	Kennedy	Jeter	Tugwell	Baynard
r		0.97/0.94/ 0.95/0.96	0.88/0.91/ 0.94/0.90	0.96/0.93/ 0.88/0.94	−0.01/0.27/ 0.35/0.29	−0.03/0.61/ 0.84/0.53

worked to advance his power in Washington rather than Baton Rouge: he endorsed anti-Longite congressman Hale Boggs in the race for governor in 1952. Finally, the liberal elements of the Longs' populism succumbed to racial backlash.[68]

The end of a family dynasty is not the whole story, however. Already in the 1950s, bifactional politics was threatened by a rising personal vote for state-wide candidates. State treasurer Pat Tugwell and secretary of state Wade Martin acquired such reputations in their offices that they accepted rather than sought endorsements on factional slates. Attorney general Jack P. F. Gremillion, first recruited onto Earl Long's ticket in 1956 in rather haphazard fashion, also sidled onto Jimmie Davis's ticket in 1959 and ultimately served four terms in the office (until a fraud conviction brought him down in 1971). Lieutenant Governor Clarence C. "Taddy" Aycock won his first term as Davis's running mate in 1959, declared himself an "independent" in the 1963 primary, and served until 1972. By 1963, the entire concept of a "ticket" was in tatters: John McKeithen headed a slate of three members (including himself), Chep Morrison a slate of four. Finally, in 1966, voters approved "Amendment 1," raising the limit on consecutive gubernatorial terms from one to two, allowing McKeithen to become the first Louisiana governor to win two consecutive nominations and two consecutive terms.[69] Factional politics broke down as officeholders discovered that they did not need the help of a slate to win.

---

[68] Although their attitudes were consistent with their time and their place, the Longs themselves are generally acknowledged to have avoided race-baiting, even when it cost them the support of long-time allies such as Plaquemines Parish boss Leander Perez. In 1964, in fact, Gillis Long lost his U.S. House seat to another Long cousin, Speedy O. Long, who accused him of being too liberal for his district.

[69] The McKeithen campaign in 1963 also made ample and pioneering use of that great instrument of individualism, television. Gone was the era of campaign caravans, stump speeches, and string

Finally, as in North Dakota, Minnesota, and Wisconsin, two-party competition within the dominant party atrophied as competition between the two parties developed. In Louisiana, the Democratic gubernatorial nominee ran unopposed or faced token opposition in general elections from 1920 through 1956. In 1960, however, the Democratic gubernatorial nominee, Jimmie Davis, and nearly the entire Democratic slate confronted Republican challengers in November. True, Davis's GOP opponent, F. C. Grevemberg (a candidate for the Democratic nomination in 1956), won only 17 percent of the vote, and the state did not elect its first Republican governor, David C. Treen, until 1979. But with each passing year, the Republicans put up stronger and stronger competition. In 1956, Dwight D. Eisenhower won the endorsement of Governor Bob Kennon and carried Louisiana for the Republicans for the first time since Reconstruction. In 1964, Barry Goldwater received the blessing of two former governors, the lieutenant governor, and the secretary of state and carried Louisiana by 120,000 votes (13 percentage points). Republican Charleton H. Lyons won 39 percent against John McKeithen in 1964, and David Treen took 43 percent against Edwin W. Edwards in 1972. And when a veteran anti-Longite, Congressman John R. Rarick, lost his primary in 1974, Republican W. Henson Moore III won his seat representing the Florida parishes. Two-party competition superseded factional competition.

DISCUSSION

For periods of a few years to several decades, factions in North Dakota, Minnesota, Wisconsin, and Louisiana were parties within parties. They named slates of candidates, they electioneered, and they organized electoral competition in major party primaries.

In all four states, the most important work the factions did for voters was identification, attaching labels to candidates and thereby classifying individuals as members of teams. Where strong personalities dominated factional politics, the identifications in the political discourse and the press were often personal: a member of the "Langer faction" in North Dakota, a figure in the "La Follette group" in Wisconsin, a "Long man" in Louisiana. In every state, though, the factions transcended personalities. "Leaguer," "Independent," and "Progressive" had recognized meanings in North Dakota. So did "Leaguer" and "regular" in Minnesota; "progressive," "regular," and "stalwart" in Wisconsin; and "Longite," "anti-Longite," and "reform" in Louisiana.

The meanings in factional membership were conveyed in two ways, also broadly similar across the four cases. First, the factions produced publicity. In North Dakota and Minnesota, the NPL and its opponents published their own

---

bands. Howard, *Political tendencies*: 375–97. McKeithen beat segregationist congressman John R. Rarick in the 1967 Democratic primary by a margin of four to one.

newspapers, issued circulars, and placed advertisements. In Louisiana, the Longites and anti-Longites regularly ran advertisements and organized rallies for their slates. In Wisconsin, the progressives and the regulars appear to have invested in advertising and events only in certain years; almost always, the primaries with the greatest investment in common campaign activities were primaries with high correlations in the votes across offices.

Second, the factions all had a process by which they issued endorsements. The Louisiana factions (and factions within factions) appear to have assembled tickets in the classic southern fashion, horse-trading with candidates and local power brokers. In the first days of Wisconsin primaries, the regulars held conventions as a matter of course and the progressives usually settled matters within the La Follette inner circle; as the competition intensified, both sides came to more formal arrangements. The slating processes in North Dakota were in a class by themselves, embedded in a structure akin to that of state party organizations: county meetings electing delegates to state conventions that made endorsements. The well-elaborated and highly participatory factional organizations no doubt helped to make the North Dakota factions uniquely resistant to the corrosive effects of intrafactional rivalries and secure incumbencies. The North Dakota factions were the archetypes of parties within a party.

In sum, in important respects, the factions in North Dakota, Louisiana, and Wisconsin looked, functioned, and reverberated like traditional party organizations. Their development, in fact, might even be likened to a party system in formation.

The factions closest in character to traditional party organizations, as Mayhew describes them, were the Longites and anti-Longites in Louisiana.[70] Patronage was a very important instrument in the arsenal of the Long "machine." Corruption *petite et grande* was commonplace. The opposition found patronage useful too, even as it claimed the high ground of "reform."

Despite a reputation for "clean" government, patronage politics was hardly unknown in America's northern tier. Bill Langer nearly went to prison for his alleged role in a scheme to support the NPL with assessments on public workers' wages. Even the righteous La Follette used public employment to advance his interests: a special progressive asset were the game wardens, "strolling around the state . . . hunting for men who will vote for La Follette."[71]

All the same, though, the parties within parties were not primarily patronage operations, and the nefarious activities of Long, Langer, La Follette, or any of their opponents should not obscure the substantial ideological component in

---

[70] The residual effects of the factional competition earned Louisiana a "TPO score" of 3, the highest in all the southern states, with "persistent factionalism." Mayhew, *Placing parties*: 104–10.

[71] Robert S. Maxwell, "La Follette and the progressive machine in Wisconsin," *Indiana Magazine of History* 48 (March 1952): 55–70, quotation at 63; Nancy C. Unger, *Fighting Bob La Follette: the righteous reformer* (Chapel Hill: University of North Carolina Press, 2000): chap. 8.

the basis for organized factional competition. Whatever the moral failings, whether his or his followers', and however misguided, Huey Long saw himself not as a patronage boss but as a reformer, the champion of the meek and downtrodden against the haughty and powerful. His program appealed to the "little guy" who had a hard time getting his crops to market, who worried about putting his children through school, who could not afford to pay his poll tax. Earl Long's attacks on "High Hat Sam" Jones were calculated not just to stir the resentment of the "hell-of-a-fellow" but also to carry a message, a message about priorities in government.[72] Behind all the theater, behind all the demagoguery, was a policy program that was sweeping in substance. That is why it generated such resistance.

In the northern tier of the Midwest, likewise, the politics of faction was an ideological politics of real force. In Wisconsin, "Fighting Bob" La Follette was a leader in the crusade against the corporations, the trusts, and the party machines, the architect of a program of reform that set the agenda in state and national politics for three decades. In North Dakota and Minnesota, the NPL was perhaps the most effective reform club – certainly in its Dakotan incarnation, the most durable reform club – that ever existed in U.S. politics. The progressive program and the NPL program rallied thousands and thousands of voters. As in Louisiana, reform also triggered reaction.

The dialectic of reform and reaction was critical to the creation of a coherent factional politics inside the dominant political parties. The insurgents had to organize to fight their way in and the regulars had to organize to beat them back. Factional competition depended on the NPL *and* the IVA, on the progressives *and* the stalwarts, on the Longites *and* the anti-Longites. In every state, the equal and opposite reaction of organized opposition was just as important as the action of organized insurgency. Organization made choices clear to voters.[73]

The factional competition in all four cases occurred in states with an uncompetitive, one-party politics. In the upper Midwest, the Republican Party

---

[72] See Key's diagnosis of the "hell-of-a-fellow" in his discussion of Louisiana politics: *Southern politics*: 165–66.

[73] In each state, moreover, the insurgencies influenced not only the supporting faction but also the opposition faction. Many of the regular leaders in Wisconsin began their careers as acolytes of La Follette and progressivism. Many of the leaders in the IVA, progressive, and ROC factions in North Dakota renounced earlier enthusiasms for the NPL. For years afterward, conservatives in Wisconsin and North Dakota were moderates and progressives nationally. The insurgencies also influenced the factions by shaping the terms of the political debate in profound and lasting ways. Huey Long and his successors shifted all of Louisiana politics to the left, so much so, Sindler argues, that the election of the first anti-Longite governor, Sam Jones in 1940, did not defeat Longism but rather ratified it. Wisconsin pioneered many political and economic reforms that persist to this day. The independents in North Dakota quickly abandoned their plans to repeal the NPL program. As a result, North Dakota still today has a state-owned mill and elevator (in Grand Forks) and a state-owned bank (in Bismarck).

dominated state politics and Democratic victories, while they occurred, were the exceptions. In Louisiana, the Democratic Party controlled access to public office almost as a public monopoly. Of course, in the first half of the twentieth century, states such as North Dakota, Minnesota, Wisconsin, and Louisiana were in no way exceptional. The Democratic Party utterly dominated the politics in the South and several of the border states. The Republican Party held sway in New England, the upper Midwest, and the Plains states. Among all of the single-party states, why did North Dakota, Minnesota, Wisconsin, and Louisiana develop the equivalent of a two-party system within the leading party?

We do not have a complete answer, but we find one common aspect of the electorates in these four states suggestive. In Louisiana, the crucial feature was the sizable francophone population, both Cajun and Creole. In North Dakota, Minnesota, and Wisconsin, the equivalent feature was their large populations of Germans and Scandinavians, most of them within a generation's remove of immigration. In 1910, in fact, northern tier states in the Midwest had the largest combined foreign-born and first-generation electorate in the entire country, as shown in Table 7.19.[74] Moreover, whereas in most parts of the United States the ethnic divide mapped onto an urban–rural divide – which became the basis for competitive two-party politics – it did not in North Dakota, Minnesota, Wisconsin, or Louisiana. Milwaukee and St. Paul did not stand out relative to the rest of their states in their ethnic or immigrant composition; neither did New Orleans relative to the rest of southern Louisiana.

The same claim for distinctiveness might also be made for New Mexico, of course. It had centuries-old Hispanic communities in the north and predominantly Anglo settlements in "Little Texas" in the east. We find substantial cohesion in primary voting in New Mexico. So far, however, we have not found the detritus of organized factional activity in New Mexico – no factional leadership, no factional advertising, no factional slating meetings. Rather, the largest correlations for factional "tickets" arose when candidates with Spanish surnames entered races for nominations for multiple offices. For example, in the year with the strongest factional "slate" voting, 1948, the average correlation between the vote for gubernatorial candidate Ralph Gallegos and candidates Fernandez, Martinez, Montoya, Romero, and Trujillo was 0.86.[75] Factional politics in New Mexico seems primarily to have been ethnic politics.

---

[74] In 1918, the NPL also sought to infiltrate the Republican Party in South Dakota, the next most similar state in its social demographics. Governor Peter Norbeck, a Republican progressive, turned the challenge aside by coopting several elements of the NPL program (including a constitutional amendment to allow state-owned enterprises) and by amplifying attacks on the League's loyalty. He prevailed easily against a primary opponent backed by the NPL. Gilbert C. Fite, "Peter Norbeck and the defeat of the Nonpartisan League in South Dakota," *Mississippi Valley Historical Review* 33 (September 1946): 217–36.

[75] The average correlation for the second "slate" of Gene Allison and Bryant, Dear, Lusk, McGrath, and Ripley was 0.69. The winner of the 1948 Democratic gubernatorial primary

TABLE 7.19 *Naturalized Foreign-Born and First-Generation Males of Voting Age 1910 Census*

Minnesota	59.5
Wisconsin	59.2
North Dakota	54.9
Utah	48.2
South Dakota	47.7
Michigan	44.7
Illinois	41.6
Rhode Island	41.5
New York	40.7
Nebraska	40.5

In contrast, factional politics in North Dakota, Minnesota, Wisconsin, and Louisiana was not ethnic politics. To be sure, the Norwegians were particularly loyal to the progressives in Wisconsin; Russian-Germans were core supporters of the Nonpartisan League in North Dakota; the Longite slates generally ran stronger in northern than in southern Louisiana. As the names on the tickets all by themselves make clear, however, the insurgent and regular factions alike paid attention to balance in their slating. They had supporters of all kinds. The insurgents had German, Norwegian, Swedish, and Yankee leaders, and the regulars did, too. The politics in factional organization states seems to have been panethnic.

The comparison suggests another possibility. Immigrants and first-generation native-born citizens of the northern states were available for mobilization as factional partisans. Because of the situation in their states, they had no experience in two-party politics and they were, in that way, open to new affiliations. In Louisiana, similarly, factions created meaningful choices in societies that had no memory of two-party politics. Strong factions had their roots, perhaps, in the *combination* of weak prior political identities, which increased receptiveness, and close-knit social structures, which facilitated reinforcement.

was yet a third candidate, Thomas J. Mabry, the incumbent. See Jack E. Holmes, *Politics in New Mexico* (Albuquerque: University of New Mexico Press, 1967): chaps. 8–9.

The social substrates and ideological underpinnings of factions contributed to another outstanding feature of organized factional politics: its fragility. The maximum span of two-party politics within a political party was forty years in North Dakota, about half that time in Wisconsin and Louisiana. Just as party systems are wont to disintegrate as new generations replace the older generations that were steeped in its founding conflicts, so assimilation, migration, and generational succession weakened the social identifications that sustained factional identifications.[76]

More importantly, the expressive nature of the attachments to intraparty factions made them terribly vulnerable to shifts in political agendas. Repeatedly, factional politics was preempted by two-party politics – by the creation of the Farmer-Labor Party in Minnesota, by the realignment of the national Republican Party and its rise in Louisiana, and by the realignment of the Democratic Party in North Dakota and Wisconsin (via the way station of the Progressive Party). The NPL could not cope with the erosion of the progressive tradition in the national Republican Party any more than the factions in Louisiana – particularly the conservative anti-Longites – could abide the national Democratic Party's embrace of racial liberalism. The ideological nature of identification with factions bound them to the old conflicts of yesterday, not the new alignments of today.[77] Politics evolved, but factions were frozen in time.

Parties adapted. The advantage of organization based on the material rewards of office is the ability to rewrite principles on a moment's notice in order to win elections. The alacrity with which the Republican bosses became the Democratic bosses in Philadelphia and the black Republican leadership became the black Democratic leadership in Chicago illustrates the point. In the long run, political parties come in two types: the righteous and the victorious.

By the looks of things, though, parties ultimately always have an advantage over factions as coordinators of electoral politics. Part of their superiority is legal privilege: the identification of candidates on the ballot by party is surely better in itself as a coordinating mechanism than any amount of factional advertising or newspaper coverage. A second, more important advantage is the priority of partisan to ideological identification. Factional politics was a local politics that was still nevertheless embedded in a national party politics. As long as the policy divisions between the national parties were misaligned

---

[76] Steven J. Rosenstone, Roy L. Behr, and Edward H. Lazarus, *Third parties in America*, 2d ed. (Princeton: Princeton University Press, 1996): chap. 7.

[77] On the tendency of purposive organizations toward fissure and fragility, see James Q. Wilson, *Political Organizations* (New York: Basic Books, 1973): chaps. 3, 6. Wilson classifies party factions such as the NPL and New York's reform clubs as "ideological parties." On shifting ideological alignments and partisan attachments, see James L. Sundquist, *Dynamics of the Party System*, rev. ed. (Washington: Brookings Institution Press, 1983): chaps. 11–12.

with local demographics and regional traditions, as they were in many parts of the country for a century after the Civil War, partisan attachments promoted factional politics. The members of neither faction could see fit to switch partisan sides. Once realigned to correspond more closely with the local social divisions, however, the national parties exerted a strong magnetic pull on loyalties in local politics as well.

And that leads to one final point about factions and parties. Factions may control access to nominations, but only parties control access to office, as a matter of definition and as a matter of law. This is the final advantage of parties over factions. As E. E. Schattschneider wrote, "the big game is the party game because in the last analysis, there is no substitute for victory in elections .... The parties lack many of the qualities of smaller organizations, but they have one overwhelming asset of their own. They are the only organizations that can win elections."[78]

APPENDIX

If factions are successful in slating, we should expect to observe a high correlation at the county level in the vote shares for candidates from the same faction seeking nominations for different offices. Working within the data, we assign candidates to "slates" in this way:

1. For each state, party, and year find the *highest* positive correlation between any two candidates running for different offices. Call these candidates A_1 and A_2.
2. Find the highest positive correlation involving A_1 or A_2 and another candidate running for a third office. Call this candidate A_3.
3. Repeat Step 2 until a candidate for *each* of the major statewide offices has been assigned to the slate. This will yield candidates A_4, A_5, etc.
4. Excluding the "Slate A" candidates, repeat the first three steps to identify the candidates on "Slate B."

Once we have defined "Slate A" and "Slate B," we find the *average* correlation among all of the candidates on each of the slates. If both slates have the same number of candidates and we find a higher average correlation for Slate B than Slate A, we reverse the slate names. Thus, Slate A always has the highest average correlation.

When there are in fact two competing factions, as we find in North Dakota, the method will almost always identify the membership of the two slates as Slate A and Slate B. (Using newspaper reports, factional advertisements, and historical accounts we have verified a substantial portion of slate membership in each of the four states.) When there is just one faction, for example, a

---

[78] E. E. Schattschneider, *The semisovereign people* (Hinsdale, Ill.: The Dryden Press, 1975): 57.

"machine" against an unorganized group of opponents, the method will almost always identify the members of its slate as Slate A.

Our measure is relatively demanding, in that we search for factions that run "complete" slates in all contested primaries. We have relaxed this requirement in several robustness checks and the overall patterns are similar if we examine the median correlation rather than the mean. We have also examined the correlations using only the top two offices, governor and U.S. senator, and the main findings again are similar.

8

Where Measures Meet History

Party Polarization during the New Deal and Fair Deal

Joshua D. Clinton, Ira Katznelson, and John S. Lapinski

"We are now substituting a 'despotism' for a free nation," proclaimed the Pennsylvania Republican, James Beck, on the floor of the House during a debate on the core legislation of Franklin Roosevelt's Hundred Days, the National Industrial Recovery Act. "It Russianizes the business of America," declared his fellow Pennsylvania Republican, Harry Clay Ransley. "We are, in this bill, not to mention a long list of others recently passed under gag rule, placing American industry under the President as dictator," pronounced their New Jersey colleague, Charles Eaton. New York Republican James Wadsworth, Jr., similarly lectured the House on "The end of individualism in America! I cannot help but believe that this means the end of real liberty and the substitution of bureaucracy – the hard, heavy, cold hand of bureaucracy – upon the daily lives of millions and millions of Americans."[1]

The back and forth in the chamber was rhetorically fierce; on key amendments, the depleted Republican opposition largely stood solidly together in efforts to weaken the bill against a virtually united Democratic Party, and in the face of mass opinion and interest group support across a wide spectrum. Final passage in the House witnessed Democrats voting in favor by a 206–23 margin. By contrast, Republicans split 53–50 in favor, reminding us that final passage votes often take distinct form. The House later approved the conference report by voice vote, but it only cleared the Senate 46–39, with 23 of the 28 participating Republicans voting "no."

Not a national emergency, not a president with a landslide mandate, and not the active support of the business community could override partisan divisions.

---

[1] *Congressional Record*, 73d Congress, 1st session, May 25, 1933, pp. 4212, 4188; May 26, 1933, pp. 4358, 4348.

And so it went during much of the New Deal and Fair Deal years. Working with uncommonly large Democratic majorities, President Roosevelt succeeded on the Hill unless, as in 1937 debates over the Fair Labor Standards Act, or, later, in disputes about union organizing, southern Democrats defected to Republican positions. Over and over again, Republicans and Democrats divided over the revolution in domestic affairs and national responsibilities that the New Deal ushered in.

This is hardly an unconventional view. It is, after all, the way that historians have long understood the role of partisanship at this critical juncture in American political history. So it is particularly jarring to have the New Deal and Fair Deal era represented in landmark systematic scholarship on congressional behavior as a halcyon time of comparatively low polarization (Poole and Rosenthal 1997; McCarty, Poole, and Rosenthal 2006).

That historical moment is now conventionally contrasted with today's ubiquity of high polarization. We all have become familiar with the historical portrait of a U-shaped pattern of elite polarization with a nadir during the New Deal and Fair Deal. Much literature also has linked polarization to legislative productivity (McCarty, Poole, and Rosenthal 2006), and to heightened incivility in politics and rhetoric (Hetherington 2009).

Motivated by the puzzling asymmetry of historical accounts of partisan division during the 1930s and 1940s and the designation of the New Deal as a low-polarization moment, this article is written as a series of four interlocking discussions. First is an engagement between history and NOMINATE, one of our discipline's most canonical measures. Second is an account of elements of change during the Roosevelt and Truman years that raise questions about both the level and the constancy of that era's polarization. Third is an assessment of alternative measures in tandem with a consideration of why NOMINATE generates results for this critical period in American history – a period that it designates as a polarization outlier – that appear to be in tension with patterns apprehended by focused historical treatments, and that do not capture shifts germane to polarization within these two decades. Fourth is an assessment of some implications for extant understandings of the impact of polarization on legislative productivity and for whether and how inequality shapes polarization.

These probes have a hortatory purpose. As the turn to history has taken hold – a quest that David Mayhew projected in his first book and that was keenly advanced by Poole and Rosenthal's pioneering analytical characterization of roll call behavior over the full span of America's past – it has become ever more important to create a dialogue between history and method (Mayhew 1966; for an example, Katznelson 2012; for an assessment, Wawro and Katznelson 2013). To that end, we offer these reflections in the hopes that they spur further inquiries and questions directed at better understanding the causes and consequences of the difficult task of characterizing history.

DEFINING AND MEASURING ELITE POLARIZATION

The NOMINATE project has defined polarization as being partisan in nature. We, too, ultimately adopt that definition, but we note that defining polarization is not an easy task, for it is an inherently ambiguous concept. In a review essay, Marc Hetherington (2009) underscores subtle differences between elite polarization more broadly and partisan polarization. He writes, "The 1960s and 1970s witnessed plenty of polarized rhetoric and behavior about divisive issues like Vietnam and Civil Rights. But differences did not break down along party lines" (Hetherington 2009: 417). This observation is important both conceptually and as we think of measurement issues, especially as most conventional definitions of elite polarization are based on partisanship.

For the purposes of this chapter, we follow the extant literature in this regard. That is, we look to differences in voting behavior between and among various partisan groups to assess polarization. We do so because, while we agree with Hetherington that polarization may occur in the absence of partisan divisions, our aim is to contribute to the scholarship on elite polarization, which emphasizes the role of partisanship. Empirical studies of polarization in Congress typically make use of roll call voting data, most notably the estimates produced by the DW-NOMINATE algorithm (Poole and Rosenthal 1997) applied to matrices of recorded roll call votes. This work measures polarization as the distance between the median first dimension DW-NOMINATE scores of the two major parties in the House of Representatives (Poole and Rosenthal 1997; McCarty, Poole, and Rosenthal 2006; Hetherington 2009; Lapinski 2008 and 2013).

Before moving further, it is important to understand what a NOMINATE-based measure of polarization does, and does not, tell us about the larger political context and the sources of partisan conflict in a legislature.[2] Poole and Rosenthal explain that the variation that is characterized by the first dimension of DW-NOMINATE "can be thought of as ranging from strong loyalty to one party ... to weak loyalty to either party to strong loyalty on the second, opposing party" (2007: 55). In other words, the "ideal points" that are recovered on the first dimension capture the extent to which there is variation in members' voting behavior on those issues on which the parties disagree. Political scientists, including Poole and Rosenthal, often label the resulting dimension as "liberal-conservative ideology" because the issues involved typically deal with such matters as income redistribution, but this label is an *ex post* interpretation of the recovered pattern. Nothing in the statistical or underlying behavioral model necessarily requires the recovered dimension to have anything to do with liberal and conservative issues (or, in fact, even ideology). This

---

[2] To be clear, while some of the analysis in this chapter is specific to DW-NOMINATE (e.g., the unclear role of the second dimension), its broader points also apply to many other roll call-based estimates of polarization.

subtle point is consequential because it reminds us that the standard measure of polarization captures the tendency of Democrats to vote against Republicans, and nothing more. The oppositional voting that we observe could be the result of policy preferences, party pressure, or the types of issues that are brought to votes on the floor. It is impossible to adjudicate between these alternatives from roll calls alone. In fact, the pattern of "yeas" and "nays" being analyzed is a product of the preferences of the members in the chamber, the extent to which voting behavior reflects those preferences, and the issues that are taken to a vote. Ideal points that result from analyzing the pattern of observed votes are sensitive to each (Clinton 2012).

Consider how extant statistical models are agnostic about the nature of the agenda, the substance of issues, and their degree of importance both in terms of the significance of legislation and in terms of the larger situation within which it is being offered and appraised. Constraints on how ideal points are assumed to change over time tend not to take such matters into account. We know, however, that there is variation along these lines at different historical moments (e.g., Clinton and Lapinski 2008), and under different conditions of partisan electoral competition and success (Lee 2008; 2009).

Law making during the New Deal took up issues that were different in kind from those debated in more recent Congresses. Legislation considered in the 1930s and 1940s fundamentally restructured the relationship between the state and its citizens in the context of the Great Depression, which had exposed the laissez-faire status quo as radically inadequate to the calamity at hand. As a result, legislation was introduced to promote a far more expansive role for the federal government, not only in terms of its involvement in and regulation of economic activity, but also in terms of the level of support that it provided for citizens. Government was reacting to a set of existing policies widely thought to be inadequate.

More recent law making has been very different. Aside from the Affordable Care Act enacted in 2010 and arguably the American Recovery and Reinvestment Act of 2009, contemporary debates have largely amended or reformed existing policies. The contrast is stark. During the New Deal, political debates were over whether or not to create Social Security; current debates are over whether or not to raise the age of retirement or the formula used to calculate cost of living increases in the amount that is paid out. Put differently, the policies of the New Deal were largely, though certainly not exclusively, about *creating* new programs and redefining the nature of the relationship between citizens and the state, given a status quo that was thought to be unacceptable. The politics of more recent periods largely, though not always, involves attempts to *amend* the relationships that characterize the existing policy regime.

Change to the nature of issues is consequential because the ideal points we estimate from observed voting behavior can change if we hold preferences fixed and alter the substantive agenda. Put differently, it is possible to generate what appears to be an increasing amount of polarization in voting behavior even if the preferences of legislators are held constant simply by adjusting the nature of the bills being voted upon. In particular, as the number of proposals to adjust centrist status quos increases – as we might expect would happen if policy converges to more median positions (Krehbiel 1998) – then the level of estimated polarization can increase even if preferences remain unchanged.

An illustrative Monte Carlo simulation briefly highlights this fact by demonstrating how both the preferences and the agenda affect the level of estimated polarization in a legislature. Think about a hypothetical legislature with 100 members and 55 Democrats. Suppose that the agenda initially consists of 100 votes with uniformly distributed cutpoints ranging between [-1,1]. Assume Democrats' true preferences range uniformly between [-1, 1-α] and Republicans' range uniformly between [-1+α, 1]. Allowing α to vary from 0 to 1 examines situations ranging from a complete lack of polarization to an instance where every Democrat is to the left of every Republican. Given the assumed cutpoints and ideal points for each choice of α, we follow Hirsch (2012) by introducing idiosyncratic voting error and generating a matrix of roll calls using the probabilistic behavioral voting model of Clinton, Jackman, and Rivers (2003) that we then use to estimate ideal points.

Figure 8.1a plots the estimated level of polarization from the ideal points that are estimated in each simulation. As expected, for a fixed agenda, as the amount of party overlap in true preferences decreases from 1 (complete overlap) to 0 (complete separation), the estimated ideal points of the average Republican and average Democrat increasingly diverge. This is the common interpretation of polarization; that is, increased polarization reflects increased disagreement between the two parties about what policies ought to be pursued by the government.

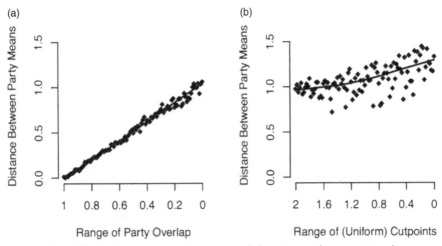

FIGURE 8.1 Polarization two ways: the impact of changing preferences (a) and a changing agenda (b) on polarization.

What is less commonly realized is that, as Figure 8.1b reveals, polarization is also sensitive to the agenda being voted upon even when true preferences are polarized (by setting $\alpha = 1$). Instead of assuming that the cutpoints uniformly range from $[-1,1]$ as in Figure 8.1a, Figure 8.1b illustrates the consequences of choosing 100 cutpoints from the uniform interval $[-1+ \beta, 1- \beta]$ when β varies from 0 to 1 across simulations. When $\beta = 0$, cutpoints are uniformly spread across the entire $[-1,1]$ policy space and we observe members from the different parties sometimes vote together on the issues we observe; $\beta = 1$ reflects the extreme instance in which all of the cutpoints are all located at 0 and every vote is a party-line vote in the absence of voting error. Figure 8.1b reveals that the measure of polarization increases as the distribution of cutpoints converges to the middle of the policy space. Theoretically, converging cutpoints can be interpreted as reflecting an increasing emphasis on amending more centrist policies as opposed to creating controversial new government programs – perhaps because policy outcomes converge dynamically to median positions over time in the absence of exogenous shocks (Krehbiel 1998).

To be clear, our polarization measures depend on both (1) the distribution of underlying preferences and (2) the issues that are brought to a vote. While Figure 8.1 suggests that, for the particular values chosen for the simulation, the impact of preferences appears larger than the impact of the agenda, the larger point is that our ability to control for the possibility of these two types of changes when conducting analyses across extensive time periods is typically limited. The difficulty of identifying the cause of observed polarization is likely to be consequential because it matters whether a legislature is polarized because of divergent preferences or whether it is polarized because the votes that are being taken are intentionally chosen to divide the parties. Whereas the latter may be a consequence of electoral position taking and may have limited implications for policy outcomes, the former reflects divergent opinions on the policies that the government should pursue. DW-NOMINATE does not let us adjudicate between these two alternatives.

Another important and underappreciated feature of DW-NOMINATE scores is that they estimate two dimensions. The second dimension deals with issues that often split parties internally, especially matters that concern race and region (Poole and Rosenthal 1997). Curiously, even though the "residual" second dimension characterizes voting on issues on which the parties are internally divided – and in which party-based polarization therefore does not occur – second-dimension scores are almost universally ignored in empirical studies of polarization. We know no major study focusing on the second dimension of the NOMINATE project. To be sure, Poole and Rosenthal do look at how issue areas map onto the second dimension in their landmark book, *Congress: A Political-Economic History of Roll Call Voting* (1997). That noted, why estimate a two-dimensional model (except for goodness of fit reasons), only to ignore the second dimension when studying important substantive topics such as polarization? Why not look at overall polarization as characterized by the entire roll call voting record of a Congress? These questions are rarely asked by the large and significant body of scholarship that constructs polarization scores for Congress based on DW-NOMINATE measures.

Equally curious is how few scholars evaluate the assumptions of DW-NOM-INATE's algorithm (for exceptions, see Carroll et al. 2009; Clinton and Jackman 2009; Carroll et al. 2013). To most, the method underneath the various NOMINATE estimators is a black box. This is unfortunate because the assumptions necessary to implement any scaling method such as NOMINATE have empirical consequences (Poole 2005; Clinton 2012). While the sensitivity of some assumptions have been explored, there are others made by both the behavioral and the statistical model that have not.[3] Of particular interest here is the manner in which strong assumptions are necessary to make scores comparable across time.

To evaluate how the ideal point estimates in one time period compare to another, a baseline is required. Because everything is unobserved but a matrix of "ones and zeros," to compute and interpret distance measures over time requires many assumptions about both a behavioral model of voting and the statistical model used to implement it. For example, if we assume, as DW-NOMINATE does, that any change in a member's ideal point must be steady, gradual, and persistent, might this affect our ability to characterize important moments in political history that are both dramatic and relatively short-lasting? As a key example, might the tremendous exogenous shocks to the political system caused by the Great Depression and World War II combined with the changing (endogenous) willingness to consider issues involving race and the electoral insulation of southern Democrats affect our assessment of partisan conflict over this period? How sensitive are our conclusions to alternative assumptions that we might make when comparing ideal points over time?

THE NEW DEAL, FAIR DEAL, AND POLARIZATION IN THE U.S. HOUSE

The NOMINATE project finds political polarization to have been very low during the New Deal and Fair Deal periods in both the House and the Senate.

---

[3] For example, when estimating a two-dimensional model using a NOMINATE-based estimator, the weight given to the first and second dimensions is assumed to be fixed across time and the weight is chosen so as to maximize fit (variously computed). There is also a "SAG Correction" built into the estimator that can override and impose a constraint on how distant members can be from one another and rescale the computed estimates. The SAG Correction prevents there from being too much distance between ideal points in the $[-1,1]$ space and it changes the meaning of the recovered space if the variation between ideal points in a Congress becomes too large. It is unclear how consequential these assumptions are when computing estimates over long periods of time where the meaning of the dimensions and the scale could vary.

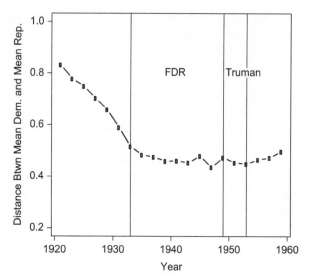

FIGURE 8.2 Polarization in the early twentieth century U.S. House (1920–1960). The trend line shows the difference between the average Republican and average Democratic DW-NOMINATE scores in the first dimension.

Figure 8.2 reveals this portrait by graphing the amount of polarization in the U.S. House between 1920 and 1960 through a calculation of the difference in the average ideal point of Democrats and Republicans according to DW-NOMINATE.[4] A crucial feature of historical analysis is distinguishing the particularities of distinctive situations. Doing this for the 1930s and 1940s, we can discern circumstances that, at minimum, complicate this low and flat characterization of the period. Moreover, these historical circumstances complicate any measure of Republican and Democratic polarization that, for this moment, fails to grapple with the particular place that southern Democrats occupied in Congress.

A first attribute of the period is a constellation of uncommon shifts in the circumstances of partisanship. These were not just ordinary changes, as in the 80th Congress, when Republican majorities displaced Democratic control in each chamber. Rather, two shifts occurred that could not but have affected both the extent and meaning of polarization.

First, the pre-New Deal 72nd Congress had been divided between 218 Republicans, 216 Democrats, and 1 Farmer Labor Party member. After the 1932 Democratic rout, fully 313 Democrats and 5 Farmer Labor members sat

[4] The Voteview.com website offers an identical figure of polarization using DW-NOMINATE scores for the entire history of the U.S. Congress. Using party medians instead of party means makes no substantive difference and the measures correlate at 0.995 for the 1877–2009 time period.

in the chamber. Bucking midterm trends, Democratic numbers grew two years later to 322, and, in 1936, to a remarkable 334, with only 88 Republicans left (as well as 8 Wisconsin Progressives and 5 Farmer Labor members). For obvious reasons, change in the Senate was slower, but by the 75th Congress, only 16 Republicans remained. From this low base, the swing back to a more ordinary division was impressive. The 78th Congress, elected in 1942, witnessed 38 Senate Republicans, and a Democratic majority of just 222–209. Normal partisanship had been restored.

A second peculiarity concerns the balance of regional forces within the Democratic Party. This period, of course, witnessed Democrats starkly divided between a primarily urban, immigrant, Catholic and Jewish northern wing and a primarily rural, native-born, Protestant southern contingent. During the Republican 1920s, southern Democrats had constituted the great majority of the party in Congress. The early New Deal realignment brought in a nonsouthern party majority. But that did not last. Starting in the 76th House and the 77th Senate, southern Democrats constituted the party's majority in the legislature once more. Never again during the Roosevelt or Truman Administrations did their share fall below half of all House Democrats; by the end of the Truman administration, fully 63 percent of Democrats in the Senate hailed from the South (understood as the seventeen states that mandated racial segregation).

Long ago, V. O. Key, Jr.'s classic chapters on the House and Senate noted how southern Democrats constituted the most cohesive bloc within the legislature (Key 1949). That being the case, the level of polarization depended not just on the degree of likeness exhibited by members of the two parties, but on the extent to which southern and nonsouthern Democrats joined forces to share a partisan position.

An additional key feature of the period is the global conflict that consumed most of the 1940s, opening with World War II and closing with the Cold War and the hot war in Korea (Mayhew 2005). These developments exerted strong normative pressures for national unity in tandem with growth in the number of military and security issues to be adjudicated in Congress. This set of pressures cross-cut continuing partisan differences about the role of the United States in foreign affairs, often serving to soften them. Thus, as an example, even as isolationists (primarily Republican) and internationalists (primarily Democratic) disagreed about such key matters as the fate of American neutrality in the late 1930s and early 1940s, they could agree across party lines to dramatically increase military spending in a dangerous world.

Within this particular context, high polarization between the parties required Democratic Party solidarity across regional lines, but the absence of polarization could have been caused by two different mechanisms – either growth in cross-partisan behavior or the defection of Democrats to the Republican camp on a meaningful number of issues – working separately or together.

To help track the patterning of partisanship under these conditions during the New Deal and Fair Deal, Katznelson and Mulroy (2012) fashioned a classification of roll call types according to the degree of likeness of southern members from the seventeen states that then mandated racial segregation manifested with respect both to fellow Democrats and Republicans. The assumption that voting behavior reflects preference homogeneity rather than party discipline (Krehbiel 2000) yields the schema shown in Figure 8.3.

With a conventional Rice score of 70 serving as the distinction between high and low similarity, this typology classifies votes in four categories: partisan votes in which southern and nonsouthern Democrats vote with high likeness but southern Democrats and Republicans do not; cross-partisan votes in which all members vote with high likeness across party lines; sectional votes in which southern Democrats do not vote either with Republicans or other Democrats; and defection votes in which southern Democrats join Republicans while deserting the party position.

Over the course of the twenty years of the Roosevelt and Truman presidencies, we can observe significant shifts in the percentage of roll calls falling within each quadrant. During the four New Deal Congresses that preceded American participation in World War II, between 67 and 73 percent of all roll calls in the House were partisan; yet during and after the 77th Congress, at no time did more than 42 percent of the votes prove to be partisan.

It is clear, in consequence, that measures displaying consistently low polarization, as shown by DW-NOMINATE in Figure 8.1, either are not accurate or mask important transformations to roll call behavior within and across the parties. Indeed, it seems clear that both mechanisms – the growth of cross-partisan voting under conditions of global duress and the upward trend of southern defection – should be invoked and better understood as underpinning

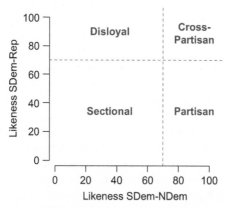

FIGURE 8.3 Typology of southern roll call behavior. Likeness scores between southern Democrats and nonsouthern Democrats (on horizontal access) and between southern Democrats and Republicans (on vertical axis). The dotted gray lines mark a likeness score of 70. A roll call that falls above or to the left of the dotted gray lines indicates that the two blocs under comparison voted with low likeness on the roll call.

TABLE 8.1 *Southern Roll Call Behavior: The Percent of Roll Calls Falling in Each Quadrant*

Congress	Number of RCs	U.S. House of Representatives			
		Disloyal	Sectional	Partisan	Cross-Partisan
73 (1933–34)	143	1.5	3.7	73.3	21.5
74 (1935–36)	212	2.4	0.6	66.7	30.4
75 (1937–38)	158	4.4	4.4	67.2	24.1
76 (1939–40)	227	7.2	4.6	67.7	20.5
77 (1941–42)	152	8.8	11.7	42.3	37.2
78 (1943–44)	156	17.3	6.4	39.1	37.2
79 (1945–46)	231	20.6	5.9	40.2	33.3
80 (1947–48)	163	21.9	8.0	41.7	28.5
81 (1949–50)	275	9.8	16.0	40.2	34.0
82 (1951–52)	181	24.1	13.3	36.8	25.9
Total	1755	12.1	7.8	50.7	29.5

any aggregate outcome of diminished polarization during the second half of this twenty-year period.

Compared to the more flat and low pattern projected by DW-NOMINATE, the categorizations of Table 8.1 discern a pattern that is more varied. Roll call voting in the 73rd and 74th Congresses at the start of the New Deal in 1933–1936 was largely defined by partisanship. The southern and northern blocs of the Democratic party united against the members from the Republican bloc, with only a few roll calls venturing into the Sectional (3.7 percent in the House and 1.8 percent in the Senate) and Disloyal (1.5 percent in the House and 3.5 percent in the Senate) quadrants. This pattern continued through much of the early New Deal period with southern Democrats diverging from non-southern Democrats on fewer than 13 percent of all roll calls in both chambers of the first four New Deal Congresses, as represented by the extreme bias of roll calls grouped on the right-hand side of that moment's scatterplots.

But this pattern did not prove to be stable. Rather, the early New Deal configuration changed dramatically, with several breakpoints marking the evolution of southern bloc behavior as members from the region began to selectively disengage from their coalitional relationship with nonsouthern Democrats. As southern members began to behave less reliably as party voters, two patterns emerged. First, southerners began, on occasion, to find new allies within the Republican Party. By the 76th Congress, the proportion of Disloyal roll calls (7.2 percent) had nearly doubled that in the 75th. Even more substantial at this moment was the sudden accumulation of Sectional votes. On these roll calls, southern members broke away as a distinct and independent bloc, diverging both from Republicans and from their co-partisans on nearly 12 percent of the roll calls. Southern Democrats in the House were shedding some partisan loyalty in favor of regional preferences.

By the 78th Congress, the Disloyal category had become the reservoir for a massive deluge of roll calls. Quite suddenly and considerably, southern Democrats began to ally with Republicans in proportions that far exceeded any previous New Deal Congress. This pattern continued into the Truman years, thus dramatically softening intraparty polarization. Democrats as a whole were not moving closer to Republicans; rather, the party's southern majority was doing so selectively.

One of the striking features of these shifts over the course of the New Deal and Fair Deal is how they match much of what we know in a more qualitative way about the period. The early moments of the New Deal, marked by the passage of an extraordinary range of legislation that transformed the scale and responsibilities of the national state – laws about banking and Wall Street, agriculture and labor, economic oversight and social security – pitted very different perspectives, if not quite formed ideologies, against each other in what was then a rather one-sided political competition between the parties. We also know, as historian James Patterson (1981) noted long ago, that a southern revolt against the wage-labor bill in the 75th Congress was a turning point. It marked the first moment southern members, fearing disruption to their low-wage and racialized labor market, and concerned about the upsurge in union activity, started to calculate how votes on what ordinarily would be thought of as first-dimension issues might affect their intense preferences about race and region. "Southern solidarity," noted the *Atlanta Constitution*, was becoming "solidarity unhitched to Democratic Party leadership" (December 22, 1937: 6).

CHARACTERIZING PATTERNS OF ELITE POLARIZATION

Given the discrepancy between the degree of polarization during the New Deal and Fair Deal as depicted by DW-NOMINATE, on the one hand, and historians, on the other, it is useful to contrast how the politics of this period are categorized according to other measures. In characterizing how DW-NOMINATE's measure of elite polarization compares for this era, we can open the way to an evaluation of the difference that variations in assumptions about ideal points make to empirical results over time.

To evaluate whether measures exist that come closer to historical treatments of the New Deal and Fair Deal, we focus on the relationship between polarization in the House according to DW-NOMINATE and the average level of party unity voting in the House; the amount of electoral polarization that is present in House districts; and wealth inequality over time. Each of these inquiries strengthens our awareness that the characterization of polarization during the New Deal and Fair Deal by DW-NOMINATE is anomalous.

Party Unity Voting and Elite Polarization

Consider simple differences in party unity voting over time as a first comparison to DW-NOMINATE trends in party polarization. We identify the set of votes in each Congress on which the parties are opposed to one another and calculate the percentage of such votes for which the average member of Congress votes with his or her own party. This is a relatively coarse description of elite polarization (Krehbiel 2000), but it does capture the level of conflictual voting behavior.

Figure 8.4 shows that party unity in voting slowly declined from 1877 through the early 1960s when it fell rather dramatically before beginning a steep ascent in the 1970s. Figure 8.4b considers the relationship between such average party unity and the level of polarization characterized by DW-NOMINATE scores. A very strong relationship is found, except during the period of the New Deal and the Fair Deal! During this period, the level of polarization is estimated to be far less than the average party unity would suggest based on the relationship between party unity and polarization. In fact, over the entire period, the correlation between average party unity and polarization measured using DW-NOMINATE is 0.69, but this correlation increases to 0.76 when the ten Congresses associated with the New Deal and Fair Deal are excluded.

Electoral Polarization and Elite Polarization

Another measure of polarization is provided by the extent to which the districts of Democratic and Republican incumbents vote for different presidential candidates. If districts represented by Democrats vote differently from districts represented by Republicans in presidential elections, this arguably provides some evidence that the two electorates disagree on issues related to national

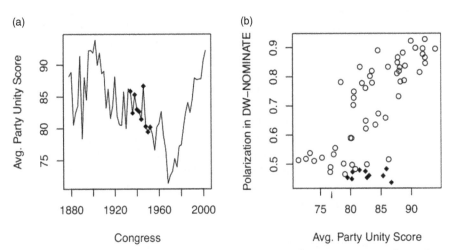

FIGURE 8.4 Trends in party unity voting, 1877–2010. (a) The average party unity voting between 1877 and 2010. (b) The correlation between this average and the DW-NOMINATE measure of polarization. Dark points indicate Congresses during the New Deal and the Fair Deal (1933–1953).

politics. To measure district electoral polarization, we calculate the difference in the average percentage of votes cast for the Democratic presidential candidate for districts represented by Democrats and Republicans.

To be clear, this measure is imperfect. Not only does the meaning of voting for the Democratic candidate change over time depending on which Democrat is running, but even if the same candidate were to run in every election, what it means to cast a vote for that Democratic candidate would depend on who else is running. Despite these shortcomings, district presidential voting behavior provides one of the only characterizations we have about the views of the electorate across enough time to allow us to track the decline and rise of polarization.

To compute this measure of electoral polarization we rely on several data sources. For the first half of this period (presidential elections from 1872 through 1948), we utilize district-level estimates of presidential votes derived from county-level election returns by Ansolabehere, Snyder, and Stewart (2001).[5] For the modern period (1952 through 2008), we use district-level returns as reported by the Census Bureau.

Figure 8.5 presents the comparison in an analogous way to Figure 8.4. The top graph plots the difference in the average two-party Democratic vote between Democrats and Republicans over time. It reveals a fairly constant level of electoral polarization (with notable exceptions in notable elections such as 1912), especially in the period leading up to, and including, the New Deal and Fair Deal. The level of electoral polarization proceeds to decrease before gradually climbing throughout the 1980s and 1990s.

In general, Figure 8.5 reveals that periods of high electoral polarization in district-level voting behavior in presidential elections occur when high levels of polarization in elite voting behavior also occur. There are some exceptions to this pattern – most notably the Congresses of the New Deal and the Fair Deal graphed in solid plots. During this critical period, DW-NOMINATE suggests that there is far less polarization than the voting behavior of districts in presidential elections would otherwise imply based on what we observe in other time periods. The stark difference is more clearly revealed when we consider the correlation between the two measures. When we include the New Deal and Fair Deal Congresses, the correlation is only 0.24 over the entire time period, but it increases to 0.45 when the outlying Congresses of the New Deal and Fair Deal are excluded. This discrepancy implies that there is something different about either the politics or the measures of the New Deal and Fair Deal era relative to the rest of the time period.

---

[5] These data are incomplete due to difficulties in matching county-level election returns with congressional districts; 18 percent of districts are missing, primarily in large cities and the Northeast. Our graphical representations of responsiveness include breaks between the early and later data to underscore this limitation. In addition, we omit the 88th Congress (1963–1964) due to missing data stemming from widespread congressional redistricting in the early 1960s.

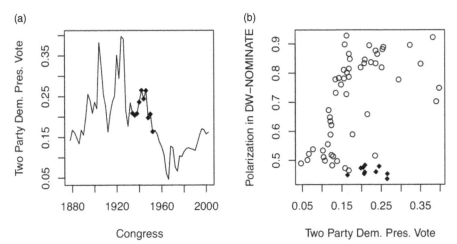

FIGURE 8.5 The relationship between district electoral polarization and DW-NOMINATE polarization. (a) The difference in the average percentage of two-party Democratic presidential vote between districts with Democratic and Republican representatives. (b) The relationship between this measure of electoral polarization and the measure of polarization based on DW-NOMINATE. Dark points indicate Congresses during the New Deal and the Fair Deal (1933–1953).

Income Inequality and Elite Polarization

The rise of income inequality has been causally associated with increases in polarization. Notably, McCarty, Poole, and Rosenthal (2003; 2006) argue that income inequality and congressional polarization in Congress are tightly linked. Our revisionist view of polarization reveals that this relationship is weakest during the New Deal era. To explore the correlation between elite polarization and income inequality, we use the fraction of wealth in the United States held by the top 1 percent as measured by Piketty and Saez (2003) and extended by Saez to 2011. This data series begins in 1913. Figure 8.6 reveals a nearly identical pattern to those of Figures 8.5 and 8.4, at least for the 1940s when income inequality according to this measure began to dramatically decrease (Figure 8.6a).

Figure 8.6 again reveals that the polarization that DW-NOMINATE estimates to be present during the period of the New Deal and the Fair Deal appears different from the polarization present during periods of similar income inequality. The relationship between income inequality and polarization evident during other historical moments appears absent during this time period. Over the entire time period the correlation between the measures is 0.51, but it increases to 0.68 when the Congresses of the New Deal and Fair Deal are excluded.

Examining the relationship between DW-NOMINATE polarization and three time-series that are thought likely to be associated with elite polarization

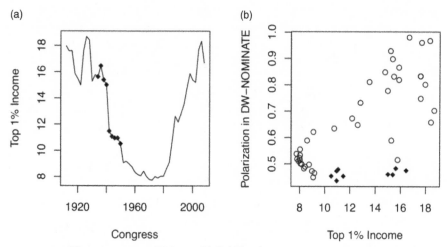

FIGURE 8.6 The percentage of U.S. wealth held by the top 1 percent, 1913–2009. (a) The percentage of wealth held by the top 1 percent of U.S. households computed by Piketty and Saez (2003). (b) The relationship between polarization and income inequality over the same time period. Solid points denote the New Deal and Fair Deal period.

in Congress – the extent of party unity voting in the House, the extent to which congressional districts are electorally polarized, and the extent of income inequality in the United States – reveals that there is a strong relationship in each case except for the period pertaining to the New Deal and the Fair Deal. The characterization of polarization in the House during the New Deal and the Fair Deal according to DW-NOMINATE is far less than the level of polarization we would predict based on other measures that are commonly thought to be related to polarization.

LAW MAKING AND ELITE POLARIZATION

Conventional wisdom holds that elite polarization produces gridlock. Lying in opposition to this conventional wisdom about the inability of the House and Senate to enact significant legislation during periods of stark partisan and ideological division, however, is the fact that some such periods have in fact been punctuated by dramatic law making. The highly polarized 111th Congress – characterized by Norman Ornstein as "the most dysfunctional political environment that I have ever seen" – was, as Ornstein himself noted, "one of, at least, the three most productive Congresses' since 1900." (Fahrenthold et al. 2010). How then should we think about the relationship between polarization and legislative accomplishment? Is there a systematic relationship between the two that would lead us to think that polarization in and of itself is sufficient to impede law making, or is the relationship less solid or more complex? Moreover, given the apparent discrepancy between the historical record and how

DW-NOMINATE classifies the polarization of the New Deal and the Fair Deal, how dependent is our conclusion about the relationship between polarization and law making on how we classify that era's politics ?

Correctly diagnosing polarization during the 1930s and 1940s is important for understanding the consequences of polarization and the relationship between the size of the majority and the distribution of policy preferences held by legislators. In terms of law making, this was among the most productive moments in American history; many New Deal and Fair Deal statutes have had a lasting and profound effect on the relationship between the federal government and its citizens. If these changes did not occur during a period of low polarization, what we attribute to polarization *per se* rather than features of the political environment has to be carefully reconsidered (e.g., Jones 2001; Schnaffner 2011). For example, when the partisan division in the House is 340–95, how consequential are the policy differences between the majority and minority party?

Many have argued that polarization decreases the ability of Congress to pass laws essential for governance. Most empirical work confirming this relationship analyzes the period after World War II (see, e.g., Binder 1999; McCarty, Poole, and Rosenthal 2006; McCarty 2007), a period in which polarization is estimated to be either constant or increasing according to the commonly used DW-NOMINATE measure. Given the nature of this variation, exploring the consequences of polarization can be difficult, as any increasing trend would produce a high inverse correlation with productive law making.

Lapinski (2008) has provided a valuable extension to this literature by exploring the correlation between polarization and law making since Reconstruction – a long period with far more variation in polarization according to DW-NOMINATE. Utilizing that measure, he indeed reports that Congresses with high levels of polarization are among the least productive (using the legislative accomplishment data of Clinton and Lapinski, 2006). We build upon this analysis while showing how alternative measures for classifying polarization during the New Deal and Fair Deal affect the empirical conclusion and causal argument.

Here, we model the number of "significant" enactments passed by each Congress as a function of polarization in the House and other prominent variables that are thought to affect the supply and demand for legislation. We use a negative binomial model to account for the discrete nature of the count data.[6] The regression results in Table 8.2 reveal that the characterization of polarization during the New Deal and the Fair Deal is critical for what we can conclude about the empirical relationship connecting polarization and law making. Looking at Congressional activity between 1877 and 1994,

---

[6] The covariates included in Table 8.2 do not include a size of the majority party. We ran the models with this variable included and it does not change any of the findings presented here.

TABLE 8.2 *Relationship between Polarization and Legislative Accomplishment,*
1877–1994.

Model 1 includes all years and Model 2 excludes the New Deal and the Fair Deal.

	Model 1	Model 2
	1877–1994	1877–1932, 1954–2004
House Polarization	−1.31	−0.34
(Rbst Stnd Err.)	(0.84)	(2.01)
Start of Term	0.52***	0.51***
	(0.13)	(0.15)
Divided Gov't	−0.13	−0.12
	(0.13)	(0.15)
Vietnam War	0.59***	0.57***
	(0.10)	(0.13)
Time	0.05*	0.05*
	(0.02)	(0.02)
Time^2	−0.001*	−0.001*
	(0.000)	(0.000)
Post-1946	−0.49*	−0.002
	(0.23)	(0.87)
Constant	2.05*	1.21
	(0.85)	(1.73)
ln(alpha)	−2.65***	−2.92**
	(0.60)	(1.09)
N	59	48

Model 1's results are consistent with the conventional understanding of the relationship between polarization and legislative accomplishments: as the parties become more polarized in Congress, the Congress is increasingly unable to pass significant legislation to address important problems facing the nation. The effect of House polarization on the ability of Congress to pass a piece of legislation in the "Top 500" is negative and statistically distinguishable from zero using a two-tailed test at $p=0.12$ and using a one-tailed test at $p=.06$.

The results of Model 2 show that the coefficient on House Polarization shrinks to a fourth of what it was when the New Deal and the Fair Deal are excluded, and the standard error nearly doubles to provide a substantively uninformative confidence interval that ranges from −4.27 to 3.60. If the New Deal and the Fair Deal are excluded from the analysis – as we might be inclined to do if we suspect that the polarization of this period is mischaracterized – the relationship between polarization and legislative accomplishment is neither substantively nor statistically distinguishable from zero.

To interpret the substantive significance of the results reported in Table 8.2, Figure 8.7 graphs the predicted number of notable laws enacted across the

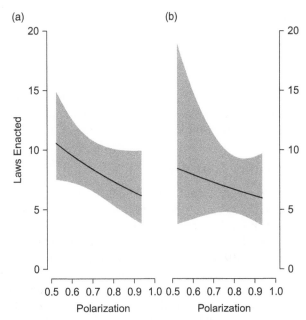

FIGURE 8.7 Interpreting the effect of polarization in Table 8.2. (a) The predicted number of notable enactments as a function of polarization in the House using the specification reported in Model 1 and data from all Congresses between 1874 and 1994. (b) The relationship when the Congresses of the New Deal and Fair Deal are omitted. The line denotes the predicted number of enactments and the shaded region is the 95% confidence interval for that prediction.

range of observed values of House polarization for the two models for modal categories.[7] Figure 8.7a presents the relationship using every Congress between 1874 and 1994, while Figure 8.7b replicates the analysis after omitting the Congresses associated with the New Deal and the Fair Deal. As Figure 8.7 reveals, whereas there is a negative relationship between polarization and legislative productivity when we measure the period of the New Deal and the Fair Deal as being a period of low polarization, if we remove these Congresses from the analysis we can no longer be confident that there is any notable relationship between the two. The line indicating the predicted number of enactments is much flatter and the shaded area denoting the 95 percent confidence interval is much wider.

The dramatic changes in the relationship between polarization and legislative accomplishment evident in Models 1 and 2 reveal that our inferences regarding the relationship between polarization and the capacity for legislative

---

[7] To generate predicted values we set *Start of Term*, *Divided Government*, *Vietnam War*, and *Post-1946* to 0 and we chose the median year for Year and Year².

accomplishment hinge critically on how we characterize the politics of the New Deal and the Fair Deal. If we think it is a period of low polarization as DW-NOMINATE classifies it, we would conclude that periods of low polarization are also periods of legislative accomplishment. If, however, we remove this period from the analysis to see how robust the relationship between polarization and legislative accomplishment is to the characterization of this period, we find that we can no longer conclude that the relationship between polarization and accomplishment is a meaningful one.

OTHER ASSUMPTIONS, OTHER MEASURES?

The preceding sections suggest that scholars should be exceptionally careful when using DW-NOMINATE to explore the politics of the critical period surrounding the New Deal and Fair Deal. Not only does the characterization of low polarization seem at odds with the historical record and the patterns of voting we observe, but the measures of polarization for this period do not correlate with measures that correlate quite highly with the polarization measure in other historical moments. Moreover, the impact of this discrepancy is important. What we conclude about such vital subjects as the relationship between polarization and law making depends heavily on how we classify the New Deal and Fair Deal eras. In these instances, two possible conclusions are conceivable. Either the larger analyses are spurious because of the mischaracterization of that key period or the larger relationships are in fact robust but the exceptional qualities of behavior during the New Deal demand explanation. One such possibility concerns the constellation of unusual factors regarding partisan patterns across and within the parties during this era, especially the role played by southern Democrats.

The analysis we present stops well short of integrating the various elements we have considered; we are not in a position either to adjudicate between possible measures or to diagnose the reasons that have propelled the divergent characterizations of polarization in the space we possess. But we do wish to consider some consequences of making alternative assumptions about the nature of politics across time to determine if the resulting characterizations better account for the trends we highlight. To be clear, the alternative assumptions we consider involve different assumptions about how to compare ideal points across time. It does not, however, grapple with the question of whether or not the agenda itself is shifting in consequential ways that are not adequately captured by the assumptions made about ideal point change across time.

The ideal point estimates that are recovered by the DW-NOMINATE model are temporally comparable over time because it is assumed that members' ideal points can only change in a linear fashion over time. Different members may change by different amounts, but, if change occurs, it is linear and it persists across a member's entire tenure in office. For the analysis in this paper, we take the same behavioral model used in DW-NOMINATE – as implemented in W-NOMINATE – but we consider the effect of taking an alternative approach to comparing ideal points over time. Rather than impose assumptions about how the preferences of individual members may change, we follow the approach taken by Groseclose, Levitt, and Snyder (1999) when extending the work of Poole and Daniels (1985) to adjust interest group scores across time.

Groseclose, Levitt, and Snyder (1999) propose a linear transformation to compare estimates that would otherwise be dissimilar because of differences in the underlying scale due to differences in the agenda being voted upon. By assuming that the underlying ideological space is constant, but that the scale for any particular Congress may be stretched, thinned, or shifted from that space depending on the votes being taken, they provide a method for adjusting estimates that would otherwise not be directly comparable.

The critical assumption of the approach proposed by Groseclose, Levitt, and Snyder (1999) is that the mean member of Congress is unchanged over time. This implies that for an individual with a long-term average ideal point of x_i, if y_{it} is the estimated ideal point of legislator i in Congress t,

$$y_{it} = \alpha_t + \beta_t x_i + \varepsilon_{it} \tag{8.1}$$

where α_t effectively recenters the ideological space of Congress t and β_t accounts for any "stretching" or "shrinking" of the space that may have occurred because of the political agenda in Congress t. From this, we can compute an "adjusted" score that accounts for possible scale differences using: $\frac{y_{it} - \alpha_t}{\beta_t}$.

Conceptually, this method estimates a series of regressions between Congresses to determine how the scales of adjacent Congresses differ from one another and then it uses the estimated difference to remove the effects of these differences from the ideal points that were estimated in time t. It creates ideal points that: (1) have a constant mean for those members serving across time and (2) best account for the evident variation subject to the constraint that the mean is fixed across time.[8] To be clear, these are very strong assumptions with seemingly implausible behavioral implications; the approach of Groseclose, Levitt, and Snyder (1999) assumes that each legislator has a fixed mean over his or her entire career and that the members' ideal points in each Congress are iid around that mean. Put differently, a shift in a member's ideal point for a given Congress is assumed to be unrelated to shifts in earlier or later sessions.

Given an alternative method of computing ideal points over time, we now explore how applying the Groseclose, Levitt, and Snyder (1999) transformation to W-NOMINATE ideal points estimated in each House compares with the

---

[8] Given the nature of the relationship in equation (8.1), the change in individual behavior is idiosyncratic across legislators and time and it is due to differences in the error (see, e.g., the discussion of Groseclose, Levitt, and Snyder (1999, p. 48)). The fact that members' average ideal points are unchanged means that it is assumed that Congress is not drifting systematically to the right or the left over time; Congress is operating in the same ideological space as past Congresses. To be clear, this is also an implicit assumption in DW-NOMINATE – scaling methods cannot easily identify if the ideological conflict shifts.

conclusions we would reach using DW-NOMINATE. Because our purpose is to explore the ability of these alternative assumptions about how ideal points vary over time to characterize the nature of politics, we focus on a comparison that uses as much of DW-NOMINATE as possible. So doing allows us to attribute differences that we uncover to the alternative assumptions used to compare the estimates over time. In particular, we ask whether the assumption of linear preference changes is problematic in the presence of large exogenous changes to the status quo such as might be caused by the Great Depression and its aftermath.

Comparing how this adjustment affects the estimated ideal points for individual members provides a clear illustration of the maintained assumptions when trying to compare ideal points across time. Figure 8.8 graphs the relationship between several estimates for the 27,940 ideal points we analyze. Figure 8.8a illustrates the consequences of the adjustment behind Equation (8.1), which rescales the underlying W-NOMINATE scores in a linear way to produce the

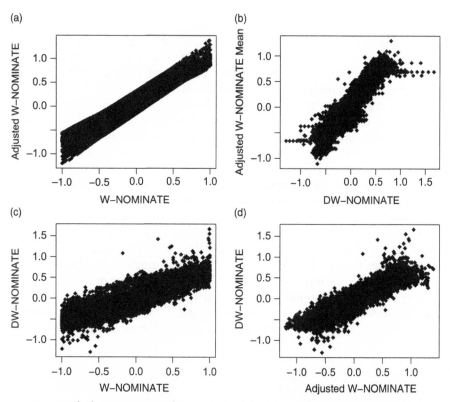

FIGURE 8.8   Ideal point estimates four ways. Each point is an ideal point for a member in a Congress calculated using either W-NOMINATE; DW-NOMINATE; or WNOMINATE adjusted using the procedure suggested by Groseclose, Levitt, and Snyder (1999) to estimate the Adjusted W-NOMINATE score and Adjusted W-NOMINATE Mean.

adjusted scores. It does so by assuming that the mean ideal point of members is constant over time but subject to random fluctuations. Figure 8.8b illustrates this assumption as it is possible to visually identify legislators with a constant adjusted W-NOMINATE mean and changing DW-NOMINATE scores.

The consequences of the linear rescaling proposed by Groseclose, Levitt, and Snyder (1999) and presented in Figure 8.8a can be seen in the bottom two graphs, which show how the unadjusted (Figure 8.8c) and adjusted (Figure 8.8d) W-NOMINATE scores compare with those produced by DW-NOMINATE.

While not a surprise given the scaling assumptions being employed and the common behavioral voting model being assumed in each instance, there is a great deal of overall similarity between the individual ideal point estimates. The ideal points of individual members in the Congresses we examine using DW-NOMINATE and adjusted W-NOMINATE, for example, correlate at roughly 0.95. However, the high level of similarity does mask some dramatic differences among some individuals. For example, if we examine the predicted ideal points of the second longest-serving member in the U.S. House – Jamie Whitten (D-MS-2) – we can observe the consequences of the different assumptions being made to compare ideal points over time.

When the House debated a bill to outlaw the poll tax in May 1943, Rep. Whitten rose to attack both organized labor and nonsouthern Democrats for supporting the legislation. Their meddling in southern race relations, he cautioned, will "make it much more difficult for us who consider ourselves liberals in the South as we struggle to free the poor people in the South and admit them to the economic life of the region and to a participation in its political processes."[9] Like many southern members of this era, he was supportive of liberal economic policies, but fiercely opposed to civil rights initiatives. Later, he signed the Southern Manifesto condemning the U.S. Supreme Court for the 1954 decision in *Brown v. Board of Education,* and he opposed the Civil Rights Acts of 1957, 1960, 1964, 1965, and 1968. (He later apologized for these actions and supported the Civil Rights Act of 1991.) He also frequently opposed the foreign and domestic policies proposed by President Reagan in the 1980s.

Whitten's specification in DW-NOMINATE is at odds with his self-described commitments. Because DW-NOMINATE assumes that ideal points can change only linearly over time – if at different rates for each member – its estimates for Whitten in Figure 8.9, denoted by the thick line, suggest that he began his service in the House as a conservative and gradually and steadily became more liberal over the course of his House career. The adjusted W-NOMINATE estimate suggests a very different account. They suggest more accurately and in a more nuanced way that Whitten opened his career as a New Deal liberal but became dramatically more conservative in the civil

---

[9] *Congressional Record,* 78th Congress, 1st session, May 25, 1943.

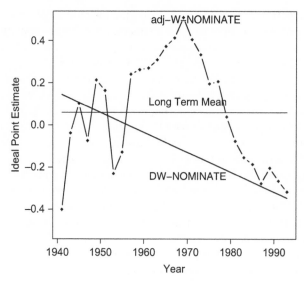

FIGURE 8.9 Three ideal point estimates for Rep. Whitten (D-MS).

rights era, only later to once again move to the left once civil rights issues had been settled at the federal level.[10]

Aggregating the individual ideal points plotted in Figure 8.8 to compute the level of polarization according to the two measures provides the long-term trends graphed in Figure 8.10. Figure 8.10 plots House polarization between 1877 and 2010 according to DW-NOMINATE (Figure 8.10a) and the transformed W-NOMINATE estimates (Figure 8.10b).

The first point worth noting about Figure 8.10 is that despite the different assumptions being used to relate ideal points over time, the two trends exhibit a substantial level of covariation over this time period: they correlate at 0.80.

Even so, it is clear that the trends suggest qualitative differences in the level of polarization across time. The horizontal line denotes the minimal level of polarization that is estimated to occur in each of the two measures. According to DW-NOMINATE, the periods of the New Deal and Fair Deal represent the start of a low period of polarization that extends to 1980. In contrast, if we "bridge" W-NOMINATE scores estimated in each House using the algorithm proposed by Groseclose, Levitt, and Snyder (1999), we observe a very different characterization. Not only is the New Deal a period of polarization that is more on par with the level of polarization that we currently measure in the House,

---

[10] The constant mean assumed by the adjusted-WNOMINATE approach is denoted in Figure 8.8 by the thin line. The deviations from the long-term mean certainly appear nonrandom, but the important point is that the conclusions that one would draw from this pattern differ significantly from those which DW-NOMINATE would suggest.

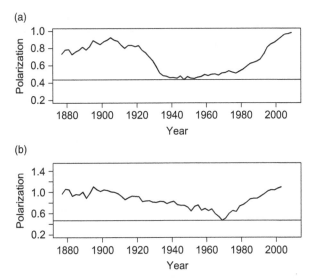

FIGURE 8.10 Measures of polarization in the U.S. House, 1877–2010. Measured using DW-NOMINATE (a) and adjusted W-NOMINATE scores (b). The horizontal line denotes the period of minimum polarization.

but the nadir of polarization does not occur until the 1960s, having begun, as the work of Katznelson and Mulroy (2012) has suggested, in the late 1930s and 1940s.

To explore the differences in these two measures further, we compare how well each covaries with the measures we examine in the section Characterizing Patterns of Elite Polarization. Predicting each as a function of polarization measured using both DW-NOMINATE and adjusted W-NOMINATE scores reveals that the adjusted W-NOMINATE measure is a better fit in every case.

Table 8.3 shows that polarization in the House is highly related to these three measures, but the adjusted W-NOMINATE measure of polarization appears to do a better job than DW-NOMINATE at describing the observed variation. Including both measures reveals that only the adjusted W-NOMINATE score is correlated with the measure of party unity presented in Figure 8.4 (Model 1) and the level of income inequality graphed in Figure 8.6 (Model 5). Disentangling the relationship with voter polarization evident in Figure 8.5 is more difficult, but Models 2, 3, and 4 suggest that the relationship is slightly stronger when using adjusted W-NOMINATE to measure levels of elite polarization.

In all, the differences in the two measures of polarization are largely due to differences in how the two measures characterize the level of polarization during the New Deal and Fair Deal period. The fact that the level of polarization according to the adjusted W-NOMINATE scores better predicts the observed variation of interest than the level of polarization suggested by

TABLE 8.3   *Correlates of Alternative Measures of Polarization*

	Party Unity	Voter Polarization	Voter Polarization	Voter Polarization	Top 1% Wealth
	(1)	(2)	(3)	(4)	(5)
Intercept	58.27*	0.10*	0.07	0.50*	0.45
(Std. Error)	(2.03)	(0.04)	(0.05)	(0.06)	(2.58)
DW-Nominate	−3.66	0.13*		0.02	−0.78
	(4.11)	(0.06)		(0.12)	(5.18)
Adjusted	32.67*		0.14*	0.10	15.58*
W-Nominate	(4.38)		(0.06)	(0.13)	(5.22)
N	63	63	63	63	44
R^2	0.73	0.08	0.08	0.06	0.35

Standard errors in parentheses,
* indicates two-sided significance at $p < 0.05$

DW-NOMINATE implies that the characterization of polarization according to DW-NOMINATE during this period is at odds with what we observe in similar situations in other periods.

Despite both the improved fit and the more reasonable account that the measure provides concerning levels of polarization during the New Deal and Fair Deal, we are not claiming that the W-NOMINATE adjustments provide the silver bullet solution to the notoriously difficult task of establishing comparable estimates over time. This remains a challenge when agendas and larger political and economic contexts can change so dramatically, as they did in the 1930s and 1940s. Our discussion also remains incomplete regarding what "second-dimension" estimates imply about polarization and how to make them more constitutive of Congressional analyses. The descriptive data we presented on southern roll call shifts in the period we have considered further underscores the significance of this lacuna. If the second dimension essentially reflects "error" in the first dimension that can be fit in a second dimension, what does it mean substantively that the relevance of the second dimension varies so much over time and that the relevance of the second dimension rises precisely when polarization is estimated to fall? Clearly, there is a cost to ignoring aspects of the congressional agenda that do not fit neatly into a one-dimensional partisan divide.

INSTEAD OF A CONCLUSION

The roll call estimates pioneered by Poole and Rosenthal revolutionized Congressional studies and, indeed, those of American politics more broadly. The intent of our chapter is not to claim that a different bridging mechanism is "better" than the approach employed in the DW-NOMINATE procedure, nor is it to suggest that we have not greatly benefited from the analysis of the roll call voting behavior data generated by the NOMINATE project. It was, and still is, a critical scholarly enterprise that has revealed much about the nature of politics.

However, we do think that it is perhaps important to reconsider some of the assumptions underlying NOMINATE and compare its results to what we know historically when conducting wide-ranging analyses spanning many different political, economic, and social contexts. Precisely because of the significance of the NOMINATE project, it is important to continue to assess the vulnerabilities as well as the strengths of this, or any other, approach to measurement that seeks to apprehend long-term historical trends. To this end, we have been attentive to a particular historical moment when the NOMINATE approach seems at odds both with focused historical accounts and with other approaches to measurement. In so doing, we hope to have cleared some ground, and to have suggested pathways for continued research and analysis.

Our intention was not, and is not, to suggest that existing analyses are necessarily problematic or that alternative existing methods produce superior results. We instead intend our analysis to prompt further questions about the importance and accuracy of various assumptions and to encourage continued conversations about how to measure and assess the nature of the changing political environment over time.

When considering polarization, for example, a host of vexing questions loom. What exactly does it mean? How close a fit should the concept of elite polarization have with partisan divisions, as distinct from substantive disagreement about issues divisions? When do considerations of ideology and partisanship become tautological? How might we best transcend an exclusive focus on the left-to-right first dimension, especially in circumstances such as the New Deal years when race and region were so manifestly important, not only in the issue space of the time, but in the very dynamics of the party system? How should we think about comparing estimates over time? Should we be aiming at portable hypotheses that hold up over huge swaths of time, or focus with at least equal intensity on historical moments that seem either exceptional or serve as critical junctures? If so, how should such times be identified? Does it make sense to be agnostic about what substantively is being scaled when we are scaling votes? There are no easy answers to these questions when measures meet history.

REFERENCES

Ansolabehere, Stephen, James Snyder, and Charles Stewart III. 2001. "Candidate Positioning in U.S. House Elections." *American Journal of Political Science* 45(1): 136–159.
Binder, Sarah. 1999. "The Dynamics of Legislative Gridlock, 1947–96." *American Political Science Review* 93(3): 519–533.
　　2003. *Stalemate: Causes and Consequences of Legislative Gridlock.* Washington, DC: Brookings Institution.

Carroll, Royce C., Jeffrey B. Lewis, James Lo, Keith T. Poole, and Howard Rosenthal. 2009. "Comparing NOMINATE and IDEAL: Points of Difference and a Monte Carlo Test." *Legislative Studies Quarterly* 34(4): 555–592.

Carroll, Royce C., Keith T. Poole, Howard Rosenthal, Jeffrey B. Lewis, and James Lo. 2013. "The Structure of Utility in Spatial Models of Voting." *American Journal of Political Science* 57(4): 1008–1028.

Clinton, Joshua. 2012. "Using Roll Call Estimates to Test Models of Politics." *Annual Review of Political Science* 15: 79–99.

Clinton, Joshua D. and John S. Lapinski. 2006. "Measuring Legislative Accomplishment, 1877–1946." *American Journal of Political Science* 50(1): 232–249.

2008. "Laws and Roll Calls in the U.S. Congress, 1891–1994." *Legislative Studies Quarterly* 33(4): 511–541.

Clinton, Joshua D. and Simon Jackman. 2009. "To Simulate or NOMINATE?" *Legislative Studies Quarterly* XXXIV(4): 593–622.

Coleman, John. 1999. "Unified Government, Divided Government, and Party Responsiveness." *American Political Science Review* 93(4): 821–835.

Edwards, George C. III, Andrew Barrett, and Jeffrey Peake. 1997. "The Legislative Impact of Divided Government." *American Journal of Political Science* 41(2): 545–563.

Fahrenthold, David A., Philip Rucker, and Felicia Sonmez. 2010. "Stormy 111th Congress Was Still the Most Productive in Decades." *Washington Post* December 23, http://www.washingtonpost.com/wp-dyn/content/article/2010/12/22/AR2010122205620.html.

Groseclose, Tim, Steven Levitt, and James Snyder Jr. 1999. "Comparing Interest Group Scores Across Time and Chambers: Adjusted ADA Scores for the U.S. Congress." *American Political Science Review* 93(1) 33–50.

Hetherington, Marc. 2009. "Putting Polarization in Perspective." *British Journal of Political Science* 39(2009): 413–448.

Jones, David R. 2001. "Party Polarization and Legislative Gridlock." *Political Research Quarterly* 54: 125–41.

Katznelson, Ira. 2011. "Historical Approaches to the Study of Congress: Toward a Congressional Vantage on American Political Development." In *The Oxford Handbook of The American Congress*. Eric Schickler and Frances E. Lee, eds. New York: Oxford University Press.

2012. *Fear Itself: The New Deal and the Origins of Our Time*. New York: Liveright/ W.W. Norton.

Katnelson, Ira and John Lapinski. 2006. "The Substance of Representation: Studying Policy Content and Legislative Behavior." In *The Macropolitics of Congress*. E. Scott Adler and John Lapinski, eds. Princeton: Princeton University Press.

Katznelson, Ira and Quinn Weber Mulroy. 2012. "Was the South Pivotal? Situated Partisanship and Policy Coalitions during the New Deal and Fair Deal." *Journal of Politics* 74(April): 604–620.

Key, V.O. 1949. *Southern Politics in State and Nation*. New York: Knopf.

Krehbiel, Keith. 1998. *Pivotal Politics: A Theory of U.S. Lawmaking*. Chicago: University of Chicago Press.

2000. "Party Discipline and Measures of Partisanship." *American Journal of Political Science* 44(2): 212–227.

Lapinski, John. 2008. "Policy Substance and Performance in American Lawmaking, 1877–1994." *American Journal of Political Science* 52(2): 235–251.

2013. *The Substance of Representation: Congress, American Political Development and Lawmaking.* Princeton: Princeton University Press.

Lee, Frances E. 2008. "Agreeing to Disagree: Agenda Content and Senate Partisanship, 1981–2004." *Legislative Studies Quarterly* 33(May): 199–222.

2009. *Beyond Ideology: Politics, Principles and Partisanship in the U.S. Senate.* Chicago: University of Chicago Press.

Mayhew, David. 1966. *Party Loyalty Among Congressmen.* Cambridge: Harvard University Press.

1991. *Divided We Govern: Party Control, Lawmaking, and Investigations, 1946–1990.* New Haven: Yale University Press.

2005. "Wars and American Politics." *Perspectives on Politics* 3(September): 473–493.

McCarty, Nolan. 2007. "The Policy Consequences of Political Polarization." In *The Transformation of American Politics: Activist Government and the Rise of Conservatism.* Paul Pierson and Theda Skocpol, eds. Princeton, NJ: Princeton University Press.

McCarty, Nolan, Keith Poole, and Howard Rosenthal. 2003. "Political Polarization and Income Inequality." Princeton University Working Paper.

2006. *Polarized America: The Dance of Ideology and Unequal Riches.* Cambridge, MA: MIT Press.

Patterson, James T. 1967. *Congressional Conservatism and the New Deal: The Growth of the Conservative Coalition in Congress, 1933–1939.* Lexington: University of Kentucky Press.

Piketty, Thomas and Emmanuel Saez. 2003. "Income Inequality in the United States, 1913–1998." *Quarterly Journal of Economics* CXVIII (1): 1–39.

Poole, Keith. 2005. *Spatial Models of Parliamentary Voting.* New York: Cambridge University Press.

Poole, Keith and Stephen Daniels. 1985. "Ideology, Party, and Voting in the U.S. Congress." *American Political Science Review* 79(2): 373–399.

Poole, Keith and Howard Rosenthal. 1997. *Congress: A Political-Economic History of Roll Call Voting.* New York: Oxford University Press.

2007. *Ideology and Congress.* Piscataway, NJ: Transaction Press.

Schaffner, Brian. 2011. *Politics, Parties, and Elections in America*, 7th ed. Belmont, CA: Wadsworth.

Wawro, Gregory J. and Ira Katznelson. 2013. "Designing Historical Social Scientific Inquiry: How Parameter Heterogeneity Can Bridge the Methodological Divide between Quantitative and Qualitative Approaches." *American Journal of Political Science.* Published online 20 August.

PART III

PARTISANSHIP AND GOVERNMENTAL PERFORMANCE

9

Polarized We Govern?

Sarah Binder

> Most of the imbalances I have analyzed ... have *not* been major, permanent, systemic problems. More precisely, at least during recent generations, many alleged problems have proven to be nonexistent, short-term, limited, tolerable, or correctable.
>
> Mayhew 2011, p. 190.

> We hope that Mayhew is right and that this difficult patch will prove to be routine, short term and self-correcting. ... But we doubt it. These are perilous times and the political responses to them are qualitatively different from what we have seen before.
>
> Mann and Ornstein 2012, p. 111.

In October 2013, Congress and the president hit an impasse over funding the government and increasing the nation's borrowing limit. Law makers' inability to reach common ground shut down the government and brought the country perilously close to defaulting on its debt. Such legislative drama – coupled with Congress's paltry legislative records since 2011 – has fueled debate over whether the U.S. national political system is irreparably dysfunctional. Thomas Mann and Norman Ornstein (2012, xiv) offer the most pungent critique, arguing that transformation of the Republican Party into an "insurgent outlier" has paralyzed our governing institutions. In contrast, David Mayhew (2011) urges caution, arguing that antimajoritarian biases in American politics are rarely permanent. In short, Mayhew says that our political system is self-correcting;

Revised version of paper originally presented at Representation and Governance: A Conference in Honor of David Mayhew, Yale University, May 29–30, 2013. I thank Joshua Bleiberg, Danny Guenther, Muxin Yu, and Miriam Gough for their invaluable research assistance.

Mann and Ornstein suggest instead that the Republican Party has forced our legislative machinery off the rails.

In this chapter, I tackle the debate between Mayhew and his critics and offer new data to evaluate the problem-solving capacity of Congress and the president in recent, polarized times. To be sure, it can be hard to see the forest through the trees: a better assessment might be made a decade hence. Still, the evidence points us toward middle ground. On one hand, a model of legislative stalemate (Binder 2003) that was developed to explain patterns in legislative performance in the second half of the twentieth century accounts fairly well for Congress's legislative performance in recent years. This suggests that recent congressional deadlock may be different in *degree* from past deadlock, but not necessarily in *kind*. On the other hand, we see a marked increase in the frequency of legislative deadlock over the past decade, and the most recent Congress for which we have data (the 112th, 2011–12) ranks as the most gridlocked during the postwar era (albeit tied with the final two years of the Clinton administration). Moreover, even when Congress and the president manage to reach agreement on the big issues of the day, these deals are often half-measures and second-bests. In short, whether our political system will self-correct in the coming years remains an open question.

SETTING THE SCENE

At the close of the 112th Congress in early January 2013, numerous Washington observers charged that the 112th Congress was the most dysfunctional Congress ever. Brinkmanship and last-minute deals prevailed. With a newly elected Republican majority in the House and a small Democratic majority returning in the Senate, law makers' disagreements nearly caused a governmental shutdown in April 2011 and came close to forcing the government to default on its obligations that summer. In the following Congress in October 2013, law makers actually went over the brink, failing to pass a bill to fund government operations and bumping right up against Treasury's debt limit. Beyond fiscal policy deadlock, legislators' efforts in both Congresses to reach long-term solutions on perennial issues of transportation, agriculture, education, environment, and others often ended in stalemate. As Senator Joe Manchin (D-WV) summed up Congress's performance early in 2013, "Something has gone terribly wrong when the biggest threat to our American economy is the American Congress" (as cited in Steinhauer 2012). Judging by the public's reaction, Congress's performance was abysmal. At times, only 10 percent of the public would admit to pollsters that they approved of Congress's on-the-job performance (Riffkin 2014).

It is tempting to pin the entire blame for inaction on heightened partisan polarization. The first two years of the Obama administration, however, complicate the finger pointing. In the 111th Congress, under unified Democratic control and with a short-lived filibuster-proof Senate, Congress and the president produced a legislative record deemed to rival Lyndon Johnson's accomplishments in the mid-1960s. Norman Ornstein, for instance, argued that Congress's record was "at least on par with the Great Society" (Murray 2012). With GOP support ranging from some to none, the Democratic Congress enacted a mammoth economic stimulus bill, adopted landmark health care reform, revamped the financial regulatory system, abandoned the military's "Don't Ask, Don't Tell" policy, ratified a new arms control treaty, temporarily extended Bush era tax cuts, and more.

The divergent records of the 111th and 112th Congresses pose a challenge for judging the recent performance of the legislative branch. Three questions arise. First, how well do scholars' descriptions capture Congress's legislative performance across the four years? One approach counts the number of accomplishments that meet a threshold of landmark significance, as ably executed by Mayhew (1991, 2005). In more recent work, Mayhew (2011) implies that a denominator might be useful: he analyzes the fate of key presidential proposals over the past sixty years. Once we account for the demand for legislation as well as its supply, are the 111th and 112th Congresses still rivals for the best and worst Congresses, respectively, of the postwar period? In the following, I update a time series on legislative gridlock to provide a better metric for judging the records of recent congresses.

Second, with a longer time series on legislative deadlock, how well do existing empirical models of legislative gridlock perform? To assess whether "this time is different," I use my model from *Stalemate* (originally tested with data from 1947 to 2000) to generate predicted levels of legislative deadlock over the past decade. To the extent that the model consistently over- or underestimates legislative gridlock, such a finding would encourage us to consider how and why legislative dynamics might be different today than before. If instead the model yields relatively accurate predictions – even in a period when the institution seems to have hit its modern nadir – then we might hesitate to conclude that the system is no longer self-correcting. To be sure, this is an easier judgment after significant passage of time. Still, such analysis should help us to put recent Congresses' collective capacity for identifying and resolving problems into perspective.

Third, Mann and Ornstein (2012, XIV) suggest that the source of Congress's recent dysfunction lies largely in the behavior of today's Republican party – termed an "insurgent outlier." After confirming the asymmetric polarization that Mann and Ornstein point to as evidence of the GOP's outlier status, I consider other ways to think about the import of Republican preferences and strategies on congressional performance. Assessments of the short-term corrigibility of our political system depend in part on what we conclude from such evaluations. I suggest that some caution may be in order before drawing firm conclusions about the ability of our political system to self-correct in the near term.

THE LANDSCAPE OF CONGRESSIONAL DEADLOCK

The contemporary study of legislative performance began with the publication of David Mayhew's *Divided We Govern* (2005), the first book to bring systematic, quantitative evidence to bear in testing claims about the impact of divided party control on the production of landmark laws. To be sure, *Divided We Govern* came on the heels of a series of works by presidential and legislative scholars perplexed and frustrated by the frequent periods of divided party government that prevailed after World War II. Between 1897 and 1954, divided party control of government occurred 14 percent of the time. Between 1955 and 1990, it occurred two-thirds of the time. And as V. O. Key observed in the 1960s, "Common partisan control of executive and legislature does not assure energetic government, but division of party control precludes it" (Key 1964, 688). Decades later, scholars (including, most prominently, James Sundquist) were still calling for a new theory of coalitional government to explain how Congress and the president could secure major policy change in the presence of divided government (Sundquist 1988–89).

In *Divided We Govern* (2005, 36), Mayhew returns us to these pursuits by asking a simple and accessible question about Congress's performance in the postwar era: "Were many important laws passed?" Mayhew's empirical goal is to set up a test of the effect of divided party control on the level of law making. Toward that end, he identified landmark laws in a two-stage process that combined contemporary judgments about the significance of Congress's work each session with policy specialists' retrospective judgments about the importance of legislation. Based on these data, Mayhew generated a comprehensive list of landmark laws enacted in each Congress between 1946 and 1990 (subsequently updated through 2012). Mayhew then tested whether the presence of divided government reduced the number of major laws enacted each Congress.

The key contribution of *Divided We Govern* was the null result for the impact of divided government on law making. Unified party control of Congress and the White House fails to yield significantly higher levels of law making. It matters little whether a single party controls both the White House and Congress: not much more is accomplished than under divided party control. Having absolved divided government as a cause of legislative inaction, Mayhew disentangles several other influences on Congress's performance. Some of those forces – including legislators' electoral incentives – point toward constancy in the record of law making. But other forces, Mayhew demonstrates, appear to be important alternative sources of variation in explaining congressional productivity, including shifting public moods, presidential cycles, and issue coalitions that cut across the left–right divide.

Mayhew's work provoked theoretical and methodological debates about how to explain and measure variation in Congress's legislative performance over the postwar period (among many others, see Binder 2003 and 2011, Brady and Volden 1998, Edwards et al. 1997, Krehbiel 1998). Perhaps the most prominent theoretical response to Mayhew's work is Krehbiel's *Pivotal Politics*. Krehbiel's work, however, is less a challenge to Mayhew's argument than a formal elaboration: he provides a theoretical framework for explaining why party control is less important to explaining patterns of law making than the distribution of law makers' policy preferences interacting with the rules of the legislative game. In contrast, I suggest elsewhere (1999, 2003) that the composition of the parties after each election shapes the capacity of Congress and the president to legislate. Unified party control fuels legislative capacity, but sharply polarized parties in a system of bicameralism limit Congress's performance.

Divergent analytical perspectives are compounded by debates over how best to measure Congress's legislative capacity. Much of the methodological debate centered on whether a measure of Congress's legislative capacity requires a denominator – a baseline against which to compare Congress's output. Mayhew's concerns about the difficulty of defining and identifying a relevant and measurable denominator were well taken. Still, I offered in *Stalemate* (2003) a measure that captures the degree of legislative deadlock by isolating the set of salient issues on the agenda and then determining the fate of those issues in each Congress. The result is a ratio of failed measures to all issues on the agenda for each Congress. My sense is that this measure of gridlock is up to the task, largely because it meets key benchmarks that we might impose to judge its construct validity. The measure identified Lyndon Johnson's Great Society Congress as the most productive of the postwar period and determined that Clinton's second session Congresses were the most deadlocked. Both assessments comport with historical and contemporary coverage of Congress's postwar performance.

As I explained in detail in appendix A to *Stalemate*, I devised a method for identifying every policy issue on the legislative agenda, based on the issues discussed in the unsigned editorials in the *New York Times*. Using the level of *Times* attention to an issue in any given Congress as an indicator of issue salience, I identified for each Congress between the 80th (1947–48) and the 106th (1999–2000) the most salient issues on the legislative agenda.[1] I then turned to news coverage and congressional documents to determine whether Congress and the president took legislative action in that Congress to address each salient issue. The measurement strategy produced a denominator of every major legislative issue raised by elite observers of Capitol Hill and a numerator that captured Congress's record in acting on those issues. The resulting gridlock score captures the percentage of agenda items left in limbo at the close of the Congress.

---

[1] I consider salient issues those matters on which the *New York Times* editorialized four or more times in a given Congress. This salience filter brought the number of major issues successfully addressed roughly in line with Mayhew's number of landmark laws enacted in each Congress.

Figure 9.1 displays the size of the policy agenda from 1947 to 2012, coupled with the number of failed legislative issues in each Congress. Figure 9.1a includes all issues; Figure 9.1b presents salient issues only. Looking first at the smoothed trend line in the overall number of legislative issues mentioned during each Congress in the *Times* editorials, we see that the size of the overall agenda increases as expected with the return of large liberal majorities during the mid-1960s. It stays at this expanded level through the civil rights, environmental rights, and women's rights movements of the 1960s and 1970s. In recent years, we see a further slight increase in the size of the agenda, no doubt reflecting both later efforts to renew the spate of landmark laws of the earlier, activist period and newer issues brought to the fore by the war on terror, global climate change, and so on.[2]

The trend in the number of salient issues in the bottom panel is more eye-catching. The overall size of the agenda increases only incrementally over the most recent decade, but the number of salient issues rises markedly in the 108th (2003–04), 110th (2005–06), and 112th (2011–12) Congresses. This jump in the number of issues attracting heightened levels of editorial writers' attention raises questions about the comparability of my original time series and the updated series for the most recent decade. However, as I detail in the Appendix, I can rule out potential methodological issues that might limit the reliability and validity of the longer times series. First, the *Times* does not appear to have changed its practices in terms of the overall number of editorials written daily over the longer period (ranging from three to five editorials per day), although it seems plausible that Congress attracts a greater share of the writers' attention over the past decade. Second, although there have been some changes in the electronic databases containing the editorials, such differences do not appear to be inflating the number of mentions of legislative issues on the editorial page. Third, the *Times*' expansion of its weekend opinion pages in recent years does not appear to have affected the number of published, unsigned editorials.

In short, the data suggest a marked increase in the number of big-ticket legislative issues attracting the attention of the *Times'* editorial board. It is also possible that the increased gridlock in recent years has indirectly fueled the size of the salient agenda, as the big issues of the day remain unresolved and thus recur repeatedly. Congress's failure to reform immigration law, entitlement programs, and the tax code, for example, likely helped to fuel the size of the salient agenda in recent years. Finally, a spate of new issues in the past decade likely caught the attention of the *Times'* editorial writers, including homeland

---

[2] Note that across all levels of salience, the relationship between party control and the number of issues on the legislative agenda is not statistically significant at conventional levels. When I control for Democratic presidents (under the assumption that Democratic presidents generate larger agendas than do Republicans) and a simple time trend, party control appears to weakly affect the size of only the moderately salient agenda (1-tailed t-test $< .05$). (The following analysis examines only more salient issues.)

(a)

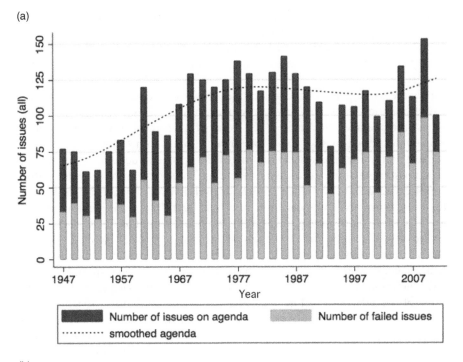

(b)

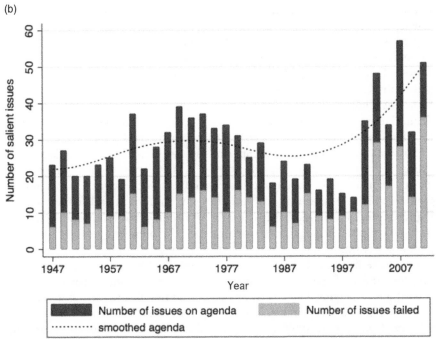

FIGURE 9.1 (a) Size of the legislative agenda (all issues). (b) Size of the legislative agenda (salient issues).

security, global warming, cyber security, the return of deficits after the 1990s, the U.S. wars in Iraq and Afghanistan, the onset of the financial crisis, and the worst economy since the Great Depression.

Figure 9.2 shows the mean level of gridlock (aggregated over the 80th–112th Congresses, 1947–2012) across different levels of salience. The far left line shows the average level of deadlock (roughly 54 percent) on the least salient issues (mentioned by the *Times* only once in a Congress). The far right line shows the average level of deadlock (roughly 43 percent) on the most salient issues (mentioned by the *Times* five or more times in a Congress). The data suggest that more salient issues are slightly less prone to deadlock than are less salient issues; in other words, issue salience is not simply a proxy for legislative conflict. Granted, the confidence intervals overlap as we move from the least to the most salient policy issues. But we can at least draw a distinction between gridlock on issues receiving only passing reference from the *Times* (such as the future of AmeriCorps) and issues that attract considerable, sustained attention (such as immigration reform). The higher level of deadlock on the low-salience issues suggests that these are issues that get little attention on Capitol Hill, have few champions or critics (beyond the *Times'* editorial writers), and thus can probably be safely ignored in examining Congress's legislative capacity.

The updated time series of the degree of legislative deadlock on salient issues in each Congress between 1947 and 2012 appears in Figure 9.3. Four features of the times series stand out. First, there is a secular increase in the frequency of deadlock over time. Second, the dire claims about the 112th Congress are essentially true. By this measure, the 112th Congress can claim to be the "worst Congress ever" for the postwar period, although the title is shared with the last Congress of the Clinton administration in 1999–2000. In both Congresses, almost three-quarters of the most salient issues remained unresolved at the end of the Congress. Coming on the heels of the 1998 GOP effort to impeach President Clinton and in the run up to a fiercely competitive contest for the White House, we probably shouldn't be surprised about the essentially dead heat between the Congresses to claim the dysfunctional honor.

Still, caution is in order in comparing the two Congresses. Some legislative action that constituted "success" in the 112th Congress might have been viewed as inadequate even at the end of the Clinton presidency. For example, Congress and the president have traditionally authorized and funded federal highway programs in multiyear reauthorization bills. But following expiration of highway programs in 2009, Congress and the president passed a series of temporary reauthorizations to keep federal programs running. Even when the parties were finally able to agree to a multiyear bill in 2012, that agreement only reauthorized two years of highway programs; conflict over raising the federal gas tax stymied efforts to finance a traditional six-year bill. I code the highway bill as a successful legislative response, even though the two-year bill allowed Congress to avoid making any decisions about how to ensure the solvency of federal highway trust funds after the end of the two years. Another

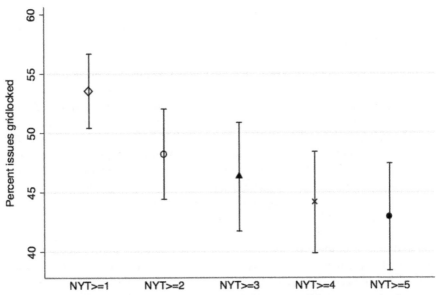

FIGURE 9.2 Average level of deadlock, by issue salience. Confidence intervals of 95%.

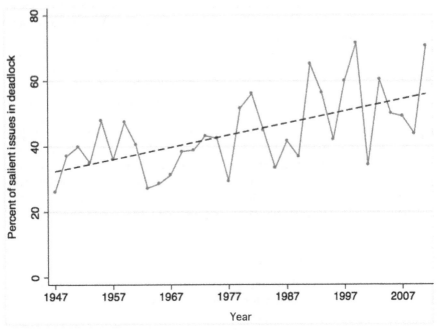

FIGURE 9.3 Frequency of legislative gridlock, 1947–2012.

problem – how to raise the federal debt ceiling in the summer of 2011 – was resolved in part by establishing the "Supercommittee" to come up with over a trillion dollars in federal savings. The 2011 deficit reduction package is scored a success, even though the Supercommittee that resulted from the agreement eventually failed. In other words, the 71 percent deadlock score for the 112th Congress likely underestimates the true level of legislative stalemate.

Third, although the 111th Congress was relatively productive compared with Congress's performances over the past decade (with the exception of the 9/11 Congress), it nonetheless fell far shy of the records of the Great Society Congresses. To be sure, the 111th Congress was nearly thirty points more productive than the 112th. But even the widely heralded 111th Congress left a lengthy list of major issues in legislative limbo, including proposals to address education, campaign finance, global warming, immigration, and gun control. In short, even with the 111th Congress's unified party control and its short-lived, filibuster-proof majority, law makers struggled to surmount significant barriers to major policy change.

Finally, a brief look at the 107th Congress, spanning before and after the attacks of September 11th, 2001, is instructive. Overall, the Congress (with unified Republican control of both branches for just a few months early in 2001) was fairly productive, leaving just 34 percent of the policy agenda in 2001 and 2002 in stalemate. Indeed, the 107th Congress outperformed the 111th – somewhat unexpectedly given the accolades earned by Congress at the end of Obama's first two years in office. But the 107th Congress's performance was shaped by the events of September 11th. Eight of the thirty-five salient issues in that Congress stemmed directly from the attacks. And on those eight issues, Congress and the president mustered a perfect record, enacting the Patriot Act, writing the Authorization for the Use of Military Force, addressing the needs of 9/11 victims, and more. Even on less salient issues stemming from September 11th, congressional deadlock stood at barely 10 percent, with just a single issue left in legislative limbo.[3] But any cooperative spirit and unity of purpose did not extend to the rest of the policy agenda. If we exclude the issues related to September 11th, Congress and the president deadlocked on just under half of the salient policy matters. Congress does appear to retain the capacity to act swiftly when a true crisis occurs, as it also demonstrated in the 2008 bailout of Wall Street after the Federal Reserve and Treasury allowed Lehman Brothers to go under. However, as we might expect, legislative unity dissipates when Congress turns its attention back to the regular policy agenda.

EXPLAINING PATTERNS OF GRIDLOCK

The longer time series allows me to pose again the question that motivated *Stalemate*: how do we account for Congress's uneven legislative performance

[3] There were eight issues related to September 11th that attracted fewer than four *Times* editorials.

over time? In that work, I used the measure of the frequency of legislative gridlock to test alternative institutional and electoral explanations for variation in congressional stalemate. I found that unified party control of Congress and the White House reduced the frequency of deadlock. Divided government – aided by parties' influence over the content of the floor agenda – empowers the opposition party to block agenda issues that they oppose. But party control alone, I argued, was insufficient to explain variation in Congress's performance.

I pointed instead to two other factors that shape Congress's record. First, I argued that the smaller the ideological center, the tougher time Congress has in securing policy agreement. The rise of polarized political parties – even before the Bush and Obama presidencies – complicated the challenge of building coalitions of sufficient size to overcome the multiple veto points institutionalized on Capitol Hill. Second, I suggested that bicameral policy differences interfere with the crafting of policy coalitions, even in periods of unified party control.[4] Although electoral and policy differences between the branches tend to garner the most attention in Washington, policy differences between the House and Senate also seem to complicate lawmakers' capacity to find common ground acceptable to both chambers. The results of the 2010 and 2012 congressional elections – delivering control of the House to Republicans while keeping the Senate in Democratic hands – make plain the barriers imposed by bicameral differences.

How does this basic model hold up when we incorporate the records of the Congresses between 2001 and 2012?[5] In Table 9.1, I show the results for a streamlined version of the original models (Binder 1999, 2003), estimating a grouped logit model to account for the variation in the size of the agenda in each Congress (i.e., the size of the denominators).[6] The estimates deliver a

---

[4] I measure the degree of bicameral divergence by comparing House and Senate voting behavior on conference reports considered in both chambers (which allows me to compare House and Senate preferences on identical legislative measures). I find the percentage difference in House and Senate support for each report and then calculate the mean difference on all conference reports in a given Congress (counting voice vote approval as 100 percent support).

[5] A brief note about the measurement of moderation. I identified the size of the political center in Binder (1999) by using Poole and Rosenthal's W-NOMINATE scores: moderates were those legislators closer to the midpoint of the two parties than to their own party medians. In response to criticism, I revised the measure in Binder (2003). Still using W-NOMINATE, I divided the percentage of moderates for each chamber and Congress by the distance between the two party medians (as measured by W-NOMINATE). Because the state of the art for NOMINATE is now DW-NOMINATE, I have recalculated the entire time series of polarization (using DW-NOMINATE both to identify the centrists in each party and chamber and to measure the distance between party medians). Regardless of how it is measured, polarization drives up deadlock – even though the two measures do not track each other as closely as one might expect.

[6] Because the dependent variable is constructed from grouped data (total number of failed legislative issues per Congress, divided by the total number of policy issues on the agenda in each Congress) with groups of unequal size, the OLS assumption of uniform variance is violated. That is, given agendas of varying size over the thirty-three Congresses, heteroskedasticity will be

TABLE 9.1 *Determinants of Legislative Gridlock, 1947–2012*

Independent Variable	Coefficient
Divided Government	0.231 (.156)[a]
Bicameral Differences	7.350 (3.267)*
Moderation	−0.876 (.368)*
Constant	−0.541 (.380)
N	33
F	7.28***

Notes: The entries are weighted least squares logit estimates for grouped data (standard errors in parentheses).
[a] $p < 0.1$,
* $p < 0.05$,
** $p < 0.01$, $p < 0.001$ (one-tailed tests).

TABLE 9.2 *Predicting Deadlock, 2001–2012*

Congress	Actual # of Failed Issues	Predicted # of Failed Issues	Error (Failed–Predicted)
107 (2001–02)	12	17	−5
108 (2003–04)	29	25	4
109 (2005–06)	17	17.1	−0.1
110 (2007–08)	28	28.14	−0.14
111 (2009–10)	14	15.5	−1.5
112 (2011–12)	36	29	7
Average			0.84

reasonably similar story to that of my earlier work: Congress still struggles to legislate when partisan polarization rises and when the two chambers diverge in their policy views.[7] To more carefully judge how well the model predicts today's lawmaking, I estimate the model based only on the original data (1947–2000) and use those estimates to generate predicted values of deadlock for the most recent decade. These steps allow me to assess whether recent legislative deadlock is greater or less than what we might expect based on the legislative world captured by the original model. As shown in Table 9.2, the

present across the disturbances. The solution in this case is to model variation in gridlock with weighted least-squares estimates in a grouped logit equation. Because the percentage data are bounded between 0 and 1, the logit function is more appropriate than weighted least squares through OLS.

[7] As in the earlier work, I test for (and reject the presence of) serial autocorrelation. A Dickey-Fuller test strongly rejects the possibility that a unit root exists. Durbin-Watson, Breusch-Godfrey Lagrange multiplier, and Portmanteau Q tests fail to reject the null hypothesis of no first order autoregressive or moving average errors.

original model does a decent job of predicting the number of failed legislative issues in three of the past six Congresses (109th, 110th, and 111th). In the remaining Congresses, the model misses the mark. The model overpredicts failure in the 107th Congress (2001–02), not surprising given Congress's legislative responsiveness in the wake of September 11th. Interestingly, the model underpredicts legislative failure in the 108th Congress, likely reflecting in part (as discussed in the following) Democrats' willingness to filibuster GOP initiatives in a period of unified party control. And the model underpredicts legislative deadlock in the 112th Congress (2011–12), confirming the common observation that legislative dysfunction reigned in the 112th. That said, the model's average error over the past decade is roughly a single failed legislative issue, suggesting that the original model continues to help to explain patterns in legislative deadlock even in more polarized times.

What broader conclusions can we draw from the updated analysis? First, the results validate the media's recent focus on the impact of polarized parties on Congress's ability to legislate. That said, because we typically use lawmakers' floor voting records, it is difficult to disentangle the extent to which partisan polarization captures ideological differences across lawmakers' or members' partisan "team play" behavior. As Lee (2009) shows using other vote-based data, a good portion of the party polarization we see in floor voting likely reflects a dose of both. Here, I avoid treading into methodological and theoretical debates about distinguishing between partisan behavior and policy preferences. Regardless of whether we deem polarization a function of ideological differences, strategic disagreement by partisans seeking electoral advantage (Gilmour 1995), or a mix of the two, the results are clear: when ideological and electoral incentives propel the parties to the wings, abandoning the political center, law makers struggle to find broadly palatable solutions to the range of problems that they face.

Second, the results confirm my earlier conclusion about the impact of bicameral differences on the difficulty of legislating. Even after controlling for the level of polarization and party control of the two branches, policy differences between the two chambers affect Congress's ability to legislate. As House and Senate chamber medians differ in their policy views – regardless of whether party control is unified or split between the chambers – legislative deadlock grows. Notably, the 112th Congress's split party control is not driving the statistical effect: bicameral differences drive up the level of deadlock even if we drop the observation for the 112th Congress.

Although statistically significant, the impact of bicameral differences is likely muted in these estimates because of the method used to tap policy differences between the chambers. My measure exploits chamber votes on conference reports since such votes allow me to compare the views of House and Senate lawmakers on identical legislative measures. For each conference report that was considered on both the House and Senate floors, I determined the percentage of each chamber voting in favor and then calculated the difference between House and Senate levels of support.[8] Averaging over all conference reports voted on in a given Congress produces a measure of bicameral policy disagreement, ranging from a low of 2 percent in 1955–56 to a high of 11 percent in 1993–94. Applying the method to the most recent Congresses, the 112th Congress's bicameral disagreement reaches just under 10 percent.

One might think that the gulf between House Republicans and Senate Democrats after the 2010 elections would have been reflected in a much higher bicameral difference score. Most likely, the conference report-based measure understates bicameral differences: lawmakers' use of conference committees to resolve interchamber differences has declined sharply in recent years. Between 1947 and 2000, the number of conference agreements averaged roughly one hundred per Congress; between 2001 and 2012, there were just over twenty. The trend may have hit rock bottom in the 112th Congress, with just seven final agreements reached via conference committee. The drop reflects both the low level of lawmaking overall and the regularized involvement of party leaders in negotiating bicameral agreements. When agreements are crafted at the last moment – the April 2011 expiration of spending authority for the government, the July 2011 debt ceiling brinkmanship, and the December 2012 fiscal cliff – there is no need (let alone time) for formal conference committee proceedings. Note, finally, that each of these is an example of a *successful* policy engagement: rising deadlock does not necessarily explain the decline in the use of conference committees. We have successful deal making even when leaders prefer other bicameral mechanisms than convening a conference.

Third, the effect of party control appears attenuated. *Stalemate* identified an independent effect of party control on legislative performance: the frequency of deadlock was higher in periods of divided, rather than unified, party control. In his recent work (Mayhew 2011, 78), Mayhew also identifies a party effect: unified party control increases the chances that presidential proposals will be enacted. Still, in the longer time series presented here, divided party government shows only limited impact on lawmakers' capacity to govern. The parameter estimate is positive, as we would expect from *Stalemate*, but misses standard levels of statistical significance (one-tailed test, p = 0.07). Looking more closely at the level of gridlock over the past decade, the record of the 108th Congress (under unified Republican control in 2003–04) seems to diminish the effect of party control. In 2003–04, 60 percent of the agenda was left in limbo at the end of the Congress; in comparison, deadlock in periods of unified party control over the longer postwar period averaged 40 percent. If we reestimate the model excluding the 108th Congress, the parameter estimate for divided government is statistically significant, driving up the frequency of gridlock.

---

[8] Voice votes are coded as 100 percent chamber support for the conference agreement.

Why do we observe such a high level of deadlock in a period of unified party control? This is not a puzzle for Krehbiel (1998), whose pivotal politics model suggests that policy change is a function of the location of the status quo and the preferences of supermajority pivots on the left and right of the median voter. Given the implicit threat of a filibuster and thus the inevitable need for a supermajority coalition in the Senate, party control of a chamber should not affect the frequency of legislative agreement in equilibrium. Of course, if the median (in recent years, a member of the majority party) and the filibuster pivot are relatively close to each other along the left–right policy dimension, then we should rarely expect filibusters to derail Senate bills: the median can easily accommodate the demands of the filibustering senator by amending the measure. That perhaps is why Mayhew (2011) finds little systematic or sustained evidence of an antimajoritarian Senate. However, once the median and the filibuster pivot begin to diverge markedly as the parties polarize, the sixtieth senator's policy demands might be harder for the majority to accommodate, increasing the frequency of deadlock.

I suspect that the recent, rising proclivity of opposition party senators to insist on sixty votes for the adoption of most amendments and measures has undermined the legislative power of majority parties in periods of unified party control (see also Smith 2010). For example, increased minority party exploitation of its parliamentary rights would help to explain the litany of legislative measures left in limbo after Democrats lost their filibuster-proof majority in the winter of 2010, as well as the heavy load of measures left undone at the close of the Republican-led 108th Congress.[9] As electoral incentives increase for the minority party to play a more confrontational role in the Senate and as the costs of filibustering decline (Smith 2010), unified party control might prove a less powerful tool for driving the legislative process.

DISCUSSION AND CONCLUSIONS

The middle of the road is a dangerous place to be. Still, my analysis suggests that there is a good deal of truth both to Mayhew's sanguine view of the future of American politics and to Mann's and Ornstein's more dire analysis of the state of Congress and its legislative capacity. To be sure, in many ways, Congress's recent legislative performance fits the well-established pattern from *Stalemate*: when elections yield more polarized parties and chambers, bargaining is more difficult and compromise is more often out of reach. To the extent that recent Congresses fit the broader pattern established in the postwar period, we might be on safe ground in concurring with Mayhew that the recent "imbalances" during the Obama administration are unlikely to be "permanent,

---

[9] In the 108th Congress, six salient measures attracted filibusters on the Senate floor, leaving three of the six in legislative limbo at the close of the Congress.

systemic problems." Of course, that is an empirical claim to be confirmed over time.

Still, four reservations temper such a conclusion. First, levels of legislative deadlock have steadily risen over the past half-century: stalemate at times now reaches across three-quarters of the salient issues on Washington's agenda. Granted, legislators differ over what issues and conditions constitute "problems" (Mayhew 2006). That might increasingly be the case as the parties polarize: lawmakers today even disagree about basic scientific facts (such as whether the earth is warming). But the absolute level of deadlock does raise eyebrows. Moreover, issues left in limbo rarely disappear from the agenda. Although a larger agenda might in itself account for Congress's sluggish record, pushing issues off to the future sometimes makes problems worse.

Second, even when Congress and the president muster agreement on a policy solution, such agreements sometimes manage to create new problems. For example, some economists argued that fiscal policy brinkmanship in the 112th Congress – last-minute decision making that increased uncertainty about future policy – harmed the economy and set back the economic recovery (Stevenson and Wolfers 2012). Moreover, markets' dismay over Congress's dysfunction that summer led to the first downgrade of the U.S. sovereign credit rating in history. If both congressional action and inaction make problems worse, it is hard to see how the political system can quickly rebound from its current partisan impasse. The system no doubt is corrigible, but it might take a long time to right itself.

Third, it is not clear whether current levels of polarization are going to subside anytime soon. On two dimensions – both the degree of polarization and the parties' relative contributions to polarization – Poole and Rosenthal (Voteview 2012) concur with critics about the nature of recent polarization. The ideological distance between the parties rivals heights not seen since the end of the nineteenth century. Partisan polarization is on the verge of passing record historical levels in the Senate and has surpassed House records stemming from the turn of the century. In addition, such polarization might be deemed "asymmetric": Republicans (particularly in the House) have moved farther to the right than Democrats have moved to the left. One might wonder whether the asymmetric pattern stems in part from Republicans' minority status: having lost the White House in 2008, the GOP is unleashed to shoot for the conservative moon (in part pulled by their Tea Party voters). So long as some degree of polarization is driven by sheer partisan team play – in which Republicans are likely to object to most proposals endorsed by a Democratic president – then extreme levels of polarization are likely to continue to lead to unprecedented levels of deadlock. It remains to be seen whether both the House and the Senate wings of the Republican Party can self-correct and how long it will take them to do so.

Fourth, changes in the structure of electoral competition in recent decades have likely altered lawmakers' calculations about coming to the bargaining table. As Lee (2013, 777) observes, margins of party control in the House and Senate since 1980 have been half the size (on average) of margins between 1933 and 1980. Presidential elections have also been close, with the last landslide Electoral College win in 1984. As Lee (2013) argues, close party competition for control of Congress and the White House appears to affect party politics in Congress. Fierce electoral competition brings control of national institutions within reach for both parties, limiting lawmakers' incentives to compromise with the other party. Why settle on half a loaf of policy when a full loaf can be delivered to the party base upon winning unified party control? As Fiorina (2006) notes, "with majority status that much more valuable, and minority status that much more intolerable, the parties are less able to afford a hiatus between elections in which governing takes precedence over electioneering." Congress's legislative capacity seems to be a victim of increased party competition in a period of polarized elites.

Ultimately, Mayhew may well be correct that our political system will weather this rough patch with little harm done. Even so, we are left in the meantime with a national legislature plagued by low legislative capacity. Half-measures, second bests, and just-in-time legislating are the new norm, as electoral, partisan, and institutional barriers limit Congress's capacity for more than lowest-common-denominator deals. Even if lawmakers ultimately find a way to get their institution back on track, Congress's recent difficulties have been costly – both to the fiscal health of the country and to citizens' trust in government. The economy will eventually regain its footing. Regenerating Congress's public standing will surely be much harder.

REFERENCES

Binder, Sarah A. 1999. "Dynamics of Legislative Gridlock, 1947–1996." *American Political Science Review* 93(3): 519–533.
    2003. *Stalemate: Causes and Consequences of Legislative Gridlock*. Brookings Institution Press.
    2011. "Legislative Productivity and Gridlock." In *Oxford Handbook of the American Congress*, Eric Schickler and Frances E. Lee, eds. Oxford University Press.
Brady, David and Craig Volden. 1998. *Revolving Gridlock*. Westview Press.
Edward, George C. III, Andrew Barrett, and Jeffrey Peake. 1997. "The Legislative Impact of Divided Government." *American Journal of Political Science* 41(2): 545–563.
Fiorina, Morris. 2006. "Parties as Problem Solvers." In *Promoting the General Welfare*, Eric Patashnik and Alan Gerber, eds. Brookings Institution Press.
Gilmour, John. 1995. *Strategic Disagreement: Stalemate in American Politics*. University of Pittsburgh Press.
Key, V.O. 1964. *Politics, Parties and Pressure Groups*. Ty Crowell Co.
Krehbiel, Keith. 1998. *Pivotal Politics*. University of Chicago Press.
Lee, Frances E. 2009. *Beyond Ideology*. University of Chicago Press.
    2013. "Presidents and Party Teams: Debt Limits and Executive Oversight, 2001–2013." *Presidential Studies Quarterly* 43(4): 775–91.

Mann, Thomas E. and Norman J. Ornstein. 2012. *It's Even Worse than It Looks.* Basic Books.

Mayhew, David. 1991, 2005. *Divided We Govern.* Yale University Press.

2006. "Congress as Problem Solver." In *Promoting the General Welfare,* Eric Patashnik and Alan Gerber, eds. Brookings Institution Press.

2011. *Partisan Balance.* Princeton University Press.

Murray, Mark. 2010. "The do something Congress." NBC News First Read. http://firstread.nbcnews.com/_news/2010/12/21/5689395-the-do-something-congress? lite [Accessed May 11, 2014].

Riffkin, Rebecca. 2014. "Public faith in Congress falls again, hits historic low." www.gallup.com/poll/171710/public-faith-congress-falls-again-hits-historic-low.aspx [Accessed June 25, 2015].

Smith, Steven S. 2010. "The Senate Syndrome," *Issues in Governance Studies,* No. 35 (June). www.brookings.edu/research/papers/2010/06/cloture-smith [Accessed May 11, 2014].

Steinhauer, Jennifer. 2012. "A Showdown Long Foreseen." *New York Times,* Dec. 30. www.nytimes.com/2012/12/31/us/politics/fiscal-crisis-impasse-long-in-the-making.html [Accessed May 11, 2014].

Stevenson, Betsey and Justin Wolfers. 2012. "Debt-Ceiling Déjà Vu Could Sink Economy." *Bloomberg,* May 28. www.bloomberg.com/news/2012-05-28/debt-ceiling-deja-vu-could-sink-economy.html [Accessed May 11, 2014].

Sundquist, James L. 1988–89. "Needed: A Political Theory for the New Era of Coalition Government in the United States." *Political Science Quarterly* 103(4): 613–35.

Voteview. 2012. "Polarization in Real (and Asymmetric)," Voteview Blog, May 16. http://voteview.com/blog/?p=494 [Accessed May 11, 2014].

APPENDIX: MEASURING THE SIZE OF THE LEGISLATIVE AGENDA

In *Stalemate*, I detail my method for retrieving and coding *New York Times* editorials between 1947 and 2000 to determine the size and content of the legislative agenda over the postwar period. Briefly, for the period 1947–1980, I used *New York Times* microfilm to locate and code the daily, unsigned editorials written by members of the *Times* editorial board; for the period 1981–2000, I used Lexis to locate editorials electronically. I found no issues of comparability between the two times periods raised by relying on different methods for retrieving editorials. More recently, to update my measure of legislative gridlock for the period 2001–2012, I relied on ProQuest's electronic version of the *New York Times.*

Figure 9.1a shows the number of legislative issues retrieved for each Congress from the *New York Times* between 1947–2012. Figure 9.1b shows the number of salient issues on the legislative agenda (those issues on which the *New York Times* wrote more than four times in a given Congress on that particular legislative issue). The secular increase in the number of legislative issues over time and the jump in the number of salient issues after 2000 raise questions about comparability of the two time series (before and after 2000). First, does the change in data source for locating editorials affect our ability to locate relevant editorials? Second, has there been a change in practice in terms of the overall number of editorials produced daily by the *New York Times*? Affirmative answers to either question complicate my ability to combine the pre- and post-2000 editorials into a single time series to tap the size and content of the legislative agenda.

I conduct several tests to ensure that neither of these potential methodological pitfalls is driving the increase in editorials over the longer time series. First, I took several steps to confirm that the ProQuest search was accurately capturing the universe of unsigned daily editorials. The *New York Times* typically publishes three or four unsigned editorials each day, only some of which address legislative issues. It turns out that each data retrieval strategy (e.g., Lexis versus ProQuest) captures a different total number of editorials each year because of differences in the search query and in the queried database. Despite these differences, however, each method appears to successfully identify the three to four daily, unsigned editorials.

To confirm that the proper editorials were queried, I compared editorials drawn from the different search mechanisms. To confirm that the ProQuest search captured the correct editorials (dropping signed editorials or political cartoons), I located editorials in the hard copy of the *New York Times* for one week in February 2014 and one week in March 2014 and compared those to the search results from Lexis, ProQuest, and the *New York Times* website. The Lexis search retrieved some unsigned editorials that appeared only in the international and online editions of the *Times*. Incorporating such editorials after 2000 would make it difficult to include the pre- and post-2000 editorials in a single measure. However, a random check of 100 editorials from the ProQuest search suggested that it is unlikely that any of these erroneously retrieved editorials (that appeared in the online or international editions) addressed legislative issues. In other words, although the electronic searches for the period after 2000 caught an array of editorials that would not have been coded based on the Lexis or microfilm coding, it does not appear that these additional editorials addressed legislative matters (and thus were excluded by the coding scheme that dropped nonlegislative editorials).

As a second precaution, I calculated the number of editorials per day for the 110th Congress (2007–08) to identify days on which the number of retrieved editorials was unusually high. I used ProQuest to compare their collection of scanned hard copies of the newspapers with my original ProQuest search results for days with more than ten editorials.[10] This step revealed three

[10] Unfortunately, my access to Brookings' ProQuest subscription expired after the original searches for 2001–12 had been conducted. Instead, for this test I had to rely on George Washington University's ProQuest subscription. Identical queries on the two ProQuest *Times* databases

patterns. First, many of the editorials were duplicate copies of nearly identical editorials (for instance, that had appeared in different editions of the same day's paper). Second, given ProQuest's coding scheme for editorials, the search queries were mistakenly capturing *signed* editorials. Finally, my original Pro-Quest search retrieved some editorials that appeared only in regional editions of the *New York Times*. These regional editorials should not have been included in the list of agenda items because the prior search methods would not have captured them and their relegation to the regional section could imply local issues rather than national ones for Congress.

After identifying the regional edition editorials, I checked to see whether they had been originally coded as legislative issues. If so, they were removed from my database of issues on the legislative agenda. This search yielded fifteen editorials that appeared in regional editions of the *New York Times*. In two cases, agenda issues mentioned in these regional editorials (Indian Point safety assessment and suburban development in the 109th Congress) were removed from the database because those editorials constituted the only mention of the issue in that Congress. In only one case did removing the regional editorial mention of an issue (Amtrak in the 110th Congress) affect the salience of an issue in that Congress: the total number of Amtrak mentions fell from 4 to 3, thereby dropping Amtrak from my list of "salient" issues for the Congress. In the remaining cases, salience scores fell by a single mention, but none of those changes removed an issue from the list of "salient" issues for the Congress.

Third, I investigated whether changes to the weekend edition of the *New York Times* could have resulted in increases in the number of editorials captured in the search query as compared to before 2000. Although the editorial board has experimented with various weekend formats over the past several years, the number of unsigned editorials has remained at roughly three or four per each weekend day. On occasion, the editorial board has run a special series that included many editorials, but judging on a comparison of the number of editorials in each December month from 1994 to the present, such instances appear to be rare and appear to occur at roughly the same rate over time.

These tests increase confidence that neither the change in methodology for retrieving editorials after 2000 nor changes in the *Times'* daily editorials practices are driving the steady increase in the size of the agenda after 2000 or the elevated number of salient issues after 2000. Eliminating those two potential explanations for the increased size of the agenda leaves us with the more palatable conclusion that the elite policy agenda has simply grown and become more complicated – not surprising given the introduction of new issues (e.g., the war on terror and homeland security) and more complex ones (e.g., global warming) over the course of the last decade.

typically return a different number of editorials, potentially due to different underlying collections of *Times* editions in the two databases or different coding of alternative types of publications on the opinion pages.

10

What Has Congress Done?

Stephen Ansolabehere, Maxwell Palmer,
and Benjamin Schneer

INTRODUCTION

In the spring of 2013, we taught an undergraduate lecture course on Congress.
It was our first time teaching such a course. The course needed to be covered,
and departmental leaves created a significant teaching gap in an important
subject. Approaching this course for the first time, the problem was how to
teach a large lecture course on Congress. The political science of the United
States Congress is a rich subject, at once highly analytical and deeply rooted in
the institution's history. How can we balance those two strains of thinking as
we approach this subject? Moreover, university instruction is changing. New
technology is changing what students expect in the classroom and what they
are capable of accomplishing outside the classroom. Students are seeking more
active learning experiences, and the traditional lecture course seems to be under
some strain. The Congress course offered an opportunity to experiment. We
turned to David Mayhew for guidance and inspiration.

Any student of Congress, especially someone studying the institution for the
first time, has much to learn about its history and its politics. David Mayhew is
a superb analyst and an encyclopedic historian, and his writing seamlessly
marries the two traditions of scholarship. Our idea was to model the course
after one of Professor Mayhew's most acclaimed projects, *Divided We Govern*.
This modern classic of congressional scholarship asks one of the most basic
questions about the legislature: What has Congress done? What are the signature and significant acts of the U.S. Congress? And why did the legislature do
what it did when it did it? *Divided We Govern* examines the history of
legislation in the second half of the twentieth century and explores several

Professor Ansolabehere wishes to thank Liz Salazar for her assistance with course websites, reserve
materials, and other support for the management of Government 1300.

competing arguments about when Congress takes significant actions. The most widely debated of these conjectures is whether unified party control of the Congress and presidency contributes to increased legislative productivity.

We decided to organize the class around a collective and collaborative research activity that would extend David Mayhew's database of significant legislation to cover the entire history of the United States. Professor Mayhew describes what Congress accomplished over a forty-five-year span of its recent history. What did Congress accomplish before Harry S. Truman ascended to the presidency? There have been numerous reanalyses of Mayhew's own data, but very little effort by political scientists to extend his project to the entire history of the U.S. Congress. Several important exceptions stand out. William Howell, Scott Adler, Charles Cameron, and Charles Reimann offer their own attempt to measure legislative productivity in the era studied by Professor Mayhew.[1] Josh Clinton and John Lapinski pushed the study back further in time, spanning the years 1877 to 1994. They also introduced a statistical method for identifying the significance of a law that relies on references to laws by other laws, rather than Mayhew's historical approach.[2] Still, there has been no comprehensive assessment of the entire history of Congress. What happened before 1876? What does the period 1877 to 1946 look like using the historical, rather than statistical, approach? And what happened after 1990? The time frame of the studies that have been done limits what one might infer, because there were few changes in control of the government between 1946 and 1990. Grant and Kelley attempt to fill this void in the literature by developing statistical methods for combining various data sources on significant legislation, including mentions of bills in the press, key votes, and experts' assessments.[3] We take a different approach from Grant and Kelley. We crowdsource the problem and return to the historical approach offered by David Mayhew in *Divided We Govern*.

Our class became "mini-Mayhews," digging into the historical records of Congress and assessments of Congress offered by historians. The classroom experience was simultaneously one of learning and research. Professor Mayhew's methodology and database of significant legislation provided a starting point, and our mission was to engage the students in the same exercise that Professor Mayhew had accomplished single-handedly. We divided the 220-year history of the United States Congress into twenty-two decades. Every student was assigned to a decade, and over the course of the semester they were

[1] William Howell, Scott Adler, Charles Cameron, and Charles Reimann, "Divided Government and the Legislative Productivity of Congress, 1945–1994," *Legislative Studies Quarterly* XXV (2) (2000): 285–312.
[2] Joshua Clinton and John Lapinski, "Measuring Legislative Accomplishment, 1874–1994," *American Journal of Political Science* 50 (2006): 232–249.
[3] J. Tobin Grant and Nathan J. Kelley, "Legislative Productivity of the United States Congress," *Political Analysis* 16 (2008): 303–323.

to become experts in their decade. Drawing on their own reading of original materials available from Congress and drawing second-hand from historical research by others, the students were to develop a database of all significant legislation on which Congress took action in their decade. Each student also wrote a brief essay about Congress in his or her decade. We then pooled all of their databases, reviewed each act identified, and developed a single database of the history of significant legislation passed by the United States Congress.

The success of this project depended vitally on the students who enrolled in the course. Thanks to the efforts of Cheryl Welch, the undergraduate program officer in the Department of Government, we managed to recruit a class of thirty-one students. They represented many of the stars of our undergraduate program. They are: Samuel Berman-Cooper, Alexander Chen, Catherine Choi, Matthew Clarida, James Clarke, Mark Daley, Parker Davis, Erica Edwards Sims, Naji Filali, Alexandra Garcia, Spencer Gisser, Kevin Hornbeck, Brian Hughes, Brandon Jones, Omar Khoshafa, Logan Leslie, Rich Maopolski, Matthew Marotta, Luis Martinez, Kyle Matsuda, Devi Nair, Diana Nguyen, Jordan Rasmusson, Owen Rees, Laura Reston, Andrea Rickey, Jared Sawyer, Kent Toland, Shang Wang, Chanel Washington, and LuShuang Xu.

This paper describes the fruit of our collective labor, and offers an assessment of the effect of divided control of the presidency and Congress on the passage of legislation. Assembling the Data describes the data collection effort. Trends in Legislative Action discusses historical trends in significant legislation. Effects of Divided Government offers a reassessment of the question of whether and how much unified versus divided government affects what Congress does. What we present here is really a first pass at the subject. This approach to the analysis of Congress can easily be replicated in future classes, and the database presented here can be used as a base on which to build.

ASSEMBLING THE DATA

On the second day of class, every student was arbitrarily assigned a decade. Once students were settled in their seats, we passed out slips of paper, each with a decade printed on it. We anticipated some decades would be especially difficult, such as the 1930s or 1960s, so we distributed multiple slips of paper for those decades. We then allowed students to trade decades. If someone had the 1830s and wanted the 2000s, he or she would have to find someone with the 2000s and make a deal. This was their first lesson in the politics of Congress, or any organization. Letting the students trade also assured a fair way of distributing decades and of assigning students to decades in which they had a particularly strong interest. The professor for the course, Stephen Ansolabehere, took the least popular decade, the 1840s. Two students, Jordan Rasmusson and Devi Nair, were assigned to Rules. Their task was to assemble a database of all the changes in the rules of each chamber, from the First

Congress to the present. The teaching fellows, Max Palmer and Ben Schneer, took on the tasks of quality control and assembling the combined databases into a common database.

Creating a database in this way is a complex task, as students could approach their assignments differently. We worked with the students to standardize their coding methods and databases across decades. We developed a common template, agreed on a common definition of "significant legislation," and collected data from the same set of initial sources. The key variables in the database template are bill names, descriptions, categories, outcomes, and roll call votes and dates. We also asked students to collect information on committees and primary sponsors in each chamber when these data were available.

We utilized a simple definition of significant legislation based on meeting one of two criteria. First, is the bill important in historical context? When we look back on the legislation from our current perspective, did this bill accomplish something important, such as establishing a major governmental agency, introducing a major policy change, declaring war, or passing a constitutional amendment? Second, was the bill viewed as an important legislative accomplishment in its own time? This type of bill is harder to identify; the task requires the use of histories or the Congressional Record. For example, some slavery-related bills that preceded the Civil War did not have long-lasting significance due to the abolition of slavery, but they were major legislative accomplishments addressing a critical issue of their time. In making these assessments, students relied on historical treatments of the Congress and politics of their decade and time period, such as the antebellum period, the New Deal, and so forth.

The use of common sources across time periods simplified the process of determining significance, as the authors of these works had already decided what bills they thought were important based on their own criteria. While these criteria may not match ours perfectly, they at least provided consistency across time periods. In addition to collecting major legislation, we also asked students to record major legislative failures, Supreme Court nominations, and other notable legislative actions.

For legislation from 1789 through 1945, students began with the bills listed in *The Yeas and the Nays: Key Congressional Decisions, 1774–1945*, by Albert Castel and Scott L. Gibson. *The Yeas and the Nays* identified key legislation from each Congress and provided descriptions and vote totals for each. *The American Political Science Review* between 1910 and 1940 occasionally presented summaries of significant Congressional action during the term. For the 1950s through 2010s, students began with the CQ *Almanac* for each year, and recorded all of the bills listed in the key votes section of each almanac. The 1940s were a particular challenge, as our key sources either ended in the 1940s or began in the 1950s. As a result, the students working on the 1940s used a variety of sources, including *The Yeas and the Nays*, Mayhew's (2000) database on congressional actions, and Charles Cameron's database on major legislation.[4] The students supplemented these books with a variety of other sources that the librarians at Harvard University helped us to identify.

Additional sources included histories of Congress, online resources from the Library of Congress, and the *Congressional Record* (and its antecedents). Galloway's *History of the House of Representatives*, and Wise's *History of the House of Representatives,* and Josephy's *The American Heritage History of the Congress of the United States* were particularly useful for many students. Galloway also included many useful figures in appendices, including counts of total public and private legislation in each Congress. Students collecting data from the 101st Congress through the present used the Library of Congress's THOMAS site. The Library of Congress's site "A Century of Lawmaking For a New Nation" was also very helpful for collecting information on the first fifty Congresses. Students looking for more detail on particular bills used the *Congressional Record* to collect information and understand the debates surrounding major bills. We spent substantial time during both lecture and discussion sections working with the *Congressional Record* (as well as the *Annals of Congress, Register of Debates*, and *Congressional Globe*), in order to introduce our students to one of the most important primary sources for understanding the politics of Congress. The websites for the House, Senate, National Archives, and Govtrack.us were also useful.

We encouraged all of the students to make a pass through the Congressional Record for their given decade. They were asked to find the laws identified by *CQ Almanac* or *Yeas and Nays* or other sources as significant legislation in the Congressional Record. They were also asked to identify subjects on which there was much debate or activity in the index of the *Record*.

A note is in order about Wikipedia, a crowd-sourced encyclopedia available free online. Wikipedia features a list of important legislation by Congress, as determined by its community of writers and editors.[5] We found Wikipedia to be tremendously helpful. The Wikipedia list of significant legislation is cross-referenced to other Wikipedia pages, and most are well documented as to original source materials used. Students were encouraged to use Wikipedia, especially to supplement and cross-check information from *Yeas and Nays* and CQ, but they were cautioned to take care to determine the reason that something was considered significant by the Wikipedia contributors and to verify against other sources. The Wikipedia page was frequently helpful for identifying major legislation missing from the initial sources, but it also included several bills that did not appear to match our criteria for significance. Some bills seem to be included on the Wikipedia page based on the political motives of the writers and editors of the list, or their significance was not related to the reason for the bill. For example, one of the early homesteading acts was deemed

---

[4] www.princeton.edu/~ccameron/datareadme.html.
[5] http://en.wikipedia.org/wiki/List_of_United_States_federal_legislation.

significant by a Wikipedia contributor because it was the first federal law that explicitly stated that women were allowed to own property on their own. When such cases were identified, we relied on other sources to make a judgment about their inclusion. In the case of the homesteading law, we felt the law was sufficiently important for many reasons to be included on the list.

The final step in assembling the database was to compile the individual databases from each student into one comprehensive database and review the students' work for consistency. Our students collected a total of 1,538 major legislative actions. We reviewed the database to remove duplicate entries (some decades were assigned to more than one student), along with any legislation that did not meet our significance criteria or was missing critical information. After this step, we were left with 1,040 significant bills that Congress enacted into law.[6] We then used keywords in the students' categories and descriptions to categorize the bills into forty-six categories (Table 10A.2 in the Appendix to this chapter). We also included counts of total public and private bills passed in each Congress. For the Congresses between 1789 and 1976 we used Appendix F of Galloway's and Wise's *History of the House of Representatives*; for the remaining years we used counts from the Library of Congress. The Appendix tables contain a list of the total number of significant acts passed by each Congress according to our project, and a count of the number of acts taken by the subject area of the legislation.

It should be noted that this approach differs from those offered by scholars who have worked on this problem in the years since Mayhew published *Divided We Govern*, such as Clinton and Lapinski and Green and Kelley. These scholars take a more statistical approach, attempting to combine multiple sources of information using statistical models. We take a more historical approach designed for the classroom. The value of our approach is to add to the growing research on what Congress has done and to propose a way that all of us as scholars can engage our students directly in the contribution to knowledge.

TRENDS IN LEGISLATIVE ACTION

The First Congress of the United States of America was called to order on March 4, 1789, in New York City. It met for two sessions of approximately 220 days in duration in New York, and held a third, 88-day session in Philadelphia from December 1790 through February 1791. By the end of the First Congress, a blueprint for the plan of government was in place, including the organization of the executive, judicial, and legislative branches, and a plan for public finance.

---

[6] This excludes major legislation that failed, legislation that was was vetoed and not overridden, and judicial nominations.

The productivity of the First Congress surely owes to the need for legislation. When the members of the First Congress initially convened, there were no national laws governing the budget, economy, citizenship, federal crimes, or many other domains that today we take as given. The Constitution had left large portions of the federal government undefined, especially the president's cabinet and the organization of the judiciary. The First Congress could not help but pass significant legislation, as they started on a nearly blank slate.

The First Congress also lacked rules for passing legislation or organizing the chambers. The rules and procedures (or lack thereof) slowed the legislature. Daily calls of the roll from March 4, 1789, to April 6, 1789, show that, for its first month, Congress could not begin for want of a quorum. Sufficient numbers of House Members for a quorum had arrived in New York by April 1, 1789, and the Senate reached critical mass soon after, on April 6, 1789. Yet even as the Congress began to meet, it became obvious that the Constitution had left much unsaid about how the legislature was to proceed. It was unclear, for example, how the two chambers were to communicate with each other, how differences between the chambers were to be resolved, what would and would not be recorded, how committees might work, and what the role of those outside the chamber (especially the members of the administration, such as Alexander Hamilton) was to be. The lack of specificity in procedures resulted in an immediate confusion, which by the end of the First Congress had evolved into a set of practices, if not rules, for getting things done.

In its first two years, Congress created the Departments of Treasury, State, and War; passed the Judiciary Act; enacted the Bill of Rights; passed a Tariff Act, called the Hamilton Tariff, which was to define the fiscal basis of the federal government for the next 125 years; passed the Naturalization Act, the Crime Act, the Indian Intercourse Act, the Copyright Act, and the Patent Act; and established the First Bank of the United States. Finally, Congress decided to build a new seat of government in the District of Columbia. For a loosely organized legislature without a committee system, party organizations, or even a comprehensive set of rules, this was an auspicious beginning.

The First Congress was also subject to distraction. Its proceedings document lengthy debates over the manner of taking oaths and how members of Congress were to address the President of the United States: "Your Excellency?" "Your Exalted Highness?" Just a month into the new Congress, the Virginia legislature applied to the Congress to hold a new convention to address the flaws in the Constitution. The first petitioners (proto-lobbyists) appear in July of 1789. Throughout Congress' first years, its members came and went, many returning home to attend to business. There were constant attempts by Alexander Hamilton to meddle in the legislative process.[7] And, by the end of the First

---

[7] Alvin M. Josephy, Jr., *The American Heritage History of the Congress of the United States* (New York: American Heritage, 1975), chapter 1.

Congress, the legislature had begun to sort into parties, aligned roughly with the factional split inside the executive between Hamilton and Jefferson.[8] Nonetheless, the First Congress forged ahead, in what was one of the most productive Congresses in the history of the nation.

In 1789, Congress felt the need to act. The Constitution was a crude architecture, not a complete plan of government. Without federal legislation to enable the functioning of the judiciary and executive, the new constitution would likely have failed. What was to happen over the next 200 years? As history marches forward, what explains when Congress does and does not act? The conjecture that David Mayhew laid out in *Divided We Govern* is that the partisan organization of Congress and the Presidency explains a substantial portion of the variation in when Congress acts and when it does not. Before assessing that conjecture, we first examine the overall patterns of legislation and significant legislation over time.

What legislation *is* has evolved substantially since the First Congress. Early bills and acts were often unnamed when they were introduced. In fact, the first bill introduced into the new Congress was an act to levy fees on the tonnage of ships introduced by Mr. Adams of Massachusetts. The resolution simply lists various types of vessels on which tonnage fees were to be charged, but actual fees are left as blanks to be filled in later.

Congress also often proceeded in an ad hoc manner. Appropriations, for example, were made on a need basis; there was no budget process. An act to fund a specific activity or project would ask for a certain amount to be spent on that activity. Internal improvements were not approved in omnibus bills but were taken up one by one – a lighthouse here, a harbor dredged there. Many of these idiosyncratic actions fall out of the scope of "significant legislation" because they do not rise to the level of singularly important actions taken by Congress. Cumulatively, though, they are important.

Over the decades, legislation became more rationalized and bureaucratic. Bills became longer and more specific. Congress eventually came up with a more comprehensive approach to budgeting. Perhaps the clearest example of the rationalization of legislation is the treatment of private bills. Throughout the nineteenth century, Congress used private legislation to pay for military pensions, benefits for military widows, compensation for property, and a variety of other particular transactions.[9] The number of such transactions grew exponentially over the decades following the Civil War, and Congress

---

[8] John H. Aldrich and Ruth W. Grant, "The Anti-Federalists, the First Congress, and the First Parties," *Journal of Politics* 55 (1993): 295–326.

[9] Theda Skocpol, "America's First Social Security System: The Expansion of Benefits for Civil War Veterans," *Political Science Quarterly* 108 (1993): 85–116. Theda Skocpol, *Protecting Soldiers and Mothers: The Political Origins of Social Policy in the United States* (Cambridge, MA: Harvard University Press, 1995).

eventually decided to create a pension law to remove the thousands of requests for relief from the legislature's agenda.

The changing nature of legislation is not as cleanly reflected in our measures of total and significant acts. But the evolution of the form of legislation and nature of statutory law is an important feature of the history of Congress. It is worth flagging how the changed nature of legislation might affect the picture of various trends. A law that creates a comprehensive approach to such private legislation becomes a significant act, but the many private bills leading up to it are not. The many ad hoc appropriation bills in the first half of the nineteenth century do not rise to the level of significance, but the budget acts that rationalize the process do.

The growing rationalization of legislation and government are worth keeping in mind when considering the historical trends in legislation. We gauge the amount of legislation and the number of significant laws passed in each Congress. There are also important changes in the content or nature of legislation that are not reflected in these trends. That awaits further investigation in future years of our courses on Congress. However, each time that Congress moves to rationalize a legislative arena, such as appropriations or pensions or committee systems, it frees up time for the entire legislature to address other matters. Hence, it may be the case that the growing rationalization of the legislative process itself creates the capacity – but not the need – to create more legislation in the future.

Congress passes two sorts of acts, public acts and private acts. Public acts take the form of statutes, judicial and executive appointments, approval of treaties, and other actions that have the standing of public laws. Private acts are actions taken by the legislature on behalf of individuals, such as a property transaction of the federal government with an individual or a grant of a special privilege, such as a pension, to an individual. Scholars usually refer to public acts when making claims about congressional action. In fact, most theoretical work really pertains just to statutes.

Figure 10.1 presents the number of public acts passed by each Congress from 1789 to 2012. Each Congress is noted by a marker and its number. The Congresses are further distinguished as occurring under unified government (president and both chambers of the same party) with a plus sign or divided government with a square. This is simply the total number of acts passed and does not depend on classifications of significance.

The patterns in Figure 10.1 help us put David Mayhew's original study of divided government in context. Mayhew's study began with the 78th Congress, which passed approximately 600 acts. The succeeding twenty years saw a rapid increase in legislative action cresting with the 84th and 85th Congresses, which produced over 1,000 acts each. Since then, there has been a steady decline in total legislation passed, and the number of public acts passed today is less than half the number passed in the peak years of the late 1950s and early 1960s. Interestingly, the low numbers of bills passed in the 111th and 112th

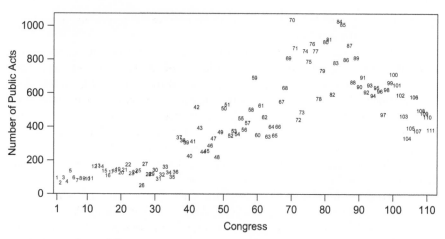

FIGURE 10.1 Acts of Congress.

Congresses appear predictable from the steady trend downward in the number of laws passed per Congress since the summit in 1959.

The figure also reveals that the post–World War II period differs markedly from what had come before. In terms of total legislative output, there appear to be four periods of congressional history. During the antebellum period (1789 to 1861), a typical Congress passed only 150 public acts. Despite their obvious importance, the first two Congresses were not particularly productive. And the true Do Nothing Congress was the 26th, which managed to pass only a few dozen public acts. From the Civil War through the end of World War I (1862 to 1925), there was a steady rise in the number of public acts from 200 to 500 acts per Congress. This was an era of rapid industrialization and, interestingly, corresponds almost exactly to the period that Steven Skowronek identifies as the era of the development of the American national executive.[10] Then, in 1927–29, comes a quantum leap in the number of public acts passed by Congress. Congress maintains this very high level of productivity from 1926 through 1966, an era described by some as the Modern Era in Congress, and also the era of modernism in many other aspects of public and private life. This era also coincides with the rise of the conservative coalition, the partisan realignment that leads to the ascendancy of the Democratic party nationally, and the beginning of the incumbency advantage. The postmodern Congress takes hold in 1967. Legislative activity drops substantially between 1965–66 and 1967–68 and has continued to trend downward since. By 1968, a new political alignment had begun to take hold, which John Aldrich and Richard Niemi (among others) characterize as a protracted period of partisan dealignment,

[10] Steven Skowronek, *Building a New American State: The Expansion of National Administrative Capacities, 1877–1920* (Cambridge: Cambridge University Press, 1982).

rising incumbency advantages and campaign expenditures, and growing public dissatisfaction with Congress. The levels of legislative output in the 112th Congress, which have triggered a new round of criticism of the institution, are comparable to the levels associated with the period from 1870 through 1920, and the numbers of public acts in the most recent Congresses continue a downward trend begun in 1967.

This broad picture of law making exposes several puzzles. Why the jump in legislative activity in the 1920s? Why the downward trend in legislation since the 1960s? It surprised us that the most productive Congresses are the 70th (1927–29) and 84th (1959–61), not, as we might have guessed, the 73rd (1933–35) or 89th (1965–67). Moreover, the 97th Congress (1981–83) had much less legislative action than we expected. We are also struck by the tremendous differences between the nineteenth and twentieth centuries, made all the more striking by the fact that the First Congress appeared on our first reading to play such an important role in the development of the institution and the government.

The incidence of significant legislation tells a subtly different story about Congress. Figure 10.2 presents the history of significant acts passed by Congress. Each point in the plot is a Congress, with those occurring under unified party control of government noted with a plus and those under divided control with a square. This graph consists of all public acts determined by our project to be significant acts of Congress.

The same general patterns emerge in both total and significant legislation. The nineteenth century produced far fewer pieces of significant legislation than the twentieth century. The amount of significant legislation passed by a typical Congress rises from the end of the nineteenth century through the middle of the twentieth century, peaks in the 1960s, and then steadily declines. Today, the number of significant acts passed by a typical Congress is now back to the levels

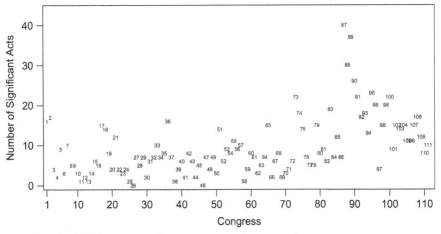

FIGURE 10.2 Significant acts of Congress.

typical of the end of the nineteenth and beginning of the twentieth centuries (Congresses 55, 56, and 57), but remains above the historical average.

The peaks, however, are notably different for significant legislation. The First and Second Congresses stand above the rest of the nineteenth century in terms of the number of pieces of significant legislation passed. From the Age of Jackson to the New Deal, the 36th (1859–61), 51st (1889–91), and 65th (1917–19) Congresses stand out as passing substantially more significant legislation than other years in the same era. There are tremendous jumps in the numbers of significant acts with the advent of the New Deal (the 73rd, 74th, and 75th Congresses) and the creation of the Great Society programs (the 87th, 88th, and 89th Congresses). In these two eras, Congress passed very large numbers of acts that had long-lasting significance to the nation. There are historical explanations as to why these bursts of activity occurred. The political science explanations are much less compelling and powerful.

One methodological aside is worth noting in reference to Figures 10.1 and 10.2. The patterns in these data provide us with some confidence in our coding of significant legislation. We do not see troubling or unusual changes in classifications from one decade to the next, that is, from one coder to the next. Had there been irregularities between the sources or the coders, we would have expected unusual jumps in the numbers of significant bills from one coder to the next. We do not observe those. The changes in the number of significant bills seem to track with broad historical trends and changes in the political context. Also, the number of significant bills in our coding is highly correlated with Mayhew's coding for the period 1945–1990. The most notable deviation is the Kennedy Congress (1961–62), when our reading of the history noted many more pieces of significant legislation than Mayhew's coding identified.

The patterns displayed in Figures 10.1 and 10.2 lay out the foundations for the second stage of our inquiry: Explaining why Congress does what it does when it does it. Professor Mayhew laid down an important conjecture – that divided government affects the ability of Congress to legislate, and especially the ability of Congress to pass significant legislation. That argument has its theoretical foundations in David Brady's and Craig Volden's *Revolving Gridlock* and Keith Krehbiel's *Pivotal Politics*. In the next section, we estimate how large an effect unified or divided control of government has on the rate at which Congress takes historically and politically significant actions.

The overall historical patterns reveal that unified partisan control cannot explain the broad contours of legislative productivity. In Figure 10.2, the 91st and 100th Congresses – both divided – passed as many significant laws as the 73rd. But there does seem to be a relationship. The First and Second (unified) are more productive than the Third and Fourth (divided), and so forth.

Before turning to the question of divided government, one final comment about the overall patterns here is in order. The rise in productivity in Congress in Figures 10.1 and 10.2 corresponds quite closely with the decline in polarization in the House and Senate, and especially with the percent of legislators from each party who are "overlapping" – that is, Democrats to the right of at least one Republican and Republicans to the left of at least one Democrat. In particular, Poole and Rosenthal identify the 70th Congress (1927–29) as the beginning of a substantial decline in polarization within the Congress, with a gradual increase in polarization beginning after the 90th Congress (1967–69). This era from 1927 to 1969 is often viewed as the standard for how Congress ought to behave by commentators such as Tom Mann and Norman Ornstein, and it does appear that broad historical fluctuations in polarization correspond with broad ebbs and flows in the tide of significant legislation. The correlation, at least from 1879 to 2012, appears obvious to us, but the causality is less clear as roll call votes and significant legislation are both outputs of the same legislative process.

EFFECTS OF DIVIDED GOVERNMENT

How does divided government influence legislative output? The data gathered by our team allow us to answer this question by looking across the entire history of Congress. Over the 220 years of Congress, the legislature produced an average of 8.7 pieces of significant legislation when the control of government was divided among the parties and 9.8 pieces of significant legislation, roughly one additional significant act, when there was unified party control of government.[11] While this comparison of means is in line with the idea that unified party control leads to greater legislative productivity, the difference is not large enough to support the conclusion that legislative output depends on party control in a systematic way: the 95 percent confidence interval on the difference in means includes zero. That difference also does not take into account the variation in the trends and levels of legislation over time. In addition, divided control of government yielded more total legislation (public laws) than unified control did. (See Table 10.1.)

Breaking out legislative output by era corrects for variation in overall legislative product across different periods of the history of Congress. We divide the data into four time eras: pre–Civil War (1st–36th Congress), post–Civil War but pre-1900 (37th–55th Congress), the turn of the century to the end of World War II (56th–79th Congress), and post–World War II (80th–111th Congress). (See Table 10.2.) Across all four eras, unified government is associated with an uptick in significant legislation; however, the magnitude of the increase varies substantially depending on the time period. In the pre–Civil War era, the difference between unified and divided party is about half a bill – slightly more than a 10 percent increase. In the second period, the gap between unified and divided

---

[11] In most cases, assessing whether Congress operated under a divided or unified government was straightforward. One exception was the 20th Congress, when John Quincy Adams held the Presidency as a Democratic-Republican and factions such as the Jacksonians were splitting off from the party. We coded this Congress as unified. That said, coding it the other way makes no material difference in our results.

TABLE 10.1 *Mean Legislative Output per Congress*

Party Control	Total Leg.	Significant Leg.	Obs.
Divided	421.02	8.64	42
Unified	407.74	9.80	69

TABLE 10.2 *Mean Legislative Output per Congress, by Era*

Era of Congress	Party Control	Total Leg.	Significant Leg.	Obs.
1st–36th	Divided	115.00	6.00	10
1st–36th	Unified	120.92	6.62	26
37th–55th	Divided	312.30	4.50	10
37th–55th	Unified	395.22	7.44	9
56th–79th	Divided	412.25	6.50	4
56th–79th	Unified	634.20	7.95	20
80th–111th	Divided	653.39	12.89	18
80th–111th	Unified	624.93	19.86	14

control is almost three bills, which represents an increase in output of over 60 percent. In the third period, the gap narrowed slightly, but by the post–World War II period it widened to a difference of five bills – again an increase in productivity of over 60 percent. Examining significant legislation, we observe that unified government resulted in roughly one additional piece of significant legislation both before and after 1900. The data follow a similar pattern when we turn to *total* legislation, with one key exception. In the post–World War II era, unified governments have actually produced less *total* legislation when compared with divided control. The other noticeable trend for total legislation is the existence of a general upward trend over time.

The comparison of means obscures some crucial factors related to legislative output that we must account for when assessing legislative productivity. First, as detailed in the previous section, we observe some sharp differences across time in legislative output driven by factors unrelated to party control; as a result, any comparison of productivity between divided and unified government must account carefully for the time trends in legislative output. We attempt to address this issue with two different approaches: by including indicator variables for the era of Congress and by taking first differences and looking at *changes* in legislative productivity after *changes* in party control. A second concern is that comparing across presidential terms may overlook the fact that historical circumstances, the effectiveness of a president's administration, or both play a role in legislative output. For example, Congress's legislative productivity during FDR's first 100 days is perhaps not directly comparable to the first 100 days of Jimmy Carter's administration. If the effectiveness of a president's administration happens to be correlated with

TABLE 10.3 *Party Control and Legislative Output*

	Total Legislation			Significant Legislation		
	(1)	(2)	(3)	(4)	(5)	(6)
Unified	−13.28	41.06	20.22	1.15	3.37**	3.27**
Government	(51.70)	(27.49)	(31.00)	(1.33)	(1.30)	(1.34)
37th–55th		242.51***	148.50***		0.29	−2.50
Congress		(21.61)	(7.85)		(1.15)	(3.23)
56th–79th		473.37***	82.50***		0.89	−3.50
Congress		(41.88)	(7.85)		(1.39)	(3.23)
80th–111th		533.35***	161.91		10.45***	−9.74***
Congress		(33.77)	(119.51)		(1.82)	(3.64)
Constant	421.02***	89.62***	157.78***	8.64***	4.01***	3.73***
	(39.63)	(20.71)	(31.00)	(0.89)	(1.21)	(1.34)
President FEs	No	No	Yes	No	No	Yes
Observations	111	111	111	111	111	111
R-squared	0.001	0.723	0.912	0.006	0.378	0.773

Robust standard errors in parentheses
* $p < 0.10$.
** $p < 0.05$.
*** $p < 0.01$.

party control, then we might wrongly attribute an increase in legislative productivity to unified or divided government. By including president fixed effects, we can estimate the effect of variation in party control on legislative output within a president's term, which rules out differences due to different administrations.

We use ordinary least squares (OLS) to estimate the effect of unified government on legislative output. The estimates are provided in Table 10.3. The main result, illustrated in Models 4–6, is that unified government is associated with roughly 3.3 additional pieces of significant legislation as compared with divided government when we include era dummy variables. This effect is substantively large. Considering that Congress has averaged slightly fewer than nine significant pieces of legislation during divided control, the observed effect of unified control represents an increase of more than one third.[12] Conversely, we do not find consistent evidence that unified government affects *total* legislation (see Models 1–3).

---

[12] In fact, if we log-transform legislative output and reestimate the model, unified government is associated with an even larger percentage increase in significant legislation.

Including the period dummy variables plays an important role in the estimation of unified government's effect on significant legislation, especially with regard to legislative output since the end of World War II. Before the 80th Congress, there were twenty-four cases of divided government and fifty-five cases of unified government. After the 80th Congress, the numbers were more equal, with eighteen cases of divided government and fourteen cases of unified government. The fact that there have been proportionally more cases of divided government since 1945, combined with Congress's tendency to produce more legislation over time, means that not accounting for the systematic differences in eras could lead us to underestimate the effect of unified government for the full time period. Interestingly, incorporating president fixed effects does not substantively alter the estimated effect.

Estimating the effect of a change from unified (divided) control to divided (unified) control provides additional evidence that party control of government influences the output of significant legislation. Taking first differences essentially eliminates time trends from the data. As Figure 10.3 illustrates, changes in legislation from Congress to Congress appear to follow a stationary process with a mean centered at zero and close to constant variance over time. The graph also provides a nice visualization of the estimated effect: changes to unified party control are consistently associated with increases in the amount of significant legislation (i.e., above zero) and changes away from unified party control to divided government are consistently associated with decreases.

Using OLS to estimate the effect of a change in unified government yields an estimate of an increase in significant legislation of more than three. This finding is robust to including a lagged term for significant legislation as well, under the

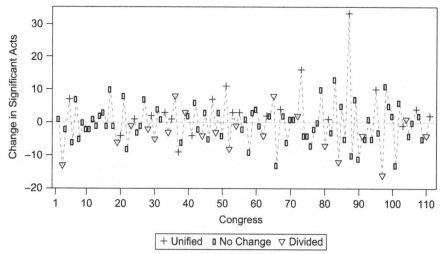

FIGURE 10.3 Change in number of significant acts.

theory that Congress's momentum from previous years might play some role in legislative output. Again, the estimated effect is substantively quite large – one way of conceptualizing the effect is to consider that Congress has changed from divided to unified control or vice versa forty-two times (twenty-one times from divided to unified and twenty-one times from unified to divided) and that each change is associated with a gain or loss of between three and four pieces of significant legislation. (See Table 10.4.) All told, the estimates suggest that Congress's legislative record might be markedly different were there substantially more years of either divided or unified control. Finally, in contrast to the findings for significant legislation, the results suggest that a change in party control has no meaningful effect on changes in *total* legislation.

One potential objection is that variation in student effort when assembling the data might bias our estimates. To check this concern, we also estimated the model using student fixed effects, which control for varying levels of dedication in assembling the data. Under this specification, the results remain unchanged.

In sum, we find very substantial effects of changes in party control on the passage of significant legislation, but no effect of such changes on the passage of total legislation. These contrasting results underscore the value of studying significant legislation, as opposed to all legislation. Congress passes many symbolic acts, such as naming a post office, declaring a "day" in order to recognize a particular cause or industry, or passing a resolution that lacks the force of law but expresses the legislature's concern about an issue. Members of Congress have no trouble voting for such inconsequential bills. It is when Congress grapples with a substantial change in the nation's laws that we see the effects of partisan politics in clearer relief. When government changes from

TABLE 10.4 *Change in Unified Government and Change in Legislative Output*

	Change in Total Legislation		Change in Significant Legislation	
	(1)	(2)	(3)	(4)
Change in Unified Government	29.95	26.88	3.83***	3.23***
	(19.04)	(19.09)	(0.98)	(0.92)
Constant	2.63	3.44	−0.05	−0.09
	(11.77)	(11.79)	(0.60)	(0.57)
Lagged DV	No	Yes	No	Yes
Observations	110	109	110	109
R-squared	0.022	0.045	0.125	0.254

Standard errors in parentheses
* $p < 0.10$,
** $p < 0.05$,
*** $p < 0.01$.

divided to unified partisan control, there is a 30 to 40 percent increase in the number of significant laws passed.

CONCLUSION

The history of Congress is the history of America. Open page one of the Congressional Record and one cannot help but get hooked. Here is the history of a great nation unfolding one step at a time. Usually the steps are slow, even tedious, but then come moments of exhilaration, when Congress takes a grand action – organizing the entire judiciary, invading the Florida territories, granting women the right to vote, passing the Social Security Act, or revamping the nation's tax code. The characters in this tale are epic, sometimes tragic, and often humorous.

There lies one of the great lessons of David Mayhew's works, such as *Divided We Govern* and *America's Congress*. Reading the *Annals*, *Digests*, and *Records of Congress* provides a rich and rewarding way to understand the institution as it operates, its context, and what it has accomplished. *Divided We Govern* tells the story of *what* Congress has done. Elsewhere, David Mayhew has pointed us toward a different path: *America's Congress* is the story of *who* and the *Electoral Connection* of *why*. Following in David Mayhew's footsteps was hugely instructive for each of us and for our students. Reading these books provided an exciting way to teach our students about Congress and to engage them from the very outset of our course in conducting original research.

When our class concluded on May 1, 2013, the three of us met to consider what we had learned. One of us tossed a question into the conversation. We had spent the past four months distinguishing significant Congressional actions from the myriad seemingly unimportant resolutions, appointments, and bills considered by the House and Senate over a span of 220 years. Was there one that stood out as the most significant act of Congress?

After a couple of minutes of reflection each of us had an answer, but a different one: the Bill of Rights, the Judiciary Act of 1789, and the Louisiana Purchase. All of us also felt that the Social Security Act and the 13th Amendment might also be included in that list. Interestingly, all five of these laws were enacted before the period originally studied by David Mayhew, and four of the five predate the Clinton–Lapinski project. The Bill of Rights, the Judiciary Act, and the Louisiana Purchase were all in some sense institutional, rather than what political science would normally designate as "policy." Each affected a different aspect of the form of American government – the Constitution, the organization of one of the branches of the national government, and the size of the territory. There was not a singular answer to this question (though the Bill of Rights might ultimately win the day), but we would never have even asked the question or felt comfortable venturing an answer without first undertaking a quest inspired by *Divided We Govern*.

Our effort to document what Congress has done provides a first glimpse at the entire history of significant legislation passed by the United States House and Senate. It is likely not the definitive database on the subject, but rather a foundation. It can and, we hope, will be improved upon.

With that in mind, we have several next steps in this project. First, document the appropriations and budget process. Appropriations are made regularly by every – or almost every – Congress. The appropriation bills in the early Congresses, though, are entirely ad hoc. Few appropriations bills in the modern era rise to the level of significant legislation, because they are often incremental and must be renewed the following year. Yet they are vitally important to the operation of the national, state, and local governments in the United States. One may treat the entire appropriations and budget process as a significant action taken by each Congress, but consisting of many smaller bills. The next time we teach this course, we plan to structure the research project around the appropriations process.

Second, consider specific policy domains. Congress itself divides its labor and responsibility among its many committees, each of which has distinct jurisdictions. It may be easier to determine significant legislation within specific policy domains than for all legislation. With that in mind, we were struck by the lack of "significant" legislation in some specific policy areas, such as crime and communications. Also, we have inquired with our colleagues in specific sub-fields and are struck by the fact that there are no standard databases of legislation and statutes within these areas of research. There is not, for example, a standard database of tariffs and tax laws. (This is currently underway in our project.)

Third, introduce multiple criteria for significance. Josh Clinton and John Lapinski consider cross-references among laws. One might also imagine other quantitative indicators, such as duration of laws, or qualitative indicators, such as expert assessments.

Finally, the significance of a law might be measured in terms of its immediate importance in a given Congress. How much time or attention of a Congress did a given topic or act consume? By most accounts, the National Energy Act of 1977 was, when it finally passed, a watered down and ineffective piece of legislation, and the Health Security Act of 1993 fell to an ignominious death. But these two laws preoccupied their legislatures, and would have amounted to major changes in the nation's energy and health policy had they passed in their original form. Failing to pass these important laws was also an important act of Congress, reflected in the massive amount of time spent debating these bills.[13] Looking at Congressional time might also reveal the import of other activities, especially investigations and ethics proceedings.

There are many ways to tell the narrative of Congress, many ways to express what Congress has accomplished. Just as there is probably not one act that

---

[13] This approach might also produce some odd results. For example, by far the most extensively debated act in the First Congress was the Tonnage Act and it received the most pages of attention in the first session of the First Congress – more than the Judiciary Act or Hamilton's Tariff.

should be singled out as most important, there is not one way to read the history of Congress. Rather, there are many variations on how we research and teach Congress, and how we marry these two activities. And every variation in reading the history of Congress reveals new lessons about American politics.

APPENDIX

TABLE 10A.1 *Party Control, Significant Legislation, and Total Legislation by Congress*

Congress	Pres. Party	Sen. Majority	House Majority	Sig. Acts	Tot. Public Acts
1	Pro-Admin	Pro-Admin	Pro-Admin	16	94
2	Pro-Admin	Pro-Admin	Pro-Admin	17	64
3	Pro-Admin	Pro-Admin	Anti-Admin	4	94
4	Federalist	Federalist	Dem. Rep.	2	72
5	Federalist	Federalist	Federalist	9	135
6	Federalist	Federalist	Federalist	3	94
7	Dem. Rep.	Dem. Rep.	Dem. Rep.	10	78
8	Dem. Rep.	Dem. Rep.	Dem. Rep.	5	90
9	Dem. Rep.	Dem. Rep.	Dem. Rep.	5	88
10	Dem. Rep.	Dem. Rep.	Dem. Rep.	3	87
11	Dem. Rep.	Dem. Rep.	Dem. Rep.	1	91
12	Dem. Rep.	Dem. Rep.	Dem. Rep.	2	163
13	Dem. Rep.	Dem. Rep.	Dem. Rep.	1	167
14	Dem. Rep.	Dem. Rep.	Dem. Rep.	3	163
15	Dem. Rep.	Dem. Rep.	Dem. Rep.	6	136
16	Dem. Rep.	Dem. Rep.	Dem. Rep.	5	109
17	Dem. Rep.	Dem. Rep.	Dem. Rep.	15	130
18	Dem. Rep.	Dem. Rep.	Dem. Rep.	14	137
19	Dem. Rep.	Democrat	Nat. Rep.	8	147
20	Dem. Rep.	Democrat	Democrat	4	126
21	Democrat	Democrat	Democrat	12	143
22	Democrat	Democrat	Democrat	4	175
23	Democrat	Nat. Rep.	Democrat	3	121
24	Democrat	Democrat	Democrat	4	130
25	Democrat	Democrat	Democrat	1	138
26	Democrat	Democrat	Democrat	0	50
27	Whig	Whig	Whig	7	178
28	Whig	Whig	Democrat	5	115
29	Democrat	Democrat	Democrat	7	117
30	Democrat	Democrat	Whig	2	142
31	Whig	Democrat	Democrat	6	88
32	Whig	Democrat	Democrat	7	113
33	Democrat	Democrat	Democrat	10	161
34	Democrat	Democrat	Republican	7	127

TABLE 10A.1 *(cont.)*

Congress	Pres. Party	Sen. Majority	House Majority	Sig. Acts	Tot. Public Acts
35	Democrat	Democrat	Democrat	8	100
36	Democrat	Democrat	Republican	16	131
37	Republican	Republican	Republican	8	335
38	Republican	Republican	Republican	1	318
39	Democrat	Republican	Republican	4	306
40	Democrat	Republican	Republican	6	226
41	Republican	Republican	Republican	2	313
42	Republican	Republican	Republican	10	515
43	Republican	Republican	Republican	6	392
44	Republican	Republican	Democrat	2	251
45	Republican	Republican	Democrat	5	255
46	Republican	Democrat	Democrat	0	288
47	Republican	Republican	Republican	7	330
48	Republican	Republican	Democrat	4	219
49	Democrat	Republican	Democrat	7	367
50	Democrat	Republican	Democrat	3	508
51	Republican	Republican	Republican	14	531
52	Republican	Republican	Democrat	6	347
53	Democrat	Democrat	Democrat	9	374
54	Democrat	Republican	Republican	8	356
55	Republican	Republican	Republican	10	449
56	Republican	Republican	Republican	9	383
57	Republican	Republican	Republican	10	423
58	Republican	Republican	Republican	1	502
59	Republican	Republican	Republican	4	692
60	Republican	Republican	Republican	8	350
61	Republican	Republican	Republican	7	526
62	Republican	Republican	Democrat	3	457
63	Democrat	Democrat	Democrat	5	342
64	Democrat	Democrat	Democrat	7	400
65	Democrat	Democrat	Republican	15	349
66	Democrat	Republican	Republican	2	401
67	Republican	Republican	Republican	6	549
68	Republican	Republican	Republican	8	632
69	Republican	Republican	Republican	2	808
70	Republican	Republican	Republican	3	1037
71	Republican	Republican	Republican	3	869
72	Republican	Republican	Democrat	6	442
73	Democrat	Democrat	Democrat	22	486
74	Democrat	Democrat	Democrat	18	851
75	Democrat	Democrat	Democrat	14	788
76	Democrat	Democrat	Democrat	7	894
77	Democrat	Democrat	Democrat	5	850

TABLE 10A.1 *(cont.)*

Congress	Pres. Party	Sen. Majority	House Majority	Sig. Acts	Tot. Public Acts
78	Democrat	Democrat	Democrat	5	568
79	Democrat	Democrat	Democrat	15	734
80	Democrat	Republican	Republican	8	905
81	Democrat	Democrat	Democrat	9	921
82	Democrat	Democrat	Democrat	6	594
83	Republican	Republican	Republican	19	781
84	Republican	Democrat	Democrat	7	1028
85	Republican	Democrat	Democrat	12	1009
86	Republican	Democrat	Democrat	7	800
87	Democrat	Democrat	Democrat	40	885
88	Democrat	Democrat	Democrat	30	666
89	Democrat	Democrat	Democrat	38	810
90	Democrat	Democrat	Democrat	26	640
91	Republican	Democrat	Democrat	23	695
92	Republican	Democrat	Democrat	16	607
93	Republican	Democrat	Democrat	18	649
94	Republican	Democrat	Democrat	13	588
95	Democrat	Democrat	Democrat	23	634
96	Democrat	Democrat	Democrat	20	613
97	Republican	Republican	Democrat	4	473
98	Republican	Republican	Democrat	15	623
99	Republican	Republican	Democrat	18	664
100	Republican	Democrat	Democrat	22	713
101	Republican	Democrat	Democrat	9	650
102	Republican	Democrat	Democrat	15	590
103	Democrat	Democrat	Democrat	14	465
104	Democrat	Republican	Republican	15	333
105	Democrat	Republican	Republican	11	394
106	Democrat	Republican	Republican	11	580
107	Republican	Republican	Republican	15	377
108	Republican	Republican	Republican	16	498
109	Republican	Republican	Republican	12	482
110	Republican	Democrat	Democrat	8	460
111	Democrat	Democrat	Democrat	10	383

TABLE 10A.2 *Categories of Significant Legislation*

(Totals exceed 1,040 as many bills are assigned to multiple categories.)

Category	Sig. Acts	Category	Sig. Acts
Administration	32	Housing	12
Agriculture	43	Immigration	23
Appointment	5	Impeachment	2
Appropriation	4	Indian	12
Aviation	5	Infrastructure	37
Banking	12	Judiciary	27
Budget	7	Labor	34
Civil Rights	26	Land	37
Commerce	67	Military	89
Communication	4	Private Law	1
Constitutional Amendment	29	Public Law	12
Crime	3	Regulation	25
Currency	11	Rules	29
Economy	74	Security	24
Education	28	Slavery	19
Election	19	State Territory	58
Energy	17	Tariff	27
Environment	13	Tax Revenue	38
Executive	11	Trade	41
Finance	29	Transportation	24
Firearms	6	Treaties	77
Foreign Relations	78	Veterans	7
Health	32	Welfare	37

REFERENCES

Aldrich, John H. and Richard G. Niemi. 1996. "The Sixth American Party System: Electoral Change, 1952–1992," in Stephen Craig, ed. *Broken Contract? Changing Relationships between Americans and Their Government.* Boulder, CO: Westview Press.

Aldrich, John H. and Ruth W. Grant. 1993. "The Anti-Federalists, the First Congress, and the First Parties." *Journal of Politics* 55(2): 295–326.

Brady, David W. and Craig Volden. 1998. *Revolving Gridlock: Politics and Policy from Carter to Clinton.* Boulder, CO: Westview Press.

Castel, Albert and Scott L. Gibson. 1975. *The Yeas and the Nays: Key Congressional Decisions, 1774–1945.* Kalamazoo, MI: New Issues Press.

Clinton, Joshua and John Lapinski. 2006. "Measuring Legislative Accomplishment, 1874–1994." *American Journal of Political Science* 50(1): 232–249.

Galloway, George B. and Sidney Wise. 1976. *History of the House of Representatives.* New York: Crowell.

Howell, William, Scott Adler, Charles Cameron, and Charles Reimann. 2000. "Divided Government and the Legislative Productivity of Congress, 1945–1994." *Legislative Studies Quarterly* XXV(2): 285–312.

Josephy, Alvin M. 1975. *The American Heritage History of the Congress of the United States*. New York: American Heritage.

Krehbiel, Keith. 1998. *Pivotal Politics: A Theory of U.S. Lawmaking*. Chicago: University of Chicago Press.

Mann, Thomas E. and Norman J. Ornstein. 2012. *It's Even Worse than It Looks: How the American Constitutional System Collided with the New Politics of Extremism*. New York: Basic Books.

Mayhew, David R. 2000. *America's Congress: Actions in the Public Sphere, James Madison through Newt Gingrich*. New Haven: Yale University Press.

  1991. *Divided We Govern*. New Haven: Yale University Press.

  1974. *Congress: The Electoral Connection*. New Haven: Yale University Press.

Skocpol, Theda. 1993. "America's First Social Security System: The Expansion of Benefits for Civil War Veterans." *Political Science Quarterly* 108: 85–116.

  1995. *Protecting Soldiers and Mothers: The Political Origins of Social Policy in the United States*. Cambridge, MA: Harvard University Press.

Skowronek, Stephen. 1982. *Building a New American State: The Expansion of National Administrative Capacities, 1877–1920*. Cambridge: Cambridge University Press.

11

Can Congress Do Policy Analysis?

The Politics of Problem Solving on Capitol Hill

Eric M. Patashnik and Justin Peck

Each year, scores of well-trained graduates of the nation's public policy schools go to Capitol Hill. Many take jobs with congressional committees or legislative support agencies such as the General Accountability Office, the Congressional Research Service, and the Congressional Budget Office. They seek to punch a ticket and build their resumes, but many also believe that policy analysis will improve legislative outcomes. Is their faith justified? Does policy analysis happen in Congress, or is it the exclusive province of executive agencies and think tanks? If Congress does engage in policy analysis, can it do so successfully?

The title of Charles O. Jones's penetrating 1976 essay expresses the predominant view among political scientists: "Why Congress Can't Do Policy Analysis (or words to that effect)." Congress is not an institution "well-structured to conduct policy analysis," Jones argues, because it is too political a body to bring systematic, unbiased evidence to bear on policy decisions (1976, 253). Congress is a *representative* assembly, not a research bureau. Its internal organization is inconsistent with analytical perceptions and definitions of policy issues (Polsby 1969). Members of Congress are parochial; geographical representation and single-member districts compel lawmakers to respond to local pressures, and undermine the incentive to legislate in the national interest (but see Lee 2005). Congress also caters to the demands of interest groups, and regularly makes economic decisions that policy analysts find indefensible on efficiency grounds (VanDoren 1989). Unsurprisingly, empirical studies on the instrumental use of policy analysis within Congress have uniformly found that policy analysis reports have little

We thank Richard Bensel, John Ellwood, Alan Gerber, Beryl Radin, Jesse Rothstein, Eric Schickler, Ray Scheppach, Colleen Shogan, Stephen Skowronek, and Craig Volden for helpful comments. All errors of fact or interpretation are our own.

independent impact on legislative behavior and decision making (Shulock 1999; Whiteman 1985).

Yet negative assessments of Congress's capacity for policy analysis cut much too deeply. First, they set unrealistic performance standards for Congress that ignore the constraints of democracy, the complex political context in which Congress operates, and the large variety of ways (both direct and indirect) that policy analysis can contribute to problem solving. Many critics evaluate Congress's performance against the benchmark of a hyper-rational, apolitical model of policy analysis that does not reflect how policy analysis is taught in public policy schools or, for that matter, practiced in executive agencies (Meltsner 1976). While policy analysis does involve intellectual work and a reasoned search for solutions, it is also a "social and political activity" (Bardach 2009, xv). The purpose of policy analysis is neither to generate knowledge for the academic disciplines nor to prescribe government decisions, but rather to provide targeted advice to particular organizational clients, which invariably have projects and agendas (Weimer and Vining 1999).[1]

Second, many who assess Congress's performance fail to recognize that Congress is a "they," not an "it" (Shepsle 1992) and that policy analysis in practice is better understood as a collective institutional process rather than as an activity engaged in by a handful of people who see the publication of a report as their primary goal. As a collective process, different congressional actors – including committee staffs, personal staffs, individual members, and congressional party organizations – may contribute pieces at different times during the legislative process. Policy analysis seeks to inform congressional action at different stages of the legislative process, from issue development to oversight of the bureaucracy to program evaluation. Third, many negative assessments overreach by evaluating Congress's performance in a constitutional vacuum, as though Congress is not just one of three national governing institutions (see Mayhew 2009). Congress is the country's *representative* body, and its contributions to problem solving should be viewed in conjunction with what is gained from the larger institutional system of which it is a part.

The most common error that scholars make in assessing Congress's performance as a policy analyst is to construe policy analysis as a simple matter of knowledge acquisition and information processing. In fact, policy analysis is a complex, iterative process comprised of multiple steps or tasks, including: defining problems, assembling evidence, constructing alternatives, selecting criteria, projecting outcomes, confronting trade offs, making decisions, and telling causal stories to an audience (Bardach 2009). No extant study analyzes congressional performance at the task level, even though some of the steps of

---

[1] We thus distinguish between client-based policy analysis and policy research. On the similarities and differences between these activities, see Weimer and Vining (1999).

policy analysis are clearly more compatible with legislative incentives and structures than others. That is the purpose of the present essay.

The shortcomings we have identified within scholarly treatments of congressional policy analysis often lead observers to overlook the important links between analysis and Congress's institutional responsibilities. Endowed as they are with the constitutional authority to craft legislation relevant to the full range of domestic and global issues, which are growing ever more complex, members of Congress are at a significant disadvantage if they lack the information necessary to understand the consequences of their decisions. Similarly, scholars risk misjudging the capacity of members to address public problems if they fail to understand the strengths and weakness of Congress's capabilities as an analyst. In short, while Section I of the Constitution makes no mention of policy analysis, it is today an unavoidable component of the "legislative powers" (which is not to say that Congress always uses policy analysis effectively).

Policy analysis can also help Congress to satisfy its oversight responsibilities. The large and densely populated administrative apparatus affords modern presidents with significant policy-making powers. Congress, in turn, is frequently charged with ensuring that bureaucrats are efficiently and effectively working to fulfill policy goals. Without the information provided by policy analysis, Congress would find it difficult to engage in oversight. Generally speaking, members are not policy experts. The information provided by analysis, however, allows them to question, oversee, and redirect bureaucrats who have significant "informational" advantages in specific areas of policy. Without analysis, oversight would be a completely empty or symbolic enterprise – which is not to deny that some committee hearings on bureaucratic performance are largely exercises in congressional blame-casting (Derthick 1990).

There is no perfect methodology for assessing how well or poorly Congress carries out the multiple tasks of policy analysis. Our strategy is to draw upon three different sources of information to reach conclusions about the institution's central tendencies. The most extensive data source we use is a survey that we conducted in April 2013 of more than 150 Washington area policy analysis professionals who work for universities, think tanks and research organizations, and government agencies. The survey aims to probe a variety of ways and openings through which policy analysis can flow into the legislative process as an input, including during the predeliberation stage. (The survey design is described in the following.)

There are both strengths and limitations to relying upon the perspective of this elite sample to evaluate Congress. One major advantage of the survey is that it relies upon the opinions of experts who are highly knowledgeable about the concepts, skills, and methodologies of policy analysis, such as cost–benefit analysis. These are technical matters about which even savvy journalists, congressional staff members, and political observers may be poorly informed. Our survey sample is large enough to capture the impressions of the policy analysis expert community while avoiding placing too much weight upon the views of a few individuals. Another advantage is that professional policy analysts are a tough-minded group. To the extent that such experts perceive Congress' performance as not uniformly negative, it is noteworthy.

This survey also comes with some important limitations, however. First, professional policy analysts (like everyone) have biases. As noted in the following, approximately 75 percent of our survey respondents profess a liberal bias of one sort or another. While we find no evidence that the ideology of survey respondents correlates with their beliefs about congressional performance, it is important to recognize that the political orientation of our sample is unrepresentative of the American public. Another limitation is that the survey focuses on questions about Congress's overall performance. As a result, the survey results lack the detail and texture of in-depth interviews. We work to overcome this limitation by supplementing our survey findings with the perspectives of current and former congressional policy analysts. In addition to conducting several individual interviews, we held a confidential focus group in Washington, D.C., on November 18, 2013, with six senior policy analysts who work for the three key congressional support agencies – the Congressional Budget Office, the Congressional Research Service, and the General Accountability Office. All the participants have had extensive experience advising Congress across a range of policy areas including budget, health care, and defense. As professional analysts employed by the Congress, they can be expected to possess intimate knowledge of how Congress operates and a more sympathetic view of the institution's performance.

Finally, we draw upon empirical and theoretical insights from the vast political science literature on Congress, including both classic works on the institution and more focused studies that assess Congress's use of policy analysis on the basis of congressional staff interviews. Taken together, these three data sources give us confidence that we can draw inferences about what policy analysis tasks Congress struggles to perform and what tasks it handles more adroitly. While we do not set out to "save" Congress's reputation, our analysis provides a more balanced and fine-grained view of Congress's strengths and limitations as a problem-solving institution.

The paper proceeds as follows. The first section defines policy analysis and establishes standards for evaluating Congress's performance. The second section describes the survey methodology (the survey text is available from the authors). The third section – comprising the core of the paper – evaluates how well Congress performs each of the eight major tasks of policy analysis (Bardach 2009) drawing on all three data sources mentioned earlier. The concluding section summarizes our main findings and offers some more speculative comments about how secular trends including partisan polarization, the widening of the policy agenda, and the growing complexity of government have interacted with Congress's policy analytic strengths and weaknesses to affect institutional performance.

WHAT IS POLICY ANALYSIS? RATIONAL, INTERPRETATIVE, AND HYBRID MODELS

What is policy analysis? Can Congress do it? What are the standards against which Congress's performance should be assessed?[2]

The traditional model of policy analysis defines it as an objective, scientific endeavor in which decision makers set goals and maximize social welfare by using analytical methods and rigorous empirical research to identify the best means to address societal problems (see, e.g., Stokey and Zeckhauser 1978). There are many reasons that the "rational" model of policy analysis is apt to fail on Capitol Hill. Members are occupied with fundraising and constituent service. They lack the time to think deeply about issues, and instead rely on cues and heuristics to "muddle through" (Lindblom 1959; Schuck 2014). Even more fundamentally, members' main objective is reelection, and political payoffs come from taking pleasing positions and delivering perceptible benefits to constituents, not from crafting efficient policy solutions (Mayhew 1974; but see Arnold 1990). As they pursue their political goals, few legislators bother to master the concepts and tools of policy analysis. The typical member finds scientific information "hard to assimilate or relate to policy questions" (Bimber 1991, 601). Legislative structures designed to facilitate reelection – including overlapping committee jurisdictions, the oral tradition, and the reliance on compromise and logrolling – also inhibit the use of analysis (Weiss 1989).

Yet Congress is not impervious to policy analysis. As Allen Schick wrote in 1976, "The argument that Congress will not become a major user of analysis is as untenable as the position that a new analytic era is just over the horizon" (234–236; see also Weiss 1989; Whiteman 1985). Members of Congress can benefit from policy analysis in at least three ways. First, information about problems and solutions helps lawmakers cope with the growing scope and complexity of government and the increasing rate of technological change. Over the decades, Congress has bolstered the informational resources at its disposal as well as its internal capacity for generating and using expertise, including funding professional committee staffs and establishing congressional support agencies (Price 1971; Schickler 2001; Shepsle 1988; Sundquist 1981; Rieselbach 1994). During the 1970s, for example, Congress established the Congressional Budget Office (CBO), the Congressional Research Service (CRS), and the Office of Technology Assessment (OTA). Second, policy analysis can help members reduce political uncertainty (Arnold 1990; Krehbiel 1991). All else being equal, members would prefer to select policies whose effects are known in advance because this would allow them to minimize the potential for surprise or embarrassment. Even if members are not interested in making "good" public policy, the capacity to anticipate allows members to "mak[e] the most of credit-claiming"

---

[2] On the technical side of policy analysis, see Vining and Weimer (2010). For an insightful review of the evolution of the profession of policy analysis, see Radin (2000).

opportunities and promote their reelection chances (Krehbiel 1991, 62). Finally, policy analysis can help Congress maintain its institutional power in the separation of powers system. The rise of the administrative presidency was a major factor in prompting Congress to beef up its analytical capacity. During the 1940s and 1950s, agencies such as the Bureau of the Budget provided trusted analysis to both branches. When the presidential branch "captured" these agencies during the Johnson and Nixon administrations, Congress was threatened. Congress responded by creating legislative support agencies to maintain its relative standing in the constitutional order (Moe 1985). While reforms to boost Congress's information-processing capacity are rare (Quirk and Binder 2005), they clearly suggest unwillingness on the part of members to entirely offload the institution's policy analysis responsibilities to the executive.

An alternative, "interpretive" model of policy analysis is more modest in its expectations of Congress – and more nakedly political. According to Nancy Shulock, policy analysis is not a problem-solving, scientific activity, but rather an "instrument of democratic process" that is used "(a) as language for framing political discourse; (b) as legitimate rationalization for legislative action where prospective rationality is inhibited by 'garbage can' decision environments; and (c) as a symbol of legitimate decision processes that can increase support for governance processes in a society that values rationality" (Shulock 1999, 229; see also Stone 2001). Don't be fooled by appearances, Shulock implies. Members of Congress may *look* like they are carefully weighing options and projecting consequences, but they are just using the positivist forms of policy analysis to create a favorable public impression. While there is no doubt that members of Congress want to look good in the eyes of observers, this view is too cynical. The massive investment in Congress's analytical capacity over the past half-century is far more than institutional window dressing.

Ultimately, the rational and interpretive models are best understood as ideal types. Neither fully captures the complexity of the roles that policy analysts play (or seek to play) in the United States (Radin 2000). Whereas the rational model asks too much of Congress by denying the legitimacy of power and persuasion in policy making, the interpretive model asks too little of the institution by rejecting both the normative, problem-solving focus and the scientific foundation of policy analysis. The challenge is to define policy analysis in a way that reconciles the power of ideas with a sober appraisal of the messy realities of legislative politics.

In our view, policy analysis is best understood as an *amalgam* of intelligence and pragmatic action. Policy analysts seek to develop options that, if adopted, will mitigate problems that people are experiencing in their daily lives. In a democracy, the audience for policy analysis includes "diverse subgroups of politically attuned supporters and opponents of the analyst's work" (Bardach 2009, xv). As such, policy analysis stands between pure planning, in which apolitical, synoptic rationality guides governance, and raw politics, in which the preferences of the powerful dictate policy prescriptions. Aaron Wildavsky developed this more balanced, hybrid model in his classic book *Speaking Truth to Power: The Art and Craft of Policy Analysis*:

> If analysis were purely intellectual, analysts would be everything, or if analysis were purely interactive, analysts would be nothing. Are we faced, then, with a choice between mind without matter or force without foresight? No. Our task is to develop a hybrid, called policy analysis, which uses intellect to help guide rather than replace social interaction. (Wildavsky 1989, 124)

Just as the effort to separate politics and administration (Wilson 1887) collapses in skirmishes over policy implementation, so the attempt to quarantine the intellectual work of policy analysis from the politics of democracy crumbles when actors frame problems and advocate solutions. Ideas about how to recast government are the currency of policy analysis, but these ideas are accepted or rejected by actors who have particular projects or interests. Wildavsky wrote that policy analysis has many faces: among other things, it is *descriptive* (in seeking to explain how a difficulty has come about); *selective* (because oriented to particular people and organizations); *objective* (in aiming to get people to agree on the consequences of options); and *argumentative* (in recognizing that the capacity to convince is essential for political support) (Wildavsky 1979). Assessments of political feasibility – Who supports an idea? What are the obstacles to change? How might these obstacles be overcome? – are integral to policy analysis. The aim of such assessments is not to claim that the feasible is desirable, but rather to help make the "desirable do-able" (Wildavsky 1989, 126).

Viewed in this light, the question is not only whether and under what conditions Congress heeds the scientific advice offered by economists (Derthick and Quirk 1985; Schick 1976), but also what Congress contributes to the multifaceted task of problem solving. David Mayhew adopts a similar position:

> To contribute effectively to societal problem solving, [members of Congress] need to be able to help define as "problems" the often inchoate fancies, preferences or demands of society or its elite sectors. The members need to make such definitions widely known and accepted. They need to frame these problems in ordinary, common sense so as to bring the public along, yet also frame them in a way that adapts to the instrumental-rationality needs of political executives and bureaucrats. They need to merchandise causal stories to a wide audience.... Beyond this, they need to probe evidence reasonably hardheadedly in a search for "solutions".... It is a tall order, but as a descriptor of congressional activity it does not refer to a null set. (Mayhew 2006, 223)

We use this hybrid model as a more realistic baseline against which to evaluate congressional performance.

SURVEY OF PUBLIC POLICY EXPERTS

We conducted an Internet-based survey of members of the Association for Public Policy Analysis and Management (APPAM), a leading professional association. An invitation to participate in the survey was sent to APPAM members who had a mailing address in the greater Washington, D.C., area (D.C., Maryland, or Virginia).[3] In total, approximately 450 people were contacted. The overall response rate was 36 percent (N=162). The sample included policy analysts from a range of employment backgrounds: 42 percent work in universities or colleges, 36 percent work in think tanks or research organizations, 14 percent work in the federal executive branch, 8 percent work in the federal legislative branch, 8 percent work in state or local government, 8 percent work for government contractors, 4 percent work for nonprofit service providers, and 2 percent work for foundations or advocacy organizations. The sample is 58 percent male. Sixty percent of the respondents have a doctorate as their highest degree, and 38 percent have a master's or professional degree. Forty-seven percent earned their highest degree in public policy, 21 percent in economics, 14 percent in public administration, 8 percent in political science, and the rest in other fields. The sample is also skewed ideologically to the left. On a 7-point scale of political views, 8 percent identified as extremely liberal, 43 percent as liberal, 24 percent as slightly liberal, 15 percent as middle of the road, 4 percent as slightly conservative, 2 percent as conservative, and 0 percent as extremely conservative. Most respondents also report having had direct interactions with members of Congress or congressional staff. Only 20 percent reported never interacting directly with members of Congress or congressional staff. Thirty percent said they had such interactions at least several times a year, 19 percent once a year, and 30 percent on occasion but less than once a year.

While the respondents have no lack of criticisms of the institution's performance, they are not reflexively "anti-Congress." The respondents accept that Congress has a major role to play in national policy making. Only 13 percent said that important domestic policy decisions should be made mostly by the president with some input from Congress. Fifty-nine percent said they thought such decisions should be made by the Congress and the president equally, and 26 percent said such decisions should be made mostly by the Congress with some input from the president.[4]

CONGRESS AND POLICY ANALYSIS TASKS

Most studies of Congress and policy analysis have examined whether Congress produces and consumes policy-analytic knowledge (Weiss 1989; Whiteman 1985). This is an essential question, but it is posed at too high a level of abstraction. Policy analysis is a multistep activity combining intelligence and interaction. To separate the pieces of this hybrid model, we use Bardach's well-

---

[3] APPAM and University of Virginia employees were excluded from the survey invitation list.

[4] Respondents had a different view when it comes to important foreign policy decisions. A majority (54 percent) said that such decisions should be made mostly by the president, with some input from the Congress.

known conceptual framework (Bardach 2009). Bardach argues that policy analysis consists of eight tasks: (1) defining problems, (2) assembling evidence, (3) constructing alternatives, (4) selecting criteria, (5) projecting outcomes, (6) confronting trade-offs, (7) making decisions, and (8) telling causal stories to an audience. (We treat the tasks as discrete, even though in practice they overlap.) Congress has potential roles to play at each step. How well does Congress perform them?

Defining Problems

The first step of policy analysis is to define the problem. On the surface, Congress looks like a premier problem definer. Countless bills contain proc-lamations along the lines of "Whereas X is occurring...," where X represents some allegedly serious problem that warrants a legislative solution. Yet, while such bold assertions may serve the electoral goals of members, they are often little more than "issue rhetoric," that is, too imprecise or emotion-laden to catalyze *pragmatic* problem solving. Instead, to serve as the foundation for policy analysis, a problem must be defined in a way that is "analytically manageable and that makes sense in light of the political and institutional means available for mitigating it" (Bardach 2009, 4).

Survey respondents gave Congress dismal marks as a problem definer. Eighty-one percent of respondents agreed or strongly agreed that Congress is more concerned with "looking good in the eyes of voters than with actually solving problems." Only 3 percent believed that Congress has done a good or better job over the last ten years in "defining problems in ways that are logical and analytically manageable," and 56 percent rate Congress' performance as "poor."[5] What accounts for Congress's poor performance on this step?

Defining problems is a challenging task for a legislature. It requires Congress to bring order to the conflicting demands of voters, experts, and interest groups. It also requires a clear-eyed diagnosis of the source of the difficulties. Even when there is a consensus on the existence of a problem, there may be disagree-ment about its causes. For example, are the disability rolls expanding because of rising clientele needs or because more people are gaming the system? Are health care costs high because providers charge too much or because consumers do not have enough "skin in the game"? Is unemployment a structural or cyclical problem? Experts themselves may disagree on the answers to these questions; it may be too much to expect a representative assembly to resolve them.

On the basis of interviews with eighty-three staff of congressional commit-tees and congressional support agencies during the 1980s, Weiss found that

---

[5] While the N is very small, the ten self-identified Republicans/lean Republican respondents who answered this question had similar assessments to the overall sample. Six of ten rated Congress's problem defining performance as poor, and four as fair.

committee staff reported using analysis primarily to certify positions and influence the priority of proposals on the agenda, but tended not to use analysis to reconceptualize problems (Weiss 1989).[6] Consistent with the findings of Weiss's earlier study, the experts we surveyed overwhelmingly agreed that members use evidence to fortify positions they already hold.[7] Eighty-four percent of respondents said they believe that congressional leaders usually know how they wish to address national problems, and that the leaders use the recommendations of policy experts to add legitimacy to positions they would have taken anyway. Only 4 percent agreed with the statement that congressional leaders often do not know the best way to address national problems, and look to policy experts for guidance on the most effective course of action. Of course, this raises the question of where members' views come from in the first place (Peterson 1995). Constituency opinion, party positions, and ideology are all potential sources of legislative preferences, but so too is the tenor of the times, to which policy analysis contributes. Policy analysis might still shape legislative problem definitions, but (as we discuss in the following) it may filter into Congress through more indirect channels at earlier stages of the legislative process (Weiss 1989).

Yet Congress does possess some institutional capacities as a problem definer, especially when its role is evaluated in the context of a separation of powers system. While Congress lacks the executive's ability to frame problems in analytically crisp ways, its openness to outside pressures and demands arguably makes a contribution to the American political system's capacity to address a changing menu of topics over time. About four in ten (37 percent) of experts surveyed rated Congress's performance in bringing attention to new issues as good or better.

Because developing effective problem definitions is challenging, many experts recommend an iterative process in which understandings of a problem are subject to revision and refinement (Bardach 2009). When confronting complex problems, trial-and-error learning is a defensible approach. By its nature, legislative coalition building is an iterative process in which bill sponsors often modify their initial assumptions in response to input from colleagues

---

[6] This is not to say that Congress never uses expertise to reconceptualize problems. As a staff member of the House Subcommittee on Elections in the late 1980s, Patashnik corresponded with political scientist Raymond Wolfinger about his empirical research on the causes of low voter turnout. Contrary to the widely held belief that low voter turnout reflected political alienation and mistrust in government, Wolfinger's research suggested that a more prosaic reason why some citizens did not vote was because they were residentially mobile and failed to update their voter registration information following a change of address. Wolfinger's research helped reframe the problem of low voter turnout among congressional staffers working on the issue, leading to the enactment of the National Voter Registration Act of 1993 (the "motor-voter" bill). See Wolfinger 1991.

[7] This is broadly consistent with Kingdon's (1997) finding that solutions may chase problems as the policy agenda is formed, rather than the other way around.

whose support they hope to win (Schick 1976). As one analyst we interviewed stated, "Making policy adjustments for political reasons that moves toward a second best solution is often the best way to proceed as it creates more ownership over the final bill. This can be critical as you often need to make technical corrections [after policy enactment]."

Indeed, the process of trial-and-error learning does not end when a bill becomes a law. As E. Scott Adler and John D. Wilkerson observe in their recent book *Congress and the Politics of Problem Solving*, there has been a significant rise in "temporary" legislation since World War II. While there are many explanations for this trend, including conflict between Congress and the executive, Adler and Wilkerson argue that the increasing reliance on short-term authorizations reflects Congress's desire to preserve the flexibility to update a preexisting policy in light of new information and changing conditions (Adler and Wilkerson 2012).

Yet congressional learning about problems takes place in a political context shaped by the policy feedback from past legislative activity (Pierson 1993). Whether short term or permanent, statutes carry the force of law, and laws generate reactions (stop! continue! do more!) among constituencies, to which lawmakers must respond. As government has grown, the policy "space" has become increasingly congested. It is rare today for Congress to legislate in an area not already populated by existing policy commitments (Patashnik 2008; Patashnik and Zelizer 2013). In the contemporary American state, legislators do not define new problems so much as cope with the consequences of earlier "solutions." Consider, for example, Congress's decision to end air traffic furloughs in 2013. That decision reflected Congress's effort to manage the political fallout from budget sequestration, which was itself a (temporary) resolution of the debt-ceiling crisis. In sum, as the complexity of government grows, law making increasingly turns in on itself. Legislators still respond to the demands of constituent groups, but those demands are mediated by the consequences of past decisions. As Wildavsky put it, "policy becomes more and more its own cause" (1989, 81).

Assembling Evidence

Evidence-based decisions cannot be made unless evidence is assembled. Data must be collected and then turned into information relevant to the policy questions at hand (Bardach 2009). Few members of Congress have the time or desire to keep up with the academic literature, let alone to conduct original research studies.

Yet Congress is "awash in policy information" (Baumgartner and Jones 2015, Bimber 1996, 1). Information is absorbed and packaged not only by congressional committees, but also by the staffs of 535 individual member offices. While many of these "congressional enterprises" are not inclined to tap into policy-analytic knowledge, others are highly active and engaged. Staff members at the core of "issue networks" devour policy reports and interact regularly with experts in academia and think tanks (Heclo 1972; Whiteman 1985). Among the most important sources of information for lawmakers are the congressional support agencies – the Congressional Research Service, the Congressional Budget Office, the General Accountability Office, and the Office of Technology Assessment (before its termination in 1994). While these agencies have suffered significant staff cuts since the 1970s (Drutman and Teles 2015), they continue to issue thousands of detailed reports each year and play a key role in gathering and summarizing evidence and conducing financial analysis for members. Through its analytic support agencies, Congress forges institutional and ideational connections to other sites of the vast U.S. policy analysis enterprise, including the academy, think tanks, and private research organizations such as Mathematica and MDRC.

The politics of legislative support agencies highlights the complex relationship between expertise and power in American democracy (Fisher 2011; Hird 2005). To ensure continuing political support, agencies must refrain from criticizing firmly held congressional positions, avoid catching members by surprise, and be attentive to Congress's prerogatives, including its goal of maintaining a balance of power with the executive (Bimber 1996). Members of Congress expect professional, nonpartisan guidance from the support agencies; they also insist upon responsiveness to their institutional interests. Support agencies that fail to satisfy the demands of members of Congress, their clients, may be denied the political sustenance required for their survival. In 1995, for example, the OTA was terminated, among other reasons, because Congress did not view assessments of technology as essential to maintaining a balance of power with the executive (Bimber 1996; Mucciaroni and Quirk 2006). Sometimes, support agencies such as the CRS and GAO are criticized when they do not follow a model of "neutral competence." Such criticism is unwarranted because *all* policy analysts must satisfy the needs of their organizational clients, and the legislative support agencies are no exception.[8] As one senior analyst who participated in the focus group stated, "I don't like that word [neutral] at all. I prefer the word 'objective.' Neutral implies that we don't make pronouncements or draw conclusions, but we do – all the time." In a separation of powers system, the requirement that the legislative support agencies be sensitive to Congress's institutional needs – and thus abandon any pretense of

---

[8] At times, experts who work for congressional support agencies face hard questions about how to balance responsibility to their clients and analytical integrity (see Fisher 2011). Having Congress as one's boss is certainly not easy, but policy analysts (no matter who their client is) struggle with such professional dilemmas all the time. "Analysts must expect … that their clients will be players in the game of politics – players who not only have their own personal conceptions of the good society but who almost always must acknowledge the often narrow interests of their constituencies if they hope to remain in the game" (Weimer and Vining 1999, 44).

"neutrality" toward basic constitutional values – is not a weakness but a strength (Fisher 2011).

While the congressional support agencies strive to be nonpartisan, partisan and ideological conflicts over the generation of information can arise when Congress decides whether to request an official government report from an agency. A reporting requirement on a subject of broad legislative interest might seem like a good government issue on which liberals and conservatives would generally agree. As Frances Lee points out, however, members are well aware that "information is a powerful weapon" (2009, 121). A study could favor one side or the other in a partisan debate. Hence congressional votes on information control tend to be either noncontroversial or highly contentious on partisan lines (Lee 2009).

The main way that members learn about policy issues is through interaction with interest groups, not from reading government reports. The conventional wisdom holds that lobbying distorts information-gathering (but see Hall and Deardorff 2006) because narrow special interests are more likely to possess the resources and incentives to convey information to legislators than organizations representing diffuse public interests (Wright 2003). If members simply listen to the advice they get from interest groups, the result may be bad policy. Kevin Esterling (2004) challenges this pessimistic conclusion about the policy consequences of interest group lobbying. Drawing on Gary Becker's model of interest group competition, Esterling argues that advocates of policies that evidence suggests will work well are more likely to invest scarce resources in lobbying efforts than are the groups that would be harmed by the adoption of these policies (Becker 1983; Esterling 2004). In sum, even if members are not motivated to promote good policies, they will do so as a by-product of servicing the organized. Esterling supports his counterintuitive claim through case studies of Congress's use of evidence in the adoption of socially efficient policies, such as the 1990 acid rain emissions trading program.

As Sarah Binder persuasively argues, however, law makers are interested in receiving information not only about the programmatic effects of policy solutions, but also about their *political* consequences, such as how support for proposals would affect a member's reelection chances (Rhodes, Binder, and Rockman 2006; see also Peterson 1995; Price 1991). There is no reason to think that the information emanating from the political environment will be unbiased or naturally lead members to support Pareto-improving reforms (Binder 2006). Members of Congress are often uninterested in learning information that challenges constituent views on salient issues and are reluctant to incorporate evidence that casts a negative light on programs that benefit well-organized groups. As one focus group participant told us, "Our analytical work has the most influence in micro, technical areas where there are no entrenched views." Members who represent districts with oil companies are unlikely to be interested in evidence about the inefficiency of oil subsidies. The problem of congressional indifference to evidence is arguably most severe when special interests are not geographically concentrated, because then there may be no countervailing constituency. For example, there is compelling evidence that U.S. physicians perform many unnecessary medical procedures, but Congress has been hesitant to use this information to strengthen the government's role in reviewing Medicare billings and reducing wasteful health care spending out of fear of antagonizing doctors, providers, and senior citizens across the country (Gerber and Patashnik 2006). Sometimes, clear evidence of a serious national problem exists – but Congress prefers to keep its collective head in the sand.

This mixed assessment of Congress's performance as an evidence assembler is reinforced by our survey results and interviews. Sixty-five percent of survey respondents said that Congress has done a poor job over the past ten years in making policy decisions on the basis of objective evidence. To make our inquiry more concrete, we asked survey respondents to reflect on the following scenario: What if a prestigious academic journal publishes a research study that shows that an existing federal transportation program is highly cost-ineffective, meaning that it would be possible to achieve the same transportation benefits at much lower cost, or to spend the same amount of money while generating much larger transportation benefits? We asked respondents how likely they thought it was that the chairs of the congressional committees with jurisdiction over the program would become aware of the study. About half of the experts (46 percent) were very or somewhat confident that committee chairs would become aware of the study. In a multivariate analysis, respondents who reported having been a legislator or served on a legislative staff were more confident that the committee chair would learn of the study, but the effect was not statistically significant in all models. (See Table 11A.4 in the Appendix to this chapter.)[9] Just 4 percent of experts were very or somewhat confident that Congress would makes a serious attempt to replace the transportation program with a more cost-effective approach, however. While we did not pose a follow-up question as to why respondents believed that Congress would fail to act on the findings of the study, we suspect the most likely answer is that the existing transportation program can be assumed to have vested interests, which Congress will be reluctant to upset.

In sum, the main information problem Congress faces is not the absence of evidence, but rather the failure of members to make good use of available information (see Mucciaroni and Quirk 2006). Indeed, only 6 percent of survey

---

[9] Of course, even if the committee chair does not learn of the study, it is possible that her staff would. During the 99th Congress (1985–1987), Whiteman surveyed congressional staff about their awareness of specific policy analysis reports. He found considerable variance, but in most issue areas over 80 percent of the staff members were aware of the relevant studies, and only one project showed less than 50 percent awareness. Interestingly, Whiteman found an inverse relationship between the perceived constituency interest in an issue and familiarity with policy analysis: on issues salient to the constituency, congressional offices tend to rely more heavily on constituent views and do not seek out other sources of information (Whiteman 1985, 162–163).

respondents said that lack of information is an extremely important reason for Congress's failure as a problem solving institution. As Figure 11.1 shows, experts were far more likely to name the following factors as extremely important reasons for Congress's failures to solve problems: partisan polarization (71 percent), lawmakers focused on their own reelections (55 percent), and interest group pressure (48 percent).

Constructing Alternatives

A creative aspect of policy analysis involves the identification of alternative ways to mitigate a problem. Putting multiple policy options on the table ensures that a leader's pet idea doesn't win the day without consideration of other possible solutions. How good is Congress at constructing policy alternatives, and where do members look for inspiration when they seek to develop ways to address an issue on the agenda?

Survey respondents provide a negative assessment of Congress's performance in constructing policy alternatives. Nearly half (47 percent) of the experts surveyed think Congress has done a poor job over the past ten years in developing new policy options for addressing national problems. Only slightly more than 10 percent think that Congress has done a good or mostly good job at this task.

Three developments may explain Congress's poor performance as an option constructor. First, modern presidents have taken on an active role as "legislator-in-chief," while Congress often assumes a reactive posture in which members respond to executive-initiated agenda items rather than develop a menu of their own. Indeed, as Cohen (2012) has demonstrated, the president's legislative policy agenda grew so much during the second half of the twentieth century that legislative activities came to occupy a central aspect of his political responsibilities. This expansion of the president's legislative responsibilities came at the expense of Congress. As Cohen argues, while Congress "might have been the center of legislative activity" through the Progressive era, presidents "became more central to the legislative process from the second half of the twentieth century onward" (109–110).

Second, committees appear to have lost power at the expense of parties over the past few decades. Policy alternatives need to be grounded in an understanding of the linkages between problems and solutions, and the mechanisms by which a particular government intervention can change the behavior of targeted constituencies. The committee process – investigations, bill mark-ups, the questioning of witnesses at hearings – give members the opportunity to develop such expertise. Andrew Taylor's (2013) recent study of congressional performance suggests, however, that intense partisanship and growing interest group pressure have undermined the quality of committee deliberations. Members come to committee hearings with "fixed preferences and a general unwillingness to change their minds" about how to approach issues (132).

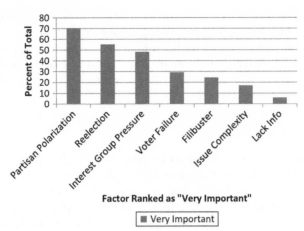

FIGURE 11.1 Experts believe lack of information is not the problem.

Third, the growth of "Big Government," and the generation of vested interest groups that lobby against reform, means that the most important alternative is often current policy. Ironically, members themselves may lack the requisite expertise even to understand the policy status quo. As one focus group participant stated, "Here's a common scenario. Congress passes a vague law, bureaucrats determine how the law is implemented and legislative branch research staff... have to 'explain it back' to Members and staff."

In terms of where Congress *does* look for new ideas about how to improve policy, most (68 percent) experts think that Congress never or almost never seeks to learn from the best practices and policy successes of other nations. Less than 1 percent of experts surveyed said that the typical member's support for a bill would be influenced a lot by whether other nations had adopted similar legislation. When members *do* look for best practices, they search much closer to home. Forty-eight percent of survey respondents said they believe that Congress seeks to learn from the policy successes of state governments some-times, and 21 percent believe that Congress seeks to learn from these state-level experiences fairly or very often. This suggests that successful policies may not only transfer across the states (Shipan and Volden 2012), but may also spread from one level of government to another. When such policy diffusion occurs, Congress may end up (indirectly) using information that entered the process at an earlier (pre-Congress) stage.

Welfare reform offers a good illustration of how research can shape congres-sional policy making without leaving a direct imprint on legislative behavior. A number of observers have argued that evaluation research on welfare-to-work experiments helped create the policy conditions that made the Family Support Act of 1988 possible (Haskins 1991). However, while many law-makers were clearly familiar with these experiments, research was not a decisive factor during either committee mark-up or floor debate (Haskins 1991). Kent Weaver, in his detailed study of the 1996 welfare reform law, similarly finds that lawmakers did not use research in a straightforward, technocratic fashion. Evaluation research did, however, improve the prospects for Republican policy ideas, including deterrence and devolution, by showing that welfare-to-work programs alone would be "inadequate to reduce welfare dependence and recidivism substantially" (Weaver 2000, 168).

In a related vein, policy analysis at times can shape the menu of congressional options through anticipated reactions. Congressional support agencies assist members with the development of policy options, but they may have even more influence by working with the executive branch to flag problems with proposals before they are presented to the Congress. One focus group participant told us about how a CBO analysis of problems with a ground combat vehicle that the Pentagon was developing led the Pentagon to significantly scale back the proposal before most members were even aware of it. "Our work sometimes gets into Congress through agencies or the press – we don't necessarily hand an idea to a member and get legislative traction," she said.

Selecting the Criteria

Policy analysis is a value-laden activity. The decision to support or oppose a policy expresses normative judgments about what constitutes good policy. A critical issue is what evaluative criteria Congress brings to bear when considering options to address a problem (see Table 11.1).

For many policy analysts, the most important evaluative criterion is *effectiveness* – whether an option actually helps solve the policy problem (Bardach 2009, 26). Back in the 1950s and 1960s, members such as Wilbur Mills took pride in the craft of legislation (Zelizer 1998). While symbolism has always been a staple of legislative life, Capitol Hill culture encouraged a seriousness of legislative purpose during this era. In today's Congress, however, it appears that partisanship, ideological rigidity, and the weakening of committees vis-à-vis parties have undermined instrumental activity (Mayhew 2006). Congressional debates are often vehicles for position-taking and member advertising, rather than opportunities to evaluate the effectiveness of proposed legislation. In their study of congressional deliberation, for example, Mucciaroni and Quirk (2006) found that members of Congress frequently make misleading empirical arguments about the consequences of proposals, and only abandon such unsupported claims when there is no longer a political gain from repeating them.[10]

---

[10] Of course, there are exceptions to the rule that Congress is less interested in policy effectiveness. Several analysts whom we interviewed independently pointed to the design of the 2009 economic stimulus legislation as a counterexample. Senators from natural resource states such as North

TABLE 11.1 *Congress and Evaluative Criteria*

Criterion	Key Findings from Literature Review and Survey
Effectiveness	Outside of particularistic programs, MCs rewarded for positions, not effects (Mayhew 1974); instrumental rationality waning (Mayhew 2006)
Economic Efficiency	Congress frequently ignores economic efficiency (VanDoren 1989)
Robustness/Ease of Implementation	MCs not receptive to arguments that something they want to do is not administratively feasible (Derthick 1990)
Fairness	MCs favorite claims appeal to "fair treatment" (Mucciaroni and Quirk 2006)
Budgetary Cost	In multivariate analysis, respondents who had been a legislative staff member were more likely to say that cost considerations would affect congressional support for a bill ($p < .01$).
Political Acceptability	Congress is responsive to public opinion (survey) and seeks to incorporate popular understandings into policy design (Mayhew 1974)

Congress also gives little weight to *economic efficiency*.[11] The usual way that analysts assess efficiency is through cost-benefit (or cost-effectiveness) studies. A majority (54 percent) of survey respondents said that cost–benefit and cost-effectiveness analysis have "only a little" influence on congressional decision making. Twenty-nine percent said these methods have a moderate amount of influence. In multivariate analysis, we found that respondents who reported a high frequency of interactions with members of Congress or congressional staff were *less* likely to believe that cost–benefit studies have a significant impact on Congress ($p < .05$; see Table 10A.3 in the Appendix).[12]

Dakota that were suffering less from the Great Recession were willing to embrace a Medicaid formula that targeted funds at hardest hit states in an effort to blunt the procyclical budget cuts of the states and boost the national recovery, even though this meant that their states would be losers under the formula. But it is difficult to maintain a congressional focus on effectiveness outside national crises.

[11] The literature has identified many factors that may cause government to pay little attention to economic efficiency, including: reelection incentives, geographically based constituencies, the influence of interest groups, electoral cycles, and the tendency of voters to treat losses and gains asymmetrically (Weimer and Vining 2010).

[12] When members of Congress *do* actively push for greater use of cost–benefit analysis, they often do so in a selective way, to erect procedural barriers against policies disfavored on ideological or partisan grounds. For example, House Republicans who wanted to neuter financial reform proposed that the Security and Exchange Commission conduct cost–benefit studies of its rule makings (Haberkorn 2013). It should be emphasized that cost–benefit analyses conducted by the executive branch may leave a significant imprint on congressional decision making. See Hird (1991).

This is not to suggest that Congress *prefers* inefficient policies, or that there are no conditions under which Congress will vote for Pareto-improving policies (see Arnold 1990). But most members of Congress tend not to value efficiency as an end in itself.

Congress also gives scant attention to what Bardach (2009) calls *robustness*, or the capacity of policies to survive the implementation process. As Wellman and Derthick observe, members of Congress are focused on achieving their political goals and are "not receptive to objections that something they want to do is not administratively feasible" (1990, 92). Indeed, only 16 percent of survey respondents said that over the past ten years, Congress has done a good job passing bills that can be implemented by the bureaucracy without excessive difficulty.

While Congress tends to downplay effectiveness, efficiency and administrative feasibility, it often focuses on *fairness*. Based on their review of legislative debates over welfare reform, repeal of the estate tax, and telecommunications deregulation, for example, Mucciaroni and Quirk argue that "legislators' favorite claims appeal to matters of personal tragedy, struggle or fair treatment, and evoke emotions like envy, resentment and empathy" (2006, 157). Members typically devote far more time to discussing the *distributional* consequences of proposals, and whether the outcomes they would produce accord with citizens' views of moral deservingness, than to the proposals' impacts on allocational efficiency (VanDoren 1989). As Schick notes, "[p]ropelled by pervasive political impulses of 'Who gets what,' Congress seems more concerned about the distributive effects of public policies than about *pro bono publico* benefit-cost ratios. Unlike the analyst who seeks to maximize national welfare, the legislator knows that it is *someone's* welfare that is to be benefited" (1976, 217; emphasis in original). This congressional concern for fairness clearly does not ensure a commitment to reducing income inequality or to equalizing the political influence of the rich and the poor (Bartels 2010; Gilens 2012; Hacker and Pierson 2011; Hochschild 1981). But Congress often concerns itself with assisting groups perceived to be the victims of inequitable treatment. In the debate over whether to subject Internet purchases to sales taxes, for example, Congress was concerned about rectifying "unfairness" to bricks-and-mortar retailers.

Congress also focuses on the budgetary costs of proposals. Thirty percent of experts in our survey said the cost of the bill would have a lot of influence on the typical member. In multivariate analysis, we found that respondents who had been a legislative staff member were more likely to say that cost considerations would affect congressional support for the bill ($p < .01$; see Table 11A.2). As we explain in greater detail in the following, the CBO has become a key arbiter of the economic consequences of policies, and its analyses of budgetary effects often shape the political context in which proposals are considered (Joyce 2011).

The criterion that Congress weighs most heavily is *political acceptability*. There is no guarantee that this political filter will eliminate only "bad" ideas or ensure that experts' proposals will be adopted. Yet, in a democracy, political acceptability is a crucial procedural value. Even the most brilliant, expert-certified, Pareto-improving policies cannot be enacted (or sustained) without it. The challenge for experts is that law makers are not only responsive to organized groups; they also cater to public opinion and seek to incorporate popular understandings of instrumental rationality into policy design (Mayhew 1974).[13] Counterintuitive proposals that do not reflect common sense tend to be resisted by voters and therefore struggle to gain traction on Capitol Hill (Mayhew 1974). Consider the difficulty that economists had following the 2008–2009 financial crisis in getting even some Democratic members of Congress to accept the Keynesian argument – which challenged the average citizen's belief about how a family should respond to a period of economic stress – that while the financial crisis was "caused by too much confidence, too much borrowing and lending and too much spending, it can only be resolved with more confidence, more borrowing and lending, and more spending" (Summers 2011).

Yet the resistance of Congress to expert input is not an entirely bad thing in a system of separated powers in which executives and courts tend to more quickly absorb elite thinking. As Mayhew writes:

the battle between the popular and the high-minded needs to be fought out somewhere. In any society, common sense versus expertise is an opposition that will not go away. In the American system, it is up for grabs how much we are willing to trust scientific, bureaucratic, legal, or moral experts. Congress helps supply an assurance that their ideas need to be sold, not just proclaimed. (2009, 361)

Projecting Outcomes

Policy analysis is *predictive* (Wildavsky 1989). It asks: What will happen if a policy option is enacted? Will a new program deliver on its promises? How much will it cost? And what unintended consequences could it create?

Congress relies heavily on the budget projections of the CBO, which is required by law to produce a formal cost estimate for nearly every bill that is reported by a full committee. By all accounts, CBO budget scores have a massive influence on congressional debate (Joyce 2011). Indeed, a case can be made that CBO budget projections have *too much* influence, and sometimes cause members to focus too much on (highly uncertain) short-term budget projections at the expense of an analysis of the broader costs and benefits of a policy option. As one interviewee stated, "CBO cost estimates are very

---

[13] In multivariate analysis, we found that survey respondents who reported having served on a legislative staff or in a legislature were more likely ($p < .05$) to say that Congress does a good job of reflecting public opinion than those who had not served on a legislative staff or in a legislature. (See Table 11A.1.)

important as it is difficult to get to the floor of the House or Senate without them. It is really the drafts of the cost estimates and mandates that cause committee staff to re-consider approaches. The public seldom sees this happening, but it is very important." There have been many occasions when CBO budget scores have had a significant impact on the political development and outcome of major reform proposals. One famous example is the CBO's review of President Clinton's health reform plan in 1994 (Joyce 2011). The administration had argued that the plan would save money, but the CBO determined that it would increase the deficit. Moreover, while the administration had claimed that the transactions of the health alliances were private and therefore should not be included in the federal budget, the CBO ruled that the transactions were budgetary in nature, making it easier for opponents to argue that the plan would vastly expand federal government activity. Some political analysts believe that the CBO's rulings contributed to the demise of the Clinton health plan (Skocpol 1996).

In addition to budget scores, the CBO prepares analytic reports on the effects of legislative proposals at the request of congressional leadership or chairmen or ranking members of committees or subcommittees. These reports make no recommendations, but may contain findings that favor one side or another of a political debate. For example, a 1995 CBO report projected that few small businesses and farms would have to be liquidated to pay the estate tax under the rules scheduled to be in effect in 2009 (Congress of the United States Congressional Budget Office 1995). A recent history of the CBO, supported by many case examples, concludes that the studies produced by the agency cannot get Congress to do something it does not want to do, though at times they can improve the content of a law that Congress was poised to enact (Joyce 2011).[14] In sum, CBO's budget scores are highly consequential, but its analytic reports have a more circumscribed and contingent impact.

Congress frequently lacks information about potential administrative challenges or weak spots of legislative proposals. Policies that work on paper may not work in practice (Pressman and Wildavsky 1973). Implementation breakdowns not only make it less likely that policy goals will be achieved, but damage the morale and prestige of agencies, although typically not the reputation of legislators themselves.[15] Congress's indifference to implementation appears to have grown over time. An appreciation for the limits of bureaucratic capacity has traditionally resided in committees, but the institutional

---

[14] It is sometimes claimed that a role of the support agencies is to stop bad ideas, but it is unclear how frequently this happens. Certainly there are examples of the support agencies' work improving legislation. For example, the Carter energy proposal changed as a result of a CBO analysis (Joyce 2011).

[15] Fiorina (1979) famously suggested that members of Congress *want* the bureaucracy to perform poorly so that they can come to the rescue of aggrieved citizens.

knowledge base of committees has been weakened by two factors. First, the new Republican majority significantly cut committee staff size in 1995 (Baumgartner and Jones 1995). In addition, committee staff turnover increased. "At one time you had staff directors who were there for 10, 15 and 20 years and not only developed a lot of expertise but who would have also worked for both Rs and Ds. Today you have a high rate of turnover," said one analyst we interviewed. According to one expert, "The lack of knowledge about how to implement legislation is becoming a huge problem. This is due to the body becoming more partisan and thus less willing to reach out. . . . This was a huge problem with [enactment of the] ACA and it will cause more problems down the line." Because members, unlike presidents, do not have a direct electoral stake in the quality of public administration, there is no procedure to ensure that implementation issues receive attention in legislative debates. To address this gap, R. Kent Weaver proposes having the GAO perform "Implementation Analyses" of major legislative proposals, similar to the CBO's budget scoring, but it remains unclear whether Congress would heed or ignore such reports.

Confronting the Trade Offs

The sixth step of a policy analysis is to confront trade offs. It sometimes happens that one of the policy options under consideration is expected to produce a better outcome on every relevant economic and political dimension than other alternatives, but that is seldom the case (Bardach 2009). Almost every policy idea is flawed in some way. A typical situation is that Option 1 is projected to make a big dent in solving a problem, but would be expensive for the government to carry out; Option 2 has a low budgetary cost, but would impose regulatory burdens on small businesses; and Option 3 is popular with voters but won't work. Typically, Congress also faces the option to maintain the legislative status quo, which may have been established decades earlier when conditions were quite different.

Does Congress wrestle with such trade offs in a serious way? Respondents gave Congress low marks on this score: 75 percent disagreed with the statement that "Congress is careful to understand the trade-offs between the outcomes associated with different policy options before deciding on a course of action." The discipline of the budget process forces Congress to accept trade-offs *across* programs, but Congress seldom compares the relative social welfare benefits of options in an effort to find the best, feasible solution to a given problem. Instead, members of Congress often use the recognition of trade-offs simply to highlight the weaknesses of proposals of the other political party, even if the proposals have net social benefits or were ones that opponents previously endorsed (Lee 2014).

In addition, as Derthick observes, there is no "budget of administrative capacity" to force Congress to establish sensible implementation priorities. "By definition," she argues "law is binding; the nature of it is to embody command. Thus, when Congress passes a law containing numerous new provisions, all equally require implementation. The legislature does not stipulate priorities. It does not say, "If you must choose, do this before that'" (Wellman and Derthick 1990, 84).

Making Decisions

One of the aims of policy analysis is to inform decisions, but Congress is no ordinary decision maker. With 535 members, it isn't easy for the institution to act even when a majority agrees on a plan. Moreover, legislative rules and procedures erect barriers to change. As Terry M. Moe and Scott A. Wilson have argued, "The transaction costs of moving a bill through the entire legislative process is enormous.... The best prediction is that, for most issues most of the time, there will be no affirmative action on the part of Congress at all. The ideal points may logically support a given outcome, but in reality *nothing will happen*" (1994, 26–27). Recent congressional reforms have made law making even more difficult. Historically, one of the ways that coalition leaders have built support for broad-based national legislation is by doling out pork barrel projects to members who vote for the bills (Ellwood and Patashnik 1993; Evans 2004). The recent ban on congressional earmarks, however, has removed some of the vital grease needed to lubricate a creaky legislative process. Yet, despite its reputation as a "gridlocked" institution, Congress has passed sweeping legislation: the American Recovery and Reinvestment Act, the Affordable Care Act, Dodd-Frank, Troubled Asset Relief Program (TARP) reform of the federal student loan program, and the Medicare Modernization Act, to give just a few recent examples (Melnick 2013).

From a policy analysis perspective, however, the key issue is not the quantity of decisions Congress makes, but their *quality*.[16] Experts we interviewed suggest that the existence of policy analysis informing congressional decision making is not assured by institutionalized practices and norms but rather depends largely on the attitude and involvement of staff who work on the issue. Once bills are drafted by committee staff, there is seldom an opportunity to make major revisions. While staff are clearly agents of their members, they may have considerable discretion in what issues they choose to develop. Explained one former senior policy analyst: "The earlier that policy analysts get involved, the larger the impact and the better the policy. This means that generalizations are difficult as the process is lumpy depending on the issue and the staff involved – it can be very good or very bad."

How do members of Congress decide whether to vote for bills? There are clearly important differences between the factors that survey respondents believe members of Congress weigh in making voting decisions and the factors

---

[16] In addition to welfare economics and public administration lenses for evaluating the quality of statutes (Frankel and Orszag 2002; Light 2002), political scientists have recently begun to focus on policy sustainability (see Berry, Burden, and Howell 2010; Jenkins and Patashnik 2012; Maltzman and Shipan 2008; Patashnik 2008; Patashnik and Zelizer 2013;).

that experts themselves use to evaluate the quality of legislative proposals. The respondents indicated that the most important influences on their own assessments of the quality of a bill are the CBO's estimate of how much the bill will cost (43 percent said this would tell them a lot about the quality of the bill) and whether policy experts played a significant role in the bill's development (34 percent said this would tell them a lot) (Figure 11.2).[17] In contrast, the respondents perceived that the most important influences on a *typical member of Congress* in deciding whether to support a bill are whether major interest groups are for the bill (82 percent of experts said they believed interest group support would have a lot of influence on legislators) and how popular the bill is with citizens (57 percent of experts believed that such public support would have a lot of influence on the typical member) (Figure 11.3).

Telling Causal Stories

The final step of a policy analysis is to convince others that the analyst's recommendations are sound. In a democracy, the audience for policy recommendations includes not only elites, but also ordinary citizens who (to press an earlier point) tend to reject ideas that do not reflect common sense. As Bardach (2009) argues, policy analysts must be able to "tell a causal story" linking public problems with proposed solutions (on stories in policy making, see Stone 2001). To be effective, such stories must pass what he calls the "New York Taxi Driver Test" (Bardach 2009, 41). While stalled in New York traffic, the analyst must be able to provide a coherent, easily understood explanation of her policy idea to the typical New York City cabbie, before the taxi driver loses interest or rejects the idea as yet another scheme of intellectuals to waste taxpayer money. Would-be policy analysts who fail this test prove incapable of "carrying on with the task of public, democratic education" (Bardach 2009, 42).

As Mayhew notes, "struggles over causal stores are often at the center of drives to enact legislation" (2012, 259). Think of the struggle over the narrative of the Affordable Care Act, or the failed push for Social Security privatization. Members may be challenged to explain proposals to constituents at town hall meetings. On the positive side, the need to tell compelling stories affords members of Congress the opportunity not only to build trust and enhance their political standing, but also to play a formative role in the construction of public preferences (Sunstein 1988, 1539–1590). Haskins (1991, 618), for example, argues that members built support for welfare reform legislation in the 1990s by telling a plausible causal story that linked citizen dissatisfaction with the

---

[17] Just 11 percent of survey respondents said that a *New York Times* editorial board endorsement would tell them a lot about the quality of a bill. To the extent that such editorials give respondents new information, this finding implies that while professional policy analysts skew to the left, they are not reflexive liberals.

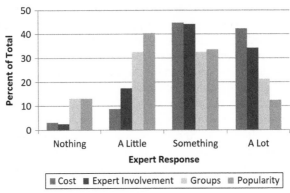

FIGURE 11.2 Experts focus on cost and expert input.

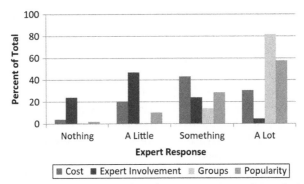

FIGURE 11.3 Experts believe that members focus on groups and popularity.

increase in welfare spending to the top-down, "federally imposed" structure of the program.

Richard Fenno's study of members' "homestyles" also highlights the importance of causal explanations. On the basis of participant observation research conducted in the 1970s, Fenno reported that many members believed that their explanations for their votes mattered as much as or more than their roll call votes themselves (Fenno 1978; see also Kingdon 1997).[18] At times, members of Congress have played a key role not only in explaining their actions to voters in their districts, but in making experts' ideas acceptable to broader publics. For example, in the 1970s, key coalition leaders, such as Ted Kennedy (D-MA),

---

[18] In today's more polarized environment, however, it may be more challenging for members to come up with explanations that will satisfy both primary and general election voters, unless they are able to successfully tailor their messages and communications to suit different audiences (on tailoring of legislators' explanations, see Mayhew 1974).

sold microeconomists' proposal for pro-competitive transportation deregulation to the public – over the intense opposition of organized interests – by
offering "simple and vivid cues of the merits of the issue"; explaining how
vulnerable geographic constituencies (small towns) would be protected from
harms; and "making a rhetorical connection between deregulation and larger
concerns of the general public," including worries about inflation and Big
Government (Derthick and Quirk 1985, 244).

  Does the contemporary Congress have a similar capacity to market ideas to
the public? The public policy experts in our survey expressed skepticism about
members' effectiveness at telling causal stories. Only 19 percent of respondents
said that Congress has done a good job or better over the past ten years at
explaining policy decisions in common sense language that ordinary Americans
can understand. Thirty-five percent said Congress has done a fair job in
explaining policies, and 44 percent said Congress's performance on this dimension has been poor. This poor performance is not due to a lack of assistance
from the legislative support agencies. According to a focus group participant,
agencies such as CRS offer a lot of help to members who know there is a
problem but don't know how to fix it or how to explain a technical policy
solution to voters. "Case in point is the rising salinity of the ocean. A liberal
member knows this is a problem, but has no idea what options are to solve it.
Policy analysis helps him to credit claim (I have a solution), take a position (we
need to lower the temperature of the ocean) and explain causal action (if we
don't do this, we won't be able to continue commercial fishing off the coast of
our state)." If the public mistrusts Congress, however, the persuasive influence
of members will be constrained.

  As a gauge of how effective experts believe members are at telling convincing
stories, we asked respondents to evaluate how effective different actors would
be at convincing the average citizen that a recently enacted public health law
was necessary and in the public interest. As Figure 11.4 shows, respondents
overwhelmingly believed that the local of member of Congress would be less
persuasive to the average citizen not only than the U.S. President and the
president of the American Medical Association, but also than a radio talk show
host. The CBO director was perceived to have no ability to persuade the public
about the need for the program.

What Does Congress Not Do Poorly?

As we have seen, our survey respondents give Congress low marks as a
problem-solving institution. This is unsurprising. Policy analysts (especially
those who work in universities and think tanks) are tough critics, and Congress
is a disparaged institution. In the face of these negative reviews, does the survey
say *anything* positive at all about Congress's contribution to problem solving?

  Another way to interrogate our results is to ask not what experts believe
Congress does well, but what they believe Congress at least does not do

poorly. Here, the results are illuminating. As Table 11.2 shows, experts overwhelmingly agree that Congress' performance over the past decade has *not* been poor in avoiding negative consequences for business, satisfying interest groups, reflecting public opinion, and bringing attention to new issues. These are not insignificant contributions to problem solving in a political system in which different institutions and actors bring different strengths. A concern for public opinion, for example, is essential if people are to accept the outcomes of policy decisions.[19] More striking is that a clear majority of experts does not give Congress poor marks on such key tasks as achieving policy goals at acceptable cost, reflecting the ideas of policy experts, and passing bills the bureaucracy can handle without difficulty. (For the most part, the experts rate Congress's performance as "only fair" in these areas.) The performance dimensions on which an overwhelming majority of experts finds Congress's record poor are distributing benefits equitably across income groups, taking into account the interests of future generations, and making evidence-based decisions. Two-thirds of respondents believe that Congress is dismal at those tasks.

CONCLUSIONS

Congress's performance as a policy analyst is problematic to say the least, but it is important to appraise the institution against a reasonable set of expectations. Policy analysis involves (and should involve) both intelligence *and* social interaction (Wildavsky 1979). Once Congress's performance is broken down into discrete tasks – something that previous research on the subject has not done – it becomes clear that Congress is neither estranged from policy analysis nor consumed by it. Great efforts have been made over the past half-century to boost Congress's analytic capacity through the establishment of support agencies such as the CBO. The contemporary Congress clearly possesses the information and access to expertise required to absorb social science findings and craft thoughtful solutions. What is arguably needed to improve Congress's performance as a problem-solving institution are not additional analytic boosters, but rather changes in legislative norms and practices (such as reducing the number of complex omnibus bills covering diverse subjects) to promote a "culture of problem solving on Capitol Hill" (Mayhew 2006, 230).

Overall, survey respondents give Congress low marks on tasks involving the use of knowledge, such as making policy decisions on the basis of evidence. At the same time, their responses point to some areas of *relative* institutional

---

[19] As Wildavsky (1989, 406) wrote: "Nor do I believe policy analysis is a waste of time, because no one cares what is true and beautiful but only what is popular and preferable. Popularity in a democracy is no mean recommendation; a policy that is marginally preferable has much to commend it compared to one that is perfectly impossible."

TABLE 11.2 *Expert Assessment of Congressional Performance*

Experts Reporting Poor Congressional Performance On...	Percent of Total
Pleasing Interest Groups	1
Avoiding Negative Consequences for Business	9
Reflecting Public Opinion	15
Bringing Attention to New Issues	21
Distributing Benefits Equitably Across Districts	33
Achieving Policy Objectives at Acceptable Cost	34
Reflecting Ideas of Policy Experts	35
Passing Bills That the Bureaucracy Can Handle	36
Promoting Economic Efficiency	43
Explaining Decisions in Ordinary Language	45
Developing New Policy Options	48
Targeting Resources Effectively	50
Defining Problems Logically	56
Distributing Benefits Equitably Across Income Groups	62
Taking into Account the Interests of Future Generations	65
Making Evidence-Based Decisions	66

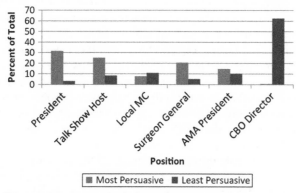

FIGURE 11.4 Expert assessments of relative persuasiveness.

strength, such as Congress's ability to craft policies that reflect public opinion. The most troubling results of the survey, in our view, touch not on Congress's lack of interest in cost–benefit analysis, which is old news, but rather on the perception among many experts that the institution today is not contributing as much as it might to the representational and legitimating sides of problem solving. This can be seen, for example, in the belief among many respondents that Congress has done a poor job in explaining issues to mass publics in plain language or in developing solutions that the citizenry can understand and embrace. The quality of governance depends on the efficiency of policy choices, but it also depends on the accountability relationship between legislators and citizens.

Several issues require more attention. The first is the influence of polarization and party competition on congressional performance. The literature on partisan polarization has focused on its impact on legislative productivity as measured by the quantity of laws passed, but we need more fine-grained evidence on how polarization and party competition affect the quality of deliberation, the definition of problems, and the way that Congress incorporates expertise and uses information (Quirk 2011). The standard process by which expertise influences policy making in the United States is through elite-led social learning. Policy experts first reach a scientific consensus on a technical issue, which then diffuses down to policy makers and the general public (Zaller 1992). This elite-led social learning process is mediated, however, by the structure of electoral competition between the two parties. The current political era is characterized by a polarization of policy elites, a sorting of constituencies, and the longest period of parity in party competition since the Civil War (Lee 2014). In this combative environment, each party has a strong electoral incentive to attack the proposals of the other side, even in the absence of an underlying substantive disagreement about public policy (Lee 2014). Gerber and Patashnik have argued that even bipartisan, technocratic reform ideas such as evidence-based medicine may become the objects of political contestation (Gerber and Patashnik 2006). We need to learn more about the conditions under which such politicization of expertise emerges, and what if any countervailing forces might suppress it.

While the focus of this paper is on how Congress's capacities vary across eight dimensions of policy analysis, a key issue for inquiry is whether and how Congress's use of policy analysis varies across policy sectors (Katznelson and Lapinski 2006). Is it the case, for example, that Congress's use of policy analysis is better in the defense arena than in domestic sectors (Schick 1976)? How is the willingness of Congress to confront trade offs shaped by the density of think tanks and experts in particular arenas? Do senior staff and members of congressional support agencies systematically skew the advice that they give to members to comport with Congress's strongly instrumental approach when issues directly implicate members' reelection concerns? How severe is this skewing? How much rationality seeps through, and does this vary in any systematic way across policy domains?

A third issue concerns the variation in congressional performance over time. There is nothing remotely new about elite complaints about Congress's failure to utilize expertise.[20] Yet Congress's performance as a problem-solving institution seems to have atrophied in recent decades (Mayhew 2006). At earlier moments in American history, Congress appeared to have the capacity to address the issues on its agenda, including big social conflicts such as civil rights, yet today the congressional agenda is dominated by technical issues, where Congress does not seem as well-suited to act. At the same time, expectations of political fairness and economic performance have become more exacting. How have congressional tools to reconcile the pressures of democratic politics with the dictates of policy analysis been affected by the new kinds of political demands and issue contexts we are confronting today? Does Congress end up focusing on more technical issues because its analytic capacity has grown – or because secular trends such as polarization, the closeness of electoral competition between the two parties, and globalization have weakened the institution's ability to deal with larger challenges? Our sense is that Congress's agenda is driven more by presidential leadership, policy feedback from past decisions, and electoral pressures than by the growth of its analytical machinery, but the necessary research has not been conducted.

A final issue concerns the separation of powers.[21] The idealized view of institutional relationships in modern American government suggests that Congress "owns" the representation function while the executive branch "owns" most technocratic governing capacity. From this perspective, many scholars believe that stark differences remain between Congress and the executive in both orientation and performance. In his recent book on why domestic policies go awry, for example, Peter Schuck argues that congressional defects and dysfunction are the main institutional source of government failure, while administrative agencies remain the "best loci within the government of fine-grained policy analysis" (Schuck 2014, 169). Yet other scholars argue that the thrust of institutional development over the past half century – including the expanded representational role of the presidency, agencies, and courts – has been to erode the separation of powers and functional differences among the branches. To evaluate the consequences of Congress's work as a policy analyst, we therefore need to understand not only how Congress's roles and capacities have changed, but also how other institutions have responded to Congress's evolution. Have the other branches found ways to enhance (or offset) the strengths (and limitations) of Congress's contributions to problem solving? Or are the virtues (and defects) of our political institutions today mutually reinforcing? Answering these questions will reveal not only how public policy is made in American government, but to what ends.

---

[20] Back in the nineteenth century, Mark Twain famously quipped, "Suppose you were an idiot, and suppose you were a member of Congress; but I repeat myself" (Paine 1912, 724).
[21] We thank Stephen Skowronek for stimulating us to think about this issue.

APPENDIX

TABLE 11A.1 *Determinants of the Belief that Congress Fails to Reflect Public Opinion*

Explanatory Variable	Model 1	Model 2	Model 3
Legislative Staffer	−0.35**	−0.37**	−0.36**
	(0.16)	(0.17)	(0.17)
Party Identification	0.21***	−	0.18***
	(0.06)		(0.06)
Ideology	0.06	−0.01	−
	(0.06)	(0.05)	
Female	−0.002 (0.14)	0.04	−0.02
		(.14)	(.14)
Constant	2.32***	3.73***	2.69***
	(0.61)	(0.17)	(0.54)
R^2	0.10	0.03	0.10
N	155	155	155

Note:
All tests run using OLS regression. Robust standard errors in parenthesis.
* $p < .10$,
** $p < .05$,
*** $p < .01$ (two-tailed tests).
Models were also run using ordered logistic regression and the results were nearly identical.

TABLE 11A.2 *Determinants of the Belief that the Cost of a Bill Influences Votes*

Explanatory Variable	Model 1	Model 2	Model 3
Legislative Staffer	0.49***	0.49***	0.51***
	(0.14)	(0.14)	(0.14)
Party Identification	−0.03	−	−0.04
	(0.05)		(0.05)
Ideology	0.02	0.03	−
	(0.05)	(0.05)	
Female	0.15	0.15	0.18
	(0.13)	(.13)	(.14)
Constant	3.04***	2.85***	3.17***
	(0.36)	(0.15)	(0.31)
R^2	0.06	0.06	0.06
N	157	157	157

Note:
All tests run using OLS regression. Robust standard errors in parenthesis.
* $p < .10$,
** $p < .05$,
*** $p < .01$ (two-tailed tests).
Models were also run using ordered logistic regression and the results were nearly identical.

TABLE IIA.3 *Determinants of the Belief that Cost–Benefit Studies Influence Congress*

Explanatory Variable	Model 1	Model 2	Model 3
Frequent Interactions with Congress	−0.42**	−0.45***	−0.41**
	(0.17)	(0.17)	(0.17)
Party Identification	−0.06	−0.05	−
	(0.08)	(0.07)	
Ideology	−0.01	−	0.01
	(0.06)		(0.06)
Female	0.22	0.24	0.21
	(0.19)	(0.18)	(0.18)
Constant	3.10***	3.04***	2.71***
	(0.56)	(0.40)	(0.24)
R^2	0.04	0.05	0.04
N	155	155	155

Note:
All tests run using OLS regression. Robust standard errors in parenthesis.
* $p < .10$,
** $p < .05$,
*** $p < .01$ (two-tailed tests).
Models were also run using ordered logistic regression and the results were nearly identical.

TABLE IIA.4 *Determinants of the Belief that Committee Chairs Would Learn of Academic Study*

Explanatory Variable	Model 1	Model 2	Model 3
Legislative Staffer	0.37	0.37	0.38*
	(0.24)	(0.23)	(0.21)
Party Identification	0.08	−	0.06
	(0.07)		(0.06)
Ideology	0.03	0.01	−
	(0.07)	(0.06)	
Female	−0.12 (0.16)	−0.1	−0.11
		(.16)	(.16)
Constant	1.82***	2.38***	2.02***
	(0.57)	(0.21)	(0.38)
R^2	0.03	0.02	0.03
N	157	157	157

Note:
All tests run using OLS regression. Robust standard errors in parenthesis.
* $p < .10$,
** $p < .05$,
*** $p < .01$ (two-tailed tests).
Models were also run using ordered logistic regression and the results were nearly identical.

BIBLIOGRAPHY

Adler, E. Scott and John D. Wilkerson. *Congress and the Politics of Policymaking*. New York: Cambridge University Press, 2012

Arnold, R. Douglas. *The Logic of Congressional Action*. New Haven, CT: Yale University Press, 1990

Bardach, Eugene. *A Practical Guide for Policy Analysis: The Eightfold Path to More Effective Problem Solving*. Washington, DC: CQ Press, 2009

Bartels, Larry. *Unequal Democracy: The Political Economy of the New Gilded Age*. Princeton, NJ: Princeton University Press, 2010

Baumgartner, Frank R. and Bryan D. Jones. *The Politics of Information: Problem Definition and the Course of Public Policy in America*. Chicago, IL: University of Chicago Press, 2015

Becker, Gary. "A Theory of Competition among Pressure Groups for Political Influence." *Quarterly Journal of Economics* 98 (1983): 371–400

Berry, Christopher R., Barry C. Burden, and William G. Howell. "After Enactment: The Lives and Deaths of Federal Programs." *American Journal of Political Science* 54.1 (2010): 1–17

Bimber, Bruce. "Information as a Factor in Congressional Politics." *Legislative Studies Quarterly* 16 (November 1991): 585–605

   The Politics of Expertise in Congress: The Rise and Fall of the Office of Technology Assessment. Albany, NY: State University of New York Press, 1996

Cohen, Jeffrey E. *The President's Legislative Policy Agenda, 1789–2002*. New York: Cambridge University Press, 2012

Congress of the United States Congressional Budget Office. "Who Pays and When? An Assessment of Generational Accounting." Washington, D.C.: Government Printing Office, 1995

Derthick, Martha and Paul J. Quirk. *The Politics of Deregulation*. Washington, DC: Brookings Institution, 1985

Drutman, Lee and Steven M. Teles, "A New Agenda for Political Reform." *The Washington Monthly*, May 2015

Easterling, Kevin. *The Political Economy of Expertise: Information and Efficiency in American National Politics*. Ann Arbor, MI: University of Michigan Press, 2004

Ellwood, John W. and Eric M. Patashnik. "In Praise of Pork." *National Affairs* 110 (1993): 19–33

Evans, Diana. *Greasing the Wheels: Using Pork Barrel Projects to Build Majority Coalitions in Congress*. New York: Cambridge University Press, 2004.

Fenno, Richard F. *Home Style: House Members in Their Districts*. New York: Longman, 1978

Fisher, Louis. *Defending Congress and the Constitution*. Lawrence, KS: University Press of Kansas, 2011

Frankel, Jeffrey A. and Peter R. Orszag. *American Economic Policy in the 1990s*. Boston: MIT Press, 2002

Gerber, Alan S. and Eric M. Patashnik, eds. *Promoting the General Welfare: New Perspectives on Government Performance*. Washington, DC: Brookings Institution, 2006

Gerber, Alan S. and Eric M. Patashnik. "Sham Surgery: The Problem of Inadequate Medical Evidence," in Alan S. Gerber and Eric M. Patashnik, eds., *Promoting the General Welfare: New Perspectives on Government Performance*. Washington, D.C.: Brookings Institution, 2006

"The Politicization of Evidence-Based Medicine: The Limits of Pragmatic Problem Solving in an Era of Polarization." *California Journal of Politics and Policy* 3.4 (2011)

Gilens, Martin. *Affluence and Influence: Economic Inequality and Political Power in America*. Princeton, NJ: Princeton University Press, 2012

Haberkorn, Jennifer. "Eric Cantor Pledges another Obamacare Repeal Vote." *Politico*, May 3, 2013 (www.politico.com/story/2013/05/obamacare-repeal-vote-eric-cantor-90900.html)

Hacker, Jacob S. and Paul Pierson. *Winner-Take-All Politics: How Washington Made the Rich Richer – and Turned Its Back on the Middle Class*. New York: Simon and Schuster, 2011

Hall, Richard L. and Alan V. Deardorff, "Lobbying as Legislative Subsidy," *American Political Science Review*, 100.1 (February 2006): 69–84

Haskins, Ron. "Congress Writes a Law: Research and Welfare Reform." *Journal of Policy Analysis and Management* 10 (1991): 616–632

Heclo, H. Hugh. "Policy Analysis." *British Journal of Political Science* 2 (January 1972): 83–108

Hird, John A. "The Political Economy of Pork: Project Selection at the United States Army Corps of Engineers." *American Political Science Review* 85 (Spring 1991)

Power, Knowledge and Politics: Policy Analysis in the States. Washington, DC: Georgetown University Press, 2005

Hochschild, Jennifer. *What's Fair? American Beliefs about Distributive Justice*. Cambridge, MA: Harvard University Press, 1981

Jenkins, Jeffery A. and Eric M. Patashnik, eds. *Living Legislation: Durability, Change, and the Politics of American Lawmaking*. Chicago, IL: University of Chicago Press, 2012

Jones, Charles O. "Why Congress Can't Do Policy Analysis (or words to that effect)." *Policy Analysis* 2 (1976): 251–164

Joyce, Philip G. *The Congressional Budget Office: Honest Numbers, Power, and Policymaking*. Washington, DC: Georgetown University Press, 2011

Katznelson, Ira and John S. Lapinski. "At the Crossroads: Congress and American Political Development." *Perspectives on Politics* 4 (2006): 243–260

Kingdon, John W. *Agendas, Alternatives, and Public Policies*, 2nd edition. New York: Addison-Wesley Educational Publishers, 1997

Krehbiel, Keith. *Information and Legislative Organization*. Ann Arbor, MI: University of Michigan Press, 1991

Lee, Frances E. "Interests, Constituencies, and Policy Making," in Paul J. Quirk and Sarah A Binder, eds., *The Legislative Branch*. New York: Oxford University Press, 2005

Beyond Ideology: Politics, Principles, and Partisanship in the U.S. Senate. Chicago, IL: The University of Chicago Press, 2009

"American politics is more competitive than ever. That's making partisanship worse." *Washington Post*, January 9, 2014 (www.washingtonpost

.com/blogs/monkey-cage/wp/2014/01/09/american-politics-is-more-competitive-than-ever-thats-making-partisanship-worse/)

Light, Paul C. *Government's Greatest Achievements: From Civil Rights to Homeland Security.* Washington, DC: Brookings Institution, 2002

Lindblom, Charles E. "The Science of 'Muddling Through.'" *Public Administration Review* 19 (Spring 1959): 79–88

Maltzman, Forrest and Charles R. Shipan. "Continuity, Change and the Evolution of the Law." *American Journal of Political Science* 52 (April 2008): 252–267

Mann, Thomas E. and Norman J. Ornstein. *It's Even Worse than It Looks: How the American Constitutional System Collided with the New Politics of Extremism.* New York: Basic Books, 2012

Mayhew, David R. *Congress: The Electoral Connection.* New Haven, CT: Yale University Press, 1974

"Congress as Problem Solver," in Alan Gerber and Eric M. Patashnik, eds., *Promoting the General Welfare: New Perspectives on Government Performance.* Washington, DC: Brookings Institution, 2006

"Is Congress 'the Broken Branch'?" *Boston University Law Review* 89 (2009): 357–369

"Lawmaking as a Cognitive Enterprise," in Jeffery A. Jenkins and Eric M. Patashnik, eds., *Living Legislation: Durability, Change, and the Politics of American Lawmaking.* Chicago, IL: University of Chicago Press. 2012

Melnick, R. Shep. "The Gridlock Illusion." *Wilson Quarterly* (Winter 2013)

Meltsner, Arnold. *Policy Analysts in the Bureaucracy.* Berkeley: University of California Press, 1976

Moe, Terry M. "The Politicized Presidency," in John E. Chubb and Paul E. Peterson, eds., *The New Direction in American Politics.* Washington, DC: Brookings Institution Press, 1985

Moe, Terry M. and Scott A. Wilson. "Presidents and the Politics of Structure." *Law and Contemporary Problems* 57 (1994): 1–44

Mucciaroni, Gary and Paul J. Quirk. *Deliberative Choices: Debating Public Policy in Congress.* Chicago, IL: The University of Chicago Press, 2006

Nivola, Pietro S. and David W. Brady. *Red and Blue Nation?: Consequences and Correction of America's Polarized Politics.* Washington, DC: Brookings Institution Press, 2008

Paine, Albert Bigelow. *Mark Twain: A Biography.* New York: Dodo Press, 1912

Patashnik, Eric M. *Reforms at Risk: What Happens after Major Policy Changes Are Enacted.* Princeton, NJ: Princeton University Press, 2008

Patashnik, Eric M. and Julian E. Zelizer. "The Struggle to Remake Politics: Liberal Reform and the Limits of Policy Feedback in the Contemporary American State." *Perspectives on Politics* (December 2013)

Peterson, Mark A. "How Health Policy Information Is Used in Congress," in Thomas E. Mann and Norman J. Ornstein, eds., *Intensive Care: How Congress Shapes Health Policy.* Washington, DC: AEI and Brookings Institution, 1995

Pierson, Paul. "When Effect Becomes Cause: Policy Feedback and Political Change." *World Politics* 45.4 (1993): 595–628

Polsby, Nelson W. "Policy Analysis and Congress." *Public Policy* XVIII (Fall 1969), 61–74

Pressman, Jeffrey L. and Aaron Wildavsky. *Implementation: How Great Expectations in Washington Are Dashed in Oakland; Or, Why It's Amazing that Federal Programs Work at All, This Being a Saga of the Economic Development Administration as Told by Two Sympathetic Observers Who Seek to Build Morals on a Foundation of Ruined Hopes.* Berkeley, CA: University of California Press, 1973

Price, David E. "Professionals and 'Entrepreneurs': Staff Orientations and Policymaking on Three Separate Committees." *Journal of Politics* 33 (1971): 316–336

"Comment," in William H. Robinson and Clay Wellborn, eds., *Knowledge, Power and the Congress.* Washington, DC: CQ Press, 1991

Quirk, Paul J. "Deliberation and Decision Making," in Paul J. Quirk and Sarah A. Binder, eds., *The Legislative Branch.* New York: Oxford University Press, 2005

Quirk, Paul J. and William Bendix. "Deliberation in Congress," in Eric Schickler, Frances E. Lee and George C. Edwards, eds., *The Oxford Handbook of the American Congress.* New York: Oxford University Press, 2011

Quirk, Paul J. and Sarah A. Binder, eds. *The Legislative Branch.* New York: Oxford University Press, 2005

Radin, Beryl A. *Beyond Machiavelli: Policy Analysis Comes of Age.* Washington, DC: Georgetown University Press, 2000

Rhodes, R.W., Sarah A. Binder, and Bert Rockman, eds. *The Oxford Handbook of Political Institutions.* New York: Oxford University Press, 2006

Rieselbach, Leroy N. *Congressional Reform: The Changing Modern Congress.* Washington, DC: CQ Press, 1994

Sabatier, Paul A. "Toward Better Theories of the Policy Process," *PS: Political Science and Politics* 24 (June 1991): 147–156

Schick, Allen. "The Supply and Demand for Policy Analysis on Capitol Hill." *Policy Analysis* (Spring 1976): 215–234

Schickler, Eric. *Disjointed Pluralism: Institutional Innovation and the Development of the U.S. Congress.* Princeton, NJ: Princeton University Press, 2001

Schickler, Eric, Frances E. Lee, and George C. Edwards, eds. *The Oxford Handbook of the American Congress.* New York: Oxford University Press, 2011

Schuck, Peter H. *Why Government Fails so Often and How It Can Do Better.* Princeton, NJ: Princeton University Press, 2014

Shepsle, Kenneth A. "Representation and Governance: The Great Legislative Trade-off." *Political Science Quarterly* 103 (1988): 461–84

"Congress is a 'They,' Not an 'It'": Legislative Intent as Oxymoron." *International Review of Law and Economics* 12 (1992): 239–56

Shipan, Charles R. and Craig Volden, "Policy Diffusion: Seven Lessons for Scholars and Practitioners." *Public Administration Review* (November/December 2012): 782–796

Shulock, Nancy. "The Paradox of Policy Analysis: If It Is Not Used, Why Do We Produce So Much Of It." *Journal of Policy Analysis and Management* 18 (1999): 226–244

Skocpol, Theda. *Boomerang: Clinton's Health Security Effort and the Turn against Government in U.S. Politics.* New York: W.W. Norton, 1996

Stokey, Edith and Richard J. Zeckhauser. *A Primer for Policy Anlaysis.* New York: HarperCollins, 1978

Stone, Deborah. Policy Paradox: The Art of Political Decision Making, *3rd edition.* New York: W.W. Norton, 2001

Summers, Lawrence. "To Fix the Economy, fix the housing market." *Reuters*, October 24, 2011 (http://blogs.reuters.com/lawrencesummers/2011/10/24/to-fix-the-economy-fix-the-housing-market.html)

Sundquist, James L. *The Decline and Resurgence of Congress.* Washington, DC: Brookings Institution, 1981

Sunstein, Cass. "Beyond the Republican Revival." *Yale Law Journal* 97 (1988): 1539–1590

Taylor, Andrew J. *Congress: A Performance Appraisal.* Boulder, CO: Westview Press, 2013

VanDoren, Peter. "Should Congress Listen to Economists?" *Journal of Politics* 51 (May 1989): 319–336

Verdier, James M. "Advising Congressional Decision-Makers: Guidelines for Economists." *Journal of Policy Analysis and Management* 3 (1984): 421–438

Vining, Aidan R. and David L. Weimer. "Policy Analysis," Foundations of Public Administration Series, 2010 (www.aspanet.org/scriptcontent/index_par_foundations series.cfm)

Weaver, R. Kent. *Ending Welfare As We Know It.* Washington, D.C.: Brookings Institution Press, 2000

Weimer, David L. and Aidan R. Vining. Policy Analysis: Concepts and Practice, *3rd edition.* New York: Prentice Hall, 1999

Weiss, Carol H. "Congressional Committees as Users of Analysis." *Journal of Policy Analysis and Management* 8 (1989): 411–431

Wellman, Michael and Martha Dertick. *Formulation of Trade-Offs in Planning under Uncertainty.* New York: Elsevier Science and Technology Books, 1990

Whiteman, David. "The Fate of Policy Analysis in Congressional Decision Making: Three Types of Use in Committees." *Western Political Quarterly* (June 1985): 294–311

Wildavsky, Aaron. *Speaking Truth to Power: The Art and Craft of Policy Analysis.* New York: Little, Brown, 1979

Wilson, Woodrow. "The Study of Administration." *Political Science Quarterly* 2 (1887): 197–222

Wolfinger, Raymond E. "Voter Turnout." *Society* 28 (1991): 23–26

Wright, John R. *Interest Groups and Congress: Lobbying, Contributions, and Influence.* New York: Longman Publishing, 2003

Zaller, John. *The Nature and Origins of Mass Opinion.* New York: Cambridge University Press, 1992

Zelizer, Julian E. *Taxing America: Wilbur Mills, Congress, and the State, 1945–1975.* New York: Cambridge University Press, 1998

12

Studying Contingency Systematically

Katherine Levine Einstein and Jennifer Hochschild

> In the realm of primitive building blocks, there is a case for ranking events as the equals of interests and preferences in a seriously explanatory political science.
>
> Mayhew 2005, 486.

> Prominent in accounts like these is human agency.... To a degree, the history of the relevant processes is a sequence of what these various figures did. It could have evolved otherwise had they done otherwise.
>
> Mayhew 2010, 1146.

Scholars of political behavior have long debated the circumstances under which individuals change their minds about salient issues, and the circumstances under which such changes matter for political or policy outcomes. The main conclusion of individual-level studies is that stabilizing forces – group membership and identity, patterns of cognitive processing, interests, habit – usually outweigh the impetus for attitude change. The main conclusion is similar at the institutional level: at least in the United States, stabilizing forces – the entrenched two-party system, legislative rules and norms, iron triangles and the iron law of oligarchy, racial or class domination – often outlast all but the strongest efforts to change policies in response to attitudinal changes.

When alteration does occur in individuals, institutions, and laws, political scientists usually reach for systematic, theoretically parsimonious explanatory frameworks to make sense of the change. High quality political science is often defined, in fact, as a persuasive causal abstraction from the particularities of place, time, person, or policy content.[1] David Mayhew (2005, 2009), however, has argued that proper nouns, dates, events, and accidents of history are essential raw material for analyzing how and why American politics and political views develop and change. In recent decades he has advocated close attention to contingency understood as human agency or even happenstance; "as a collective explanatory enterprise, the profession may be under-investing in factors that are proximate, short-term, or contingent" (Mayhew 2009: 99). Although by no means simply a claim that "stuff happens," this focus is a far cry from the bold simplifications in his earlier work (as in *Congress: The Electoral Connection*) or from the usual explanatory ambitions of political scientists.

We take up Mayhew's call for incorporating contingency into the study of American politics, examining when and how unique events can spur opinion change, and when and how opinion change can eventuate in new laws, rules, or rulers. Using case studies ranging from the 1960s civil rights movement to the contemporary politics of global warming, we begin to develop a theory of studying contingency systematically (building on Shapiro and Bedi 2009). We generate many more loose ends than completed fabrics, and conclude by ruminating on the prospects for rigorous analysis of how political outcomes "could have evolved otherwise had ... [various figures] done otherwise."

CLARIFYING TERMS

For Mayhew, contingent events span everything from the Civil War or World War II (Mayhew 2005) to particular moments such as the Great Mississippi Flood of 1927 that led to the Flood Control Act of 1928 (Mayhew 2009: 122). That is, contingency may encompass an extended set of linked actions that develop a distinctive momentum, or may focus more narrowly on a unique and unforeseen occurrence.[2] A complete systematic study of contingency would incorporate the implications of change on the scale of wars or world-wide epidemics, but we limit our attention in this chapter to specific incidents, actions, or social disturbances.[3]

Along with scope, one must specify the kind of phenomenon that counts as a politically relevant contingency. One elected official responded to a draft of this chapter by urging a focus only on human agency, on the grounds that "events are the conditioning factor but intentions and goals shape the meaning of the event." That is a plausible argument, of course; it underlies constructivist

---

[1] In this aspiration or achievement, political scientists differ radically from historians, for whom "contingency is everything," as a colleague of one of us put it in a committee meeting. Thus historically oriented political science has a very different feel from politically oriented history.

[2] Clark 2013 provides a good example of the argument that wars and their impact are radically contingent.

[3] See Schedler 2009 for a valiant effort to categorize contingencies.

theories in the social sciences and post-structuralism in the humanities. But it is not our argument. We follow Mayhew in broadening the scope of our inquiry to "triggering events" ranging from a flood to a currency crisis, an international dispute, a technological innovation, or a political actor's malfeasance (Mayhew 2009, 122–123). Theoretical refinement might usefully cluster or even filter out some types of incidents; as Robert Lieberman has observed, "things that could have come out differently – but for a chance, singular event – play a different role in systematic theorizing about politics from human action undertaken through willful choice" (personal communication). But the theory is too undeveloped to warrant such refinement at this point.

Finally, a full theory of contingency would need to grapple with the distinction between triggering events that were in some sense predictable and those that were completely novel to the relevant political actors. School shootings such as those of Columbine High School in Colorado or Sandy Hook Elementary School in Connecticut were not in a literal sense predictable or predicted; no one could anticipate that children at those particular locations would be killed. But mass shooting incidents in the United States have occurred often enough over the past few decades that it is entirely foreseeable that another will occur, and plausible that it will occur in a school. In contrast, some triggering events are "circumstances of 'unmeasurable uncertainty'. . . . [A]ny valid basis for classifying instances is absent. Effects and outcomes of action cannot be calculated because such situations are unlike any other. . . . 'The situation dealt with is in a high degree unique'" (Katznelson 2013, 33; internal quotations are from Knight 1921, 225, 233). Examples of unmeasurable uncertainty include the creation of Nazi death camps and the first detonation of an atomic bomb over a city.

Once again, a full theory of contingency's impact on political attitudes and outcomes would need to develop the implications of the differences between the anxiety of predictable uncertainty and the "radical . . . fear" (Katznelson 2013, 33) of unmeasurable uncertainty. We limit ourselves in this chapter, however, to the relatively more tractable issue of predictable uncertainty.

TWO CONTINGENT EVENTS

We begin to develop a theory of contingency by exploring two instances in which singular events, directly created or closely followed by human agency, seemed likely to shock the American public and public officials into action. They are the Sandy Hook School massacre and Superstorm Sandy. The elements of these cases – their basic contours and the public's and elites' immediate responses – provide the raw material for beginning to study contingency systematically.

Sandy Hook and Gun Control. On December 14, 2012, Adam Lanza used three of his mother's legally bought semiautomatic guns and one combat shotgun to murder her, twenty children, and six adults at Sandy Hook Elementary School in Newtown, Connecticut. He then killed himself.

Although not the only high profile mass shooting in 2012, the Sandy Hook murders set some grim records. The incident was the second deadliest mass shooting by a single person in American history, behind only the Virginia Tech massacre in 2007; it was the deadliest school shooting in any public school in the United States. The youth and innocence of the children, along with the heroism of their teachers, suggested that even gun-loving Americans might think twice about U.S. gun laws in the wake of the tragedy.

Indeed, publicity was immediate, intense, and worldwide. LexisNexis reported 2,445 newspaper articles and 2,057 television and radio stories in the week after the shootings.[4] President Obama's televised speech on the day of the killings reminding watchers that "as a country, we have been through this too many times. Whether it's an elementary school in Newtown or a shopping mall in Oregon or a temple in Wisconsin or a movie theater in Aurora or a street corner in Chicago – these neighborhoods are our neighborhoods, and these children are our children." He pledged that "we're going to have to come together and take meaningful action to prevent more tragedies like this, regardless of the politics ... And I will do everything in my power as president to help" (Obama 2012). He reiterated that pledge over the next few months, including in speeches in January 2013 and the State of the Union address in February: "I know this is not the first time this country has debated how to reduce gun violence. But this time is different."

Prominent media and political elites agreed that Sandy Hook meant that the politics of gun control had changed. Hendrik Hertzberg of the *New Yorker*, to cite only one example, wrote that "the most obviously sensible solutions ... are universally and, alas, correctly seen as out of reach.... But lesser steps ... are, for the first time in nearly a generation, imaginable. There is, for the moment, a perceptible change in the weather" (Hertzberg 2013). Some politicians were less cautious: Republican former member of Congress Joe Scarborough – a recipient of the National Rifle Association's (NRA's) highest rating during his four terms – observed that "Friday changed everything. It must change everything.... Our Bill of Rights does not guarantee gun manufacturers the absolute right to sell military-styled high-caliber semi-automatic combat assault rifles with high capacity magazines to whoever the hell they want." Democratic Senator Joe Manchin – also lauded by the NRA for his voting record – similarly called for a "common sense discussion" in which "everything should be on the table" (Kurtz 2012). Other members of Congress also promised immediate action, the vice president met with stakeholders in order to draft legislation, states began legislative efforts to control aspects of gun sales – and sales of guns, ammunition, and magazines rose rapidly in anticipation of coming restrictions.

---

[4] We searched *LexisNexis Academic* for "Sandy Hook" between December 14 and 22, 2012 in, respectively, "headline and lead" for all newspapers and "everywhere" in TV and radio transcripts.

Most Americans supported this new push for gun control. By December 19, 2012, nine-tenths claimed to have heard or read "a lot" about the shooting. Although large majorities continued to oppose bans on owning handguns throughout the winter of 2013 and the public was split on whether various measures would have prevented the Sandy Hook killings, anywhere from a small majority to 95 percent endorsed proposals to monitor purchases, limit access to ammunition, or otherwise manage gun ownership. In most cases, these are higher proportions than endorsed a similar proposal before December 14, 2012. It is not surprising, therefore, that 52 percent agreed in a January 2013 poll that "this incident has made you more likely to support some forms of gun control" (42 percent said "no difference"). (All evidence in this paragraph is from Pollingreport.com, "Gun Control.")

The best available tracking poll question, used by both the Gallup Organization and NBC News/*Wall Street Journal*, asks respondents if laws covering the sale of firearms should be made "more strict, less strict, or kept as they are now?" These polls are especially valuable because they use the same question wording over time, and the question has been asked repeatedly regardless of whether gun control is in the news.[5] Although support for stiffer gun laws had been steadily declining, Sandy Hook spurred a sharp change: while in October 2011, only 43 percent of Americans favored stricter gun laws, on December 19, 2012, that figure was 58 percent (Figure 12.1). Roughly three-fifths of respondents continued to support stricter laws through January 2014.[6] That differs noticeably from the absence of sustained change in public opinion in response to the Columbine killings in April 1999.

A different method of parsing public views provides further support for the claim that "this time ... [was] different." Through LexisNexis, Danny Hayes (2013) examined the number of newspaper articles using the phrase "gun control" in the wake of prominent mass shootings in Newtown [Sandy Hook], Virginia Tech, and Aurora, and after the shooting of Representative Gabrielle Giffords. Figure 12.2 displays a graph reproduced from his data.

Media interest in the wake of Sandy Hook was markedly different from that after other mass shootings, with mentions of gun control lasting far beyond what they had in earlier incidents. The sustained change in public opinion, the continued media attention, and the powerful response from public officials of

---

[5] Polling organizations usually ask about gun control only soon after a mass shooting or other highly visible crime; using just these surveys would bias our efforts to assess whether Sandy Hook had a measurable impact on gun control attitudes. The same methodological problem pertains to measuring the impact of many other contingencies, so we focus on events for which there are at least some before-and-after measures of opinion.

[6] The proportion of respondents favoring *less* strict gun control initially decreased in the wake of Sandy Hook, but rose sharply in January 2014, suggesting a polarization of the public. We believe that these intense opponents of gun control are one reason that Sandy Hook spurred policy change only at the state and local level, an issue we explore later in this chapter.

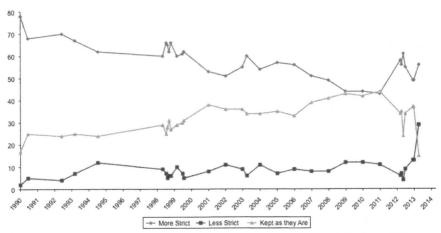

FIGURE 12.1 Public support for gun control, 1990–2014. Source: Polls from Gallup Organization and NBC/*Wall Street Journal*, in Roper Center for Public Opinion Research 2014. The question reads: "In general, do you feel that the laws covering the sale of firearms should be made more strict, less strict, or kept as they are now?" (with slight variants in wording).

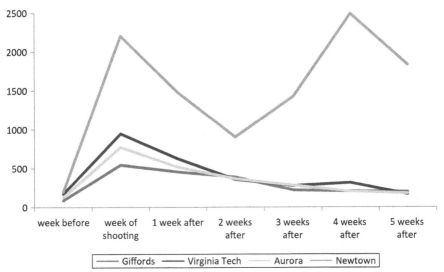

FIGURE 12.2 News stories mentioning "gun control."

both parties all suggest that the murders at Sandy Hook School are the type of seminal event that Mayhew urges us to analyze.

Superstorm Sandy and Global Warming. In late October 2012, a massive hurricane and a winter storm merged over the Atlantic Ocean, forming what the media quickly dubbed a "superstorm." This enormous storm came only a year after Hurricane Irene devastated large swaths of New England. Irene's destruction, however, occurred mainly in sparsely populated areas of Vermont; in contrast, Superstorm Sandy made landfall in media- and population-rich New Jersey, wreaking havoc on low-lying areas across the New York City metropolitan corridor. It caused seventy-two direct deaths and eighty-seven indirect deaths, rendering it the deadliest hurricane to strike the United States since Hurricane Katrina in 2005. It also cost the United States at least $71 billion dollars (in current 2012 dollars) in property damage. In constant 2010 dollars, it was the second costliest U.S. hurricane since 1900 (National Hurricane Center 2011; National Hurricane Center 2013).

The combination of Sandy's and Irene's damage, coming soon after other "weird weather" events including wildfires and droughts, spurred climate scientists to hope that Americans had reached a turning point in their views on climate change policy. Recalling Cleveland's flammable river, Michael Mann put it most succinctly: "This may be that sort of Cuyahoga River moment for climate change" (Boxall and Banerjee 2012). A researcher on environmental psychology outlines why such a public opinion shift would be both plausible and expected: "polar bear images and melting glaciers do raise people's concern, but they feel disempowered because they cannot do anything about it, whereas the local thing they understand" (Gray 2011). More formally, reminders of remote threats raise concern about global warming but not motivation to act, whereas personal experience with floods renders individuals more likely to agree that climate change is occurring *and* more likely to change their lifestyles to conserve energy (Spence et al. 2011).[7]

Nonetheless, Hurricane Sandy had little visible impact on public opinion. One careful researcher found no statistically significant difference in belief in global warming and preferences about climate change policy between respondents interviewed immediately before and after the storm (Environmental and Energy Study Institute 2013). We similarly found no difference in commitment to climate change policy before and after the storm, as shown in Figure 12.3.

In contrast to its minimal impact on public opinion, however, Hurricane Sandy elicited strong responses from important actors of both major political parties. New York Governor Andrew Cuomo immediately linked the storm to climate change and the need for policies to tackle it: "Part of learning from [Hurricane Sandy] is the recognition that climate change is a reality, extreme weather is a reality, it is a reality that we are vulnerable. . . . Protecting this state from coastal flooding is a massive, massive undertaking. But it's a conversation I think is overdue"(Vielkind 2012). Connecticut's governor Dan Malloy made

---

[7] Note that Superstorm Sandy need not have been causally related to climate change for it to serve as a focusing event that affects public or elite opinion.

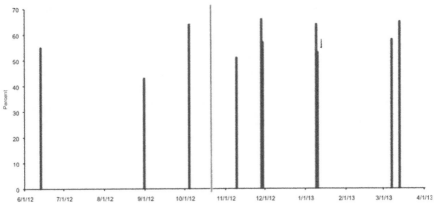

FIGURE 12.3 Commitment to climate change policy before and after Superstorm Sandy. Across eleven months and ten relevant survey items, an average of 58 percent of Americans endorsed greater governmental attention to climate change; these results do not differ markedly before and after Sandy's landfall on October 29, 2012. We examined all polls on global warming policy in Roper Center's iPOLL database from June 1, 2012, to May 1, 2013. When available, we used items that directly asked whether climate change should be a top policy priority for the United States. When policy questions were not available, we used a broader question asking if global warming was a serious issue. The surveys are: Pew Research Center (June 13, 2012; November 9, 2012; January 10, 2013); Gallup Organization (August 31, 2012; January 9, 2013); ABC News, *Washington Post* (October 4, 2012); Associated Press, GfK (November 28, 2012); Quinnipiac University (November 29, 2012); Yale University (March 7, 2013); *Washington Post*, Stanford University (March 13, 2013).

the same attribution to the storm (along with other blockbuster storms): "Climate change is giving more severe weather more frequently as the environment continues to warm" (Bass 2013). New York Mayor Michael Bloomberg overrode his Republican affiliation to endorse Barack Obama for reelection to the presidency on the basis of Obama's record on climate change: "Our climate is changing. And, while the increase in extreme weather we have experienced in New York City and around the world may or may not be the result of it, the risk that it might be – given this week's devastation – should compel all elected leaders to take immediate action" (Bloomberg 2012). The president of ConservAmerica, a "right-leaning environmental group," sought to move environmental politics back into the Nixon-era realm of nonpartisanship: "'With a majority of Americans already expressing concern about climate change and most others trying to make sense of destructive and unprecedented weather, voters of all political stripes will be looking for leaders willing to tackle the problem and offer real solutions. There is no political future in the climate denial game, and I hope my fellow Republicans can now see the political pitfalls of being bullied by the most radical and irresponsible voices in our party'" (Rob Sisson, quoted in Sheppard 2013).

Sandy Hook and Hurricane Sandy, then, have an important commonality: both events provoked an immediate and sharp elite response. In the former case, political actors who had opposed gun control displayed a public about-face; in the latter case, a prominent politician endorsed a candidate of the opposite party. The public's response to these two events, in contrast, differed markedly. Sandy Hook spurred a considerable rise in support for gun control, while Americans' opinions about environmental policy remained unchanged in the face of Hurricane Sandy. How might these differences in response to an unpredicted and shocking event matter for policy change? To answer that question, we turn to a more systematic exploration of responses to contingent events.

RESPONSES TO CONTINGENT EVENTS

The core elements of our nascent theory of the politics of contingency form a decision tree. Moving down particular branches expands, reduces, or eliminates the chance that an unpredicted event or human action will shape public opinion or policy choices. Figure 12.4 displays the decision tree, with

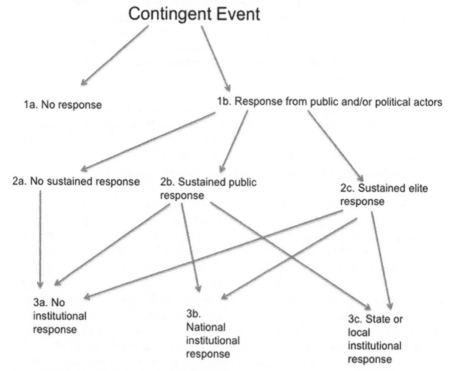

FIGURE 12.4 Contingent event decision tree.

accompanying numbers to match the text below. Row 1 presents a dichotomy between a politically relevant response and no politically relevant response. This is the stage of analysis demonstrated so far in our exploration of Sandy Hook and Hurricane Sandy: both led to a substantial public and/or elite response that seemed to imply policy action. Row 2 explores whether (and, if so, why) elites or the public sustain their response. Row 3 concludes by investigating whether elite or public responsiveness, or lack thereof, is associated with policy change at the national or local levels, and why such change occurs, if it does. We continue to use Sandy Hook and Sandy to illustrate the branches, but, when appropriate, we present evidence from other cases ranging from Pearl Harbor to urban riots.

1a. No or minimal politically relevant response from the media, public, or political actors. If a potentially significant event or action does not evoke a response from one or more politically relevant sectors of society, it will not in fact become a significant event. A complete theory of how to study contingency systematically would need to explain this nonevent; as most other scholars are likely to do, however, we simply note it here and turn our attention to more potent events.

1b. Response from the public, media, or political actors. This is the threshold condition for an unpredicted event or human action to become politically relevant. Both Hurricane Sandy and the Sandy Hook killings fall into this category: Sandy Hook spurred media attention as well as elite and public responses, while Sandy received media attention and moved the opinions of relevant important elites.

2a. No sustained politically relevant response. In a world crowded with events and actions, only a few capture the attention of citizens, the media, or elites. Moreover, only a fraction of these attention-attracting events generate *sustained* attention with political implications. History is littered with celebrity deaths, sensational court trials, and tragic plane crashes that evoked a flurry of media, elite, and public attention as the "event of the century" before soon receding from view. While some of these potentially salient events turn out to be too trivial or confusing to attract politically meaningful and sustained attention, others require deeper explanations to distinguish events that generate brief spikes in attention from those with more staying power. The rest of line 2 in the decision tree provides the opportunity to explore that issue.

2b. Sustaining public attention. A great deal of research, of course, examines the growth and maintenance of the population's attention to phenomena identified as actual or potential public issues or problems. To that large literature, we add two additional mechanisms that seem especially important for retaining people's engagement with a contingent event or action.

2b1. Citizens available to be galvanized. The first mechanism is the proportion of the public available to be affected. Many or even most Americans are unlikely to change their views in response to an event or action. They may be deeply committed to their current standpoint and unwilling to change it (Green et al. 2004), motivated reasoning may lead them to absorb a new phenomenon into extant perspectives (Lodge and Taber 2013), or they may simply be unaware of the event or action. But some can and will respond to an incident that they deem significant; how many is the crucial question here.

The people most likely to be mobilized in response to a contingent incident are those who know relevant factual information, perhaps understand its political import, but up to now have failed to use it when forging policy judgments or taking political action. They can be contrasted with those whose presumed knowledge, views, and commitments must all be changed in order for them to know and use appropriate facts in making political choices, or those who have no knowledge, views, or even awareness of the subject. Albeit for different reasons, people in both of the latter categories are unlikely to respond to new information or an unpredicted event or action (for a more extensive analysis, see Hochschild and Einstein 2015).

Thus, we expect unpredicted events to have more noticeable and lasting effects when more Americans are available to be galvanized; a comparison of views related to Sandy Hook and Hurricane Sandy demonstrates this mechanism in action. Consider Figure 12.1. While about two-thirds of survey respondents had held clear views on gun control in the decade before 2012 – 10 percent favoring less strict regulations and 40 to 60 percent endorsing stricter policies – one-third consistently fell into the question's middle category of "keep firearms policies as they are." The children's murders changed the views of many in this moderate, or perhaps uncertain, group. The proportion of Americans endorsing less strict policies changed only slightly in the shooting's aftermath – decreasing by 2 to 7 percentage points in polls through April 2013 – while the proportion endorsing stricter laws rose by 10 to 20 percentage points over the same months. Almost all of the "stricter" responses came at the expense of the "do not change" responses. In short, a third to half of the one-third of Americans who had previously expressed no strong view about firearms control moved into the ranks of those supporting stronger limits in the months after, and presumably in direct response to, Sandy Hook.

Contrast this movement with views on climate change policies. We classify an individual who knows that global warming is happening, damaging, and man-made, but who does not support government action to address climate change, as available to be galvanized by an event such as Hurricane Sandy. We lack as consistent a series of survey items as were available on gun control, but luckily the Gallup Organization had asked a set of relevant questions in March 2012, seven months before the hurricane. We operationalized correct information as agreement both that global warming is happening and that it is substantially caused by human action. Only a third of respondents were correctly informed by this measure, and only a quarter of that group, on average, did not already endorse the eight policy proposals on offer in the survey. Thus only 8 percent of the full sample were available to be persuaded of the need for policy efforts around climate change in response to a relevant event. There were simply not enough Americans lacking strong views about policy responses to global warming for even a contingent event as powerful as a massive hurricane to affect the public's policy views very much.

2b2. Repetition. Ample research in political science and psychology shows that persuasive effects generally decay over time, with the impact of one-off events usually being short lived and ineffectual (Chong and Druckman 2010; Kuklinski et al. 2000; Berinsky 2012). With rare exceptions, an event must be reinforced by further, similar events from which one can draw the same policy lessons in order for it to have a long-term consequence.[8]

The American public's and political officials' responses to racially motivated violent protests in the summer of 1967 and April 1968 demonstrate the impact of reinforcement by further, similar, events. Although violent protest – sometimes severe and extensive – had occurred in American cities for several years before then, the number and intensity spiked between July 1967 and July 1968. Figure 12.5 shows the pattern of protest-related arrests from 1964 through 1972, along with the proportion of Americans who identified "social control" as the most important problem facing the country.

The public's focus on social control rose and fell, seasonally, during the 1960s; this was, after all, the era of the Vietnam war, student unrest, and rising inflation so people had many other political issues to think about. But public attention was clearly greater after July 1967 than before and, with the exception of one anomalous survey, it remained high for half a decade even as the number of violent protests tailed off somewhat. Policy and electoral responses were extensive, deep, and long lasting.

2c. Sustaining elite attention. There are other branches in the decision tree; an issue need not have persistent or even strong short-term public support in order to generate a meaningful policy response. Many laws are passed, taxes raised or lowered, or regulations promulgated without knowledge from more than a few key actors (Brixi et al. 2004; Howard 1999; Mettler 2011). So the decision tree's row 2 includes a third branch, focusing on elite actors.

The set of relevant actors includes elected officials as well as issue advocates, policy entrepreneurs, lobbying and interest groups, regulators, and so on.

---

[8] One apparent exception is Americans' response to Japan's attacks on Pearl Harbor on December 7, 1941. Starting in March 1937, for the next four years no more than 30 percent of the public (often as low as 5 percent) agreed that the United States should enter the burgeoning European and then Asian war. Majorities often opposed even selling supplies or ships. Support for war increased only slightly over this period. A week after the Pearl Harbor attack, however, 97 percent and 91 percent respectively approved Congressional declarations of war against Japan and Germany (Gallup, December 12–17, 1941). By January 1942, almost a fifth were concerned that the United States was not "doing all it can toward winning the war" (Gallup, January 1942. All data are from Roper Center iPOLL).

We label this exception "apparent" in response to Adam Berinsky's claim (Berinsky 2009) that the American public was already fairly interventionist before the attack; if correct, his argument undermines the particular example but not our theoretical claim.

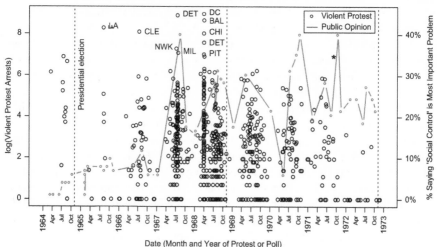

FIGURE 12.5 Violent protest arrests and public opinion on "social control," 1964–1972.
Source: Wasow 2015.

As with public opinion, large and sophisticated scholarly literatures have grown up around all of these actors and their behavior in setting agendas, framing problems and solutions, mobilizing supporters, and attaining policy goals. To this literature we add three elements that seem especially useful for explaining when elites give sustained attention to contingent events or actions.

2c1. Shock or outrage. Public actors are people as well as politicians, so their emotions can affect or even determine their political actions. Some contingent events are so powerful that they evoke a felt need to respond. The reactions of politicians such as Joe Manchin, previously an opponent of gun control, to the horrors of the Sandy Hook massacre fall into this category. Similarly, senators or representatives whose children develop rare or serious diseases sometimes sponsor legislation to provide research funds or compensatory regulations for the condition. The 1965 voting rights demonstrations in Selma, Alabama, provide another famous instance. A week after the Bloody Sunday beatings of marchers and two days after even more people braved the dangers of the Edmund Pettus Bridge, President Johnson presented a bill to a joint session of Congress that eventually became the Voting Rights Act. His speech became iconic:

> What happened in Selma is part of a far larger movement which reaches into every section and state of America. … Their cause must be our cause, too, because it is not just Negroes but really it is all of us who must overcome the crippling legacy of bigotry and injustice. And we shall overcome.

2c2. Personal political advantage or issue promotion. Although occasionally idealists, public actors are more often politicians, adept at turning an unpredicted and attention-grabbing event to their personal political advantage – or, more charitably, to the benefit of a cherished policy position. New York Mayor Michael Bloomberg had advocated a more aggressive governmental response to climate change long before Hurricane Sandy flooded his downtown. In 2011, for example, he argued in the United Nations that cities must lead the battle against global warming: "As mayors – the great pragmatists of the world's stage and directly responsible for the well-being of the majority of the world's people – we don't have the luxury of simply talking about change but not delivering it" (News Watch 2012). His plea for national and even international attention to climate change in the wake of Hurricane Sandy was thus more an instance of issue promotion than a conversion experience; in our terminology, the contingent path of the storm gave the mayor an opportunity to reinforce and demonstrate his sustained attention to a long-standing concern.

2c3. **Partisan advantage.** A further step away from acting out of moral outrage is the strategy of using a contingent event or action to promote one political party at the expense of other(s). A striking instance is that of "birthers," as they are known to their opponents. For most of Barack Obama's presidency, the Republican Party parlayed three contingent facts – the Democratic president lived in Indonesia for a time as a child, his father was African, and his name has an uncanny resemblance to that of a hated and feared enemy – into a powerful device for stoking opposition to his presidency and policies.

Before September 11, 2001, most Americans had no opinions about Muslims or were mildly favorable. Views of Muslims showed no partisan divide. After September 11, 2001, hostility rose, especially though not uniquely among Republicans (see Roper Center for Public Opinion Research iPOLL; and Hochschild et al. 2012, 153–155). Given that set of views, tying anti-Muslim sentiment to Barack *Hussein* Obama proved irresistible to many opponents. Before Donald Trump, no responsible politician espoused hostility to Muslims or Islam per se, but some suggested or hinted not only that Obama is a Muslim but also that such an affiliation makes one's patriotism or American identity suspect. In 2010, for example, former Alaska governor Sarah Palin "accidentally" promoted a tweet showing a sign that read, "The blood of Jesus against Obama History made 4 Nov 2008 a Taliban Muslim illegally elected President USA: Hussein [sic]." In the same year, while criticizing Obama administration policies, Palin noted that "I'm not calling anyone un-American, but the unintended consequences of these actions, the results, are un-American." Speaker of the House John Boehner was similarly coy when asked about some Americans' belief that Obama is a Muslim: "It really is not our job to tell the American people what to believe and what to think."

By 2010, up to a quarter of Americans agreed that Obama is a Muslim and another 25 to 40 percent, depending on the poll, did not venture an opinion on his religion. A third of conservative Republicans agreed. Those who perceived Obama to be a Muslim were less likely to vote for him than those who did not (Layman et al. 2009; Smith c. 2010). The causal connections among Americans' views of Islam, Republican elites' hints that Obama is an un-American Muslim, the public's beliefs about Obama's religion, and vote choice are complex. Probably causation runs in many directions at once and, in any case, explanation of links between elite position-taking and public opinion is not our central concern here.[9] Our point is more particular: effective politicians are adept at seizing on contingent events or actions in order to put them to partisan use. It may not always work, but it is always tempting.

3a. No or minimal institutional response. Attention to an unpredicted human action or event matters in the public arena over the long run only if it affects people's political activity or is associated with institutional or policy responses to the contingency. Line 3 of the decision tree, therefore, addresses whether sustained attention is linked to political or policy change. To begin with the negative case, the belief that Obama is a Muslim has had no traceable policy impact; those who see Obama as un-American would not have voted for him or supported his policy initiatives no matter how many baptisms he underwent. As with the other two nodes in the decision tree identified as "no response," it would be worthwhile to explicate this variety of nonevent. But we pass by it here, instead focusing primarily on why the positive cases differ from this cell.

3b. National institutional responses. Sometimes an unexpected event or action does eventuate in a policy response; Mayhew's list of such impactful contingencies ranges from depressions and recessions to wars, assassinations, floods, and groups of unruly citizens. Reams of scholarship are devoted to the issue of how a potential agenda item moves onto the actionable Congressional agenda, and how a bill becomes a law; here we offer two additional considerations that seem especially germane to the study of contingency.

3b1. Fending off further contingency. Some national institutional responses are aimed at minimizing the impact of past contingencies or the likelihood of future unexpected events or actions. The Troubled Asset Relief Program sought to mitigate the almost-unanticipated 2008 economic calamity by compensating some individuals and institutions for the disastrous and unintended results of their own or others' actions. At the same time, the Federal Reserve Bank's newly invigorated "stress tests" for major banks sought to protect the United States against another crash resulting from contingent combinations of human activities. Analogous governmental protective measures respond to natural disasters, whose occurrence can be expected but whose location cannot be predicted. An example is the National Flood Insurance Act of 1968, intended to buffer home owners from the cost of damage such as that caused by Hurricane Betsy in 1965. This type of government response to an event or action, or to public or elite attention to an event or action, is the most straightforward route down the decision tree of studying contingency systematically.

---

[9] For plausible explanations, see Nyhan 2010; Hartman and Newmark 2012; Langer 2010. The underlying theory in most of these analyses is in Zaller 1992.

3b2. An easy fix. National institutional responses to contingent events may also occur because politicians perceive an easy fix to a situation that annoys key voters. A trivial but telling example occurred in 2013. On Monday, April 22, the Federal Aviation Administration furloughed about 10 percent of its air traffic controllers in response to budget limitations caused by the sequestration law. For a few days, flights in five of the largest U.S. airports experienced considerable delays. By Friday, both houses of Congress had passed and the president had signed a law permitting the FAA to shift money within its budget categories; the furloughs, and delays, ended before business travelers had to confront a weekend spent in an airport waiting for postponed flights home. In the right conditions, participants in the unwieldy American system of checks and balances can move with alacrity, particularly when traceability is a boon (Arnold 1990; see also Huber 2009 and Wood 2009).

3c State or local institutional response. Sometimes the federal government's failure to act is not merely one of many nonevents, but is itself an occurrence that requires explanation. Sandy Hook provides one such example. Despite a galvanizing event coming after a series of many similar events, up to 95 percent public support for some policy responses, intense media focus, carefully vetted policy proposals, bipartisan sponsorship, and officials' heartfelt pledges of legislation, the Democratically controlled Senate failed to pass even a token gun control bill in a vote four months after the school murders.

Why? The explanation, in brief, is that Mayhew I ("the electoral connection") (Mayhew 1974) can halt Mayhew II ("events as causes") in its tracks. That is, even the set of characteristics just described may be no match for senators' electoral imperatives.

For one thing, despite the changes in public attitudes about gun control laws reported earlier, the usual partisan divide remained. By February 2013, seven in ten Republicans chose "protect[ing] the right of Americans to own guns," while seven in ten Democrats chose "control[ling] gun ownership" in a forced choice item about the more important goal. (Independents split evenly. Pew Research Center for the People & the Press 2013.) Given Republican senators' own ideologies and the nature of their constituencies, their opposition to even a rather anodyne bill to expand background checks could be predicted. But the bill failed in the Senate for an additional reason– four Democrats also voted against it (in addition to the Senate majority leader who voted "no" for procedural reasons). Here, too, Mayhew I provides the explanation for this more surprising result: all four were from relatively conservative states. Thus Heidi Heitkamp of North Dakota told critics, "I always had a reputation as somebody who will listen, somebody who is pretty independent-minded but also believes that at the end of the day, you got to listen to your constituents. . . . The [telephone] calls literally were before the last day at least 7 to 1 against that bill. . . . This is part of our culture in North Dakota. And they expressed those opinions to me pretty loud and clear" (Raju 2013).[10] Her three Democratic colleagues gave similar statements.

Where the public, media, or elites show sustained attention to a contingent event or action but the national government does not act, the old trope of states as laboratories of democracy becomes newly salient. The United States has thousands of elected governments; federal inaction may foster action in at least some states and localities. For example:

The more President Obama talks about the need to raise the federal minimum wage, the less likely it appears that Republicans in Congress are inclined to do it.

But the stalemate matters less and less. In the last 14 months, since Mr. Obama first called for the wage increase in his 2013 State of the Union address, seven states and the District of Columbia have raised their own minimum wages, and 34 states have begun legislative debates on the matter. Activists in an additional eight states are pursuing ballot referendums this year to demand an increase in wages for their lowest-paid workers (Shear 2014).

In the two years since that article appeared, even more states, cities, and smaller governments have debated or instituted a raise in the minimum wage. Other issues show the same pattern; in the face of federal inaction on immigration reform, for example, states and cities are acting either to encourage immigration and help the undocumented, or to discourage immigration and punish undocumented status (Community Services Administration n.d.; Gulasekaram and Ramakrishnan 2015 Varsanyi 2010).

Our two central cases reveal more fully both how states and localities respond to contingent events, and how the responses themselves add another layer of contingency. Consider Hurricane Sandy. Despite elites' calls for action, national political actors made virtually no effort to legislate climate change policies, perhaps because of Republican veto power. Some local governments, however, particularly those directly affected by Sandy, stepped into the vacuum quickly and aggressively. The plan for "A Stronger, More Resilient New York" included 257 recommendations to strengthen parts of the city most vulnerable to "climate events"; it proposed such measures as adding over 1.2 million cubic yards of sand to city beaches and increasing the height of dunes to alleviate the impact of waves and storm surge (City of New York 2013). As Deputy Mayor for Operations Cas Holloway, put it: "The risks from extreme weather and climate change are real, and the City has responded with an ambitious and achievable plan – a multi-layered strategy of strengthening coastal defenses, upgrading buildings, protecting critical infrastructure, and making neighborhoods safer and more vibrant." Connecticut's state government implemented resilience policies through the Connecticut Climate Preparedness Plan

---

[10] Mayhew I also explains why even a majority Democratic vote was insufficient; the Senate's filibuster rules dictated the need for a supermajority.

(Department of Energy and Environmental Protection 2013). Boston's Mayor Thomas Menino announced Climate Ready Boston, with a parallel observation: "While the City of Boston had been preparing for the impacts of climate change since 2007, Hurricane Sandy was a gut check. We needed to do more" (Climate Preparedness Task Force 2013).

Even if all of these plans are not fully implmented, local governments nonetheless appear to be the most fertile venue for climate policy. As of 2015, 1,060 mayors from all fifty states, representing almost 90 million people, endorsed the U.S. Conference of Mayors Climate Protection Agreement. The Agreement commits participating cities to develop policies to meet or beat the Kyoto Protocol targets, to push state governments to implement similar policies, and to urge Congress to pass greenhouse gas reduction legislation. It would clearly be more efficient and pervasive if the federal government took action, but federal stalemate need not preclude response from other levels of government.

Gun control advocates similarly found some state and local governments more amenable to regulation than was their national counterpart after the Sandy Hook shootings. The Brady Campaign to Prevent Gun Violence reports that within a year, twenty-one states had passed stricter gun control laws, with eight states' changes classified as "major" (Law Center to Prevent Gun Violence and Brady Campaign to Prevent Gun Violence 2013).

Despite the fact that both inspired local responses to contingency, however, Hurricane Sandy differs from Sandy Hook in one crucial way. We know of no local government that sought to make its community more vulnerable to the effects of global warming, whereas some states moved in the opposite direction from those lauded by the Brady Campaign's gun control initiative. That is, some states reacted to the Sandy Hook killings by loosening gun control laws. Supporters of looser gun laws refer to the Sandy Hook killings just as do supporters of stricter laws, but to very different ends: "The president is using the massacre at Newtown 'to further his liberal agenda to try and disarm and disenfranchise law-abiding Americans from their enshrined Second Amendment that is, ... rights' " (Walshe 2013, quoting Alaska House Speaker Mike Chenault). As of 2016, some states were moving to permit "open carry" in locations such as churches and schools, and "concealed carry" in locations such as university campuses.

In short, localities' responses to contingent events or actions may themselves be contingent. Idiosyncratic phenomena – the proximity of an arresting event (Wasow 2015), the ideological or partisan group currently in local power, a policy entrepreneur or crusading newspaper, a skilled interest or advocacy group that can deliver votes (such as the NRA in the case of gun control), or resource-rich foundations or business leaders – may have a large impact on which local governments act, and what policy outcomes they produce (Glick and Friedland 2014; Mansbridge 1986; Shipan and Volden 2008; Stone et al. 2001). It is no surprise that states and cities nearest to Hurricane Sandy's landfall with liberal governors or mayors responded most strongly, or that Republican-run states and cities were the most vehement in rejecting gun control after Sandy Hook.

Structural characteristics – population size and distribution, electoral design, community wealth, racial and ethnic composition, cultural and religious formations, region, physical features, transportation patterns, or general patterns of partisanship – add a further layer of contingency to the question of how local governments respond to contingent events. We expect that the smaller the unit of governance, the more important idiosyncratic actors and actions are relative to deeper and more stable institutional factors in shaping the policy response to contingent events – but that too is a subject for further exploration.

State and local policy responses to unpredicted or unpredictable events or actions are necessarily limited; as Edward Glaeser observes, "most localities are very restricted in the kinds of stuff they can do" (Lowrey 2014). But sometimes many piecemeal, partial, multidirectional policy responses have considerable impact, especially in the context of federal government inaction.

CONCLUSION

Just as Monsieur Jourdain of *Le Bourgeois Gentilhomme* was surprised to discover that he had been speaking prose all his life, political scientists might be startled to learn that they have been analyzing contingency throughout their careers. Although M. Jourdain was pleased by the thought ("How grateful am I to you for teaching me that!"), scholars in a discipline that often aspires to causal precision and analytic parsimony may not be so gratified. Nonetheless, as our comments about the large literatures in public opinion, elite incentives, or obstacles to policy change imply, the systematic study of contingency engages widely with political science scholarship. Indeed, studying contingency may simply be the flip side of studying rules, patterns of thought, or institutional design.

The central question in studying contingency systematically is whether the previous sentence is correct. That is, is the study of contingency essentially the same thing as the study of causation, with the focus of attention merely shifted to the unexplained variance that remains after theoretically based causal analyses have done their work? In that case, whose logic is captured in shorthand here as Mayhew I, the goal of studying contingency systematically is to reduce its role in both social science explanations and real world politics and policy making.

Or is politically relevant contingency something distinct and best studied on its own terms, as implied by Mayhew's later assertion of "a case for ranking events as the equals of interests and preferences in a seriously explanatory political science"? In that case, the goal of studying contingency systematically is to develop its explanatory impact in a more robust way than has heretofore been done, and perhaps even to celebrate its place in politics and policy making.

This chapter has explored the implications of the second choice; we share the view of Mayhew II, that unpredicted or unpredictable events or actions need to be analyzed in ways that move beyond trying to explain away what is left over after developing the implications of the electoral connection or some other general law. But throughout this exercise, we have been constantly reminded that, just as rules operate within unpredictable circumstances, so the impact of unpredicted events develops within a rule-constrained public realm.

Even if the viewpoint of Mayhew II is persuasive, this chapter only begins the necessary analysis. Basic questions remain, such as which of the phenomena on which we focus are necessary, sufficient, or neither for a contingent event to change views in a sustained way and affect political and policy outcomes. How does one even define and study contingency (Shapiro and Bedi 2009)? What is the role of powerful individual actors in creating exogenous shocks or taking advantage of those that occur during their period in office (Read and Shapiro 2014)? What creates and sustains momentum in public opinion, media attention, elite concern, or partisan jockeying for advantage?[11] Why are state and local responses to an event so varied and seemingly random at times? How might a combination of contingent events yield a political outcome that no single contingent event would have produced by itself (Hochschild and Burch 2009)?

Our goal has been to open those questions by outlining a framework of when, how, and why idiosyncratic events drive durable and important changes in public opinion and policy. As political scientists, we reject some historians' view that significant change is, by definition, contingent – that a policy's unfolding results arising out of particularities of context and human agency may be retrospectively explained but not prospectively predicted. Along with Mayhew I, we assume that individual and institutional incentives and logics can be identified and used to systematically explain some outcomes. But only "some" outcomes – Mayhew II haunts Mayhew I, and sorting out their relationship seems a goal worth pursuing.

REFERENCES

Arnold, R. Douglas (1990). *The Logic of Congressional Action*. New Haven, CT: Yale University Press.

Bass, Paul (2013). "Malloy: 'This Is Climate Change.'" *New Haven Independent*. www .newhavenindependent.org/index.php/archives/entry/this_is_climate_change/.

Berinsky, Adam (2009). *In Time of War: Understanding American Public Opinion from World War II to Iraq*. Chicago, IL: University of Chicago Press.

(2012). "Rumors, Truths, and Reality: A Study of Political Misinformation." Cambridge MA, MIT, Political Science Department. web.mit.edu/berinsky/www/les/ rumor.pdf.

---

[11] This question links the study of contingency to the analysis of positive and negative feedback loops. See, among others, Campbell 2003; Patashnik 2008; Hochschild 2013.

Bloomberg, Michael (2012). "A Vote for a President to Lead on Climate Change." *Bloomberg.com*. www.bloomberg.com/news/2012-11-01/a-vote-for-a-president-to-lead-on-climate-change.html.

Boxall, Bettina and Neela Banerjee (2012). "Sandy a Galvanizing Moment for Climate Change." *Los Angeles Times*. November 4.

Brixi, Hana, et al., eds. (2004). *Tax Expenditures – Shedding Light on Government Spending through the Tax System: Lessons from Developed and Transition Economies*. Washington, DC: International Bank for Reconstruction and Development.

Campbell, Andrea (2003). *How Policies Make Citizens: Senior Political Activism and the American Welfare State*. Princeton, NJ: Princeton University Press.

Chong, Dennis and James Druckman (2010). "Dynamic Public Opinion: Communication Effects over Time." *American Political Science Review* 104(4): 663–680.

City of New York (2013). "Mayor Bloomberg Details Progress on Resiliency Projects Outlined in the City's Long-Term Plan to Protect City against the Effects of Climate Change on Hurricane Sandy Anniversary." www1.nyc.gov/office-of-the-mayor/news/348-13/mayor-bloomberg-details-progress-resiliency-projects-outlined-the-city-s-long-term-plan-to/#/o.

Clark, Christopher (2013). *The Sleepwalkers: How Europe Went to War in 1914*. New York: Harper.

Climate Preparedness Task Force (2013). "Climate Ready Boston: Municipal Vulnerability to Climate Change." www.cityofboston.gov/news/uploads/30044_50_29_58.pdf.

Community Services Administration (n.d.). "New Haven's Elm City Resident Card: My City. My Card." www.cityofnewhaven.com/csa/newhavenresidents/.

Department of Energy and Environmental Protection (2013). "Connecticut Climate Preparedness Plan." www.ct.gov/deep/cwp/view.asp?a=4423&Q=528012&deepNav_GID=2121.

Environmental and Energy Study Institute (2013). "Public Perceptions about Global Warming and Government Involvement in the Issue." www.eesi.org/032813polls.

Glick, David and Zoe Friedland (2014). "How Often Do States Study Each Other? Evidence of Policy Knowledge Diffusion." *American Politics Research* 42 (6): 956–985.

Gray, Louise (2011). "Flooding at Home, Not Polar Bears, Convinces People of Man-Made Climate Change." *The Telegraph*. March 21.

Green, Donald, et al. (2004). *Partisan Hearts and Minds: Political Parties and the Social Identity of Voters*. New Haven, CT: Yale University Press.

Gulasekaram, Pratheepan and S. Karthick Ramakrishnan (2015). *The New Immigration Federalism*. New York: Cambridge University Press.

Hartman, Todd and Adam Newmark (2012). "Motivated Reasoning, Political Sophistication, and Associations between President Obama and Islam." *PS: Political Science and Politics* (July): 449–455.

Hayes, Danny (2013). "Why This Gun Control Debate Has Been Different." *Wonkblog*. www.washingtonpost.com/blogs/wonkblog/wp/2013/01/28/why-this-gun-control-debate-has-been-different/.

Hertzberg, Hendrik (2013). "Shots." *New Yorker*. January 7: 17–18.

Hochschild, Jennifer (2013). *Dynamics of International Migration: Will Demography Change Politics before Politics Impedes Demographic Change?* Cambridge, MA: Harvard University, Department of Government.

Hochschild, Jennifer and Traci Burch (2009). "Contingent Public Policies and Racial Hierarchy: Lessons from Immigration and Census Policies." In *Political Contingency: Studying the Unexpected, the Accidental, and the Unforeseen*, eds. Ian Shapiro and Sonu Bedi. New York: New York University Press, 138–170.

Hochschild, Jennifer and Katherine Levine Einstein (2015). *Do Facts Matter? Information and Misinformation in American Politics*. Norman: University of Oklahoma Press.

Hochschild, Jennifer, et al. (2012). *Creating a New Racial Order: How Immigration, Multiracialism, Genomics, and the Young Can Remake Race in America*. Princeton, NJ: Princeton University Press.

Howard, Christopher (1999). *The Hidden Welfare State: Tax Expenditures and Social Policy in the United States*. Princeton, NJ: Princeton University Press.

Huber, Gregory (2009). "Contingency, Politics, and the Nature of Inquiry: Why Non-Events Matter." In *Political Contingency: Studying the Unexpected, the Accidental, and the Unforeseen*, eds. Ian Shapiro and Sonu Bedi. New York: New York University Press, 205–221.

Katznelson, Ira (2013). *Fear Itself: The New Deal and the Origins of Our Time*. New York: Liveright Publishing Co.

Knight, Frank (1921). *Risk, Uncertainty, and Profit*. Boston: Houghton Mifflin.

Kuklinski, James, et al. (2000). "Misinformation and the Currency of Democratic Citizenship." *Journal of Politics* 62 (3): 791–816.

Kurtz, Howard (2012). "Some Pro-Gun Voices Now Changing Their View." *Daily Beast*. www.thedailybeast.com/articles/2012/12/17/some-pro-gun-voices-now-changing-their-view.html.

Langer, Gary (2010). "This I Believe." *ABC News Online*. blogs.abcnews.com/thenumbers/2010/08/this-i-believe.html.

Law Center to Prevent Gun Violence and Brady Campaign to Prevent Gun Violence (2013). "2013 State Scorecard: Why Gun Laws Matter." www.bradycampaign.org/sites/default/files/2013-scorecard.pdf.

Layman, Geoffrey et al. (2009). *A Muslim President? Assessing the Causes and Consequences of Misperceptions about Barack Obama's Faith in the 2008 Presidential Election*. Toronto, Ontario: Annual Meeting of the American Political Science Association.

Lodge, Milton and Charles Taber (2013). *The Rationalizing Voter*. New York: Cambridge University Press.

Lowrey, Annie (2014). "Cities Advance Their Fight against Rising Inequality." *New York Times*. April 6 p.A1

Mansbridge, Jane (1986). *Why We Lost the ERA*. Chicago, IL: University of Chicago Press.

Mayhew, David (1974). *Congress: The Electoral Connection*. New Haven, CT: Yale University Press.

(2005). "Wars and American Politics." *Perspectives on Politics* 3 (3): 473–493.

(2009). "Events as Causes: The Case of American Politics." In *Political Contingency: Studying the Unexpected, the Accidental, and the Unforeseen.*, eds. Ian Shapiro and Sonu Bedi. New York: New York University Press, 99–137.

(2010). "Legislative Obstruction." *Perspectives on Politics* 8(4): 1145–1154.

Mettler, Suzanne (2011). *The Submerged State: How Invisible Government Policies Undermine American Democracy*. Chicago, IL: University of Chicago Press.

National Hurricane Center (2011). "The Deadliest, Costliest, and Most Intense United States Tropical Cyclones from 1851 to 2010 (and Other Frequently Requested Hurricane Facts)."

(2013). "Hurricane Sandy: October 22–29, 2012 (Tropical Cyclone Report)."

News Watch (2012). "C40 Chair, New York City Mayor Michael R. Bloomberg: 'Cities Are Forging Ahead.'" newswatch.nationalgeographic.com/2012/03/14/c40-chair-new-york-city-mayor-michael-r-bloomberg-cities-are-forging-ahead/.

Nyhan, Brendan (2010). "Pundits Blame the Victims on Obama Muslim Myth." www.brendan-nyhan.com/blog/2010/08/pundits-blame-the-victims-on-obama-muslim-myth.html.

Obama, Barack (2012). "Statement by the President on the School Shooting in Newtown, Ct." www.whitehouse.gov/photos-and-video/video/2012/12/14/president-obama-makes-statement-shooting-newtown-connecticut#.

Patashnik, Eric (2008). *Reforms at Risk: What Happens after Major Policy Changes Are Enacted*. Princeton, NJ: Princeton University Press.

Pew Research Center for the People & the Press (2013) "If No Deal Is Struck, Four-in-Ten Say Let the Sequester Happen." www.people-press.org/2013/02/21/section-1-opinions-about-major-issues/.

Raju, Manu (2013). "Heidi Heitkamp Defends Gun Vote." *Politico*. www.politico.com/story/2013/04/heidi-heitkamp-defends-gun-vote-90600.html.

Read, James and Ian Shapiro (2014). "Transforming Power Relationships: Leadership, Risk, and Hope." *American Political Science Review* 18(1): 40–53.

Roper Center for Public Opinion Research iPOLL. www.ropercenter.uconn.edu/.

Schedler, Adreas (2009). "Mapping Contingency." In *Political Contingency: Studying the Unexpected, the Accidental, and the Unforeseen*, eds. Ian Shapiro and Sonu Bedi. New York: New York University Press, 54–78.

Shapiro, Ian and Sonu Bedi, eds. (2009). *Political Contingency: Studying the Unexpected, the Accidental, and the Unforeseen*. New York: New York University Press.

Shear, Michael (2014). "After Push by Obama, Minimum-Wage Action Is Moving to the States." *New York Times*. April 2.

Sheppard, Kate (2013). "Could Chris Christie Bring the GOP around on Climate?" *Mother Jones*. www.motherjones.com/environment/2013/02/chris-christie-climate-change.

Shipan, Charles and Craig Volden (2008). "The Mechanisms of Policy Diffusion." *American Journal of Political Science* 52 (4): 840–857.

Smith, David Thomas (c. 2010). *The First Muslim President? Causes and Consequences of the Belief that Barack Obama Is a Muslim*. Ann Arbor: University of Michigan, Department of Political Science.

Spence, A. et al. (2011). "Perceptions of Climate Change and Willingness to Save Energy Related to Flood Experience." *Nature Climate Change* 1(1): 46–49.

Stone, Clarence et al. (2001). *Building Civic Capacity: The Politics of Reforming Urban Schools*. Lawrence, KS: University Press of Kansas.

Varsanyi, Monica, ed. (2010). *Taking Local Control: Immigration Policy Activism in U.S. Cities and States*. Stanford, CA: Stanford University Press.

Vielkind, Jimmy (2012). "Cuomo: 'Climate Change Is a Reality... We Are Vulnerable.'" *Capitol Confidential*. blog.timesunion.com/capitol/archives/162798/cuomo-climate-change-is-a-reality-we-are-vulnerable/.

Walshe, Shushannah (2013). "Some States Propose Gun Control Law, Others Say No to Federal Proposals." *ABC News*. January 19.

Wasow, Omar (2015). "Do Protest Tactics Matter? Effects of the 1960s Black Insurgency on White Attitudes and Voting Behavior." Paper presented at the Center for the Study of Democratic Politics, Princeton University, Princeton, NJ, April 9.

Wood, Elisabeth (2009). "Modeling Contingency." In *Political Contingency: Studying the Unexpected, the Accidental, and the Unforeseen*, eds. Ian Shapiro and Sonu Bedi. New York: New York University Press, 222–245.

Zaller, John (1992). *The Nature and Origins of Mass Opinion*. New York: Cambridge University Press.

13

Majoritarianism, Majoritarian Tension, and the Reed Revolution

Keith Krehbiel

The publication of David Mayhew's *Congress: The Electoral Connection* in 1974 rocked the field of legislative studies. The tight and eminently readable compendium not only has enlightened generations of students as an introduction to Congress but also has earned even higher accolades as research. The scholarly impact of the book came in two surges, paralleling its two parts. The first part signified a methodological break from traditional congressionalists of the 1950s and 1960s. Using a rigorous (yet accessibly nonformal) axiomatic approach, Mayhew engaged in what he called a "mono-causal venture" when studying legislative behavior, organization, and outcomes. Of course, he did not believe that the single cause he isolated – the reelection motive – was the sole causal factor of the various dependent variables. Rather, he viewed it as a search for a pervasive force of politics of first-order significance for understanding what atomistic, self-interested legislators do and why they do it. The plausibility of his argument, the evidence adduced to support it, and its lasting impact attest to Mayhew's success in his search for a single, fundamental force.

The second part of Mayhew's monograph, which is the springboard for this paper, begins with a classic example of his uncanny ability to identify and frame new research agendas. The excerpt is well-known.

[The] organization of Congress meets remarkably well the electoral needs of its members. To put it another way, if a group of planners sat down and tried to design a pair of American national assemblies with the goal of serving members' electoral incentives year in and year out, they would be hard-pressed to improve on what exists. Mayhew 1974, 81–2.

I gratefully acknowledge David Brady, Sarah Binder, Josiah Ober, Eric Schickler, and Melissa Schwartzberg for helpful communications and recommended readings, and Richard Bensel, Nick Eubank, Molly Jackman, and Alan Wiseman for insightful feedback on early drafts.

With the benefit of hindsight, it is evident that Mayhew was two steps ahead of the field. Not only did he exhibit a firm grip on the importance of representative assemblies as institutions that define their individual members' strategic opportunities and constraints,[1] but he also had the prescience to observe that many important institutional features are endogenous.[2] Therefore, rules and procedures – much like policies – ought eventually to be studied as potential objects of choice in attempts to understand the dynamics of institutional development.[3]

But do "group[s] of planners [sit] down and ... design ... national assemblies?" My objective is to develop, and to assess preliminarily, a new way of thinking about the development of voting political institutions that sheds light on Mayhew's hypothetical institutional design scenario. As Mayhew sought to identify the fundamental force underlying the electoral connection, I am searching for fundamental forces of political institutional design. The primary distinguishing feature of my approach is its emphasis on *majoritarianism as a variable* whose value is determined by the sum total of an organization's contextual institutional features and is, therefore, partially within the control of the organization's members. The secondary distinguishing feature is a characterization of a legislative institution as a body of parliamentary or procedural *rights* and their distribution, with an emphasis on *individuals* rather than parties as recipients of rights.

I begin by discussing the concept of *majoritarianism*, not exclusively as simple majority rule but rather as a more general, two-dimensional concept that is defined by a numerical property (a stipulated required level of assent) and by the context to which the assent threshold applies (e.g., to policy choice, to decisions to consider policies, or to procedural choice). Next, I consider the broadened conception of majoritarianism in the context of institutional development. This fusion of ideas leads to the creation of a simple analytic device – the cube of *majoritarian tension* – that provides structure for the rest of the essay. The domains of collective choice to which the framework can be applied are numerous, but this essay focuses on congressional reform. A critique of existing literature is offered, after which several of the explicated shortcomings are illustrated and addressed by a reconsideration of U.S. House of Representatives' adoption of the Reed rules in 1890. A concluding discussion offers some caveats and directions for continued studies based on the revised concept of majoritarianism and the new framework of majoritarian tension.

---

[1] In this vein, the "New Institutionalism" agenda was soon to follow (Shepsle 1979) and to be advanced aggressively in several other seminal works, such as Shepsle and Weingast (1987).

[2] This was the approximate launching pad for Weingast and Marshall (1988) and Krehbiel (1991).

[3] I use the term "institutional development" instead of "institutionalization" because my emphases differ in nontrivial ways from those of Polsby (1968).

MAJORITARIANISM AS A VARIABLE

Like many other political organizations, legislatures make collective decisions by voting, usually with a well-defined counting rule or preference-aggregation function. When the counting criterion is met, a motion, candidate, or proposal passes; otherwise it fails. Typically, we think of collective decisions as choices about policies, for instance, passage of legislation or adoption of amendments to bills. The essence of institutional endogeneity, however, is that collective choice occurs at a higher level as well: legislatures also choose the rules of procedure by which they, in turn, choose policies. To obtain a deeper under-standing of political institutional development, two preliminary needs must be addressed: a need to sharpen and extend the conception of majoritarianism by building in context-specificity, and a need to isolate a parsimonious set of pervasive tradeoffs that must be confronted during consensus-building. The overarching question is: What desirable properties of institutional development besides majoritarian consensus are important in collective choice, and how do they interact?

Two Dimensions of Majoritarianism

Majoritarianism is a multifaceted concept. I will restrict my attention to two of its dimensions which I call *numerical* and *contextual*. A consequence of this elaboration is that my usage of the term is more general than that of others.

Usually, when political scientists speak of or write about majoritarianism, they have foremost in mind *simple* majoritarianism: the idea that, for a candi-date or a proposal to be deemed and accepted as the decision of a group of voters, the number of votes cast for that candidate or proposal exceeds one-half of the total number of votes cast. A straightforward way of characterizing simple majoritarianism – and, by extension, other forms of majoritarianism – is in terms of a numerical *threshold of assent*. The threshold of assent for simple majority voting expressed in terms of number of votes is $\frac{N}{2} + 1$ (or $\frac{N+1}{2}$), where N is the total even (or odd) number of voters. More conveniently expressed in terms of fractions between 0 and 1, simple majoritarianism is therefore said to have a *critical value* of $\frac{1}{2}$. Above the critical value, a motion, proposition, or resolution passes; below the critical value, it fails.[4] The numerical characteriza-tion of simple majoritarianism generalizes easily to other recognizable forms of majoritarianism. *Unanimity* is a voting rule with a critical value of 1, *super-majoritarianism* has a critical value between $\frac{1}{2}$ and 1 (often $\frac{2}{3}$), and *submajor-itarianism* (which borders on oxymoronic but is not unheard of) has a critical value of less than $\frac{1}{2}$. I emphasize that I am using *majoritarianism* as a general

---

[4] The case of strict equality of the voting ratio with the critical value requires situation-specific tie-breaking rules, but this will not cause confusion.

term that subsumes the prefixed forms: sub-, simple-, and supermajoritarianism, and also includes unanimity.

A core feature of political institutional development is that rules, such as those that govern voting, may be endogenous in the long run. The simple assent-threshold definition of majoritarianism fails to capture other important aspects of the choice process. To accommodate some of these, I introduce, define, and use a set of setting-specific types of majoritarianism which I summarize as the second, *contextual dimension of majoritarianism*. Four majoritarian contexts vary in terms of their place, purpose, and consequences for the surrounding choice processes. Table 13.1 summarizes four context-based types of majoritarianism and integrates them with numerical majoritarianism via simple parameters.

Immediate majoritarianism, which is parameterized by a fractional assent value, α, refers to the yes-vote threshold for policies, amendments, and other directly policy-outcome-consequential collective choices. It is the nominal, *de jure* voting rule that, in contemporary legislatures, is usually codified in standing rules or precedents, and applied to the motion or proposal directly before the body at a specified time. Several examples are given that illustrate variation of immediate majoritarianism both across institutions and within a given institution.

Background majoritarianism (β) is the *de facto* assent threshold required to bring a measure before the voting body. It is often manifested earlier in the process than, and as a prelude to, foreground or immediate majoritarianism. While in some respects it resembles immediate majoritarianism, it also differs in a significant way. The impact of background majoritarianism depends upon not only upon established procedural requirements but also upon behavior within a larger procedural context. So, for example, by erecting a higher threshold for considering a proposal than for passing it ($\beta > \alpha$), an opportunity is created for forward-looking legislators to adopt strategies that make the background-majoritarian threshold the *de facto* voting assent level required for subsequent amendments or for final passage. The politics of filibusters as played out in the Senate in recent years when anonymous holds are epidemic is an example of background (*de facto*) supermajoritarianism in the presence of immediate (*de jure*) simple majoritarianism, where the background rather than foreground is the constraint that binds. Similarly, background supermajoritarianism can also be due to assent requirements that may be invoked later than the legislature's passage of a bill. A common example in U.S. politics is an executive veto with a legislative supermajority override. When a veto threat is credible, the *de facto*/background assent threshold (2/3) is again greater than the *de jure*/immediate assent threshold (1/2), and so the true degree of consensus required is – like the filibuster example – supermajoritarian.

Remote majoritarianism (γ) is another step removed from immediate and background majoritarianism. It refers to the level of assent required to change standing rules or to set and affirm precedents that, jointly and in total,

TABLE 13.1 *Types of Majoritarianism*

Types of Majoritarianism (Objects of Choice)	Assent Threshold	Description	Examples and their Critical Values (Assent Minima)
Immediate or *de jure* (Policies)	α	The fraction of affirmative votes required to pass amendments, enact legislation, adopt policies, etc.	• U.S. Congress final passage of bills: $\alpha = 1/2$. • U.S. Senate ratify a treaty, $2/3$. • U.S. Senate may deviate from most rules via unanimous consent, 1. • U.S. criminal jury conviction, case and state-varying but usually 1. • 13th Century Bologna selection of magistrates, $13/20$.
Background or *de facto* Consideration of Policies)	β	The fraction of affirmative votes required to close debate or preclude delay	• House deviation from normal order via special rules $\beta = 1/2$. • Senate invokes cloture under its standing Rule 22, $3/5$. • Supreme Court *certiorari*, $4/9$.
Remote (General Procedures)	γ	The fraction of votes required to change a rule, or to set or affirm a precedent	• U.S. House and Senate, $\gamma = 1/2$ under general parliamentary law (*Jefferson's Manual*). • U.S. Senate Rule 22 stipulates that invoking cloture on an attempt to change Rule 22 requires a $2/3$ vote. • U.S. Constitution, Article V, gives provisions for Constitution's own amendment: $3/4$ supermajority of states.
Cultural	δ	Beliefs and pressures exogenous to a self-governing body within a political system that influence its α, β, γ parameters mostly indirectly, gradually, and tacitly	• Greeks culture valued participation and tacitly supported simple majoritarianism. • The Catholic Church through the middle ages was pseudo-unanimous (election by "acclamation"). • U.S. culture was initially unanimity-tending but soon became simple majoritarian, especially in legislatures • Public corporations' shareholders are fond of share-weighted simple majoritarianism.

determine the more proximal parameters, α and β. As such, remote majoritarianism covers classes of situations rather than bill-specific cases.[5] Like background majoritarianism, remote majoritarianism always *may* have a bearing on immediate decision making, but its effect is indirect, because it rests on an implicit threat. The higher level of majoritarianism (γ) will be invoked only to the extent that the lower level(s) (α or β) are perceived to be failing regularly in major ways. Roughly speaking, the greater is the assent threshold for changing rules, the more stable such rules will be in the day-to-day, year-to-year, or century-to-century operation of the institution. In many political institutions, the remote majoritarianism threshold is not quantified or codified, in which case the operable value of γ is subject to uncertainty. In the U.S. political system, for instance, remote majoritarianism is relatively explicit but not without ambiguity. The ambiguity stems from the concept of *general parliamentary law*, which is considered the fallback set of rules when the existing rules do not specify a consensus majoritarian criterion or when standing rules have not yet been adopted (e.g., at the beginning of a new Congress when the House has yet to pass new rules or affirm its previous rules). Moreover, general parliamentary law is widely regarded as an embodiment of simple majoritarianism.[6] For the U.S. Congress and many state legislatures, unless their rules stipulate otherwise, general parliamentary law holds and makes them remotely simple-majoritarian by default.

---

[5] I introduced the term "remote majoritarianism" in *Information and Legislative Organization* (Krehbiel 1991) where its definition is more general than it is here. Specifically, I did not single out and define what I now call "background majoritarianism," whose distinguishing feature from remote majoritarianism is that the former has greater bill or proposal specificity. Both types are background forces relative to immediate majoritarianism, but remote majoritarianism resides more deeply in the background than what I'm now calling background majoritarianism. Their respective objects of choice also differ. Background majoritarianism is specific to consideration of designated policies or motions; remote majoritarianism pertains to changes in more general standing rules or precedents.

[6] During his vice presidency (and when presiding over the Senate) Thomas Jefferson wrote a manual of basic parliamentary procedure that came to be known and published as simply *Jefferson's Manual*. In section 41 of the manual, Jefferson writes, "the voice of the majority decides; for the *lex majoris partis* is the law of all councils, elections, &c., where not otherwise expressly provided." *Lex majoris partis* – the law of the majority – is sometimes given a more elaborate translation as "majority rule in a society that governs itself by the consent of the governed." Somewhat curiously, Jefferson never uses the term "general parliamentary law," even though the term appears regularly, with his name, in House and Senate precedents. Upon further exploration I found less than complete consensus regarding the origin, meaning, and definitive source on general parliamentary law, sometimes also called "common parliamentary law." Other allegedly "definitive sources" that crop up occasionally include *Roberts Rules of Order* (which is written more for private meetings than for public law making) and *Cushing's Manual* (which, likewise, sought a broader audience; its author, Luther Cushing, was clerk of the Massachusetts House of Representatives). See, for example, Jennings (n.d.) for superficial but typical views of general parliamentary law and Malamut (2008) for a more serious assessment that grapples with the subtlety and ambiguity in general parliamentary law.

Cultural majoritarianism (δ) completes the list and precludes an infinite regress in causes of causes of levels of variable majoritarianism. It refers to the degree to which members of a polity – external to, but potentially influential on, the focal organization – have a demand for, or aversion to, consensus-demanding procedures. In the United States, two contemporary examples of cultural majoritarianism that simmer and sometimes boil are citizens' disillusionment with the electoral college (which *ex post* can be submajoritarian with $\alpha < \frac{1}{2}$ of the national electorate) and grumbling about the Senate's filibuster propensities ($\beta = \frac{3}{5}$ of the Senate). Implicit in these joint positions is an affinity in the American public for consistent simple majoritarianism, that is, the public believes that it ought to be the case that $\alpha = \beta = \gamma = \frac{1}{2}$. I am not willing to bet that public opinion polling would corroborate this, however.[7] Suffice it to say that cultural majoritarianism is a latent, deep-background factor and probably only rarely and indirectly affects institutional development.[8]

Recapitulation

Many types of majoritarianism can be characterized in two dimensions. The first dimension of majoritarianism is numerical and specifies the threshold fraction of votes above which a motion is deemed the collective choice. The second dimension refers to the context in the political process in which the first dimension's assent threshold applies. The four contexts in which different degrees of majoritarianism may take hold or are: *immediate* (choice over policies), which is the most familiar and most easily quantifiable; *background* (which may alter *de facto* the policy-choice assent threshold); remote (overt choices of or changes in procedures); and *cultural* (constituents' attitudes about an organization's procedures). Any given type of majoritarianism can be viewed as exogenous in one context and endogenous in another; this classification depends upon the research objective.

---

[7] Indeed, it is difficult to envision the appropriate survey item that could elicit this information.

[8] A recent, possible example in which cultural majoritarianism *may* have had some impact on intralegislative majoritarianism parameter values is the Senate's decision – via simple majority – to set a precedent for proceeding to the consideration of a selected subset of presidential appointees *without* the historically required 3/5 vote in the presence of a hold or implicit threat of a filibuster and its correspondingly requisite cloture vote (see *Congressional Record*, November 11, 2013, pp. S8413–S8418). In terms of Table 13.1, a simple majority of Democrats – possibly emboldened by anti-supermajoritarian public sentiment ($\delta \cong \frac{1}{2}$) – acted forcefully to lower background majoritarianism (β) from 3/5 to 1/2 for consideration of NLRB appointments. The subtle but important feature is that, at the level of remote majoritarianism (γ), the key action – voting to table the appeal of the decision of the chair – was simple majoritarian ($\gamma = 1/2$). A broad interpretation of instances like these is that the level of remote majoritarianism (γ) in the Senate occasionally inches downward as a result of bouts of gridlock malaise, possibly backed by (perceived?) cultural simple majoritarianism. (The NLRB nuclear option incident agitated Senate Republicans, to be sure. There was little pushback from the general public, however.)

MAJORITARIAN TENSION

Why does majoritarianism vary over time and space, that is, both across political organizations and within them? Why do some organizations (e.g., the U.S. House) tend to prefer simple majoritarianism while others (e.g., the Senate) adhere more often to *de facto* supermajoritarianism? Is it because members' majoritarian tastes differ, because organizational constraints differ, or is it just a matter of historical quirks and inertia?

As a starting point, consider what unanimity and supermajoritarianism do relative to their simple-majoritarian counterparts. By definition, unanimity sets the bar of assent higher than other voting rules and therefore demands greater *consensus* from the organization in order for it to express its collective assent – that is, in order for the supermajority to speak for the whole. Consensus is typically regarded as a desirable property of collective choice, provided it is obtained for the right reasons, such as through deliberation and debate; through acquiring, digesting, and aggregating all relevant information about constituents' preferences and the consequences of policy; through bargaining, compromising, and finding common ground, and so on. If this kind of process leads to consensus, or if the need for consensus brings about this kind of process,[9] then supermajoritarianism seems like a good practical recipe for institutional development and corresponding well-informed, prudent, or generally wise decision making.

On the other hand, a high critical value of immediate majoritarianism ($\alpha \gg \frac{1}{2}$) has a downside, too. Requiring too much consensus can result in the politics of gridlock. Most political organizations have members with diverse preferences. They also differ in their willingness and ability to specialize. Under these conditions, it is well known that reaching a consensus is difficult; preference aggregation and information aggregation are both difficult, and often impossible. Consequently, the organization is often unable to reach a high assent threshold when it could well have reached a lower one, in which case simple majoritarianism may not look so bad after all. Simple majoritarianism, in other words and other things equal, better enables the organization to be responsive to its external constituencies and to make *timely* decisions.

Rules as Balancing Mechanisms

This brief and intuitive discussion can easily be repackaged in a framework amenable to analyzing and interpreting institutional change in a wide range of

---

[9] In the context of institutional development, the assent level of majoritarianism is sometimes an exogenous variable, and sometimes an endogenous variable. Which form it takes and when depends upon the organization that is studied and the research question that is asked. Because it seems premature at this stage to develop a causal theory of majoritarianism, I settle for a more modest, exploratory approach, which is to identify likely covariates of majoritarianism and defer questions of direction of causality.

settings. The framework is an embodiment of a simple empirical conjecture about forces affecting institutional design and development.

Conjecture: *The rules governing the collective choice processes of voting institutions balance its members' simultaneous desires for consensus, timeliness, and wisdom during decision making.*

Some elaboration on the three key terms in the conjecture is useful. *Consensus* does not necessarily mean the literal number of votes received but more importantly the breadth of positive expressed assent as well as the passive and tacit consent to the outcome by opponents of the winning alternative. In other words, consensus has a quantitative or counting component, but more intangible, nonquantifiable factors determine consensus, too. *Timeliness* refers primarily to the speed of the decision but not so much its appropriateness.[10] Timeliness can also be defined indirectly as the opposite of gridlock. Finally, *wisdom* refers to the overall quality or soundness of the decision, given the best available information and technology. Analytic examples of phenomena that represent real-world notions of wisdom include Fenno's (1973) "good public policy," Gilligan and Krehbiel's (1987) "informational efficiency," and Hirsch and Shotts's (2012) "quality."

The three forces identified in the conjecture can be seen as forming a platonic ideal-form conception of a political institution. That is, if it were possible, we would design democratic institutions whose members unanimously and immediately made sound decisions. Unfortunately and obviously, this is not possible due to *majoritarian tension*. Figure 13.1 illustrates.

Notice first that the base of the cube represents minimum consensus, which could be implemented, for example, by a dictatorship, the sole head of which possesses the only vote that counts. A rash dictator (point A) acts quickly by definition, spending no time to acquire information, deliberate, or reflect on the consequences of the policy he will unilaterally impose. A reflective dictator (point B), in contrast, acts slowly and deliberately, processing all information to maximize the wisdom of his choice.

The third, vertical dimension in the diagram implicitly brings majoritarianism into the picture, albeit in a somewhat indirect and imprecise way. *Consensus* generally is regarded as a desirable feature of representative governance. Consensus covaries positively with the degree of majoritarianism required by voting rules or methods – other things equal, the greater the supermajority threshold, the greater the consensus – but this relationship is not perfect.[11]

---

[10] *Appropriateness*, subjective though it is, is better classified as a component of *wisdom*.

[11] A common example of the imperfect correlation between consensus and the numerical consent threshold is U.S. presidential nominating conventions when, following a candidate's crossing the simple-majority threshold, a delegate moves that the candidate be nominated "by acclamation" (in effect, unanimity). *Ex post* consensus-exaggerating proclamations, such as these, were also common in Ancient Greece (Ober 2008, Raaflaub et al. 2007, Schwartzberg 2014) and in

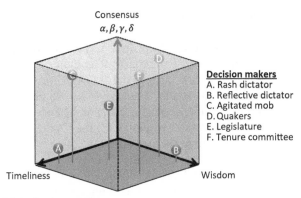

FIGURE 13.1 Majoritarian tension.

Therefore, a somewhat holistic approach is needed to interpret the consensus dimension fruitfully. Specifically, an organization's consensus level is determined jointly by its three majoritarian parameters, α, β, and γ, possibly reinforced or constrained by cultural majoritarianism, δ. The relationship between these parameters is a topic in its infancy that I hope to nurture in future work. For present purposes, all that needs to be noted is that at any given level of majoritarian consensus, some combinations of timeliness and wisdom that are feasible under dictatorships are no longer feasible. For example, majority coalition building is time-consuming, especially if preferences are heterogeneous and/or proposals are multidimensional, in which case(s) maximum timeliness is no longer attainable. Similarly, aggregation of information and convergence of beliefs are complicated and imperfect processes, so maximum wisdom is not feasible. In short, consensus is costly for any nontrivial collective choice problem.

In a more comprehensive form, the cube could be embellished to characterize simplex-like, institution-specific, feasibility-frontier surfaces that rule out unattainable mixes of consensus, timeliness, and wisdom (beginning with the obviously unattainable (1,1,1) point on the unit cube). A helpful thought experiment is to imagine an interior, approximately triangular surface and to visualize institutional development as a dynamic process in which procedures are adopted that, upon implementation, may push out toward the feasibility frontier in the direction of the arrows. Alternatively, beginning on the frontier, institutional change may be characterized as an instance of moving along the Pareto surface, necessarily trading gains in one (or two) dimension(s) for losses in the other two (or one).

Medieval papal elections (Heinberg 1926, Giuriato 2007). Presumed consent of those in the minority with the majority-established position also lies at the core of Rousseau's conception of the General Will and, to some extent, Locke's Social Contract.

Four additional observations about majoritarian tension are noteworthy.

First, the extreme low values of the three criteria – that is, convergence to the origin of the cube at its back-bottom corner – have respective antonyms that provide a brutally comprehensive summary of common criticisms of some present-day legislative institutions, such as the U.S. Congress. An approximate opposite of consensus is polarization. The opposite of timeliness is gridlock. Opposites of wisdom are policy ignorance or incompetence. An uncompromising congressional cynic, therefore, would locate the Congress at the origin of the cube and would caricaturize the organization as divisive, dysfunctional, and dumb.

Second, different institutional arrangements' procedural attributes are at least indirect or long-term reflections of their cultures' different values, traits, and technologies. Citizen democracies of ancient Greece were highly participatory, sometimes with casts of thousands, so reaching a consensus that approximated unanimity was clearly not possible. Quaker settlements (point D) in the colonial era, in contrast, were composed of a smaller number of more homogeneous, more patient members for whom time was not of the essence, but wisdom was important, and consensus was a must. In other words, different cultures or choice environments have different relative valuations of the three criteria and so will make different tradeoffs and reach different approximate optima in its various voting institutions.

Third, of the three dimensions in the cube, consensus is probably the most directly manipulable via institutional reforms. The most transparent mechanisms are the voting thresholds summarized in Table 13.1. It is not the case, however, that timeliness and wisdom adjustments or improvements are off limits, nor are they unaffected by procedural reform. Rather, the mechanisms by which legislative organization can be tweaked to capture gains in timeliness or wisdom are just somewhat less transparent and subject to more uncertainty than reforms such as changing the cloture requirement from two-thirds to three-fifths.

Finally, the costs and attainability of timeliness and wisdom in collective choice vary with environmental factors. For instance, for any given institution, some periods of history are clearly more demanding than others. Variable demands for policy-making action, in turn, affect the value placed on rapid responsiveness to external events. Similarly, the complexity of policy making exhibits variation across policy areas at a given time as well as for the same policy over time. In high-complexity periods or policy domains, wisdom will weigh more heavily into the equation than when the relevant environments are calm and static.

Implications

The cube of majoritarian tensions and, more generally, its three forces bearing on institutional design is not a positive theory in the normal sense of the term, but it can serve as a basis for forming some preliminary, crude empirical expectations about institutional development. Specifically, if decision makers' competing demands for consensus, timeliness, and wisdom are at work, then we should be able to find evidence of the following characteristics when observing actual instances of institutional change or reform.

1. **Evolutionary – not revolutionary – change.** In well-established voting institutions, we should observe a mostly steady state in procedures. When procedural changes do occur, they will tend to be incremental and consistent with longer-term historical trends.
2. **Cube interpretability of majoritarian change.** Changes in α and, less commonly, in β, should be rationalizable or interpretable as tradeoffs between one or more pairs of consensus, timeliness, and wisdom.

The expectations can be thought of as covering the overall nature of change and the main correlates of change, respectively. That is, the first expectation is that institutional development will be smooth, slow, and nonvolatile. The second expectation is that, within these overall patterns, the various twists, turns, and tweaks of institutional majoritarianism will be understandable as compromises pertaining to the timeliness and wisdom of the historical and institutional contexts.

Both expectations are closely related to and consistent with the majoritarian cube (Figure 13.1) and the nested nature of variable majoritarianism (Table 13.1). To see why, consider the life cycle of a political institution. In institutional infancy, rules are absent and regularized procedures are rare. Consequently, the requisite consensus level is undefined and fluid, collective choice is cumbersome and slow, and individuals' wisdom is underutilized if it exists at all. Figuratively, the infant institution is near the origin of the cube, so free lunches, represented as improvements on all three dimensions, await discovery via introspection, experimentation, or just luck. With the passage of time and transition of the institution into adolescence, procedures that prove useful are adopted with increasing regularity, business is transacted more and more speedily, and specialization and division of labor – at first, ad hoc, but, when effective, regularized – begin to allow decisions to be better informed.[12] When an institution reaches maturity (geometrically, when its majoritarian cube coordinates lie on the simplex or Pareto surface), free lunches are things of the past. For instance, it is no longer possible to reform the institution to reduce gridlock without lowering consensus, undercutting wisdom, or both. Because reform in mature institutions involves inescapable tradeoffs among typically competing cherished standards, institutional changes that a self-organizing body will agree to accept are likely to be gradual and often imperceptible – not abrupt and radical. Furthermore, to the extent that the four types

---

[12] See, for example, Cooper 1960 on the origin of the US House Committee system.

of majoritarianism pertinent to procedural change approximately meet the condition $\alpha \leq \beta \leq \gamma \leq \delta$, so that the higher order rules for changing lower-order rules become more and more consensus-demanding, far-reaching reform is all the less likely, simply because a larger majority is not likely to agree to a rules change that enables a smaller coalition to do what it otherwise cannot do. In summary, the deck is heavily stacked against nonincremental change.

In a more comprehensive work in progress, I am applying the majoritarian-tension framework to a wide range of settings, institutions, and their development.[13] Henceforth in this paper I restrict my attention to the U.S. Congress.

MAJORITARIANISM AND CONGRESSIONAL REFORM

Congressional reform is a well-studied instance of political institutional development in which majoritarian conflict plays a key and often controversial role. Consequently, studying instances of congressional reform is a promising way to explore the utility of the majoritarian-tension framework. Rather than move immediately to application of the new approach, however, it is instructive to summarize existing approaches and findings to establish points of comparison. To fix things in context, I consider *reform* as it is characterized in the literature as an instance of sanctioned endogenous procedural change, and I continue to consider *majoritarianism* as an assent threshold that can vary across and within institutional settings.

A Composite Sketch

For several decades, congressional scholars have viewed reform through distinctively partisan lenses. Research projects have taken on one of two equally interesting forms: reform as a dependent/endogenous variable, or reform as an independent/exogenous variable. In both types of study, institutional change variables are given party-laden definitions and interpretations.[14] For instance, a rules change is observed, and the so-called reform is classified and coded as either pro-majority or pro-minority. Researchers who seek possible causes of the reform (e.g., Binder 1996; 1997; Schickler 2000; 2001) then regress a qualitative reform variable on various party-based measures such as majority party size advantage, party polarization, or Binder's notion of "partisan capacity." Significant coefficient estimates are taken as corroboration that reforms

---

[13] Related work in progress includes: voting in ancient Greece and Rome, ecclesiastical voting in the Middle Ages, the evolution of roll call voting in the English Parliament, and majoritarianism and the U.S. Senate's filibuster and so-called nuclear option.

[14] This claim is somewhat overstated and/or reflects a recent-time bias. Earlier reform literature, however, did something similarly zero sum albeit with a committee/subcommittee focus (Rohde in the 1970s) or a committee-versus-party or party leadership focus (Cooper and Brady 1981, for example).

are party-motivated. Similarly, other researchers who seek evidence of the consequences of reform also use party-based coding of rules regimes but instead put them in the right-hand side of statistical models and test whether they systematically affect other partisan phenomena such as roll rates or spatial-directional of change in legislation (see, e.g., Cox and McCubbins 2005, ch. 4; Dion 2001).

The implicit model of Congress that motivates these research strategies is that *parties'* desires for rules changes in Congress are ever present, and opposing partisan forces are engaged in a zero-sum struggle over who has the ability to organize the legislature and dictate the policy agenda. However, although the demand for partisan agenda setting would seem empirically to be approximately constant – with *each* party wishing *always* to be a monopoly agenda setter – the actual occurrence of allegedly significant changes in congressional rules is episodic.[15] So, for instance, we see repeated references to a handful of demarcation events (Reed's Revolution, the Cannon Revolt, the Legislative Reorganization Act of 1946, the Subcommittee Bill of Rights of 1973, etc.) that define what have come to be accepted as distinct – and presumably distinctly different – periods, eras, or institutional arrangements (e.g., the Jacksonian era, the partisan era, the textbook Congress, and the resurgence of party).

The findings of these empirical inquiries are interesting, because they give rise to several generally accepted substantive conclusions, in spite of the fact that there is also a modicum of specific disagreement across studies in terms of included variables, their meaning, and their measurement.[16] Summing up, most scholars are in basic agreement on five empirical propositions regarding congressional reform in the U.S. House.

1. *Short-term constant.* At any given time – and hence on average – the majority party enjoys a distinct advantage over the minority party in terms of procedural rights.
2. *Long-term variation.* Sporadic and dramatic bursts of reform – or discontinuities in the distribution of relative partisan procedural advantages – occur periodically, but not very often.
3. *Causes or correlates.* Reforms that bolster the majority party's strategic arsenal are positively related to majority-party size and majority-party homogeneity.[17]

---

[15] Research on congressional reform and legislative organization more broadly is abundant, and my references are far from exhaustive. Recommended earlier works include Jones (1968), Polsby (1970), Mayhew (1974), and Rohde (1974). More recent studies have tended to be more data intensive and occasionally theoretical. These include Binder (1997), Binder and Smith (1997), Schickler (2001), Wawro and Schickler (2006), Dion (2001), and Cox and McCubbins (2005).

[16] Park (2013) provides an insightful up-to-date review, critique of estimation methods, and extension to this literature.

[17] E.g., Aldrich and Rohde's (1998) "conditional party government" and Binder's (1996) "partisan capacity."

4. *Consequences.* The majority party parlays its procedural advantage (sometimes called a "cartel") into an electoral advantage by restricting floor activity to those issues that burnish its brand name and thereby also contribute to continued majority-party success in the electoral arena.[18]

5. *Long-term steady state.* Propositions 1–4 imply that the long-term steady state of party-based legislative organization is one in which the majority party's procedural advantages result in systematic majority-party policy bias.

Puzzles and Problems

Nuance is ineluctably lost in composite sketches of bodies of literature. Even so, it is an understatement that most contributors to the party-oriented reform literature would endorse most of the five propositions. There may be some drop-off at Proposition 5, but, even there, agreement is widespread and often ardent.[19] What needs to be emphasized, then, is that Proposition 5 is very difficult to rationalize from the perspectives of immediate and remote simple-majoritarianism. To see this, consider the following:

The Submajoritarian Puzzle. In conventional partisan procedural politics, a *majority of the majority party* generates equilibrium policy outcomes that a *bipartisan simple majority of the legislature* would like to change to the chamber median voter's ideal point. Yet, according to Proposition 5, that bipartisan simple majority does not act – directly or indirectly – to improve its well-being. How and why does this form of *majority partyism*[20] overpower simple majoritarianism in an immediately and remotely simple majoritarian legislature?

The puzzle is disturbing because, upon brief reflection, it defies majoritarian common sense. The typically anthropomorphized "majority party," when atomized, is really only a majority *of the majority party* and, moreover, a *minority* of the legislature as a whole. Nonetheless, in the conventional strong-majority-party argument, this coalition dominates policy choice in spite of its numerical-minority status. As such, the scenario contradicts the principle of immediate simple majoritarianism as defined in the first section of this

---

[18] Some of these advantages are of the "position-taking" variety (Mayhew 1974). Others are outcome-based and are attributed to passage of policies that are noncentrist and that favor the majority party over the minority party and over the House median voter.

[19] Furthermore, many congressional scholars buy in to something much like Proposition 5 for reasons independent of the procedural mechanisms embodied in Propositions 1–4. After all, Proposition 5 in isolation is essentially a statement of any standard strong-parties-in-government claim/hypothesis/theory.

[20] As elaborated in the Majoritarian Tension and Reed Rules section of this chapter, by *majority-partyism* I mean dominance by a majority of the majority party.

chapter, as codified in the Standing Rules of the House, multi-volume sets of House precedents, and *Jefferson's Manual*, and as revered in American culture.

Meanwhile, the big loser in the equilibrium scenario within this partisan world is not only a bipartisan coalition but also a majority-of-the-legislature coalition that, under the Constitution and general parliamentary law, could change the rules. That its members decline to exercise their rights to change their rules contradicts the principle of remote simple-majoritarianism. How can it be that the two levels of simple-majoritarianism – direct and remote – generate outcomes that are known *ex ante* by all legislators to be *ex post* submajoritarian?

I will not attempt to offer a definitive answer, but I will suggest and explore a few possibilities for resolving the puzzle.[21] Part of the problem stems from key words and the way they are used. Another part is due to coding conventions and the theoretical need to anticipate correctly the partisan consequences of rules, even when the rules have no overt partisan content. And most of the problem has to do with units of analysis. Happily, all of these shortcomings are avoidable or remediable in the alternative framework I will employ.

The first problem is a common tendency to conflate – or, worse, to equate – *rights* and *power*. It is nearly impossible to conceive of rules and procedures in the absence of rights, therefore, it is critical in this literature to be precise about what is meant by procedural rights. Procedural rights are specified individuals' entitlements to take specified actions at specified times as part of collective choice processes. Once granted (via standing rules or precedents), rights acquire a stickiness that for most purposes renders them exogenous. Procedural rights are *not* entitlements to win, that is, to exert power over policy choice by getting more desirable outcomes than those who are deprived of the enabling right. Power, instead, is endogenous in the legislative game. Rights *may* make designated legislators powerful over outcomes, but they do not guarantee it. Power over outcomes depends on other features as well, such as the location of status quo policies, the structure of the game, and the strategies that players adopt. An illustrative instance of confusion attributable to right/power conflation is the common usage of the term "agenda-setting power."[22] An agenda setter *may* be powerful, but whether she is or is not depends upon situational factors and the behavior of others when she exercises her procedural rights.

A similar and correctable foible is a mild epidemic of adjective deficit disorder coincident with the usage of the terms *majority* and *minority*. All too often the literature is muddled simply because "party" (seemingly nonpurposely)

---

[21] One possibility that I will not explore here but that is implicit in some of my prior research is that the premise of the paradox – namely, the description of procedural politics in Proposition 5 – is empirically inaccurate. For now, however, I concede that most researchers in this area take seriously the substance of the proposition, and I shall follow suit.

[22] One of many examples is this often-quoted passage: The majority party's "negative agenda power is unconditional." (Cox and McCubbins 2005, 37).

is dropped from the phrases *majority party power* and *minority party power*. So, for example, the statement "The minority has the right to engage in dilatory tactics" could apply to the minority party, or it could apply to any group smaller than $N/2$ where N is the size of the legislature and the group members may belong to either party. Indeed, the numerical, nominal "minority" could be composed entirely of members of the *majority* party.

A more serious and probably more controversial feature in most recent reform literature is the selection of parties as units of analysis and/or as the stipulated recipients of procedural rights. As a preface, I emphasize that I do not dispute that endogenous procedural changes (reforms) often have partisan motivations, nor do I dispute that many of them have partisan consequences once implemented. I am, however, skeptical about the first-order importance of parties in congressional reform and therefore wish to explore the possibility of choosing different units of analysis.

To justify this change in emphasis, I begin with a basic empirical question: How often, and with what scope, do the standing rules of the House (or Senate) grant procedural rights to a party or parties?

The short answer is: only rarely and narrowly. Furthermore, when party-specific rights are granted asymmetrically, they favor the *minority* party. This discovery comes from a text search of the *Rules of the 111th House of Representatives*. In the fifty-five-page, three-columns-per-page document, the "majority party" is referenced only eight times, five of which are in Rule X, Organization of the Committees, which governs the committee appointment process. But each of these eight majority party references also reference the minority party to whom they assign *exactly the same rights*. The remaining three majority-party mentions arise in Rule XI, Procedures of Committees and Unfinished Business, and are similarly symmetric and innocuous. So, as a strict matter of codification, there is no evidence of the majority party stacking the procedural deck. Indeed, the count for mentions of "minority party" number seventeen – over twice that of "majority party."[23]

I am not suggesting that there is any nonnegligible minority party bias in this finding. The key point is that, with the exception of a few innocuous mentions in which parties are treated evenhandedly, there is no explicit basis for the claim that either party *as a collective entity* has any procedural advantage stemming from rights granted in the House's standing rules.

Closely related to the paucity of mentions of "party" in the rules are some purely conceptual drawbacks of the terms "majority rights" and "minority rights." The underappreciated fact is that rights are inherently *individual*

---

[23] I also searched for "minority member" and "majority member" on the assumption that *party* is likely to be an implicit adjective in those phrases. Here the differences were even starker: 43 mentions of "minority member" but only 1 mention of "majority member." The suggestion is that the standing rules are more concerned with explicating minority party rights to ensure even-handedness than majority party rights to promote party bias.

opportunities, not *group* entitlements.[24] So, even if the House chose to try to bolster the minority party's ability to dampen the effects of, say, the majority party's efforts to push its legislative agenda, it is not clear whether the House could, or how it would, grant a right to delay *to the minority party* as a single unit. More reasonably – and true to the nature of the explication of rights as they are actually codified in the standing rules – the House that wants to level the procedural playing field confers rights to *all* individual members of *both* parties, say, to speak on specified legislation. This may, in turn, have the effect of delaying the passage of a specific bill and, therefore, be labeled as a "minority right" ("party" intentionally omitted) only inasmuch as a minority of *legislators* (not necessarily the minority *party*) exercises their individual rights in the specific situation. So-called "minority rights," in other words, are not rights granted exclusively to the minority party, or even to any given ad hoc minority of legislators. As the term is used, minority rights are actually rights (not powers) granted to *all* legislators but that, in the course of the legislative game, are exercised by an ad hoc minority that may or may not correspond closely with minority party membership. Construed and implemented as such, so-called minority rights also can just as easily be exercised by members of the majority party. Suffice it to say that one can question the transparency if not the logic of a working definition of *minority rights* whose logical implication is that such rights are possessed by *everyone*. Yet, so it is in much of the research on congressional reform.

Finally, in light of conceptual imprecision surrounding majority and minority (party) rights, it is not surprising that the task of coding reforms of rules in terms of partisan impact is also problematic. Take, for example, the codification of the motion to suspend of the rules – a procedure that can be invoked by a supermajority of two-thirds of the House. As implemented, the motion allows departure from the regular order of business, brings before the House a different measure otherwise not in order, allows for debate, and, finally, with the requisite supermajority, passes that measure without further amendment. This is a good example of the type of rules change that Binder, Cox and McCubbins, Dion, and Schickler consider and code as an expansion (or contraction) of majority (or minority) rights (with the adjective "party" implied but often not specified). To appreciate the complexity of this partisan coding task, notice four things. First, the suspension procedure, like almost all other reforms that various authors code, does not mention parties, so the case for asymmetric impact is ambiguous from the outset. Second, neither does it mention a generic, ad hoc majority or minority or otherwise single out groups for favored treatment; rights are granted uniformly at the individual level. Third, even in terms of the impact of the procedure as employed – that is, the

---

[24] It is true that individual rights in principle can be assigned exclusively to members of a specified group, such as a party, but we have seen that – contrary to what the literature suggests – this is rarely done in Congress.

consequences of reform – it is not clear whether the majority (party?) or minority (party?) is advantaged. One spin is that the majority is advantaged because it can expedite action by circumventing dilatory motions, quickly passing bills, and protecting them from hostile amendments, all in a single vote. Furthermore, the Speaker may exhibit majority-party bias by refusing to recognize minority-party members to make motions to suspend. However, another approximately equally plausible spin is that the procedure, like the Senate's infamous Rule 22, empowers the minority (party?) by making it possible for a 1/3 + 1 minority to kill bills brought up under suspension. Fourth and finally, this is arguably a relatively *easy* reform to code because at least we have some basic modeling tools that can inform us of conditions under which one party or another will benefit from the procedure.[25] For most reforms no such theory exists, in which case the coding decision seems arbitrary and manipulable at worst and a subjective guessing game at best.

Implications

This summary of the literature has several implications for studying majoritarian tension and legislative reform. Procedural rights are and should continue to be a primary micro-level focus in the study of reform, but rights should not be presumed to confer power to those who possess them. Furthermore, by default, the possessors of rights should be thought of as individuals, not groups, unless the rule granting the rights singles out a predefined group as an *exclusive* possessor of the right. In the U.S. Congress, this is rarely if ever done, except in a slightly imbalanced, *minority*-party-favorable way. Consequently, scholarship that codes procedural reforms in majority party/minority party win–lose fashion in effect imputes both partisanship and zero sumness onto reform situations that may in fact be nonpartisan and quite possibly positive sum.

MAJORITARIAN TENSION AND REED RULES

Among the many reputedly significant procedural developments throughout the colorful history of the U.S. House of Representatives, its 1890 adoption of the so-called Reed rules during the 51st Congress stands alone in terms of captivating and eliciting superlative statements by congressional scholars, political pundits, and journalists. What is the conventional wisdom of the Reed Revolution? Is it analytically sound? Have viable alternative interpretations been overlooked? I address these questions in order.

---

[25] Suspension of the rules is well approximated as a closed-rule model with a monopoly agenda setter and a 2/3 (instead of median) pivot.

Conventional Wisdom

In addition to its portrayal of the introduction of Reed's Revolution as an abrupt, epochal, institutional event, the conventional account of this noteworthy slice of history is based on *a* form of majoritarianism – but it is a majoritarianism of a distinctively different kind from that formulated and discussed in the first and second sections of this chapter. A better, but regrettably awkward, term for it is "majority-partyism."[26]

In brief, the problem that the Republican Party regularly confronted in the 1880s was *minority-party-induced gridlock* via individual members' exercise of their rights to use dilatory tactics. As the 51st Congress convened in December of 1889, Republicans had an ambitious policy agenda for the nation but a thin majority in the House. The agenda covered diverse topics such as pensions, tariff legislation, an elections bill to protect blacks' voting rights against Southern disenfranchisement efforts, and the controversial Silver Purchase Act. In previous Congresses, such legislative agendas had proven to be susceptible to dilatory tactics, too. So, as Thomas Brackett Reed of Maine ascended to the Speakership on December 2, 1889, he anticipated that, barring some sort of unprecedented minority-party comity or majority-party procedural coup, the 51st Congress would exhibit more of the same.

Within two months of Reed's election to the Speakership, the infamous showdown occurred during an attempt to bring before the House a partisan-charged contested election case. After 162–1 vote in favor of seating the Republican candidate, Democrats noted the absence of a quorum (< 165). In unprecedented fashion and under vociferous objection, Reed ruled that members who were present but not voting on a roll call shall be counted as present for purposes of establishing a quorum and that, therefore, the House's 162–1 vote stands.[27] And so it did – ultimately, but with considerable intervening cacophony – when a simple majority of the House voted to table Democratic leader Crisp's appeal to Reed's ruling.

Comprehensive accounts of the ensuing debate, the procedural issues, and how they were resolved exist elsewhere,[28] so I will omit many tangential details. For immediate purposes, it suffices to say that, while nullification of

---

[26] I considered using the less awkward term "party majoritarianism" but rejected it because it implies majoritarianism within parties while remaining tacit about behavior and outcomes between the parties (that is, who wins and why?). "Majority partyism," in contrast, properly directs attention to the majority party as the recipient of procedural rights and as the winner in party competition over law making.

[27] The first of many clever quips that would occur over the subsequent days occurred immediately. After a member challenged Reed's having counted him present, Reed replied, "The Chair is making a statement of fact that the gentleman from Kentucky is present. Does he deny it?" (*Congressional Record*, vol. 61, Jan. 29, 1890, p. 948.)

[28] Dion's (2001) and Jenkins and Stewart's (2013) accounts are particularly carefully researched, detailed, and readable.

the vanishing quorum tactic was the crowning achievement of "Czar Reed," as he came to be known, it was only one of several changes in House procedure that were quickly adopted via simple-majority rule and codified in the *Standing Rules of the House of Representatives*. To summarize, the changes included:

1. The aforementioned right of the Speaker to count members physically present during roll calls even though they abstained from voting and/or declined to affirm their presence when called upon;
2. The Speaker's right to refuse recognition of members who sought to make dilatory motions;
3. A reduction in the size of the quorum (to 100) to conduct business in the Committee of the Whole;
4. The ability to close debate by majority vote on any part of a bill being considered in the Committee of the Whole;
5. The Speaker was given the right to refer House and Senate bills and messages from the President to committees without intervening debate;
6. Codification of the Speaker's right to chair the Rules Committee.

The prevailing interpretation is that the passage of the Reed rules marked a distinct and discontinuous event, tantamount to a change in the House's procedure-induced equilibrium. Even Schickler, who is much more skeptical about majority-partyism than most contributors to the Reed Revolution literature, writes: "Adoption of the Reed rules in 1890 is without question one of the most significant events in the institutional development of Congress. No single change did more to secure [generic] majority rule in the House" (2001, 32).[29]

As was noted in the Majoritarianism and Congressional Reform section of this chapter, congressional scholars are frequently ambiguous about whether minority or majority rights or power are generic nonpartisan terms or whether they are shortcuts for minority-*party* and majority-*party* rights, power, and so on. In most studies of the Reed rules, it seems clear that scholars do have parties in mind rather than generic majorities and minorities. More specifically, scholars seem to have in mind that the Reed rules changes constituted an abrupt and immediately successful assertion of majority *party* (not generic majority) *power* (not just rights) at the expense of the minority *party* (as opposed to a generic minority). For instance, Cox and McCubbins assert that

when it comes to rule changes affecting the majority party's control of the agenda, the adoption of Reed's rules stands out from all others in importance – so much so that congressional history can be simply divided into pre-Reed (small advantage) and post-Reed (large advantage). 2005, 25.

---

[29] Schickler's research is uncommonly cognizant of the difference between generic majoritarianism and what I am calling "majority partyism." From context it is clear that his excerpt is essentially nonpartisan. Yet, even a nonpartisan account interprets the event as highly significant.

The data on which they base this are reproduced in Figure 13.2 where the plotted variable is the proportion of times final passage votes move in the majority-party direction in the pre-Reed-rule (left of the vertical line denoting the rules change) versus post-Reed-rule (right side of line) eras, and where straight fat lines depict best fits within the two periods.[30]

Limitations of Conventional Wisdom

In the subfield of congressional reform, any given study of the pre–post form can be questioned on methodological grounds. In the case of Figure 13.2, several points deserve brief mention because, to some extent, they generalize. First, substantial congress-to-congress variation is evident in the dependent variable. Measures of majority-party power or discipline are inherently noisy and can be very misleading.[31] Second, a clean partition of pre-Reed and post-Reed Congresses does not exist because the 52nd Congress rescinded the Reed Rules (more on this in the following). A consequence of this fact is that only seven pre-Reed observations are present in the dataset, which raises a caution flag about significance.[32] Third, while the authors briefly consider a trend variable, they dismiss it as insignificant without allowing for nonlinearity. Casual observation of the figure suggests, however, that an increasing asymptotic curve would fit the data quite well (see the hypothetical dotted red curve in Figure 13.2).[33] Finally, it is not clear what the theoretical expectation of majority partyism ought to be, given the dependent variable. If the Reed rules completely stripped the minority party of its agenda-setting rights, then shouldn't *all* legislation move in the majority-party direction and the post-Reed observations *all* lie at or near 1.0? As it happens, only 7 of 54 Reed-rules Congresses have values greater than .95. A more careful look at the implications theories of majority partyism for data of this sort is clearly needed.

Upon closer inspection, explanations of the reforms based on majority partyism as it is modeled in the literature miss the mark in some noteworthy ways. No existing account of the Reed rules is explicitly grounded in a formal theory. In at least one case, however, the rules are argued as being consistent with an explicit formal model. The example is Cox and McCubbins's (2005) "cartel agenda model." This is a model of what the authors call "negative agenda control," meaning that whenever a majority of the majority party is not

---

[30] The dashed curve is for future reference, and the dotted Senate graph can be ignored.

[31] See Krehbiel (2000; 2003a,b; 2007) on party voting and Rice cohesion indices, the coefficient of party influence, and partisan roll rates, respectively.

[32] The authors base their claim of significance on estimates of five negative binomial regression equations (Cox and McCubbins 2005, Table 4.1, p. 70) that include various combinations of nine "control variables." Their key "Reed" dummy variable is significant in each equation, but each equation has a pseudo-$R^2 = 0.04$.

[33] Cox and McCubbins (2007) have made their data available online. I ran a simple regression of their dependent variable on the log of their time-trend variable; the coefficient $\beta = .074$ is significant at $p = .001$ and the $R^2 = .169$.

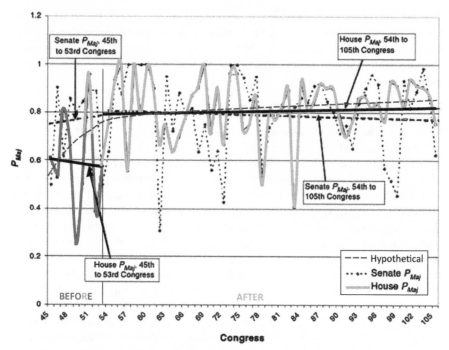

FIGURE 13.2 Example of a before-and-after study. "Effect of Reed's rules on the proportion of bills moving policy toward the majority party." (Cox and McCubbins, 2005, Figure 4.3, p. 72.) Thick solid lines superimposed to accent House findings.

made better off by a bill that is subject to amendment to the House median position, the majority party (or its designated leader) will not allow such legislation to go to the floor. Whatever its merits might be in other settings, this theory bears little resemblance to either the majority party's problem or its procedural solution at the time the Reed Revolution occurred. To be sure, obstruction was rampant in the late-nineteenth-century Congress. But its source was a *minority* of the *House*, not a *majority* of the *majority party* as in the cartel agenda model. Furthermore, once the problem of obstruction was allegedly solved by counting individuals present but not voting, the institutional fixes – such as enhanced Speaker's recognition rights, the ban on dilatory motions, the possible use of special rules to bring legislation to the floor, and the Speaker's seat on the Rules Committee – are all instances of *positive* agenda control, not negative agenda control. The Cox–McCubbins model is one of exclusively negative control and, therefore, does not fit the facts of the case.[34]

---

[34] I should emphasize: this critique is *not* a refutation of the formal cartel agenda model but rather a questioning of its relevance to the case of the Reed Revolution which elsewhere seems to be taken for granted.

Nor is the mismatch between theory and evidence lessened appreciably when the slightly different "conditional party government theory" is applied to late-nineteenth-century data. According to Rohde (1991), the ripeness conditions for majority-party-enhancing reform are: (1) homogeneity of preferences within the majority party, (2) a large majority party, and (3) parties whose preferences are far apart from one another's. With the possible exception of the third condition,[35] the situation in 1890 was distinctively *unripe* for reform. The Republican majority was very thin, and Republican preferences were unusually *heterogeneous* (Schickler 2001, 34–35).

How, then, should we think about the Reed Revolution as an instance of the exercise of procedural endogeneity? Let's begin by highlighting what is confusing in existing literature: the role of majoritarianism. It seems straightforward – and, indeed, it is quite common in the literature – to reason as follows. By abstaining or refusing to be counted in a roll call or quorum call, minority party members gained power disproportionate to their numbers. This minority-party-favoring outcome, in turn, ignited the majority party's revolt. The revolt took the form of rules changes that transferred power from the minority party to the majority party, and which abruptly changed the House equilibrium from "pre-Reed (small advantage) [to] post-Reed (large advantage)" (Cox and McCubbins 2005, 75).

Plausible and common though it is, such reasoning is questionable in at least three ways: First, the reform situation is primarily about *rights* (which legislators are entitled to do what, and when?); it is only secondarily about *power* (who benefits more from the policy that passes after the rights-enabled strategies are played?). Second, the characterization of the reforms as a reassignment of *parties'* rights fails to target the more useful unit of analysis; legislative rights are more accurately portrayed as individual-level phenomena. Third, the immediate problem of the majority party circa 1890 was neither the absence of negative agenda control nor the absence of positive agenda control. The problem, instead, was *de facto* supermajoritarianism (i.e., background majoritarianism with $\beta > \frac{1}{2}$) and a corresponding perceived need for simple-majoritarian – not *majority-partyism* – procedures. The first two of these three issues were addressed in the Majoritarian Tension section of this chapter. The third claim is uniquely important for interpreting Reed's rules and therefore merits a more detailed discussion.

Negative agenda control? There is no reason to doubt that members of the *majority* party, too, could have exercised their individual rights not to be counted, just as members of the minority party did. In other words, there is nothing asymmetric in legislators' rights in quorum call situations at either the individual level or the party level. What, then, was asymmetric at this allegedly

---

[35] The polarization condition has attracted the least attention of the three and is shown in Krehbiel and Meirowitz (2002) not to follow from the assumptions of the conditional party government model as presented in Aldrich and Rohde (1998).

critical juncture of history? A plausible answer is the likely location of status quo points in the 51st Congress. Obstruction and dilatory tactics by the minority party suggest that status quo points resided on the minority-party side of the House's median voter.[36] That is why the majority party was frustrated by its inability to pull policy toward, or into its side of, the House's median voter. Ironically, the negative agenda control was in the *minority* party.

Positive agenda control? The likely asymmetric distribution of inherited status quo points also helps to clarify my earlier assertion about positive agenda control. The situation was ripe for majority-party agenda setting, and undoubtedly the majority party leadership in the 51st Congress would have benefited from monopoly agenda-setting rights. I can find no evidence, however, that Reed and the Republicans had such high hopes. Nor did they have monopoly agenda-setting rights. True, several of the raw materials were present: suspension of the rules could serve as a precedent for closed-rule-like procedures (albeit subject to House supermajority approval); the Speaker sat on the Rules Committee, which had the right to propose restrictive rules (albeit subject to House majority approval); and the Speaker obtained enhanced recognition rights (subject to party-alternation constraints, committee-favoring precedents, etc.). But there was no talk of, nor were there subsequent historical instances of, majority-party monopoly agenda setting as in the classic Romer-Rosenthal (1978) take-it-or-leave-it game. Rather, the more modest goal of Reed and his party was simply to break minority-party-induced gridlock.[37]

This leaves one thing to explain: the assertion that the pre-Reed Revolution institutional arrangement was not really about agenda control as it traditionally has been modeled. That is, it was neither an absence of negative agenda control by the majority party nor an absence of positive agenda control by the majority party. Rather, it was an instance of *background supermajoritarianism* of an essentially nonpartisan – or, at most, incidentally partisan – form.[38]

---

[36] This tendency is also consistent with the fact that House control had switched between the 50th and 51st Congresses, so if the Democrats in the 50th were powerful, the status quo points inherited in the 51st would tend to be on the Democratic (minority party) side of the House median, and hence "ripe for obstruction" (Krehbiel 1985).

[37] Analytically, this is a mirror image of the cartel agenda model, with status quo points on the *minority*-party side of the House median, making the situation ripe for *minority*-party gatekeeping or obstruction. So another way of interpreting the Reed rules spatially is to say they signified a change of the following sort: initially, a majority of the *minority* party had blocking rights and there was a corresponding gridlock interval on the minority party's side of the spectrum; the house then switched to a new, open-rule/no-gatekeeping/no-gridlock-interval setting in which the House median was the equilibrium outcome as attractor of the old gridlocked status quo points. The essence of this interpretation holds, too, without the party overlay.

[38] How one characterizes the partisanship of the episode is secondary to the italicized phrase. I use the phrase "incidentally partisan" because if the background-supermajoritarianism-based interpretation has merit, parties play no essential role in the explanation. Again, this is not to deny the existence of partisan theatrics, animated press coverage, etc.

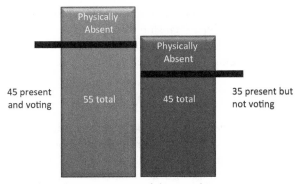

FIGURE 13.3 Example and interpretation of the vanishing quorum.

Figure 13.3 clarifies this instance of background supermajoritarianism with a simple example that illustrates the arithmetic of the vanishing quorum. To make the arithmetic easy, assume the legislature has 100 members, with 55 in the majority party and 45 in the minority party. The Constitutionally mandated quorum is a simple majority, 51. Suppose also, however, as was normal at the time, that literal absences are common, say, 10 in each party. A quorum of 80 members is clearly present, but 35 of these – all minority members – choose to "vanish" (e.g., by abstaining), leaving only 45 present and voting. Legislative business, therefore, cannot be conducted and gridlock prevails.

Background supermajoritarianism is unveiled when addressing the question: What would it take to break the gridlock? The answer is: any combination of 6 or more votes. These might be obtained by retrieving true absentees from either party (likely to have been difficult) and/or by counting those minority party members who are present in the chamber but who were exercising their right not to be counted (much easier, although contrary to existing precedent[39]). So, of the 80 members in the chamber on any given day, 51 – an approximate $5/8 = .625$ supermajority – are needed to conduct business. The similarity between this choice setting and the Senate's filibuster as it is used in recent decades is noteworthy. In each case, the nominal or *de jure* threshold required for passage is simple majoritarian, $\alpha = \frac{1}{2}$, but the *de facto* threshold is supermajoritarian, $\beta = \frac{3}{5}$ in the Senate and $\beta \approx \frac{3}{5} > \frac{1}{2}$ in the House.[40]

The congruence between the ostensibly majoritarian House and the more conspicuously supermajoritarian Senate alerts us to one other not-so-obvious observation. By institutionalizing via precedent a *de facto* background-supermajoritarian critical value $\beta > \frac{1}{2}$, the House was also implicitly demanding

---

[39] The right not to be counted was explicit and accepted (begrudgingly) at the time. It was grounded in precedents that predated the focal episode by decades.

[40] In the House case β is a variable fraction with a fixed numerator of $\frac{N+1}{2}$ and a denominator equal to the total number of members physically present.

a level of consensus higher than that for simple majoritarian and likewise demanding a modicum of bipartisanship for legislation to be successful. This heretofore hidden role of bipartisanship in the Reed Revolution resurfaces in the Discussion when I summarize the aftermath of the Reed Revolution.

Majoritarian Tension as an Alternative Interpretation

Can legislative reform be better understood by adhering to the traditional focus on majority versus minority parties and group-based procedures and power, or rather by shifting attention to individuals and a rights-based approach that considers consensus, timeliness, and wisdom, conditioned by variable majoritarianism? The discussion is structured by the two, informally derived, cube-based expectations from the second section of this chapter, concluding with a retrospective on majority partyism.

Evolutionary or Revolutionary Change?

As noted earlier and illustrated in Figure 13.2, existing accounts of the Reed Revolution strike a loud chord for a new, robust, majority-party-favorable equilibrium.[41] Taking a broader historical perspective of not only formal rules changes adopted at a slice in time, but also informal practices and the accretion of codified precedents over time, gives rise to a different interpretation. This is true within and across three types of practices and precedents that regularly governed House decision making in the nineteenth century and that regularly govern House decision making today: recognition, suspension of the rules, and special orders (bill-specific rules). A brief review of the emergence of these procedures underscores in triplicate a largely overlooked feature of majoritarian change – procedural and precedential *gradualism* – the sum total of which significantly dilutes the conventional account of Reed's rules as an abrupt, revolutionary shift to a new, majority-party equilibrium.

Recognition. Although an often-emphasized part of the Reed Revolution was to enhance the Speaker's recognition rights, there had already been a long-standing, multifaceted foundation of recognition precedents on which to place the 1890 enhancement. Centralized recognition rights actually began in the first session of the 1st Congress when the House adopted Rule XIV, Section 2 of which stated that "when two or more Members rise at once, the Speaker shall name the Member who is first to speak" (Hinds Precedents, 61).[42] In the 1840s, precedents began to establish additional criteria for recognition, giving priority to reporting committees, for example, in 1843 (Hinds, 69). Until 1857, the

---

[41] This subsection is expanded and adapted from Gilligan and Krehbiel (1987), where similar content is given a slightly different but not incompatible interpretation.

[42] Citations to Hinds without a volume number refer to the 1899 edition, *Parliamentary Precedents of the House of Representatives and United States*. Citations with a volume number refer to the five-volume set published in 1907. Numbers refer to precedents, not pages.

Speaker's recognition choice was subject to appeal and therefore implicitly constrained by remote majoritarianism. Indeed, in most of the key recognition precedents cited by Hinds, the decision of the chair was in fact appealed and therefore resolved via simple-majority vote, suggesting that the remoteness of remote simple majoritarianism was, as a practical matter, fairly immediate and, therefore, likely to have constrained the Speaker's behavior (Hinds, 65, 66, 69).

The slow but steady growth in the Speaker's recognition rights continued unabated into the second half of the century. A 1879 precedent clarified:

Discretion must be lodged with the presiding officer, and no fixed and arbitrary order of recognition can be wisely provided for in advance.... The practice of making a list of those who desire to speak on measures ... is a proper one to know and remember the wishes of the Members. As to the order of recognition, he [the presiding officer] should not be bound to follow the list, but should be free to exercise *a wise and just discretion in the interest of full and fair debate.* Hinds, 63, italics added.

So, although individuals' recognition rights are not exactly uniform (the Speaker's discretion gradually grew over time), neither are they party-based, majority-party biased, or insensitive to basic notions of fairness. Rather, when recognition rights favor some legislators over others, it is for a normatively and legislatively defensible reason. Normatively, the apparent aim is to elicit wise decisions via balanced deliberation and debate. And, as a practical matter, Speaker discretion facilitates the timely treatment of legislation in a way that elicits wisdom from a diverse and relatively informed segment of the membership.

Later in the 1880s, a precedent gave recognition preference to a bill supporter from a committee over the committee's chairman, because the chairman opposed the bill. And in 1889 a bill manager was favored over other members who wished to make motions of greater privilege. With the benefit of hindsight and the luxury of juxtaposing and placing multiple events in a broader historical perspective, this precedent and its generalized partner from 1892 are strongly suggestive with regard to the question of "revolution or evolution?" First, it should be noted that both precedents were precipitated by dilatory motions, which we know from the earlier discussion were regular occurrences in this era. Second, note that one of the Speaker-enhancing precedents occurred before the adoption of the Reed rules, and one occurred after the presumed one-time equilibrium-shifting event. They both had the same qualitative and non-abrupt effect, however: to make it easier for the Speaker to preempt dilatory tactics and to keep the House on the track of deliberation and debate that would allow the House at least to consider if not to adopt legislation in a timely manner.

A third point of interest is that the later, more general precedent, set in 1892, occurred when *Democrats* were in the majority and Speaker Crisp was in the chair. Furthermore, the person who appealed the decision of the chair (the chair being *against* dilatory tactics) was none other than Thomas Brackett Reed!

That is, the same pair of adversaries in the Reed revolution had another showdown over essentially the same procedural issue, *but they had both flip-flopped their positions on that issue.* Obviously, their over-time behavior is tortuous to rationalize as both principled and consistent. The only principle that is consistent with these events is that of a majority of individuals wanting and demonstrating the ability to reduce delay and facilitate deliberation. Consequently, the House adjusted its *de facto* level of majoritarianism in a way that incurred costs in consensus in exchange for benefits in timeliness and wisdom. Furthermore, the instantiation of those principles and tradeoffs occurred gradually and consistently throughout time and in much the same way both well before and well after the Reed rules episode.[43]

Suspension of the rules. The history of the House procedure known as suspension of the rules is quite nuanced. In the interest of space, I economize on precedent-specific details and simply summarize the broad historical trend, which mirrors that of recognition practices and precedents.

Before the 1870s, the suspension procedure was supermajoritarian, requiring a two-thirds vote, and was used to change standing rules or to deviate from the regular order of business. In these regards, it served as a sort of early functional equivalent to what later became a role of the House Rules Committee. Again, however, this transformation was gradual. Suspension sometimes entailed specifying conditions for debate, but bills brought to the floor via suspension were typically open for amendment as specified by the standing rules (Hinds, V, 5856). It wasn't until after the 1860s that suspension became more restrictive in terms of permissible amendments. In 1868 the procedure first took on its modern-day form: it became "possible by one motion both to bring a matter before the house and pass it under suspension of the rules" (Hinds, V, 6846). Eight years later a precedent was set in which the suspension procedure ordered a vote on an amendment followed by a vote on the bill, much like a later-day modified-open rule, although again by super-majority vote.

For present purposes, the point is not so much the procedural details as it is the spread of dates of precedent-setting events and the steadily increasing flexibility and diversity of procedures by which the House conducted its business. As with recognition procedures and precedents, suspension, too, had the effect of bringing legislation before the House, providing a chance for its deliberative consideration, and giving it a fair chance of passing (in this instance, by supermajority vote). No evidence suggests abrupt or significant differences in the design, use, or consequences of the procedure in the temporal proximity of the Reed Revolution. Rather, the suspension procedure seemed to have equilibrated as a sensible if not optimal tradeoff between consensus,

---

[43] This seemingly steady flow of precedents that bolstered Speakers' recognition rights continued into the twentieth century. Space constraints preclude elaboration. See Gilligan and Krehbiel 1987 for more details.

timeliness, and wisdom and was subject only to minor, incremental precedent-reinforcing refinements that occurred both long before and long after the ostensibly tumultuous event in 1890.

The Speaker and the Rules Committee. The history of the Rules Committee and the Speaker's role on the Committee make a better case for abruptness in institutional change at the time of the Reed Revolution, but only slightly better. True, the Speaker obtained the codified right to be Chairman of the Committee, and the Committee obtained privileged status and could therefore report rules (special orders) to the floor at any time to expedite consideration of other legislation. But these rights were neither without precedent nor as revolutionary as is usually portrayed. Beginning on the first day of the 1st Congress, the Rules Committee initiated changes to the House's standing rules, even though its role during the rest of the regular sessions was minimal. By as early as 1841, however, precedent had been established for the Committee to issue bill-specific resolutions at any time (Hinds, 1538), and by 1850, the Committee had obtained exclusive jurisdiction over reports to change the rules (Hinds, 1540). Only three years later, yet nearly three decades before Reed's rules were adopted, there was precedent for a report from the Rules Committee taking precedence over the regular order (Chiu 1928, 118).

Nor was the Speaker's involvement in Rules Committee affairs an innovation of the Reed period. In fact, the Speaker chaired the Committee as early as 1858 and was made *ex officio* member in 1859 (Alexander 1915, 193). In brief, the House Rules Committee was positioned to fulfill its eventual well-known role as a "traffic cop" (Oppenheimer 1977; 1994) directing the flow of legislation well in advance of the infamous 51st Congress.[44]

If there was any abrupt and significant institutional event along the Rules Committee's otherwise evolutionary path, it was more likely to have been in 1883 than in 1890, the year of the so-called revolution. In the earlier year, precedent was established for special orders from Rules to be adopted by simple majority rather than the two-thirds majority previously required and, likewise, to be required for suspension of the rules (Hinds, IV, 3152). Depending upon how the House was to use special orders (i.e., as mechanisms for hastening consideration of specific bills, or as mechanisms to change standing rules), this precedent signifies a decrement in background majoritarianism (β) or remote

---

[44] Cox and McCubbins (2005, 57) are clearly aware of many of these precedents, but, citing Roberts and Smith (2003), they discount their significance on the grounds that not many special rules were adopted through the end of the 50th Congress. Of course, significance of procedural rights does not depend upon their frequency of use. Nor is the key point in this historical review about the exercise of procedural rights. Rather, the point is that the institutional apparatus, hence the Rules Committee's strategic potential, was grounded in precedents that were executed and codified well before Reed's rules. On this critical point, Cox, McCubbins, and I are in agreement.

majoritarianism (γ), respectively. As it turned out, at approximately the same time, bill-specific special orders became more common and began to impose restrictions on amendments to legislation, thereby making them not only more flexible mechanisms than the suspension procedure but also more timely ones, because their consensus threshold was effectively reduced to simple majority. Not surprisingly, then, after 1880 "the use of the motion to suspend the rules [had] gradually been restricted, while the functions of the Committee on Rules [had been] enlarged" (Hinds, IV, 6790).[45]

In summary, for each of three important domains of House procedure – recognition rights, suspension of the rules, and special orders and other Rules Committee rights – the opening of a larger window of history reveals the same pattern. Change was evolutionary, not revolutionary, and the specific changes that coincide temporally with the passage of Reed's rules were not outliers in any significant way. At most, they were codifications and, to some extent, consolidation of then-longstanding, incrementally developing practices and precedents. The House had been remotely simple majoritarian from its inception, but it had not always been *de facto* simple majoritarian. What Reed's quorum counting strategy did in terms of the majoritarianism parameters was bring to the fore and exploit that remote majoritarianism ($\gamma = \frac{1}{2}$) to decrement background majoritarianism to $\beta \cong \frac{1}{2}$ for that subset of legislation that elicited vanishing quorums. In the proper context of the longer, mostly simple-majoritarian history of the House, the so-called Reed Revolution was admittedly somewhat more than a procedural blip; but it was considerably less than a big bang that instantly inaugurated a new partisan era.

Cube Interpretability of Changes

What can be inferred from the evolution of House majoritarianism about the motivations for, or consequences of, the Reed rules? More specifically, does the perspective of majoritarian tension – as illustrated in the consensus–timeliness–wisdom cube – provide a more viable interpretation of the specific procedural changes than the conventional account? I reconsider those specifics in the order summarized here.

1. *The right of the Speaker to count members physically present during roll calls even though they abstained from voting and/or declined to affirm their presence when called upon.* It is doubtful that it has ever been stated this way, but the 1890 House vote to uphold the ruling of Speaker Reed[46] on the

---

[45] Hinds Precedents include several pages of examples in which special orders provide for consideration of bills with varying restrictiveness in terms of time allotted for debate and amendments permitted.

[46] Technically and more indirectly, the vote was on the motion to table an appeal of the decision of the chair, which had the effect of upholding the Speaker by a simple majority.

counting of the quorum was a manifestation of remote simple majoritarianism being used to lower the assent standard in background majoritarianism, thereby increasing the set of legislation for which the majoritarian assent thresholds – both *de facto* and *de jure* – approximated or equaled a simple majority status. Specifically, the simple majority vote by which the House upheld the Speaker's ruling that all present members could be counted established a new precedent, and the House's subsequent vote to codify this precedent in its standing rules was a more conspicuous instance of the invocation of remote simple majoritarianism. That is, the House made its rules – α and especially β – more tightly simple majoritarian, and did so via simple majority vote $(\gamma = \frac{1}{2})$. Under the prior precedent that had tolerated the vanishing quorum, the *de facto* consensus threshold was effectively a variable[47] $\beta > \frac{1}{2}$. Under the overturned precedent and newly passed standing rule, the threshold was in effect lowered to an approximate simple-majoritarian constant, $\beta \cong \frac{1}{2}$.

In terms of the majoritarian tension cube, the codification of the Speaker's right to designate vanishing quorums as dilatory had fairly straightforward causes and consequences. The cause is not much in dispute, although authors' ways of stating it differ. Most research calls it frustration with "minority obstructionism" (with minority *party* implied). I recast it as frustration with gridlock caused by implicit background supermajoritarianism.[48] The consequence of eliminating *all*[49] individuals' rights not to be counted was that bills under the Reed rules became easier to consider and, therefore, more likely to debate, and more likely to pass, thereby reducing gridlock.

The primary majoritarian tension that this case illustrates is between consensus and timeliness. After the reform, legislation was subject to an overall lower consensus criterion and, therefore, was less likely to pass with a broad bipartisan consensus, some of which had been necessary prereform in order to break a House filibuster via vanishing quorum. But while the cost of reform was borne on the consensus dimension, an immediate offsetting benefit was reaped on the timeliness dimension. The House was able to make more timely decisions due to the effectively lower value of *de facto* majoritarianism (β), which made it easier to break minority-party gridlock, because a simple majority in the House no longer needed (as many) minority-party votes.

[47] The pre-Reed rules β was variable because the requisite supermajority in any given vanishing quorum situation was determined by the number of truly absent members and the number of present but vanishing members (recall Table 13.1).

[48] The exact same phrase accurately describes the Senate's filibuster and countless other rules and precedents that make their respective institutions supermajoritarian in nature. Schwartzberg (2014) has a treasure trove of examples (although she does not describe them this way either).

[49] Note that the rules change was uniform and across-the-board in its redefinition of *individual* rights. So, while the reform initiative was undoubtedly party-motivated, the resulting codified rule is party-blind which, as we saw earlier, is the usual case.

Finally, the implications of the main rules change for wisdom are ambiguous. Other things equal, lowering the assent threshold undermines wisdom by reducing the need for the potential majority to convince swing voters that its proposal is prudent. This is the direct wisdom cost of the reform. However, there may also be an indirect benefit of consensus-lowering on wisdom that acts though the timeliness benefit. More specifically, to the extent that lowering the consensus threshold frees up time that would otherwise be consumed by dilatory behavior, such time can be reallocated to floor debate, committee specialization, or other wisdom-contributing activities. This is the indirect wisdom benefit of the reform. Do the direct wisdom costs exceed the indirect wisdom benefits? I cannot say. I can only suggest that the majoritarian-tension cube provides a relatively clear, parsimonious, and general way of posing questions central to political institutional reform, with regard to both direct and indirect consequences. The remaining examples of this general claim are necessarily brief and therefore cursory.

2. *The Speaker's right to refuse recognition of members who sought to make dilatory motions.* This was a form of agenda right that, if new, would have been a free-lunch gain in timeliness (with no offsetting consensus or wisdom costs). However, inasmuch as there were increasingly strong precedents for the Speaker's right to be discriminatory in both recognition and nonrecognition well in advance of the Reed rules, a viable alternative interpretation is that reform mostly codified the procedural status quo, and, therefore, is more consistent with the evolutionary rather than revolutionary view of procedural change.[50]

3. *A reduction in the size of the quorum (to 100) to conduct business in the Committee of the Whole.* This little-discussed rules change is an approximation of a Pareto-improving procedural tweak. It made it easier for the House to deliberate, debate, and amend legislation in the Committee of the Whole, leading to gains in timeliness and possibly wisdom with no offsetting costs from the fixed, simple-majoritarian consensus criterion $\alpha = \frac{1}{2}$.

4. *The ability to close debate by majority vote on any part of a bill being considered in the Committee of the Whole.* In effect, this is simple-majoritarian cloture. It had no direct consequences on the threshold for passage of legislation but, like the previous two rules, brought about small productivity gains in terms of timeliness and wisdom.

5. *The Speaker was given the right to refer House and Senate bills and messages from the president to committees without intervening debate.* Also inconsequential on the consensus dimension, this procedural change was likely to have resulted in a timeliness gain. Another possible consequence was a small indirect benefit in wisdom, to the extent that committee deliberations became

---

[50] Some additional subtleties concern different evolutionary paths of recognition practices, precedents, and rules for privileged versus nonprivileged motions. These deserve further scrutiny but are outside the scope of this analysis.

more likely to elicit high-quality deliberation and debate than filibuster-like, dilatory behavior on the floor.

6. *Codification of the Speaker's right to chair the Rules Committee.* This right was likely not to have been very significant for two reasons. First, the Speaker already had a seat on the Rules Committee and there was codified precedent for his serving as chair since as early as 1858. Therefore, consequences of the codification are negligible unless there was a nontrivial threat that the House otherwise would have overturned these precedents. There is no indication that the Speaker's right was in jeopardy. Second, anything the Rules Committee did to affect the flow of legislation was (and still is) subject a majority vote, and neither this nor the other Reed rules changed this fact.

Majority Partyism or Majoritarianism?

The essence of majority partyism is disproportionate majority-party power that is grounded in asymmetric procedural rights and that results in electoral rewards. This venerable theoretical argument has three refutable implications that can be assessed, and ought to fare well with reference to what many scholars regard as the pinnacle of party government in the United States. Specifically, majority partyism suggests that:

1. The majority party will consistently (and successfully) support central-ization and consolidation of procedural rights in leadership, for example, the Speaker.
2. The minority party will steadfastly (but futilely) oppose the majority party's procedural ploys.
3. Subsequent to passage of the majority party's legislative agenda, electoral rewards will redound to the majority party.

How well do these propositions account for the Reed Revolution and its aftermath? To see, we look through a slightly enlarged window of procedural politics, extending from the 51st Congress, on which the conventional reform scholars have placed so much weight, through the 53rd Congress. Here are the essential facts.[51]

51st Congress. Notwithstanding their thin majority but otherwise consistent with prevailing party theories, Speaker Reed and his fellow Republicans organized and deployed their "procedural cartel" in an attempt to pass more legislation, burnish the Republican "brand name," and reap electoral rewards. As they hoped and expected, gridlock dissipated. However, the predicted electoral payoff did not materialize. Republicans were slaughtered at the polls and entered the 52nd Congress with only 88 of the House's 333 seats.

---

[51] See Schickler 2001, ch. 2, for an excellent, much more detailed account.

52nd Congress. Under the new, huge Democratic majority, the Reed rules were *not* readopted. Also anomalous from the party-theoretical perspective is that *minority*-party Republicans favored extension. Once their attempted extension failed, however, Republicans exercised their reinstated rights to "vanish" in order to block the progression of majority-party-favored legislation. Gridlock returned and the majority party was punished at the polls again, although the Democrats did manage to hang on to their majority.

53rd Congress. Reed's rules were reconsidered yet again, and the third time was the charm: the reforms were largely re-adopted. The winning procedural coalition was much different than four years earlier, however. Specifically, the critical amendment reinstating the Speaker's quorum-counting right was adopted by a large bipartisan supermajority, with the Yea votes of 82.3 percent of members (125 of 170 Democrats plus all 85 Republicans). Dilatory tactics were quashed, the Congress was productive, and Reed's rules were re-codified in the Standing Rules of the House, where, in large part, they have been stable ever since.

Each of the three propositions drawn from majority partyism is inconsistent with much of the immediate extended historical record. Proposition 1 fails in the 52nd Congress when Democrats, who had an enormous majority, spoke and voted *against* the rules changes that were theoretically in their party's interest. Proposition 2 fails in both the 51st and 52nd Congresses for the same reason: the minority party Republicans consistently and often unanimously *supported* rules said to confer procedural advantage to the majority party. And Hypothesis 3 fails in all three Congresses for a mixed bag of reasons.[52]

Are simple majoritarianism and majoritarian tension more promising building blocks for an improved theory – or at least a more consistent interpretation – of congressional reform? It seems so. With the benefit of hindsight, the events of 1894 in the 53rd Congress rather than 1890 in the 51st should be identified as the capstone of Reed's rules, for it was only then when the House codified what proved to be a *durable* set of precedent-grounded changes in its standing rules. To see why the changes endured in the second but not the first instance, two background facts must be brought to the fore. First, this point of resolution came only after a period of experiential learning by members of *both parties* (Democrats and Republicans), *in both party roles* (majority and minority), and in electorally volatile times. These conditions undoubtedly gave party members a sharper and more balanced perspective on the costs, benefits, and tradeoffs of different procedural arrangements. Second, in the crucial roll call in the 53rd

[52] In the 51st, behavior in the House follows the majority partyism script, but behavior in the electorate mostly does not. In the 52nd, behavior in the House is inconsistent with the theory, so the antecedent of the hypothesis is false (Democrats didn't do the right thing to earn their electoral reward). In the 53rd, about 75 percent of Democrats (in the majority) followed the script, but 100 percent of minority Republicans supported the rules changes contrary to theoretical expectations. Furthermore, Democrats lost 116 seats in the next election when they should have been rewarded for their eventual institutionalization of the putative procedural cartel.

Congress that reinstated the quorum rule once and for all, a large bipartisan supermajority of House members expressed an apparent belief that the House *overall* was better off conducting its business with Reed's rules than without them. Why? Because without Reed's rules the House was often *unable* to conduct its business. In other words, the real controversy was about timeliness, first and foremost, and about partisanship only secondarily, temporarily, and often anomalously with respect to majority-partyism theory.

More generally, this semi-structured reconsideration of the Reed Revolution suggests that the House's adoption of new rules – although providing unparalleled political theater featuring colorful personalities and partisan vitriol – can be described more aptly than as a case of majority-partyism. It was instead a large set of semi-regular but mostly random incremental changes in practices that were intermittently recorded as precedents and occasionally codified as changes in standing rules. Such changes are better classified as evolutionary than revolutionary. Furthermore, the sum total of events culminating in what been called Reed's Revolution is better interpreted as a long series of small changes in legislators' procedural rights that reflect sensible tradeoffs between consensus, timeliness, and wisdom within a predominantly simple-majoritarian legislative institution.

CONCLUSION

The variable levels and types of majoritarian consensus exhibited in political institutions are tempered by their members' concomitant but conflicting desires for timely and wise decisions. The tradeoffs between these three forces – consensus, timeliness, and wisdom – seem to be both acute and omnipresent in collective choice organizations. Decision makers' active management of majoritarian tensions – or, alternatively, their passive tolerance of procedural evolution via a form of natural selection among figurative mutations of precedents – are central and enduring characteristics of political institutional development.

Which is the better description of real-world procedural change: active management with periodic revolutions, or passive and gradual evolutionary change? A precise answer would likely reside on a continuum rather than within one or the other dichotomous categories. Furthermore, the correct answer is surely different for different self-governing institutions at different times in their histories. With such complexities duly noted, the thrust of this investigation is to move the U.S. House's procedural change marker a few spaces toward the evolutionary. and away from the revolutionary. end of the spectrum.

Specifically, the revised interpretation of the so-called Reed Revolution suggests that institutional change in self-governing legislatures – even when it appears from journalistic accounts to be abrupt, calculated, and conspicuous – is actually incremental, unintentional, and buried deeply within thick volumes of mind-numbing precedents. Significant institutional change is often a decades-long process of gradual accretion of experiences with more or less random procedural trials. If experimental legislative procedures are proven repeatedly to be useful, members of both parties passively and consensually begin to treat their conformance with such procedures as implied procedural rights. Over time, the acceptable uses of many such procedures are fine-tuned, clarified, and recorded in the body's precedents. Sometimes – as in the case of the Reed rules – they are also codified into the institution's standing rules. To get this far, however, is likely to require a period of affirmation of the workability of the revised procedure(s) in multiple settings. Ultimately, a supermajoritarian bipartisan consensus is likely to be required, too, as a practical matter, if the codified reform is to last well into the future. Indeed, with reference to remote majoritarianism as discussed in the second section of this chapter and summarized in Table 13.1, it may be helpful in future studies of reform to differentiate between *nominal* remote majoritarianism (which, in the House, is mostly simple majoritarian) and *effective* remote majoritarianism (which the history of the Reed rules suggests is bipartisan and supermajoritarian with a tacit but unknown y strictly greater than $\frac{1}{2}$.

A closely related issue worth future investigation concerns the generality of nineteenth-century observations and interpretations to modern Congresses and to other legislatures and voting organizations. If the tensions between consensus, timeliness, and wisdom are salient and strong in most or all mature collective choice bodies, then we would expect radical or revolutionary institutional change to be rare across a much broader class of voting institutions and to occur only in the presence of very large exogenous shocks, such as wars, revolutions, or economic catastrophes. In normal times, however, durable institutions will have discovered and adopted a set of procedures that approximate a Pareto optimal mix of consensus, timeliness, and wisdom, in which case further improvements in one of the three domains always comes at the cost of at least one of the other two.

Finally, it bears repeating that, although it shows some promise, the majoritarian-tension cube is a framework – not a theory. As such, its limited purpose is to categorize phenomena and suggest relationships rather than to explain and predict events. While the framework does more or less what it is intended to do, a genuine theory of majoritarian institutional development is still needed. One natural avenue to such a theory would be to postulate that an institutional designer optimizes over the three dimensions (consensus, timeliness, wisdom) given her values and corresponding preferences over the feasible points within the three-dimensional space. This seems to be exactly the wrong thing to do, however, because the House, the Senate, and endogenous-procedure institutions generally are not unitary institutional designers. The problem is much more difficult than that, because the rule-maker in a self-governing institution is a plurality – sometimes of unspecified hence ambiguous size and often without transparent rules for changing lower-order rules (y). These facts complicate procedural choice severely, and we have only begun to develop a precise vocabulary and analytical approach to these sorts of problems. The concluding hope is that the concept of variable majoritarianism and the framework of majoritarian tension will play constructive roles in future scholarship that seeks a deeper understanding of the fundamental nature of procedures, procedural reform, and their enigmatic endogeneity within political organizations.

REFERENCES

Aldrich, John and David Rohde. 1998. *Measuring Conditional Party Government*. Manuscript: Midwest Political Science Association.

Alexander, DeAlva Stanwood. 1915 [1970]. *History and Procedure of the House of Representatives*. Franklin Press.

Binder, Sarah A. 1996. "The Partisan Basis of Procedural Choice: Allocating Parliamentary Rights in the House, 1789–1990." *American Political Science Review* (1996): 8–20.

1997. *Minority Rights, Majority Rule: Partisanship and the Development of Congress*. Cambridge University Press.

Binder, Sarah A. and Steven S. Smith. 1997. *Politics or Principle?: Filibustering in the United States Senate*. Brookings Institution Press.

Chiu, Shi-Chang. 1928 [1968]. *The Speaker of the House of Representatives Since 1896*. AMS Press.

Cooper, Joseph and David W. Brady. 1981. "Institutional Context and Leadership Style: The House from Cannon to Rayburn." *American Political Science Review* (1981): 411–425.

Cox, Gary W. and Mathew D. McCubbins. 2005. *Setting the Agenda: Responsible Party Government in the US House of Representatives*. Cambridge University Press.

2007. *Replication Data for: Setting the Agenda: Responsible Party Government in the US House of Representatives*. Harvard Institute for Quantitative Political Science.

Dion, Douglas. 2001. *Turning the Legislative Thumbscrew: Minority Rights and Procedural Change in Legislative Politics*. University of Michigan Press.

Fenno, Richard F. Jr. 1973. *Congressman in Committees*. Little-Brown.

Gilligan, Thomas W. and Keith Krehbiel. 1987. "Collective Decisionmaking and Standing Committees: An Informational Rationale for Restrictive Amendment Procedures." *Journal of Law, Economics, and Organization* 3: 287–335.

Giuriato, Luisa. 2007. *Combining Autocracy and Majority Voting: The Canonical Succession Rules of the Latin Church*. Manuscript: University of Rome La Sapienza.

Heinberg, John Gilbert. 1926. "History of the Majority Principle." *American Political Science Review* 20(1): 52–68.

Hinds, Asher C. 1899. *Parliamentary Precedents of the House of Representatives of the United States*. U.S. Government Printing Office.

Hirsch, Alex and Kenneth Shotts. 2012. "Policy-Specific Information and Informal Agenda Power." *American Journal of Political Science* 56: 67–83.

Jefferson, Thomas and Henry Augustine Washington. 1854. *The Writings of Thomas Jefferson*, Volume 8.

Jenkins, Jeffery A. and Charles Stewart III. 2013. *Fighting for the Speakership: The House and the Rise of Party Government.* Princeton University Press.

Jennings, Alan. N.d. "Roberts Rules: Getting Comfortable with Parliamentary Procedure." www.dummies.com/how-to/content/roberts-rules-getting-comfortable-with-parliamenta.html.

Jones, Charles O. 1968. "Joseph G. Cannon and Howard W. Smith: An Essay on the Limits of Leadership in the House of Representatives." *The Journal of Politics* 30 (3): 617–646.

Koger, Gregory. 2010. *Filibustering: A Political History of Obstruction in the House and Senate.* University of Chicago Press.

Krehbiel, Keith. 1985. "Obstruction and Representativeness in Legislatures." *American Journal of Political Science* 29: 643–59.

   1991. *Information and Legislative Organization.* University of Michigan Press.

   2000. "Party Discipline and Measures of Partisanship." *American Journal of Political Science* 43: 212–27.

   2003a. "Asymmetry of Party Influence: Reply." *Political Analysis* 11: 108–09.

   2003b. "The Coefficient of Party Influence." *Political Analysis* 11: 95–103.

   2007. "Partisan Roll Rates in a Nonpartisan Legislature." *Journal of Law, Economics, and Organization* 23: 1–23.

Krehbiel, Keith and Adam Meirowitz. 2002. "Minority Rights and Majority Power: Theoretical Consequences of the Motion to Recommit." *Legislative Studies Quarterly* 27(2): 191–217.

Malamut, Michael E. 2008. "Musings on General or Common Parliamentary Law." *Parliamentary Journal* XLIX(3) July.

Mayhew, David R. 1974. *Congress: The Electoral Connection.* Yale University Press.

Ober, Josiah. 2008. *Democracy and Knowledge: Innovation and Learning in Classical Athens.* Princeton University Press.

Oppenheimer, Bruce I. 1977. "The Rules Committee: New Arm of Leadership in a Decentralized House." In *Congress Reconsidered*, vol. 1. Praeger Publishers, pp. 96–116.

Oppenheimer, Bruce. 1994. "The House Traffic Cop: The Rules Committee." In Joel Silbey (ed.), *Encyclopedia of the American Legislative System.* Scribners, pp. 1049–66.

Park, Hong Min. 2013. *Logit, Ordered Logit, and Multinomial Logit: A Case of Studying Rules Changes in the U.S. House.* Manuscript: University of Alabama.

Polsby, Nelson W. 1968. "The Institutionalization of the US House of Representatives." *American Political Science Review* 62(1): 144–68.

Raaflaub, Kurt A., Josiah Ober, and Robert Wallace. 2007. *Origins of Democracy in Ancient Greece.* University of California Press.

Roberts, Jason and Steven Smith. 2003. "Procedural Contexts, Party Strategy, and Conditional Party Voting in the U.S. House of Representatives, 1971–2000." *American Journal of Political Science* 47: 305–17.

Rohde, David W. 1974. "Committee Reform in the House of Representatives and the Subcommittee Bill of Rights." *The ANNALS of the American Academy of Political and Social Science* 411(1): 39–47.

   1991. *Parties and Leaders in the Postreform House.* University of Chicago Press.

Romer, Thomas and Howard Rosenthal. 1978. "Political Resource Allocation, Controlled Agendas, and the Status Quo." *Public Choice* 33: 27–43.

Schickler, Eric. 2000. "Institutional Change in the House of Representatives, 1867–1998: A Test of Partisan and Ideological Power Balance Models." *American Political Science Review* 94(2): 269–288.

2001. *Disjointed Pluralism: Institutional Innovation and the Development of the US Congress.* Princeton University Press.

Schwartzberg, Melissa. 2014. *Counting the Many: The Origins and Limits of Supermajority Rule.* New York: Cambridge University Press.

Shepsle, Kenneth A. 1979. "Institutional Arrangements and Equilibrium in Multidimensional Voting Models." *American Journal of Political Science* 23(1): 27–59.

Shepsle, Kenneth A. and Barry R. Weingast. 1987. "The Institutional Foundations of Committee Power." *The American Political Science Review* 81(1): 85–104.

Wawro, Gregory J. and Eric Schickler. 2006. *Filibuster: Obstruction and Lawmaking in the US Senate.* Princeton University Press.

Weingast, Barry R. and William J. Marshall. 1988. "The Industrial Organization of Congress; or, Why Legislatures, Like Firms, Are Not Organized as Markets." *The Journal of Political Economy* 96(1): 132–163.

PART IV

CONCLUSIONS

14

Intensified Partisanship in Congress

Institutional Effects

Representative David E. Price

My intent is to discuss current congressional operations, mainly in the House, in a way that reflects the concern of David Mayhew and the other contributors to this volume both to understand and to assess the quality of institutional performance. I will take as my point of departure three interrelated aspects of the current configuration of partisan forces in the House:

- Increased polarization of the congressional parties and their electoral bases, by which I mean both homogeneity within the parties and distance between them;
- The increased competitiveness of the parties in Congress, what Frances Lee terms "the continuous prospects for change in party control";[1] and
- The asymmetrical movement of one party toward an ideological extreme – that is, the emergence of the Republican Party as what Tom Mann and Norm Ornstein term an "insurgent outlier."[2]

It is an interesting question to what extent these three aspects of our current partisan reality are mutually reinforcing, and to what extent they are in tension, potentially mitigating or modifying one another. But I will treat them as a cluster and suggest what some of their institutional effects might be. While some of these effects have become more pronounced since Republicans took control of the House in 2011, all have been a number of years in the making.

It is vitally important, of course, to understand the near-term policy effects of intensified partisanship – on the capacity of Congress to produce major policies,

---

Dinner address at "Representation and Governance: A Conference in Honor of David Mayhew," Yale University, May 29, 2013.

[1] See Chapter 6.
[2] Thomas Mann and Norman Ornstein, *It's Even Worse Than It Looks* (New York: Basic Books, 2012), pp. xiv, 184–97.

to achieve interbranch coordination, in short, to govern the country – and to address Sarah Binder's question: "Is this time different?"[3] Rather than wading directly into that discussion, I want to suggest four further consequences, concentrating on the workings of the institution. These changes help explain current policy performance – or dysfunction – but they are also likely to have longer-term effects on how, and how well, Congress works. Therefore, I believe they are worthy of more attention and analysis than they have received.

My first observation is that intensified partisan competition and conflict have contributed to the increased centralization both of parties in the House and of House operations in general. In *America's Congress* and *Partisan Balance*, David Mayhew focuses on Newt Gingrich as the key figure in transforming the tactics and style of Republicans as an opposition party.[4] Upon becoming Speaker in 1995, he was equally consequential in centralizing House leadership.

There is no question a corrective was called for. I remember working with the whip organization soon after coming to Congress, when committees too often reported bills that divided the Democratic Caucus and had to be amended on the fly as the whip counts came in. It was telling that when Democrats returned to power in 2007 after twelve years of Republican control, few if any called for a return to the previous degree of decentralization.

That is not to say, however that the Gingrich–Hastert era offers a model worthy of emulation. I and others vigorously criticized its excesses and abuses.[5] One of the disputed practices – requiring approval of a "majority of the majority" before a matter could be brought to the floor – had to be set aside by Speaker John Boehner (R-OH) earlier this year in order to pass the fiscal cliff tax measure and Hurricane Sandy aid. The issue is likely to come up again in future policy battles.

Democrats avoided the worst abuses – such as three-hour roll calls in the middle of the night – and loosened the reins a bit on the committees. But under both parties, House proceedings have remained highly regimented, reflecting the political reality of heightened partisanship – a polarized, closely divided House, with each side inclined to take full advantage of any opening provided by the other.

The question of whether this pattern necessarily entails the decline of congressional committees is an important one. Both as a student of Congress and as a member, I have thought it was fallacious to regard leadership strength and committee vitality in zero-sum terms. I have seen effective party and committee

---

[3] [Conference Paper, Chapter 9 of this volume]

[4] David Mayhew, *America's Congress* (New Haven: Yale University Press, 2000), pp. 101–02, 235–40; and *Partisan Balance* (Princeton: Princeton University Press, 2011), p. 176.

[5] David E. Price, "Reflections on *Congressional Government* at 120 and Congress at 216," *PS*, April 2006, pp. 231–35; Thomas Mann and Norman Ornstein, *The Broken Branch* (New York: Oxford University Press, 2006).

leadership reinforce each other, producing both a better legislative product and a smoother route to passage. But in the modern House, such positive examples are increasingly hard to come by.

I came to the House in 1987 with a fresh recollection of the phenomenon of policy entrepreneurship that had attracted my attention as a political scientist, first in the Senate and increasingly in the House. For years I was able, at the beginning of each Congress, to identify several initiatives that I wanted to pursue, on my own committees and others, and often to achieve a decent rate of success. I also remember free-wheeling markups on the Banking Committee, frequently forming cross-party coalitions to pass amendments. All of that is much rarer now, and I believe there are real costs in terms of the engagement and initiative of individual members and, sometimes, the quality and legitimacy of the legislative product.

An interesting question is this: if committee operations have been curtailed by virtue of intensified partisanship and leadership control, has that partisanship reached the point at which, even if the committees were opened up, members would be unlikely to engage in other than formulaic ways? That is the possibility raised by Robert Kaiser's new book, *Act of Congress*, an insightful account of the financial services regulatory reform legislation of 2010. The two chairmen, Barney Frank in the House and Chris Dodd in the Senate, were strongly inclined to adhere to the "regular order" in reporting and passing their bills, more so in both cases than their party leaders wished. But it did not matter, because Republican members were so locked into a posture of opposition to whatever the president requested and to ritualized talking points that they were not able or inclined to take advantage of whatever opportunities the chairmen offered for open deliberation and debate.[6]

A second consequence of intensified partisanship has been discussed in many of the chapters included in this volume, so I will touch on it only briefly: the incidence and character of the activities that Mayhew found legislators engaging in to achieve their electoral goals. As Mayhew looked back on *The Electoral Connection* at year 25, he expressed disappointment that scholars had not made more of "position taking." Perhaps, he speculated, "its importance exceeds its modelability."[7] I am not certain about the "modelability" part, but I assure you that "position taking" has only increased in importance.

Both its pervasiveness and its current character owe much to intensified partisanship. I just returned from a week in which the main item on the House floor was short-circuiting the review of the Keystone pipeline; the week before, we voted for the thirty-seventh time on repealing all or part of the Affordable Care Act. Neither has the slightest chance of final approval. But as Mayhew

---

[6] Robert Kaiser, *Act of Congress* (New York: Alfred A. Knopf, 2013), chaps. 14–19.
[7] "Observations," p. 251.

stated in 1974, "the electoral payment is for positions rather than for effects."[8] The difference is that position-taking is now more a collective partisan enterprise and that it largely dominates the House floor, at least in the weeks between artificially induced fiscal crises. Recall that in 1974, Mayhew was already speculating that legislative mobilization was on the wane.[9] But in those years Congress at least routinely passed farm bills, highway bills, education reauthorization bills – all of which are languishing at present.

What has happened to credit claiming? It certainly hasn't gone away, despite the chest-thumping about banning earmarks. For a while, members such as myself enjoyed occasionally calling out colleagues who showed up for ribbon-cuttings simultaneous with the chest-thumping. Now we're actually seeing cases where the position taking *trumps* the credit claiming; some new members are giving the stiff-arm to the local officials, researchers, educators, and others who ask for their help. We will see how that goes. But the double-talk is still more common – pledging one's undying support for cancer research, for example, while touting and voting for budgets that take the percentage of NIH proposals funded into single digits.

The third institutional effect is the erosion of Congress' constitutional prerogatives and of its institutional role in relation to the executive – developments that particularly affect and concern me as a member of the Appropriations Committee. The portrait of Appropriations that Richard Fenno drew in the 1960s focused on its restrained partisanship, while Mayhew saw the deference members gave to Appropriations as an important component of institutional maintenance.[10] Both were tied to the Committee's responsibility, on behalf of the House, to hold the executive branch accountable, regardless of which party was in control in the White House or Congress.

Appropriations, however, is now being swamped by partisan forces in and beyond the House, and its institutional role is diminishing as a result.[11] The experience I had in 2012 as ranking Democrat on the Homeland Security Subcommittee provides a snapshot of the contending forces at work. Striving to maintain the "regular order" and to uphold the Committee's bipartisan tradition, the Subcommittee chairman and I strove mightily to bring a bipartisan bill to the floor. We succeeded, but then came the incoming fire in the form of extreme antiimmigration amendments – forbidding enforcement officers from providing translation services to immigrants not proficient in English,

[8] David Mayhew, *Congress: The Electoral Connection* (New Haven: Yale University Press, 1974), p. 132.
[9] Ibid., pp. 119–21.
[10] Richard Fenno, *The Power of the Purse: Appropriations Politics in Congress* (Boston: Little, Brown, 1966), pp. 200-03; Mayhew, *Electoral Connection*, pp. 152–54.
[11] For earlier episodes reflecting the trend, see David E. Price, "Response," in forum on "Fixing Congress," *Boston Review*, 38 (May–June 2011), pp. 28–29; and David E. Price, "After the 'Housequake': Leadership and Partisanship in the Post 2006 House," *The Forum* 8 (2010), no. 1, art. 6.

for example, or from prioritizing criminal aliens for removal (that would give everyone else "amnesty," they said). In past years Republicans would have given such amendments thirty to forty votes, rolled their eyes, and moved on. But in the new House, they *passed* the amendments with near unanimous Republican support.[12] Republican leaders knew that this spelled the end of bipartisan support for the bill, but they could not or would not control the process. It was ideological position taking against appropriating, and appropriating didn't have a chance.

In marking up Appropriations bills, we are working under the meat-ax of "sequestration," which hits almost all appropriations accounts but is the exact opposite of rational appropriating. It was designed to be so unthinkable that it would force action on the real drivers of the deficit, tax expenditures and mandatory spending. But it turned out that Republicans valued their antitax ideology more than they worried about defense cuts, and the sequestration ax fell.

The full committee chairman, Hal Rogers, has railed against sequestration and urged successive deals to get more workable budget numbers. More often, he has admitted there was little he could do. Appropriations remains stuck, and we continue to face government shutdowns and default crises. The swamping of the appropriations process by larger partisan forces, which has been increasing for a number of years, is now almost complete.

The fourth institutional consequence of intensified partisanship in its current incarnation is a drastic decline in Congress' *bipartisan capacity*. Congress also depends, of course, on *partisan* capacity, and the strength and solidarity that the parties have developed since the 1970s have enhanced performance in many ways, by overcoming fragmentation and enabling the majority to rule. As a committed Democrat, I take considerable pride in periods of partisan achievement such as 1993–94 and 2009–10. But I am also a veteran of the budget battles of the 1990s. This leads me to react with alarm to two aspects of our current budget situation. First, our fiscal challenges, including the future of our entitlement programs and the need to raise revenue commensurate with necessary expenditures, are far more difficult than those Congress faced in the 1990s. And second, our capacity to take these challenges on, in the bipartisan and comprehensive fashion that history teaches us is almost always necessary, is far weaker. Reaching agreement was extraordinarily difficult in the 1990s; it seems almost impossible now.

There are a number of areas in which Congress historically has been strengthened by a bipartisan as well as a partisan capacity. The current languishing of a number of authorizations points to committees where that capacity has slipped – Transportation and Infrastructure, for example, and Agriculture, as well as Appropriations. But the effects are greatest in fiscal

---

[12] See Roll Calls no. 362 and 363, June 7, 2012.

policy, where leaders must face unpleasant realities and take on political adversity. This was done in the bipartisan budget agreement of 1990 and in the comprehensive budget bill of 1993. The latter was enacted with Democratic heavy lifting alone, and the electoral consequences in 1994 were disastrous, thus confirming the maxim that bipartisan cover is generally required. Some now-familiar partisan trends were evident in these earlier battles – recall that in dissenting from the 1990 agreement Newt Gingrich staked out the antitax absolutism that has been with us ever since.[13] But the current state of partisan polarization and conflict has clearly – one hopes not fatally – weakened further the capacity of Congress to deal with a range of fiscal issues critical to the country's future.

As someone who experiences the institution of Congress every day, I agree with other congressional scholars that this new mode of partisanship is a variable of enormous significance. The question is what the full range of consequences might be. I have suggested some that have a direct bearing on how the institution works, and how well. I believe political scientists are well equipped to address these questions, and I hope that many of you will do so.

---

[13] See David E. Price, *The Congressional Experience*, 3rd ed. (Boulder, CO: Westview Press, 2004), pp. 147–50.

15

The Origins of *Congress: The Electoral Connection*

David R. Mayhew

I have been assigned a question: Where did my book *Congress: The Electoral Connection* come from? I wrote it forty years ago in 1973. Here is some personal archaeology. The story goes back a long ways. It says something about the times, the context, and the Yale department, as well as the political science profession and the country back in the 1970s. Here are five ingredients of the book enterprise as I now remember it.

First of all – I had been reading a lot! That is virtually the only thing I know how to do – read! It is my lasting methodology. I don't know how to do statistics, or game theory, or interviews – interviews with people strike me as being a horrible thing to have to do! Structured or otherwise, I wouldn't know how to do them. I can scarcely use a telephone! But I do know how to read! I have always known how to read. So the book has a literary background. I had been reading for a long time. I'd read a lot as an undergraduate. At graduate school my advisor was V. O. Key and I'd virtually memorized everything Key had written. Also, I used to read the *Congressional Record*. I got that publication every day, the hard copy. I think that at the time every congressman (they were virtually all men back then) had twenty-five free subscriptions of the *Record* to send out per district (my district was Connecticut #2, the same as Nelson Polsby's), and I got one at an early age, and for maybe twelve years I got the thing every day. And I'd really look at it! I probably spent an hour every day with the *Record*; it'd be crazy to read every word, but there it was. And this was before *Congressional Quarterly Weekly* amounted to much – it was out there but it was very thin. There wasn't any *National Journal*, and I was nowhere near the *Washington Post*. So I had to make do with the *Congressional Record*. There is a wrinkle. Back in those days the *Congressional Record* listed its roll call totals by the ayes and nays but it didn't identify the members by party. So in order to make sense of it all I needed to memorize the party affiliations of the individual MCs. Being forced to do that was a great education! It was like learning the numbers table at age six.

Also in the category of reading: When I got out of Harvard graduate school in the fall of 1963, I discovered I didn't know much about political science! I had taken some nice courses, I loved my teachers and courses, I loved the setting, I loved what I learnt, but I knew virtually nothing about political science as it was developing then. So what I did was to go back through all the professional journals that had articles about American politics, anything that had to do with American politics (fewer journals existed then), all the way back to 1950. That is, I systematically went through all the journals from 1950 to 1963–64, reading and taking notes on all the pieces about American politics. I still have the index cards. I built a stack of cards about ten inches thick, just tanking up whatever there was in the way of accumulated lore about American politics. This included material about Congress but also elections and other topics, state politics at that point – state politics was a bigger deal in studying American politics than it is now in political science. So I had a reading base going back to 1950.

Second, I had spent time on Capitol Hill. This was a great big piece of good fortune for me – an APSA congressional fellowship. Youngsters trying to get into the trade should really go down there and spend some time. It's very important to get oriented, to get a sense of the place. I did that in 1967–68. I worked in a House office, I worked in a Senate office for awhile, and I also worked in the office of the Democratic Study Group (DSG) for a few weeks. (Actually, this DSG stint prefaced what Gary Jacobson and I later puzzled about in the early 1970s drawing on a spotty collection of campaign finance data I had systematized for that outfit.) But what was so valuable on the Hill was watching how the members operated. As a congressional fellow I had access to the offices, I could sit right in the offices of the folks – the House member, the Senate member – and see what they did during the day. And I think that a lot of my *Electoral Connection* book comes out of that perception and assessment of what they were up to as I watched them operate. I watched people come through the offices, I watched the members operate on the floor, and I went back to the districts. I went to gin mills in New Jersey, Indian reservations in Montana. I could see the members dealing with their constituents. It was very valuable. And I remember that with my House member from New Jersey, without thinking about it very deeply, I mentally coded what he was up to. I could watch my boss as visitors came through the office. For people in Trenton there would be "goodies" – distributive politics. For the unions it would be solicitude – "we'll do what you want as far as it's possible." For the Princeton folks it was issue positions – the Princeton folks loved issue positions! My boss doubled his campaign contributions in the Princeton area after coming out against the Vietnam War, and he knew what he was doing as he made that move. They loved issue positions in Princeton! There it was – a kind of differentiation of effort. I could see my New Jersey member putting on different kinds of caps as he operated with different kinds of constituents as they came through. It was absolutely fascinating stuff! I was just watching. I didn't have a writing project in mind at this point. I was just seeing what they were up to.

All right, that is two ingredients.

A third ingredient of the book, which has been talked about in a general sense in this volume, is the American political setting of the late 1960s and 1970s. It is clear that certain things were happening. Incumbency advantage was rising, especially involving House members elected since the mid-1960s, which seemed to denote a kind of individuation of politics that hadn't quite been there before. We could see an increase in the government programs that were being generated. This was casework heaven. We could see a high point of cross-party voting on Capitol Hill – that is to say, *not* party versus party, but a messy something else, in the politics of the 1960s and 1970s. These things were happening, that was the setting, and some of us were resonating to these trends. Bob Erikson was writing about incumbency advantage in 1971 before I got into that topic myself. Mo Fiorina wrote on the exploding casework. Out there independently some of us were responding to these same changes in the political environment. As of 1973, when I wrote *The Electoral Connection*, I had already been watching politics for a quarter of a century, and one of the properties of that vantage was that I could see the change over that span. I had witnessed the *growth* of cross-party voting, of individuation, of House incumbency advantage. I had memories all the way back to 1948 and 1950. Truman beat Dewey in a vote in my elementary school home room in 1948. I still have clippings from the election of 1950 – one on Everett Dirksen's victory in Illinois. Those earlier times in my dim memory had a political cleavage that was quite straightforwardly partisan compared with the 1970s. The point I am making here is that as of 1973 I had been seeing an evolution toward the features of the 1970s for a quite a long time. I could see what was new. It needed a new analysis.

The fourth ingredient of the writing of this book has to do with the Yale intellectual environment of the 1970s. I got to New Haven in 1968. Yale was a hothouse department at that time in the profession. Here was the environment as I think it impinged on me around 1970 or so at Yale: Sharp analyticism was in the air. That was what was valued – sharp analytics of some kind or another. Bob Dahl, Ed Lindblom, and Bob Lane were the most senior of the faculty at Yale at the time. At the junior level, Gerry Kramer came aboard – he was a smart, fearsome, intellectually stern figure. Doug Rae was a walking expositor of analytics. Looming in the background was Martin Shubik, another fearsome figure. This was the environment I struggled to operate in at the time. Another figure, a writer not at Yale but who was very important in the intellectual context, was Anthony Downs. His theory was out there. His book *An Economic Theory of Democracy* was very much promoted at Yale by, for one, Lindblom. That work was very important to me as a theoretical enterprise. I remember at a particular point in the forming of *The Electoral Connection*, the Downs book erupted in a particular way. I was teaching a graduate seminar one year in the early 1970s, and I was using Downs's book. And going into class, it occurred to me that maybe I could do something useful by complicating what Downs was doing in his basic thinking, which was that parties are point-source entities that compete with each other for elections. But suppose that you take that premise to the congressional level – so that you're not dealing with just one presidential candidate or party, but rather with an assembly or two assemblies of 535 people – how does the Downsian premise launder into that environment? That musing induced me to make the distinction between position taking and credit claiming (I think I operated that way anyway, having also watched my boss in action on Capitol Hill rotating between those stances). These are not two distinct emphases that arise so quickly to the mind as one thinks about presidents or parties doing their representing. Whereas with 535 individual district-based people they do leap to the mind more easily. So this fourth ingredient was there – the Yale intellectual environment of the 1970s.

A fifth ingredient was this one – *The Electoral Connection* book is a theoretical essay. And someone said to me once, "Did you write that over a weekend?" No, I didn't write it over a weekend, but it is rather short and rather simple, after all, in some ways. The structure is simple. And it is not a quantitative enterprise except for a few charts – it's a thought enterprise. How was one to do that? What was the basis in political science? What was the tradition or the eager reception committee for writing theoretical essays? That's not where things were going in political science or where they seemed to have been – writing theoretical essays, whatever a theoretical essay is. But it is a form of presentation I moved into in the 1970s, and I think there is some precedent in my background. One model was probably Louis Hartz. I studied at Harvard with Hartz quite a bit. I took three courses with him. He was quite outside my domain doing chiefly European political thought. But his *The Liberal Tradition in America* was a book that was always in the front of my mind. It's a theoretical essay. He takes a pretty simple idea and marches it through a lot of American historical terrain. Then the more proximate model, I would guess, for getting into my own essay was Bob Dahl's work, particularly his *A Preface to Democratic Theory*. This is exactly a theoretical essay. It is broad, roaming, and discursive; it doesn't have numbers in it; it is a thought piece that covers a fair amount of terrain playing through it a query about democracy; and it is fairly short – I mean, he could have written it in a weekend (although I'm sure he didn't)! So that was a kind of model. I don't remember being conscious of models or even of in any especially coherent way setting out to write a theoretical essay, but I think that Hartz's work and in particular Dahl's work were background imprints as I went into writing *The Electoral Connection* in 1973.

Those are the five ingredients. And so the book came together in 1973. I wrote it in the summer of that year – it took about thirteen weeks to write (which is more than a weekend). I had some earlier skimpy, scruffy draft material but it didn't figure much. I had it all lined up. I had a stack of cards to write from (i.e., the quotes, the references, and such) that I had assembled during the preceding academic year. I've never succeeded in writing and teaching at the same time. I just can't do it, it's like Gerry Ford, I just can't do those two things at once. So I needed the space, the time, the slack, the summer to actually do the writing – flat out, without interruptions. And that's what I did in the summer of 1973. Otherwise, that was the summer of Sam Ervin's televised hearings into Watergate. They went on for hours. I couldn't miss those! But I couldn't watch television at all during the day because I had to write! So fortunately one of the channels took hearings from the day and ran them again at night, so I'd write during the day and watch Sam Ervin at night! This was a riveting background for writing a book about Congress.

And the writing went rather smoothly. There was only one glitch as I remember it. I had thought the whole thing out pretty well. That glitch was having to figure out how to define "credit claiming." I wrestled with that for awhile, and I was never satisfied with what I got. But then I adopted – I think I consciously did this – a move that Bob Dahl sometimes made in his writing, which is to say, "Well, I can't solve everything here. So let's just do the best I can and get beyond it! Get to the next paragraph and the next page!" Dahl commonly did that, and that's what I did with credit claiming. The concept has some holes in it, I know it has some holes in it, it has unclear boundaries, but I had to stop! I had to go on to the next page. But generally speaking, the writing of the manuscript went pretty smoothly.

And I do mean writing, not typing. In those days we composed in handwriting. I mean for youngsters that is nearly inconceivable. The early 1970s was certainly before computers, maybe before electric typewriters (I can't remember). In those days what you would commonly do if you were writing something lengthy was to put it in handwriting and then send it to a typist. So that is what I did. I put it in handwriting. I still have a photocopy of the handwritten version. I think the typist never gave me back the original draft, but operating on an insurance principle which I routinely do, I made a photocopy of the whole thing before I sent it to the typist. You really needed to do that back then! I mean there were all those stories about dissertations being lost in the trunk and the car stolen. Hence my still existent photocopy. I fished it out of the closet a few months ago.

And that was it. I had to write something or else I was going to lose my job very quickly! So the summer of 1973 was very critical to that. I had to get that project on paper. That was it! I wrote this book crafting this theoretical essay, and then I stopped. I never did anything more to advance this argument, I just stopped. I had said everything I wanted to say and that was the end of it.

QUESTION AND ANSWER:

Q: You were mentioning models for the kind of essay you wrote, but you didn't mention Schattschneider. I'm wondering why that is.

A: That's an interesting point and I think you might be right. Especially *The Semi-Sovereign People*, yes. That might have been in my mind. After all, that is another very distinguished theoretical essay. I think you're right, so let's magnify by about 50 percent my claim and add on Schattschneider. I think that's probably right. But what else can you think of? It wasn't that common, was it?

Q: Hirschman's *Exit, Voice, and Loyalty*?

A: When was that? Probably a bit later? [Audience: 1970?] I see. But I don't think I was aware of it. It was outside political science, at least I wasn't keying on it. But most people didn't write theoretical essays. My advisor, V. O. Key, didn't write them, Dick Fenno didn't write theoretical essays (I don't think so, at least).

Q: *Congressmen in Committees*?

A: Well, no. I don't think so. I think that work is more elaborate, it's got more in it, it's more of a production. It has lots of interview and empirical material. I wouldn't put it in the same bracket, I think. I don't know. But you're right about Schattschneider. I certainly knew his work, his three books.

Q: You end your story with the completion of the work, and you never came back to it. I'm sure you were asked many times to do a second edition, and you never did. I'm curious what the immediate reception was to the book?

A: Well, in the academic world I think it was picked up pretty quick – about two or three years. In the public affairs world, not picked up so much. I mean it was reviewed by Walter Shapiro in the *Washington Monthly* and it had a bit of a public face, not as much, obviously, as some works do, but yes – it was picked up by academics pretty fast. But then I stopped. I stopped chiefly because I didn't have anything more to say on this topic, but then going forward a few years in political science came the kind of rational choice analysis that I really didn't know how to do. I mean, I knew how to do a few simple premises, but I had no training, and so therefore I was obviously incapable of carrying forth the whole business in the elaborate fashion that rational choice training would have supplied. Nor was I interested in doing that, really. I was interested in moving on, finding some other kind of thing to do. And generally speaking, what I've done is to move on to do some things rather different.

Q: How many copies has it sold?

A: Something like 100,000 maybe? But don't really know, I lost track a while ago. There is a brisk second-hand market. I never got much in the way of royalties.

Q: You said a word about Louis Hartz as a teacher. I was wondering if you'd say a little about V. O. Key.

A: They were very different. Louis Hartz was charismatic in seminars as well as lectures. He had a following – a pied-piper kind of guy, for very good

reason. V. O. was very different. V. O. was soft-spoken, recessive. He
not a star undergraduate teacher and didn't try to be one. He ran
workmanlike undergraduate course. I had a couple of his graduate sem
inars – by-the-books seminars on their subjects, one on parties and one on
legislative behavior. I think he was terrific, but it just a different kind of
presentation from Hartz's.

V. O. was always very helpful to me – very respectful, he read my work
when I put it in front of him. I remember I put the first three chapters of my
dissertation in front of him, and I had a graph and the axes were reversed.
It was awful. He vetted and corrected my first three chapters and veered me
toward doing the whole business better. And then he got sick and never got
better, at age sixty-three.

Index

Index

inter-party, 8
competitiveness, 371
conditional party government, 26–27, 138, 350–51
Condorcet, Marquis de, 92
Congress, accomplishments of
  assembling data on, 245–48
  conclusion to, 260–65
  effects of divided government on, 255–60
  First Congress achievements, 245–46, 248–50, 253–54, 356–57
  introduction to, 243–45
  legislative accomplishments, 208–9
  trends in legislative action and, 248–55
Congress: A Political-Economic History of Roll Call Voting (Poole and Rosenthal), 196–97
Congress and the Politics of Problem Solving (Adler and Wilkerson), 276–77
"Congress: The Case of the Vanishing Marginals" (Mayhew), 65–67
Congress: The Electoral Connection (Mayhew), 1–2, 6–7, 15–16, 35–36, 65, 117–18, 328
  conclusion to, 61–62
  Congress in 1970s and, 18–20
  Congress today and, 21–23
  consequences and, 55–61
  contemporary electoral arena and, 39–55
  electoral roots of partisanship and, 27–29
  intellectual origins of, 11–12
  means and, 37–39
  motive and, 36–37
  origin of, 377–81
  overall assessment and, 29–31
  party-centric theories and, 24–27
  rational choice theory and, 16–18
congressional behavior, 2–3
Congressional Budget Office (CBO), 267, 270–72, 277–78, 283, 285–88
congressional enterprises, 277–78
Congressional Quarterly Weekly, 377–78
Congressional Record, 11–12, 247, 377–78
Congressional Research Service (CRS), 267, 270–72, 277–78, 292
Congressmen in Committees (Fenno), 16–17
Connecticut Climate Preparedness Plan, 320–21
consensus, 9–10, 335–38
ConservAmerica, 311–12
Conservative Opportunity Society, 116
constitutional reform, majoritarianism and, 340–46

contemporary electoral arena, 39–55
contingency, 304–5
  conclusions to, 322–23
  responses to, 312–22
  Sandy Hook massacre, gun control and, 306–9
  Superstorm Sandy, global warming and, 309–12
  terms for, 305–6
conventional wisdom, 347–54
Coolidge, Calvin, 100
Cooper, Joseph, 26
Cooperative Congressional Election Study (CCES), 41–42
Copyright Act, 249
Cornyn, John, 123
cost-benefit analysis, 284–85, 298
Cover, Albert D., 4
Cox, Gary, 18, 24–26, 131–32, 345–46, 349–51
CQ Almanac, 246–48
credit claiming, 21–22, 116–17, 121–24, 126–27, 138–39, 374, 381
  Boehner and, 38–39
  partisan communications and, 123–37
Creoles, 186
Crime Act of 1994, 249
Crisp, Charles Frederick, 355–56
cross-party coalitions, 54
cross-party cooperation, 59–60
CRS. See Congressional Research Service
cultural majoritarianism, 333–34
Cuomo, Andrew, 310–11
Cyr, Paul N. "Doc," 176

Dahl, Robert, 11–12, 379, 381
Daley, Mark, 244–45
Dammann, Theodore, 170, 173–74
Daniels, Stephen, 210–11
Davidson, James O. "Yim," 168–69
Davis, Jimmie, 178–83
Davis, John E., 160–61
Davis, Parker, 244–45
Davis, Tom, 164–65
DCCC. See Democratic Congressional Campaign Committee
deadlock. See legislative deadlock or gridlock
debt ceiling, 236
decision-making, 289–91, 335
defection rates, 41
delay, 15–16, 23
DeMeyer, Frank, 92
democratic accountability, 2–6